DRUMS
OF
TERROR

Voodoo in the
Cinema

One of *Sugar Hill*'s (1974) "Zombie Hitmen."

DRUMS OF TERROR

Voodoo in the Cinema

by Bryan Senn

Midnight Marquee Press, Inc.
Baltimore, Maryland

Cover Design: A.S. Miller

ISBN 1-887664-18-1
Library of Congress Catalog Card Number 98-65675
Manufactured in the United States of America
Printed by Kirby Lithographic Company, Arlington, VA
First Printing by Midnight Marquee Press, Inc., July, 1998

Acknowledgments: John Antosiewicz Photo Archives, Betty Cavanaugh, Don Dohler, Jerry Ohlinger's Movie Material, Lorne Marshall, Wayne Shipley, David H. Smith, Linda J.Walter

For my son Dominic

May all your monsters be in the movies.

Though skeptical at first, Santería sorcery makes Cal Jamison (Martin Sheen) one of *The Believers* (1987).

ACKNOWLEDGMENTS

A book like this could not have been completed without the generous aid of many individuals, so I'd like to extend my heartfelt thanks (and a Voudoun blessing) to the following:

Gina Beretta (my patient wife), whose broad perspective and wonderful editorial skills kept me on the straight and narrow.

Lynn Naron, for his superb photographic assistance and general support.

Ron Borst, who combed through his matchless collection to provide whatever materials I might need (and who, with permission from Sinister Cinema's Greg Luce, also bestowed upon me the dubious privilege of previewing at the last minute the "lost" film *Chloe*).

Eric Hoffman, *Famous Monsters of Filmland*'s "Answerman" himself, for answering a resounding "yes" when asked to open his personal treasure trove of photos, press materials, and films.

Marty Baumann (of *The Astounding B Monster* Internet magazine), Tim Lucas (*Video Watchdog*), Gary Don Rhodes, Tony Timpone (*Fangoria*), David Uhrbom, and Tom Weaver for providing further materials and sharing their obscure arcana.

Ken Landgraf, Ted Okuda, Stephen D. Smith, and Chuck Wilson for allowing me to take advantage of their supreme film-finding skills.

And Freddie Francis, Alex Gordon, Richard Gordon, Jack Hill, Tim Kelly, William Lustig, William Marshall, David McGillivray, Caroline Munro, Robert Quarry, Sam Sherman, and Del Tenney for sharing their time and personal reminiscences.

Darby Jones, voodoo cinema's most imposing zombie, stalks through the night (in both *I Walked with a Zombie* [1943] and *Zombies on Broadway* [1945]).

TABLE OF CONTENTS

Oil, religion, and *White Zombie* (!) in Hobbs, New Mexico c. 1938. (Photo: Russell Lee/Farm Security Administration; courtesy of Lynn Naron)

INTRODUCTION

"In many out of the way corners of the Earth there may still be found remnants of races that believe implicitly in the religious formulas that have come down to them from the dim and distant past. Of all these strange beliefs, perhaps the most inexplicable and disturbing is that of the Haitians, known to white men as 'VOODOO.'"

—opening narration for the 1935 film *Ouanga*

"This is a religion of major stature, rare poetic vision, and artistic expression…"

—experimental filmmaker turned Voudoun initiate Maya Deren

REEL VOODOO

As demonstrated by the above *Ouanga* quote, moviemakers initially took a condescending (not to mention racist) attitude toward the practice of the religion known as Voudoun (or "voodoo" as it's called in common parlance). Unfortunately, this attitude hasn't changed much over the subsequent six decades, either in the average citizen or (with *very* few exceptions) in celluloid portrayals.

This system of "strange beliefs" which proved so "inexplicable and disturbing" to the common moviegoer has inspired dozens of filmmakers over the last 60-odd years to paint their voodoo visions on the silver screen (as well as prompting scores of others to employ the concept as seasoning for their cinematic broth). In the art of cinema, voodoo films possess their own unique flavor and attraction. Filled with bizarre rituals, tropical locales, frenzied sensual dancing, deadly hexes, powerful sorcerers, and the dreaded walking dead, voodoo movies appeal to the Western audience's thrill of the exotic, the strange, the inexplicable. Not unexpectedly, filmmakers have been more inclined to exploit rather than explore the topic. After all, with all due respect to those serious practitioners of Voudou and its variations, legitimate worship is *not* the stuff of celluloid dreams—or nightmares. As veteran screenwriter Tim Kelly (*Sugar Hill*) observed, "Naturally with films, much of the historical accuracy is dropped and the sensational aspects sort of take over." Just as few people would buy a movie ticket in order to witness a full Catholic Mass

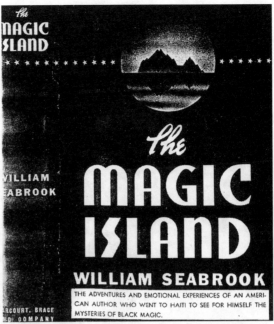

Published in 1929, William B. Seabrook's popular account of Haitian voodoo served as (uncredited) inspiration for the talking screen's first full-fledged voodoo film—*White Zombie*. Courtesy Ronald V. Borst/Hollywood Movie Posters

(in Latin, of course), most viewers don't wish to see the drawn-out dancing and intricate rituals of legitimate Voudoun worship. No, moviegoers want to see spells, human sacrifices, and zombies. Consequently, that is just what filmmakers have provided.

As a result, most voodoo movies aren't too concerned with the spiritual aspect of their topic and tend to focus on more sensationalistic traits, portraying the religion as an evil practice centered on malevolent hexes and walking corpses. While it is true that Haiti is full of protective ouangas (charms) and that practitioners do sometimes seek out the aid of bokors (sorcerers), the main thrust of true Voudoun is to provide a venue by which the initiate develops a personal relationship with the loas (the spirits or gods) and so becomes part of the spiritual (as well as temporal) community. Much as the true Christian loathes those who pray for personal gain at the expense of others, so does the devout Voudounist disdain those who seek the loas' direct aid for ill. Consequently, judging Voudoun by its cinematic incarnations would be like evaluating Christianity by watching movies like *Race with the Devil* or *The Devil's Rain* which focus on a perverted form of the religion.

Apart from the deep South, voodoo didn't enter the general American consciousness until William B. Seabrook published *The Magic Island* in 1929, his intriguing, sensationalized account of Haitian voodoo. This popular book first inspired a Broadway play, then (indirectly) the highly successful Bela Lugosi vehicle *White Zombie* (1932). With *White Zombie*, the idea (if not exactly the spirit) of voodoo took root in popu-

Reel voodoo and real Voudoun: above an actual Haitian worship ceremony. (Photo: Maya Deren).

lar culture. Even the great Orson Welles, the "boy wonder" of stage and radio, scored a success in 1936 with a voodoo variation of Shakespeare's *Macbeth*(!). Welles went so far as to hire a troupe of dancers from the west coast of Africa along with an authentic witch doctor, a dwarf named Abdul, to insure the integrity of the production's rituals. Reportedly, Abdul cursed an unkind critic, who subsequently contracted pneumonia and died! This deadly sensationalism is exactly what attracted filmmakers to the topic in the first place.

REAL VOUDOUN

In spite of what most moviemakers would have us believe, Voudoun is a legitimate religion born of a genuine spirituality. Though the dogmatic Christian may cringe at the thought, true Voudou is fairly close to Catholicism in its structure—but on a more personal, intimate, and vibrant level. (In fact, most Voudoun altars are adorned with lithographs of Catholic saints; and "Santería"—the Cuban form of Voudou—literally means "the worship of saints.") Like the Catholic, the Voudounist believes in the one true God (*Bon Dieu*) as the creator of all things. Voudoun's various loas (spirits or lesser deities) act (much as the saints do) as intermediaries between the believer and the Supreme Being. Whereas Catholics pray to the saints, however, the Voudounist goes that extra mile and welcomes the loa into his very body. Through ritual and dance, the Voudounist seeks possession by the loa. As the Haitian saying goes, the Catholic goes to church to speak about God while the Voudounist dances in the hounfour (a Voudoun place of worship) and becomes God.

This is not to say, however, that the Voudoun faith is simply an Africanized version of Catholicism. As Wade Davis explains in his book *Passage of Darkness*, "Although some Catholic iconographic elements and votive objects were adopted by Vodounists, it is patently misleading to describe contemporary Vodoun [sic] as a syncretism of African traditions and Catholic ritual." Instead, "the presence of these potent images is not evidence of the Westernization of Vodoun ritual, but rather indicates the ability of the Vodounist to transform Catholic icons by noting their similarities to African spirits." For instance, the Virgin Mary is seen as the representation of Erzuile, the goddess of love, while St. Patrick (with his attendant snake imagery) becomes Damballah, the serpent of the sky.

Reel voodoo and Real Voudoun: above a voodoo ceremony from the film *Voodoo Woman* (1957).

POSSESSED BY THE GODS

The rather disturbing (at least to Judeo-Christian observers) concept of possession is at the very heart of Voudoun, and is what makes the religion both so unique and so exotic. As Maya Deren, an experimental filmmaker who went to Haiti to film its native dance and who returned a Voudoun initiate, wrote in her book *Divine Horsemen: The Living Gods of Haiti*, possession by the loa "is the center toward which all the roads of Voudoun converge." Unlike its often violent and lascivious portrayal in cinema (as exemplified by *Angel Heart*'s bloody, sexually charged ceremonial scene), Voudoun possession (in Deren's words) "does not free the identity of the individual, but, on the contrary, replaces it with a highly formalized, disciplined identity, that of the loa... The actions and utterances of the possessed person are not the expression of the individual, but are the readily identifiable manifestations of the particular loa or archetypal principle. Since it is by such manifestations that the divinities of the pantheon make known their instructions and desires and exercise their authority, this phenomenon is basic to Voudoun, occurs frequently, and is *normal* both to the religion and to the Haitians." In his volume *Life in a Haitian Valley*, the more formally trained anthropologist M.J. Herskovits concurred: "This form of worship of the loa [possession] is neither unrestrained hysteria, nor drunken orgiastic satisfaction of the sex drive" (Lisa Bonet's big-screen writhing notwithstanding). (For a fascinating first-hand account of this phenomenon from someone who has actually

A Haitian serviteur (Voudounist) in the process of being "mounted" by a loa. Note the casual expressions and postures of those present—possession is a natural and expected (indeed, sought after) part of Voudoun worship. (Photo: Maya Deren)

13

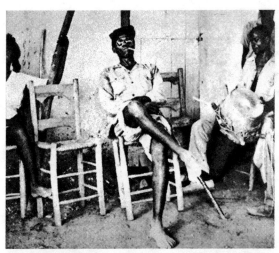

A man possessed by the loa Ghede takes on the personality and mannerisms of that Voudoun spirit. (Photo: Maya Deren)

been "mounted" by a loa, I highly recommend Maya Deren's book *Divine Horsemen*.)

THE LURE OF VOODOO

What, in effect, makes the topic of voodoo so alluring (as evidenced by the numerous books and films on the subject released over the last half-century)? Superficially, it can be put down to the attraction of the supernatural—or simply of the unusual. On a deeper and more significant level, however, it's the direct contact (or *perceived* contact) with the spiritual world that makes voodoo such a fascinating topic. As Wade Davis remarks, "Through spirit possession, the Vodoun acolyte walks in and out of the supernatural world with an ease, frequency, and impunity that have consistently astonished ethnographic and medical observers. In Vodounist thought, the immediacy with which the believer interacts with the spirits is but a consequence of the remarkable dialogue that exists between humans and the loa. The spirits are powerful and, if offended, can do great harm, but they are also predictable and, if propitiated, will gratefully provide all the benefits of health, fertility, and prosperity."

The Voudoun faith is one of reciprocity, in which man and the spirits commingle for mutual benefit in a spiritual partnership. "Just as man must honor the spirits," writes Davis, "so the loa are dependent on man, for the human body is their receptacle... Once mounted the possessed person loses all consciousness and sense of self; he or she becomes the spirit, taking on its persona and powers."

DRUMS OF *TERROR?*

The huge importance of the drums and dance in Voudoun ceremony becomes evident when one sees that this shared spirituality is expressed above all through music. Via the medium of dance, the loas become manifest in the temporal plane. As Joseph M. Murphy writes of Santería in *Working the Spirit*, "The orishas [the Santería term for the loas] are 'called' by their drumbeats, but they also 'are' these rhythms, vibrations of the experience of the community. The rhythms are echoed, redoubled, and textured...in the dances of the orishas and human beings."

The drumming and dancing also serve to forge a bond among the worshippers themselves, and so strengthen the Voudounist sense of community. As Deren explained in *Divine Horsemen*, "The rhythm and sound of the drum brings out the movements of the dancing. It is the drumming which fuses the fifty or more individuals into a single body, making them move as one as if all had become linked on a thread of a single pulse." While perhaps not grasping the full import of the drums and dance, filmmakers have generally seen the *cinematic* value of including ceremonial dancing and pounding rhythms, so that most voodoo movies contain at least a touch of colorful ceremony and excited movement.

VARIATIONS AND HISTORY

The best known form of this religion brought from the west coast of Africa to the New World via the slave trade is, of course, the Haitian worship called Voudoun. In this book, however, I also include those films that deal with the various offshoots, adaptations, and sister faiths of Voudoun: the Cuban and Puerto Rican forms known as Santería, the Brazilian version called Candomblé (or Macumba), the Jamaican offshoot labeled Obeah, and the adaptation found in North America (primarily in the South) known colloquially as Hoodoo.

Over the years, the Voudoun religion has been the brunt of bad press, largely because those who wrote of it were outsiders who feared what they often termed this "savage cult." This fear stemmed from the slavery within which the religion was born (or, more accurately, *re*born from its African roots). The white masters saw Voudoun as a powerful unifying force, one that could incite action and build hope in their oppressed slaves. (In fact, it helped do just that, for, after a 13-year struggle beginning in 1791, Haiti became the site of the only successful and lasting slave revolt in the history of the Western world. ("The Petro cult [one of several branches of Voudoun, which also includes the Rada sect and the Congo faction]," declared Deren, "was born out of a cosmic rage. It is the rage against the evil fate which the African suffered because of his enslavement. The energy from that rage enabled him to regain his freedom by winning the revolution against the Napoleonic forces.") As such, Voudou was something to be feared. [1] As

A 1990 Voudoun market in Lome, the capital city of Togo, West Africa. (Photo: David Uhrbom)

early as 1884, the smear campaign began with the publication of *Haiti or the Black Republic* by then-British Consul Spencer St. John. In it, the author outrageously details numerous heinous (and suppositional) crimes purportedly perpetrated by Voudounists, including the cannibalizing of children! According to at least one modern scholar, this fear has subsided little in the intervening century. "The Relegation of 'voodoo' to the horror genre," conjectures Joseph Murphy in *Working the Spirit*, "reflects mass America's real horror of independent black power. If voodoo was powerful enough to free the slaves, might it not free their descendants?" Fuel for thought, anyway.

One frequently cited objection to Voudoun is its use of animal sacrifice. While indeed sacrifice (primarily of chickens, but sometimes of a goat and on rare occasions a bull) remains a part of some Voudoun rituals, the act focuses not on death but on life. "The attitude of the Haitian toward the death and blood of these sacrificial beasts is never morbid," explains Maya Deren. "The intent and emphasis of sacrifice is not upon the death of the animals, it is upon the transfusion of its life to the loa, for the understanding is that flesh and blood are of the essence of life and vigor, and these will restore the divine energy of the god."

To the outside world, Voudou has rarely been taken seriously. Most people look upon it as a back-wards superstition. The term "religion" has rarely been applied to Voudoun. Rather words like "cult" or "sect" are often used in its place. Even many of the religion's more level-headed chroniclers seem to look upon it simply as a form of peasant folklore doomed to extinction. (French anthropologist Alfred Metraux, for example, wrote in his seminal 1959 work *Voodoo in Haiti* that, "I am not [Voodoo's] apologist and I know that sooner or later it must disappear.")

But Voudoun and its sister faiths have *not* disappeared. Rather, they've seen a resurgence in popularity of late, not only in their respective homelands, but in America as well, with large centers of practitioners located in major cities such as New York, Los Angeles, and Miami. For some, perhaps, it may be a reawakening to their cultural heritage. For others it could be a reaction to living in an increasingly technologized environment, an attempt to regain something of the natural or spiritual world that has become more and more distant in today's modern societies. While it may indeed be "mere superstition" (a term that can be applied to *any* religion or belief based on "faith"), Voudoun fulfills a basic need in its followers, offering an understandable and approachable worldview in both the natural and spiritual sense.

THE WALKING DEAD

In pop culture (and, consequently, in film), apart from the drums and the ever-present voodoo doll,[2] voodoo's most recognizable icon would have to be the zombie. Though its etymology remains hazy, the term "zombie" probably came from the African Kongo word *nzambi* which means "spirit of a dead person." *Webster's Collegiate Dictionary* defines a zombie as "a will-less and speechless human in the West Indies capable only of automatic movement who is held to have died and been reanimated but often believed to have been drugged into a catalepsy for the hours of internment."

The investigations of Harvard ethnobotonist Wade Davis (chronicled in his somewhat sensationalized book *The Serpent and the Rainbow* and further in his more scholarly tome *Passage of Darkness*) offer convincing evidence that zombies do indeed exist—though not as the walking corpse of Hollywood

The market proprietor (a Voudoun priest) bestows a blessing on an amulet designed to protect travelers. (Photo: David Uhrbom)

fantasy. Through an engulfing tide of cultural tradition and psychological belief, and aided by the physiological properties of neurotoxins and psychotropic drugs obtained from local flora and fauna, a victim's will and individual identity can be stripped from him. The unfortunate creature is not a decomposing cadaver, however, but a living person whose memory and personality has been sublimated and even partially erased.

While the zombie phenomenon can apparently be broken down into a set of physiological and psychological components, Voudoun believers give equal, if not more, weight to the "magical" side of the process. The Haitian Voudounist sees the soul as composed of two parts—the *gros bon ange* ("big good angel") which is the raw energy that functions to keep the body alive, and the *ti bon ange* ("little good an-

gel") which is that aspect of the soul that gives the individual his or her personality and willpower. (The *ti bon ange* is what travels during sleep to experience dreams; it is also this portion of the soul that the loa displaces during possession.) The capture of the *ti bon ange* via sorcery creates the walking shell known as a "zombie." In Haiti, it is believed that only one who dies an *unnatural* death (a demise which is not a call from God—*Mort Bon Dieu*) can become a zombie. This death is propitiated by the bokor (via the application of a magical powder or poison), which allows the sorcerer to perform the rituals that ensnare the *ti bon ange*. It is important to note that the more existential or spiritual properties of this zombification process prove just as critical as the physiological ones, for without immersion in belief by both the perpetrator and the victim, zombification would ultimately fail.

The process used to accomplish zombification typifies the Voudoun religion—a mix of the practical and the spiritual. "For the vodounist, the creation of a zombi [sic] is essentially a magical process," writes Davis in *The Serpent and the Rainbow*. "However, the bokor in creating a zombi cadaver may cause the prerequisite unnatural death not by capturing the *ti bon ange* of the living but by means of a slow-acting poison that is applied directly to the intended victim... That poison contains tetrodotoxin, which acts to lower dramatically the metabolic rate of the victim almost to the point of clinical death. Pronounced dead by attending physicians, and considered materially dead by family members and even by the bokor himself, the victim is in fact buried alive... In those cases in which the victim receives the correct dose of the poison, [he or she] wakes up in the coffin, and is taken from the grave by the bokor. The victim, affected by the drug and traumatized by the set and setting of the total experience, is bound and led before a cross to be baptized with a new name. After the baptism, or sometimes the next day, he or she is made to eat a paste containing a strong dose of a potent psychoactive drug, the zombi's cucumber, which brings on a state of disorientation and amnesia. During the course of that intoxication, the zombi is taken away into the night."

But *why* create a zombie—an expensive, complicated, and dangerous feat for all involved? According to Davis (in *Passage of Darkness*), "Zombification is a form of social sanction imposed by recognized corporate bodies—the poorly known and clandestine secret Bizango societies—as one means of maintaining order and control in local communities." In other words, it is a form of capital punishment—a living death—meted out by the community leaders. Unlike cinematic zombies, who are generally portrayed as the innocent victims of greedy sorcerers eager for slaves[3] or as mindless instruments of revenge, the Haitian zombie is a convicted criminal serving out a sentence for his crimes against the community. Also in contrast to the movies, these will-less creatures hovering between the natural and spirit worlds are not to be feared but rather are to be pitied. For the Haitian Voudounist, the fear is not of being harmed by a zombie but of *becoming* one.

A NOTE ON NOMENCLATURE

Unlike most of the world's other major religions (Buddhism, Christianity, Confucianism, Hinduism, Islam, Judaism, Taoism, et al.), the Voudoun faith possesses no significant written text or tract; its practices, rituals, and tenets have been passed down from generation to generation as an oral tradition. (In fact, since Voudoun is not a centralized religion, ritualistic detail can differ significantly from region to region and even from hounfour to hounfour. These disparate practices, however, still remain expressive of the universal *principles* of Voudoun.) Consequently, even something so basic as the proper spelling of the religion's name varies considerably from book to book and scholar to scholar. In order to make the distinction between the real and imagined (ironically, most fantasy filmmakers take great pains to do just the *opposite*), I employ the expected "voodoo" whenever referring to the concept's cinematic incarnations and revert to the Haitian-originated term of "Voudou" or "Voudoun" when speaking of the real-life religion itself.

ABOUT THE BOOK

If, as some have asserted, movies mirror life, voodoo movies often seem to take the form of a *funhouse* mirror, reflecting a bizarre and distorted image of its topic. Just like gazing at one's reflection in the carnival looking glass, however, seeing such an anomaly can be both entertaining and a little frightening. In addition, many voodoo pictures also possess a shard of verisimilitude here and there, making a glance into their depths even more worthwhile.

The purpose of this book is to chronicle, critique, and explore every theatrically released, English-language voodoo movie to date. Admittedly, sometimes the stories behind a film's making prove more entertaining than the movie itself, but such are the hazards of the job. While some are good, many are bad, and a few are downright ugly, most voodoo movies contain at least the promise (occasionally fulfilled, more often not) of a glimpse into an alternate world view and spirituality that can be both fascinating and unsettling.

For space and practical reasons, I have included only those foreign films which have been released in English, either dubbed or subtitled. Also, only those features that contain a significant element of voodoo will have their own chapter. What qualifies as *sig-*

Voodoo in pop culture. From the 1960 album's liner notes: "The walls echo to the cries and the wails of the believers. That's Voodoo!"

nificant?—a film in which voodoo plays an integral role in the story. Those pictures with a negligible or tangential voodoo element will be found in the appendix entitled "Pseudoo-Voodoo." Also included in this section are those "lost" films, such as *The Dead One* (1961) and *Voodoo Heartbeat* (1972), which have currently disappeared from view. Made-for-TV and direct-to-video releases are covered in a second appendix: "Boob Toob Hoodoo."

So, as you follow a zombie through the cane fields or watch an unfortunate writhe in pain when some painted witch doctor stabs a pin into a doll, please keep in mind that most of these movies are no more accurate a reflection of the Voudoun religion than *Rosemary's Baby* is of Christianity. That said (and with apologies to all true believers), it's time to delve into the cinematic world of diabolical dolls, evil hexes, and the walking dead.

Bryan Senn
July 1998

[1] In Jamaica, "obeahmen" were blamed by the white planters for fomenting the (unsuccessful) slave rebellion in 1760.
[2] Though strongly associated with screen voodoo, the so-called "voodoo doll" has little to do with actual Voudoun. In all probability, voodoo dolls did not even originate in Africa, since such image magic was practiced in Europe long before African slaves came to the New World. As Daniel Cohen writes in *Voodoo, Devils, and the New Invisible World*, "European colonists in America were sticking pins in dolls made from the clothes of their enemies without receiving any instruction from African slaves... It may well have been the slaves who picked up the 'voodoo doll' from their European masters."
[3] Given the ready availability of cheap labor in Haiti (the poorest nation in the Western hemisphere), economic incentive seems an exceedingly unlikely factor in the creation of zombies.

The moody intensity of Bela Lugosi as Murder Legendre from *White Zombie*.

WHITE ZOMBIE (1932)
Voodoo, Mood, and Bela Lugosi

"I kissed her as she lay there in the coffin—
and her lips were *cold*."
—John Harron as Neil

White Zombie is not only the *first* full-fledged voodoo film but also one of the best. Generally revered as an atmospheric triumph from the Golden Age of Horror and equally treasured as one of Bela Lugosi's finest hours (and nine minutes), *White Zombie* stands as a prime example of mood over money.

The Halperin brothers (director Victor and producer Edward) apparently received their inspiration from a Broadway play entitled *Zombie* which opened on February 10, 1932, and ran for a scant 21 performances. The play (itself inspired by the 1929 book *The Magic Island*, W.B. Seabrook's fascinating—if biased—account of his experiences with Haitian voodoo) is set in Haiti and features a plantation owner who suspects his wife of infidelity. When he drinks a potion concocted by his wife's lover he seemingly dies but later rises up to stalk about and frighten the rest of the cast. *The Motion Picture Herald* announced on February 20, 1932 that the play would soon be made into a film (which never materialized). Meanwhile, the Halperin brothers hired Garnett Weston to write a screenplay featuring an altered storyline. When the play's author, Kenneth Webb, learned of the Halperin project, he filed suit in March against them for copyright infringement. Webb lost the suit, however, when the Halperins argued that the play was not a success and so its commercial viability would not be hurt, and that, more to the point, Webb did not have a copyright on the idea of "zombies."

White Zombie was shot in two weeks for a mere $62,500—less than *one-fifth* what 1931's *Dracula* cost. The filming took place primarily at night at Universal City. "We never went off the Universal lot," recalled Enzo Martinelli, assistant cameraman to cinematographer Arthur Martinelli (his uncle), in the February 1988 issue of *American Cinematographer*. "Even the night exteriors on the backwoods roads were shot there." Art directors Ralph Berger and Conrad Tritschler redressed and expanded (via the wizardry of flawlessly matted glass paintings) standing sets from previous horror pictures to produce the forbidding mountaintop fortress of Murder Legendre, voodoo-master. The sorcerer's great hall, for example, is

a rearranged Castle Dracula interior furnished with huge, ornate chairs from *The Cat and the Canary* (1927). Legendre's fateful terrace sports the impressive staircase from Castle *Dracula* while the basement of *Frankenstein* Castle became the zombiemaster's subterranean vaults. A balcony from Universal's 1923 *Hunchback of Notre Dame* cathedral juts out from the magician's mountaintop aerie.

His ninth film as director, but only his third talkie, the low-budget *White Zombie* is undoubtedly Victor Halperin's finest cinematic achievement. Like *Dracula* before it, Halperin's picture generates a powerful mood of eerie dread. *Un*like that earlier Lugosi classic, however, *White Zombie* sustains and steadily builds upon that mood from beginning to end. Whether by design (unlikely), accident (possibly), or a combination of both (probably), the Poverty-Row director (undoubtedly led by cinematographer Arthur Martinelli's visual acumen) created the most atmospheric independent horror film of the decade, a darkly

Bela Lugosi and Robert Frazer gaze at *White Zombie*'s title character (Madge Bellamy).

Gothic shadowplay of good vs. evil which fully exploited the sinister side of the voodoo milieu. Halperin went on to direct seven more features after *White Zombie*, three of them horror films: *Supernatural* (1933), *Revolt of the Zombies* (1936), and *Torture Ship* (1939). None of his subsequent pictures, however (even *Supernatural*, which cost many times *White Zombie*'s budget to make), comes close to the atmospheric power generated by *White Zombie*. Garnett Weston's languorously macabre script; Bela Lugosi's iconographic evil; Conrad Tritschler's brooding matte paintings (which manage to simultaneously expand Ralph Berger's redressed Universal sets while intensifying the claustrophobic morbidity of its subject); and, above all, Arthur Martinelli's shadow-land lighting and fluid nocturnal photography all combine to produce a unique classic of voodoo cinema.

Voodoo sorcerer Murder Legendre employs his cadre of Living Dead to steal Madeline's "corpse" and so make her his *White Zombie*.

The story begins as a young couple, Madeline and Neil (Madge Bellamy and John Harron), journey to the Haitian plantation of Mr. Beaumont (Robert Frazer) where they will be married. Though posing as the couple's benefactor, we soon learn of Beaumont's *true* motive when he says privately, "I'd sacrifice anything I have in the world for her; nothing matters if I can't have her."

A carriage arrives and takes Beaumont to an eerie sugar mill, worked solely by zombies! A zombie servant shows the apprehensive visitor to Murder Legendre (Bela Lugosi), voodoo-master. Beaumont tells the unsavory sorcerer of his unrequited love, and Legendre produces a small vial. "Only a *pinpoint*, Monsieur Beaumont," beams Legendre, "in a glass of wine or perhaps a flower."

When Madeline puts off Beaumont's last-minute expressions of love, the rejected suitor offers her one last gift—a rose tainted with Legendre's zombie powder.

Madeline weds Neil as planned, while outside in the garden lurks Legendre. The voodoo-master takes a candle from its lamp bracket and, wrapping

Madeline's stolen scarf about it, begins to carve the wax with his dagger. When the sorcerer places the crude figure into an open flame, Madeline collapses at the banquet table—seemingly dead.

After placing his bride in her tomb, Neil drowns his sorrows at a cafe. Tormented by her image, he rushes back to the cemetery. To his horror, he finds the tomb empty. Beaumont and Legendre (with his zombie helpers) have already been there.

In Legendre's clifftop castle overlooking the sea, Beaumont listens as Madeline plays the piano. Though her fingers move across the keys, her eyes only stare sightlessly ahead. Aghast at what he's done, Beaumont pleads with Legendre to "put the life *back* into her eyes." Legendre, however, has taken a shine to Madeline himself and so surreptitiously places the zombie drug in Beaumont's wine, watching detachedly as the paralyzing drug takes effect.

After learning from his friend, Dr. Bruner (Joseph Cawthorn), of Murder Legendre's sinister reputation, Neil and Bruner ride through the jungle toward the voodoo-master's clifftop aerie. Though weak from fever, Neil makes it to the castle. On the terrace,

Legendre confronts the intruder with his cadre of zombies. "What are they?" shouts Neil. "To you, my friend," replies the sorcerer, "they are the angels of death." Neil shoots at the approaching figures—to no effect. As Legendre watches his zombie minions force Neil back toward the precipice, Dr. Bruner creeps up behind and strikes the sorcerer on the head, knocking him cold. The now-masterless zombies simply step over the edge and plunge into the sea far below.

Madeline begins to revive, but Legendre awakens and she again resumes her lifeless stare. The sorcerer explodes a gas pellet to keep Neil and Bruner at bay, but a shadow looms behind the evil voodoo-master. The forgotten Beaumont, half-paralyzed by the debilitating zombie-drug, makes a staggered lunge at Legendre and topples the sorcerer off the parapet to his death. Unable to recover his balance, Beaumont follows a moment later. "Neil, I—I dreamed," says Madeline wonderingly, restored by the zombie-master's death. The couple embrace.

Dramatic impact was the name of the game for Victor and Edward. In a pre-credit sequence (a novelty for the time), the picture opens on an eerie, dimly-lit long shot of a midnight burial in which tattered natives solemnly stand about an open grave while others shovel dirt into the gaping hole. On the soundtrack, a drum beats a dirge-like pattern in an almost subliminal rhythm. The word "WHITE" in stylish Gothic/art-deco letters appears at the top of the scene. Then, in time with the drumbeats, translucent rays stream upwards from the bottom of the screen (seemingly from the open grave itself) to illuminate letters one by one, slowly spelling out Z-O-M-B-I-E and complete the title of this production. (Note: The burial taking place at a crossroads accurately reflects an old voodoo fear and consequent custom: If possible, bodies of beloved relatives were buried near a road or, better yet, a crossing, in order to make it more difficult for zombie-making bokors to steal the corpses unseen.)

Shortly thereafter, a coach moves through the near-blackness of night. Suddenly, a pair of huge eyes, their whites shining as if from an inner fire, appear superimposed over the traveling carriage. (Enzo Martinelli remembered how the inventive cinematographer achieved this effect—without expensive opticals: "Arthur just took a cardboard and cut two holes in it about as wide apart as Lugosi's eyes, placed it in front of Lugosi's face and put a light through it. It put two little spots right on his eyeballs when he started to become dangerous.") The scene shifts to another stretch of road alongside which a dark figure stands. As the coach moves into view and approaches the man, the pursuing eyes dwindle in size, moving toward the motionless figure until they disappear altogether, seemingly absorbed into the blackness of the

Legendre seemingly salutes his feathered familiar before working his voodoo sorcery.

mysterious form just as the coach pulls abreast of him and stops. Via these orbs, Halperin visually evokes the near-omniscient otherworldly power of Murder Legendre—*before* we've even met him—to generate an uneasy awe at this pivotal introduction.

Halperin then places Arthur Martinelli's camera on the opposite side of the carriage, looking *through* the coach to the diabolical stranger, so that we see the silent figure lean in the coach window, invading the safety of the interior while he slowly and deliberately places his long hand on the door—on the very *barrier* separating the heroine (and viewer) from the menacing figure. After the coach has sped away when the driver spies "zombies!" coming down the hill, Martinelli's camera views Legendre from a low angle (and slightly tilted to add an almost subliminal unease) so that the figure looms menacingly large. With a smugly evil grin, Legendre tucks the scarf (ripped from around the neck of the heroine as the coach abruptly pulled away) into *not* his pocket as expected but into his shirt itself, as if desiring the garment next to his naked skin. The action thus becomes almost a violation—and a foreshadowing of worse ravishments to come ("It felt like hands clutching me," gasps the heroine as punctuation).

The Halperins' favorite cinematographer, Arthur Martinelli later photographed both *Supernatural* (1933) and the brothers' zombie follow-up feature, *Revolt of the Zombies* (1936; a non-voodoo zombie film). According to *Variety*'s obituary (September 20, 1967), the 50-year veteran cameraman "is credited with having filmed the first pix of both Ethel and John

Legendre watches with diabolical interest as Beaumont succumbs to the bokor's zombie poison.

Barrymore." One of Martinelli's last films was the Bela Lugosi Poverty Row potboiler, *The Devil Bat* (1940).

It is difficult (often impossible) to separate the contribution of a director vs. a cinematographer. Did Halperin carefully position Martinelli's camera to his own specification, or did he simply follow the cinematographer's advice in setting up the shots? Most likely it was a combination of both, but based on the two men's quality of output, one strongly suspects that the latter was more prevalent than the former. In any case, their partnership bore some wonderfully strange fruit.

When Neil stumbles back to the cemetery and sees the door to Madeline's tomb flung wide, for instance, he hesitates at the threshold, the back of his hand pressed tightly to his mouth, fearful of what he may find. Neil finally steps into the mausoleum, but we (the camera) remain outside. After what seems a lifetime of tension (though only a few seconds in reality), the gentle nocturnal melody of croaking frogs and chirping crickets is shattered by an anguished scream reverberating off the vault's interior when Neil finds his beloved gone. The tense waiting and unseen cry make for a moment of drama both heartwrenching and frightening (and an instance almost "Lewtonesque" in its unseen import).

Martinelli took pains with his lighting, enhancing mood and providing illuminating metaphors with his subtle shadings. When Madeline, cradled in Neil's arms, succumbs to Legendre's evil spell, she closes her eyes. With the camera focused on her luminous face, the light steadily darkens to a gray dimness—as if the light of her very soul had suddenly gone out.

Shooting almost entirely at night enhances the picture's sepulchral atmosphere. Even the few daylight scenes appear filtered, so that the moody gray light brings with it little illumination and no sense of warmth.

Enzo Martinelli recalled the care with which Arthur Martinelli worked. "My uncle was always sure it was possible to recognize the source of the light in those scenes. In so many shows today they just ignore the light source. When working on the indoor sets he always gave them a little scope, a little depth. He kept the actors well *into* the set, not back against the walls. The sets were nicely lit for depth and mood."

Martinelli's camera moves often and with great purpose—drawing the viewer into the uncanny proceedings. In the funereal sugar mill, the camera moves in front of Beaumont as he crosses the factory floor to Legendre's unholy lair. Retreating before him, the camera seemingly backs *through* a gate of ornate wrought-iron. The camera continues to recede, drawing Beaumont in after it, as the man opens the bars and steps through like the condemned entering a prison cell—or a fly entering the spider's lair. For a moment he stands, uncertain, the dark lines of the gate behind him reminiscent of an arachnid's web.

For Madeline's burial scene, the camera retreats in front of the casket as the silent pallbearers carry it slowly forward and the robed priest intones his liturgy. Moving ahead of the coffin, the camera seemingly backs into the niche—carrying the viewer *inside* the dark tomb itself as they lift the coffin onto the lip of the opening. Our view narrows to a small rectangle above the invading casket so all we see are the silent, stunned forms of Beaumont and Neil hanging back at the mausoleum's steps. The only sound is the ominous grating of the coffin as it slides inexorably toward us, pinning us within the black crypt.

Perhaps the eeriest sequence in a film suffused with uncanny atmosphere comes when Beaumont visits Murder Legendre's unholy mill. Following the voodoo-master's zombie servant, Beaumont enters the drab stone building. Inside we see a large two-story expanse around which runs a recessed balcony. Men, half-dressed in rags, shuffle forward to their tasks in a lethargic, steady stream. Dominating the center of the hall is a round catwalk encircling what appears to be a large wooden vat. Underneath is a large spoked wheel with a man pushing against each spoke in order to turn the cylinder. The figures move slowly, silently. Their unnatural stillness and emaciated frames are too strange to be men—at least not *living* men. As Beaumont steps onto the balcony, the camera views him from low on the catwalk across the room so that half-naked, ragged legs pass back and forth in the foreground. Figures with baskets of sugar cane on their heads move in a slow, steady stream around the circular walkway to drop their load into the vat. The camera takes us inside the huge cylinder and we see large wooden and metal blades at the bottom ro-

For their production the Halperin brothers borrowed not only Universal's backlot, standing sets, and furniture, but that studio's ace makeup man, Jack Pierce, as well—to create the film's subtly shuddery zombie visages.

tating relentlessly to chop up the cane. One of the lumbering, silent figures stumbles and topples sideways into the vat. The camera pans down to show his fellow workers continue to walk in their never-ending circuit to power the grinding blades—their unseeing, dead eyes oblivious to their fellow's gruesome fate.

Throughout the sequence, the only sound heard is the almost unearthly groan of the straining wooden gears and grinding cane—a moan rising and falling like the very souls of the damned, speaking eloquently for those empty shells who no longer possess the will to cry out.

Though far from his most expensive production, Victor Halperin seemingly took more care with *White Zombie* than his subsequent projects. Within his den of death, Legendre, in low tones, commands Beaumont to "Send me word—when you use [the poison]." Like an infernal vapor, wisps of steam punctuate the words exhaled from Lugosi's satanic lips. By taking the time to capture his icy breath for this one close-up (and single line), Halperin adds a bizarre, hellish flourish to the moment.

Halperin and Martinelli make inventive use of sound and shadows to visually evoke Neil's state of singular grief. Neil, the only person visible, sits at a table in a noisy cafe, while on the wall behind him move silhouettes of couples dancing or talking animatedly at tables. Though surrounded by the sounds of laughter and clinking glasses, Neil sits isolated from the gaiety, as removed from the spectral images of humanity as light from shadow. The moving shades cannot touch Neil and he cannot touch them, for he is utterly alone in his anguish.

The Halperins had the good sense (and good fortune) to borrow from Universal the services of makeup wizard Jack Pierce (with assistance from Carl Axcelle) to create the zombie faces as well as Lugosi's devilish countenance. Not until Karloff's Hjalmar Poelzig of *The Black Cat* (also a Jack Pierce creation) two years later would another human visage reflect such focused diabolism. Pierce's subtle makeup turns slowmoving actors into frightening gargoyles of living death. When Beaumont mounts the carriage sent him by Legendre, he looks over at the driver beside him. A close-up of the driver's hands holding the reins reveals two cadaverous claws, the spaces between the fingers and tendons darkened to create a bony skeletal impression. Halperin heightens the perception by showing the reins threaded tightly through the un-

Evil incarnate: Bela Lugosi as Murder Legendre.

moving fingers—as if they have little power to grasp or move of their own volition and are as brittle as dried bones. When Beaumont looks away from the hands toward the driver's face, his eyes go even wider and he involuntarily draws back from what he sees. The camera pans left to show the upturned face of a corpse, its bony features made prominent by Pierce's subtle shadings while the eyes stare sightlessly ahead and a black hood frames the cadaverous countenance.

Murder Legendre is the epitome of evil—vile for the sake of vileness. As such, Bela Lugosi was the ideal choice for the role. Unrestricted by the constraints placed on other men, Lugosi's Legendre indulges his evil whims to the fullest, delighting in the suffering he causes. Lugosi's glowering expression reflects his diabolical intent while the actor keeps his movements slow and measured to intensify the impression of malevolent power. His hypnotic gaze and sardonically evil smirk speak volumes of the man's malignant character. Though Lugosi plays the part perfectly, it ultimately becomes limiting.

As Murder Legendre, "[Bela Lugosi's] portrayal even surpasses that former work of artistry, [*Dracula*]," ballyhooed the *White Zombie* pressbook. While Lugosiphiles find it hard to disagree with such a grandiose assessment and have long held *White Zombie* up as one of that actor's finest vehicles (it *is*, after all, difficult to envision anyone else in the role of the evil voodoo master), Murder Legendre simply fails to do justice to the actor. Much like Karloff's Fu Manchu of the same year, Lugosi's Legendre is a thor-

oughly evil entity, devoid of any grace-saving attribute or emotion. While this provides the actor with plenty of opportunities to exercise his particular brand of menace, the one-dimensional character severely limits him—more so even than *Dracula*, who indeed possessed a sympathetic side (who can forget Lugosi's sad soliloquy ending with, "To die, to be really dead—that must be glorious"?). Even so lowly a vehicle as 1935's *Murder by Television* (arguably Lugosi's *worst* film of the decade) allowed the actor more range of expressive emotion than did *White Zombie*. To his credit, Lugosi plays the diabolical Legendre splendidly, his powerful presence in fine form as he unleashes his malevolent hypnotic stare at an unwitting victim or leeringly strokes the heroine's hand with his spider-like fingers while giving full sardonic weight to his mocking voice. Still, in the end, Legendre is merely a one-dimensional bogeyman, devoid of the romantic mystique of *Dracula*'s Count, the emotional pain of *The Black Cat*'s Vitus Verdegast, or the tortured obsession of *The Raven*'s Dr. Vollin. While Lugosi serves *White Zombie* admirably, if one examines his character closely, *White Zombie* fails to return the favor. Often thought of as the consummate Lugosi vehicle, in truth *White Zombie* simply took him for a ride further down the typecasting highway.

The single greatest fault found in *White Zombie* is the creaky, silent-era acting which permeates the picture. The cast constantly overplays. (In fact, the only "natural" performance in the film comes from Joseph Cawthorn's Dr. Bruner—a sort of comedy relief Van Helsing—whose easygoing manner remains free from the heavy theatricality of the rest.) Even Lugosi (never the most restrained of actors) succumbs to temptation and poor (or, by some accounts, *lack of*) direction from Victor Halperin and plays too broadly at times. Often, the actor's mastery of melodramatics allows him to pull it off. When Legendre begins carving his wax voodoo doll outside Beaumont's mansion, for instance, a croaking caw splits the silence and the camera pans up from Legendre to reveal a vulture perched atop a stone pillar. Lugosi, with an evil, smug smile on his lips, cocks an appreciative eyebrow and gives a knowing glance toward the bird, whose hawkish eye seems to sparkle back at him. At other times, however, Lugosi simply goes too far. Upon casting his spell over Madeline by burning the wax effigy, Lugosi stares directly into the camera (no doubt at Halperin's [mis]direction), ludicrously bats his eyelashes several times as if coming out of a daze, and opens his eyes to their white-orbed, impossible widest before stalking directly toward the camera, his face coming so close that it ultimately blocks the screen. The painfully obvious theatrical expressions simply draw unwanted attention to themselves and serve to distance the viewer from the proceedings.

As the "white zombie" of the title, Madge Bellamy plays her role of mindless automaton perfectly. Unfortunately, the same cannot be said for her stint as a "living" character. Ms. Bellamy, a star of silent films trying to break through to talkies, appears soulless from the very beginning, with a vacant look in her large doe-eyes and little inflection in her high-pitched child-voice. She needed a director more versed in sound (and more comfortable with actors) than Victor Halperin (who'd only made two talkies previous to this picture) to transform her waifish pantomime into the more natural acting now required in this new age of sound pictures.

Born Margaret Philpott, Madge Bellamy saw *White Zombie* as her comeback vehicle. Ms. Bellamy was a supremely successful star of the silent screen, but hadn't made a picture in over two years. Her "comeback" didn't take, however, and she made only a handful of (minor) films after *White Zombie*. A decade after her failed "comeback," the actress' name once again became front-page news, though not because of her acting. In 1943, Madge Bellamy shot and wounded her millionaire lover of five years when the man suddenly married another woman. "Pistol Packin' Madge" (as one paper dubbed her) received a suspended sentence for the assault and was placed on probation. "I only winged him," the actress told Richard Lamparski (in *Whatever Became Of... 11th series*) years later, "which is all I meant to do. Believe me, I'm a crack shot." After leaving motion pictures, she owned and operated a large junkyard in Ontario, California for many years. "I've avoided all my life the romantic stuff which novels and movies are about," declared the former actress. "Never went in for that mush."

An amusing (and outlandish) publicity article printed in the picture's pressbook claimed that Ms. Bellamy's screen "death" greatly affected the actress. "Madge Bellamy Scared to Death By Own Portrayal in 'White Zombie'" announced the headline. When the actress viewed the day's rushes, reported the article, "that part of the sequence in which she is seen lying in a coffin was flashed upon the screen, and, after taking one look, Miss Bellamy let cut a piercing scream and bolted for the door. And nothing could prevail upon her to return. Now Miss Bellamy is a convert to cremation."

According to studio publicity, the Halperins intentionally kept the dialogue in *White Zombie* to a minimum, even trimming pages from the shooting script. "The producers decided that the public is tired unto death of 100 percent dialogue in pictures," reported an article in the film's pressbook. "In fact, it is their firm conviction that the public is tired of even

Universal's Castle Dracula set becomes the voodoo-master's mountaintop lair—the new home of the *White Zombie*.

20 or 30 percent dialogue. The result is that only 15 percent of the length of 'White Zombie' is accompanied by dialogue. This was permitted because the story is all action, and stirring action at that." The two brothers came to Hollywood from Chicago in the early 1920s and began their own production company. Having produced over 30 previous features, the majority of them silents, the pair undoubtedly felt more comfortable with the silent medium (as evidenced from the heavy, melodramatic acting found not only in *White Zombie* but in their subsequent features as well, from *Revolt of the Zombies* [1936] to as late as *Torture Ship* in 1939).

Though (rightly) calling *White Zombie* "one of the eeriest and most fantastic stories ever pictured for the screen," United Artists promoted the picture as something of an exposé. "The story of 'White Zombie,'" announced the film's pressbook, "is based upon personal observation in Haiti by American writers and research workers, and, fantastic as it sounds, its entire substance is based upon fact." Right. The picture's advertising and ballyhoo played up the apparent recognition of zombies by the Haitian Penal Code, encouraging theater owners to place in their lobbies blow-ups of "Article 249":

> "Also shall be qualified as attempted murder the employment of drugs, hypnosis or any other occult practice which produces lethargic coma, or lifeless sleep. And if the person (**Zombie**) has

At the zombie-master's sugar mill, worked by the silent, soulless Living Dead, Beaumont seeks Murder Legendre's hellish help.

been buried it shall be considered murder no matter what result follows."

As one might suspect, the bracketed word "zombie" was strictly a Hollywood inclusion, inserted to lend a supernatural air to Article 249's medical/legal emphasis. While making good PR copy, such sensationalistic assertions did the image of the heretofore largely unknown religion no favors.

In addition, the erroneous claim to be based on "fact" notwithstanding, the film itself served its subject poorly. Casting Voudou in a decidedly evil light, *White Zombie* tainted the topic and set the cinematic tone for the decades to come. As the subgenre's cinematic debut, *White Zombie* proved an excellent introduction to screen "voodoo" but a libelously misleading inauguration to real-life Voudoun.

The "catch lines" used to advertise *White Zombie* ranged from suggestive to racist to downright amusing:

"What does a man want in a woman, is it her body or is it her soul?"

"They knew that this was taking place among the blacks but when this fiend practiced it on a white girl—all hell broke loose."

"Look around you, do your friends act queerly—strangely they may be ZOMBIES—living, breathing, walking, under the spell of the Master of the Living Dead."

Reviews of *White Zombie* ran from raves to pans. *Variety* reported that "Victor Halperin goes to Hayti [sic], hotbed of obi, for the latest addition to the blood curdling cycle, and with good results... Now and then a tendency to overplay jars slightly, but in the main the atmosphere of horror is well sustained and sensitive picturegoers will get a full quota of thrills." *The New York Times*, however, could find nothing good to say, quoting a line from the picture: "'The whole thing has me confused; I just can't understand it.' That was, as briefly as can be expressed, the legend for poster-ity of 'White Zombie.' Charity—still the greatest of the trilogy—suggests that the sentence be allowed to stand as comment."

Despite the mixed reviews, *White Zombie* was a huge financial success for the Halperin brothers. Conversely, the film only made between $800-900 (reports vary) for its star, Bela Lugosi. Despite this sore point, Lugosi considered this picture along with *Dracula* to be two of his best according to film histo-

lights they needed and they only used reflectors. I was driving the carriage with two wild horses and they just had the road marked out with reflectors. It was tough keeping those horses going in the right direction, but Bela knew what atmosphere he wanted to create and he never settled for anything less."

Though not a perfect film, *White Zombie* can stand up and be counted among the handful of voodoo pictures which managed to rise above its inadequate resources to successfully create a brooding, otherworldly atmosphere all its own. In addition, though it did nothing for the actor's career (and little for his wallet), *White Zombie* sports a quintessential Lugosi performance to be savored with each repeated viewing. In short, *White Zombie* rightly deserves the oft-misused appellative honor "classic," and stands as a superior example of moody voodoo ("moodoo?").

Legendre and one of his "angels of death."

CREDITS: Director: Victor Halperin; Producer: Edward Halperin; Story and Dialogue: Garnett Weston; Photography: Arthur Martinelli; Editor: Howard McLernon; Art Direction: Ralph Berger, Conrad Tritschler; Dialogue Director: Herbert Farjeon; Makeup: Jack Pierce, Carl Axcelle; Special Effects: Harold Anderson; Original Music: Guy Bevier Williams, Xavier Cugat; Musical Arrangements: Abe Meyer; Additional Music: Nathaniel Dett, Gaston Borch, Hugo Riesenfeld, Leo Kempenski, H. Herkan, H. Maurice Jacquet; Production Assistant: Sidney Marcus; Assistant Director: William Cody; Second Assistant Director: Herbert Glazer; Released July 1932 by United Artists; 69 minutes

rian William K. Everson, who saw the actor often in the early 1950s. "He had great respect for the speed and efficiency with which the Halperin brothers made that minor classic," wrote Everson in *Castle of Frankenstein*, "and an envy for all the money they'd made out of it while he had only signed for a flat salary."

Lugosi's official biographer, Robert Cremer (in the book *Lugosi, The Man Behind the Cape*), told a different story. According to Cremer, Lugosi was displeased with the way director Victor Halperin was handling the film and so took it upon himself to go about "reordering scenes, restaging some completely, rewriting others, and finally taking the director's baton in hand to mold the film to his personal specifications." Actor Clarence Muse (who played the coach driver) concurred: "Bela made a lot of changes in the script and directed some of the scenes himself." Muse credited much of the picture's fine atmosphere to Lugosi. The film was shot in the dead of night, and Muse recalled, "Those guys on the set cut out a lot of

CAST: Bela Lugosi (Murder), Madge Bellamy (Madeline), Joseph Cawthorn (Dr. Bruner), Robert Frazer (Beaumont), John Harron (Neil), Brandon Hurst (Silver), George Burr MacAnnan (Von Gelder), Frederick Peters (Chauvin), Annette Stone (Maid), John Printz (Latour), Dan Crimmins (Pierre), Claude Morgan (Zombie), John Fergusson (Zombie), Velma Gresham (Maid), Clarence Muse (Driver)

DRUMS O' VOODOO
(1934)
Perspective on a Shoestring

"Beat dem drums... Beat dem drums... Beat dem
drums... The ancient god Voodoo commands you...
Beat... Beat... Beat... Beat!"
—Laura Bowman as Aunt Hagar

Cinema's second voodoo entry came from the very
fringe of the movie industry—the so-called "Negro
circuit." Written by an African American, *Drums o'
Voodoo* took its subject in a diametrically opposed
direction from its predecessor, *White Zombie*, for
Drums o' Voodoo is the first picture to shine a benign
light on its topic and capture the sense of community
integral to Voudoun spirituality.

When black actor/playwright J. Augustus Smith's
stageplay *Louisiana* closed after only one week on
Broadway in 1933, Smith turned his one-act play into
a movie script and took it to independent producer
Louis Weiss. The cost-conscious Weiss hired (at a
pittance) nearly the entire stage cast, including Smith
himself (who played Amos Berry in the play just as in
the movie), to save money since the actors already
knew their lines and were in costume. If *White Zombie* was low-budget, then *Drums o' Voodoo* was *no*-
budget, costing only about one-*tenth* its already cheap
predecessor. Still, *Drums o' Voodoo* holds the distinction of being the first film based on the work of a
black dramatist—*and* the first blaxploitation voodoo
movie.

In the mid-1930s, between 200 and 600 theaters
in the United States (estimates vary) catered strictly
to the "colored" population. By contrast, over 35,000
cinemas served white patrons. So, while a market
did exist for all-black films, it was extremely limited.
Consequently, producers were forced to work within
minuscule budgets to guarantee a profitable return on
their investment. (The average cost of an "all-colored" production in the early 1930s was an incredibly
low $6,000.)

Director Arthur Hoerl shot Smith's story at New
York's Atlas Soundfilm Recording Studios in late
March of 1933. Even during production, the picture
went through a confusing series of retitlings. Filmed
under *two* working titles, *Louisiana* and *Voodoo*, the
New York State Censor Board approved the picture
(after substantial cuts) in 1934 as *The Devil*. When
the film finally saw general release in May of 1934

(over a year after completion), it carried the moniker
Drums o' Voodoo. Later reissues added *Louisiana*,
Voodoo Drums and *She Devil* to the roster. So, while
Drums o' Voodoo may be the cheapest voodoo film
ever produced, it also sports the most impressive ar-
ray of names.

In a rural Louisiana black community, voodoo
and Christianity exist side by side. "The choral pro-
cessions," the opening written narration tells us, "the
sacred chants and the incessant beating of the voodoo
drums on the eve of a sacrifice, are horrible and wonderful embellishments of a religion that is practiced
as fervently today in certain communities as Christianity."

The old voodoo priestess Aunt Hagar presides
over "the ancient worship of the jungle gods" while
Elder Berry (!) ministers to his Christian flock. Into
this peaceful coexistence comes the evil, unscrupulous Tom Catt (!!), who wants the parson's niece,
Myrtle, for his "jook joint" across the river (a den of
liquor, gambling, and loose women). Ebeneezer, Aunt
Hagar's grandson, loves Myrtle and so goes to his
grandmother and begs her to keep the innocent girl
from Tom Catt's claws. To this end, the voodoo witch
intones a spell and assures Ebeneezer that no harm
will come to the girl.

The whole God (and voodoo)-fearing community wants the vile Tom Catt gone, but are afraid to
act. Catt tries to blackmail the parson into sending
Myrtle to him. (Many years ago, before he'd found
God, Reverend Berry was with Tom Catt on a chain
gang and Catt has been periodically extorting money
from Berry by threatening to tell all to the congregation.) When the minister refuses to sacrifice his niece,
Tom Catt first tries to charm Myrtle and then to force
himself upon her. A group of passing townspeople
rescue Myrtle and Aunt Hagar warns Catt that "if the
sun goes down in this community on your worthless
carcass, I'm gonna *blind* ya—I'm gonna *blind you*,
ya hear me?!" The swaggering rogue puts no stock in
the old woman's threats, however.

That night, Tom Catt breaks into the church revival meeting to tell the congregation that "Amos
Berry ain't the man you think he is." Amos rises and
stops Tom Catt with his own confession: "I go over
to his place to pay him money not to tell you all that
I—was on the chain-gang once—for murder." This
puts the congregation in an angry uproar. Tom Catt
takes advantage of the confusion and pulls out his ra-
zor to threaten the crowd. "I told you that anything I
wants I gets," he tells them menacingly. "I want that
gal," he demands, motioning to Myrtle. Before he
can act, however, he's suddenly struck blind. This
section of the film is so choppy that it is difficult to
tell exactly what happens. In the next scene, Aunt
Hagar tells pastor Berry that Ebeneezer has taken the

stricken Tom Catt home, "But it ain't over yet." The print currently available for viewing abruptly ends here, but reviews of the day indicate that Tom Catt stumbles out into the swamp and is swallowed up by (offscreen) quicksand.

The poor condition of the one surviving print (distributed on video by Sinister Cinema) makes a complete assessment of *Drums o' Voodoo* difficult. The print is so choppy that dialogue often ends in mid-sentence and whole scenes are missing (including all but a snippet of the picture's climax). Still, the butchered remains of *Drums o' Voodoo* can give us some idea of the film's merit.

Despite its crude production values, slow pacing, and missed opportunities, *Drums o' Voodoo* remains a worthy voodoo entry because of the unique perspective it affords us. *Drums o' Voodoo* portrays a time and place in which the religion of voodoo is just as real as Christianity (in fact, more so, since it is voodoo rather than Christian prayer which accomplishes the aims of the community). Rather than the evil black magic seen in *White Zombie* (1932) or the destructive fanaticism holding sway in the same year's *Black Moon* (1934), voodoo is here portrayed as a benign, helpful force. Voodoo ceremonies are as commonplace—and just as valid—as weekly church services. Every member of the community knows of, tolerates, and acknowledges the ancient religion. Even the minister himself admits, "I believe [Aunt Hagar] is the only one 'round here that can drive Tom Catt out of this community." While some have turned away and tried to forget their religious heritage, in the end they must come back to the fold to save their town from the earthly evil (in the form of the violent—and ungodly—Tom Catt) that threatens their physical—and spiritual—selves. This stress on voodoo as a primal religion rather than as perverted sorcery gives *Drums o' Voodoo* a unique, refreshing atmosphere and affords us a glimpse into an alternative spirituality.

Screenwriter J. Augustus Smith peppers his meandering screenplay with colorful dialogue that brings to life the colloquial time period and superstitious subject. Aunt Hagar's curse upon Tom Catt, for instance, is a rhythmic whammy at once amusing *and* chilling:

> "Jungle gods, I makes a spell
> to cast this imp back to hell.
> In a pit of bile and sand,
> let him join his hellish band.
> Let no mercy stay thy heart,
> jungle gods make him depart.
> Plunge him, crush him—like a
> crumb, for you Voodoo, I beats
> dem drums."

Later, when Hagar restrains the townspeople from attacking Tom Catt for what he tried to do to Myrtle, she unleashes this invective: "Don't stain your hands with his worthless blood. *I'll* fix him. I'll fix him [turning to Tom Catt]—you creepin', crawlin', hissin', lizard-eatin', poisonous black Catt...Your soul is as black as the soot on a skillet!"

The juxtaposition of voodoo and Christianity makes a fascinating springboard for a tale of spiritual conflict which, sadly, fails to materialize in Smith's story. The written narration at film's beginning informs us that "a struggle between the White God and the Black Gods still goes on—to the steady beat of the voodoo drums." While *Drums o' Voodoo* indeed exposes us to plenty of voodoo drumming in the ritual ceremony scenes (the only visually interesting sequences in the picture), the only "struggle" takes the form of several of the Christian congregation complaining about the noise of the drums keeping them awake at night. Smith chooses to fill the running time with lengthy scenes of Bible-thumping revival meetings, complete with noisome spirituals and enraptured "Amen"s. In the end, very little conflict arises and very little happens in the picture, with most of the film's 70 minutes filled with time-killing songfests or dull exchanges between the parishioners.

The picture's opening is quite promising—a promise which sadly remains unfulfilled since *Drums o' Voodoo* makes for a poor horror film indeed. As a rhythmic voodoo chant and drumbeat (reminiscent of

Drums o' Voodoo screenwriter J. Augustus Smith (center) also stars in the film as Elder Berry (a moniker just "ripe" for ridicule!).

the native ceremonial chant from *King Kong*) plays on the soundtrack, the scene begins with the camera tight on a steaming cauldron. Lit from inside, the devilish pot seems to glow. When the camera pulls back (in the film's *only* tracking shot), we see a group of half-naked black men, their bodies glistening with sweat, dancing around the cauldron, their forms twisting and turning rhythmically with the drumbeat. Tending the voodoo vessel in the center is a black-robed, hooded figure who, lit from the fire below the bubbling kettle, conjures up images of a hellish devil-crone. In a circle around the dancers sit the chanters, their arms rising and falling along with their primal voices. A near-solid curtain of Spanish moss surrounds the scene, the wispy tendrils almost glowing in the eerie light cast upon them. Unfortunately, this all-too-brief scene quickly dissolves to a lengthy, mundane sequence at "A Louisiana Jook" (as the onscreen title informs us). When the picture again returns to the cryptic voodoo ritual, all hopes of uncanny mystery immediately vanish when the crone reveals herself to be a benign elderly Aunt Hagar (who's more than a little comical in her overacting). Never again does *Drums o' Voodoo* generate anything even approaching a spine-tingle.

On the technical side, *Drums o' Voodoo* is without a doubt the most primitive entry in voodoo cinema (and that's saying something!). A filmed play, the whole production is completely stagebound, with the "exteriors" represented by a few unconvincing stage sets. The pedantic photography and direction emphasize the picture's static nature. All cinematic considerations seem to have fallen by the wayside, for the camera never moves after the opening scene. Director Arthur Hoerl (helming his fourth—and final—feature) fails to exploit the mystery or horror in his subject and chooses to simply anchor the camera and film his players moving in front of it. The only indication the viewer has that this is a motion picture

are the infrequent close-ups which Hoerl grudgingly inserts every few minutes.

With one exception, the performances lack conviction. Laura Bowman's (in awful makeup that makes the black actress look as if she's a white woman wearing blackface!) doomful, singsong delivery and swaying gestures inspire more titters than shudders, and the story's author, J. Augustus Smith, appears so stiff and uncomfortable in the role of the persecuted minister that it is almost a relief when he finally loosens up and goes on a long and ridiculous tirade at the climactic revival meeting. The picture's one good performance comes from Morris "Chick" McKinney as Tom Catt, whose swaggering attitude is balanced by an easygoing charm, making his vile villain dangerously seductive.

Laura Bowman's acting career spanned nearly half a century, most of which she spent touring the U.S. and Europe in theater companies. "The Negro Barrymore" (as the press sometimes labeled her) frequently appeared on Broadway, supporting the likes of Tallulah Bankhead, Helen Hayes, and Miriam Hopkins, and once gave a command performance at Buckingham Palace before King Edward VII. In 1935, the 54-year-old actress married LeRoi Antoine ("the first Haitian singer-actor to come to the U.S.," accord-

1940 reissue poster bearing a new title for *Drums o' Voodoo* **(1934).**

ing to *Variety*), a man 28 years her junior. Ironically, Ms. Bowman was deathly afraid of voodoo in real life. Her husband recalled that during a trip to Haiti, Bowman was fearful that she might die and be transformed into a zombie.

J. Augustus ("Gus") Smith ran away from home at age 14 to join the Rabbit's Foot Musical Comedy troupe. After touring with traveling minstrel shows throughout the South for a number of years, Smith finally made it to Broadway by starring in his own play, *Louisiana*, produced by George Miller for the Negro Theater Guild. The play garnered several good reviews, but the powerful theater critic Brooks Atkinson savaged the production in his critique, leading to the play closing after only eight performances.

At this time a few blacks produced their own films (Oscar Micheaux being the best-known example)—most "all-colored" pictures were made by whites. *Drums o' Voodoo* was no exception and, though starring black actors, it carried an all-white crew.

After acquiring the screen rights from Edgar Rice Burroughs in 1918, producer Louis Weiss became the first man to bring Tarzan to the silver screen. Throughout the 1920s, Weiss supervised a number of lower-berth pictures, specializing in Westerns and comedies. At one point, he headed Columbia Pictures' serial division, producing the Frank Buck "Jungle Menace" series, among others. With the advent of television, Weiss adapted to the new medium and supervised the *Craig Kennedy, Detective* series. Weiss remained active in the industry through film distribution up until his death in 1963.

Having trained as a newsreel cameraman in New York, cinematographer Walter Strenge began working in Hollywood movies only a year previous to his *Drums o' Voodoo* assignment. Over the next four decades, he carved out a distinguished career in the industry, culminating in an Academy Award nomination for *Stagecoach to Fury* (1956). That same year he became president of the American Society of Cinematographers and eventually co-authored the *American Cinematographer Manual*, the primary textbook of film photography.

Strenge's co-cameraman, J. Burgi Contner, also went on to bigger and better things, particularly in television, working on shows such as *You Are There*, *Naked City*, and *The Defenders*. Also an engineer, Contner is credited with several important inventions, including the Academy Aperture used in theater projectors, the Cineglow sound system, an early color film process, and the Cineflex combat camera (for the U.S. Army Air Corps).

Few critics or trade publications bothered to review *Drums o' Voodoo*. One exception was *Variety* (which seemingly covers *everything*). In his May 15, 1934 critique, "Bige" called this "all-Negro feature...

The evil Tom Catt (Morris McKinney), whose "soul is as black as the soot on a skillet," wants to sink his claws into the virginal Myrtle (Edna Barr).

cheaply produced and looking it; also badly acted. Fails to rate either as a film laboratory experiment in racial traits or as an entertainment." "Bige" had nothing good to say technically either: "So shallow are the settings, picture appears to have been produced in one room, not too large. Besides shallow they are too phony in appearance to fool any audience... Poor lighting as well as the unfortunate scenery combine to make the photography look bad, while jerky cutting doesn't help either." On the plus side, the reviewer did admit that "the sound is satisfactory and the dialog exceptionally good."

While *Drums o' Voodoo* may not be much of a motion picture, it stands as a minor milestone in voodoo cinema as the first (admittedly weak) stab at *exploring* rather than exploiting the Voudoun religion.

CREDITS: Alternate Titles: *Louisiana*; *Voodoo Drums*; *She Devil*; Director: Arthur Hoerl; Producer: Lou Weiss; Screenplay: J. Augustus Smith (by arrangement with George L. Miller); Cinematographers: Walter Strenge, J. Burgi Contner; Editor: Adrian Weiss; Art Director: Sam Corso; Production Manager: Ben Berk; Sound Effects: Lyman J. Wiggin and Verne T. Brayman; Recorded by Cineglow Sound; Released May 1934 by International Stageplay Pictures; 70 minutes

CAST: Laura Bowman (Aunt Hagar), Edna Barr (Myrtle Simpson), Lionel Monagas (Ebeneezer), J. Augustus Smith (Amos Berry), Morris McKinney (Thomas Catt), A.B. Comathiere (Deacon Dunson), Alberta Perkins (Sister Knight), Fred Bonny (Brother Zero), Paul Johnson (Deacon August), Trixie Smith (Sister Marguerite), Carrie Huff (Sister Zuzan)

A publicity shot from *Black Moon*: pictured—Jack Holt, a knife-wielding extra, and Fay Wray. Courtesy Ronald V. Borst/Hollywood Movie Posters

BLACK MOON (1934)
The Natives are Restless

"Blood worship, sacrifice to the black gods—
you call it voodoo."
—Arnold Korff as Dr. Perez

"*Black Moon* is a film I've almost erased from my consciousness," admitted Fay Wray (in *Starlog* magazine). So has the movie-watching world in general since, until recently, the picture belonged to that sad subgroup, the "lost film." Disappointingly, *Black Moon* is not much of a rediscovery. "I've never seen it," stated Ms. Wray, "but I think it was supposed to be a pretty interesting story." Indeed it was.

Juanita (Dorothy Burgess) takes her small child, Nancy (Cora Sue Collins), back to visit the tiny West Indian island of San Christopher where she was raised. While staying at her uncle's plantation (the only whites "among 10,000 blacks") she answers the lure of the jungle drums and resumes her old role of voodoo priestess, participating in a human sacrifice.

When her unknowing husband, Stephen (Jack Holt), arrives from New York, he discovers her involvement in the local voodoo cult and tries to take his family and leave the island. The natives, however, conspire (with Juanita's approval) to keep them there, murdering the island's wireless operator, stealing the solitary boat, and killing Nancy's suspicious nanny.

Dorothy Burgess up to her voodoo treachery in *Black Moon*. (Ronald V. Borst/ Hollywood Movie Posters)

Stephen sneaks out to witness a voodoo ceremony (consisting of "500 colored dancers in a ritual number [supervised by dance director Max Scheck]," according to a blurb in *Film Daily*) and shoots the high priest who's about to sacrifice a young girl. At this, the natives rebel and attack the plantation. Stephen, his attractive secretary Gail (Fay Wray), and Nancy are all captured, though Juanita's uncle, Dr. Perez (Arnold Korff), and a friendly boat captain named Lunch (Clarence Muse) escape.

Sitting like a queen in judgment at the captured plantation, Juanita tells Stephen and Gail that they are to be sacrificed that night. But Perez utilizes a secret passageway to spirit the pair away. When the natives discover "les blancs" have escaped, they demand that Juanita offer up her own daughter in their place. At first Juanita resists, but the power of the cult proves too strong and she capitulates, carrying the child to the sacrificial spot herself. As Juanita succumbs fully to her fanaticism and shakily raises the ceremonial knife over her own daughter, Stephen arrives and shoots his wife, saving the child. The following day things have seemingly returned to normal on San Christopher, and Stephen, Gail, and Nancy leave the cursed isle far behind.

Those seeking a horror rediscovery in *Black Moon* are destined for disappointment. Despite the involvement of diabolical voodoo and human sacrifice, nothing is made of the mystical (much less horrific) aspects of the West Indian religion. No zombies, no hexes or curses, no talk of vengeful spirits or voodoo gods, not even a single ceremonial snake rears its sacred head. The story might just as well have taken place in the wilds of India as a tale of religious upheaval or in darkest Africa as some Tarzan movie subplot. The film's main interest comes from the themes of fanaticism and love and the moral dilemma posed when the two conflict, rather than from any voodoo trappings. "Out of the inferno of tropic madness comes the weirdest romance of our time!" shout the ads for *Black Moon* in a bit of revealing ballyhoo.

The players generally acquit themselves well. Jack Holt, as the husband and father, exhibits an unselfconscious, ebullient affection for his young daughter and, later, a bitter shock when he learns of his wife's savage activities. Fay Wray, beautiful as always, does well with the few significant scenes given her, showing tender concern for the child and a wistful, pained stoicism in submerging her true—and forbidden—feelings for her married employer.

As Juanita, Dorothy Burgess is too cold to elicit much sympathy from the viewer and so denies the film much of its potential power. Also, the screenplay provides little insight into Juanita's character. We never see the ties that bound her to this brutal sect as she matured on the island—we're simply told that she

Wary of the evil influence of the nursemaid (a voodoo priestess), Gail watchers over little Nancy in *Black Moon*. (Ronald V. Borst/Hollywood Movie Posters)

camerawork creates little mood. One expects more from the director of *The Black Room* (1935) and the cinematographer from *The Hunchback of Notre Dame* (1939) than a barely average melodrama.

Black Moon received a lukewarm reception from the critics. *Variety*'s "Shan" commented that "direction in *Black Moon* is commendable and the acting is good, but the scenario possesses dubious elements. Studio has made a strong effort to weave an interesting white romance around the black magic of the Negroes of the West Indies, but unsuccessfully." Thornton Delehanty of *The New York Post* dismissed *Black Moon* as "a humid melodrama… put together hastily on a formula that has frequently done service for the cinema and pulp magazines."

The Motion Picture Herald pointed out a stereotypical shortcoming in voodoo cinema (and in jungle movies in general) when it cautioned, "In that the colored natives involved in the film are rather harshly pictured as bloodthirsty worshippers of black gods who indulge in sacrificial orgies, the film may meet with objection in those situations where colored people make up a portion of the patronage."

Indeed, in making voodoo nothing more than the driving superstition of fanatical savages (while at the same time failing to generate any of the expected thrills and shudders), *Black Moon* did the religion (and its viewers) no favors.

was raised to it. The viewer shares no common base with her and subsequently can't empathize with her compulsion. At the end, however, when Juanita chooses to sacrifice her own child, Ms. Burgess effectively displays an emotional turmoil which at least momentarily draws the viewer into her plight.

The picture moves at a painfully slow pace. Scenes often drag on far too long to be effective (including the tedious ceremonial dancing) and very little happens over the course of the film's 69 minutes. Much of the picture focuses on the husband discovering what the viewer already knows.

Roy William Neill's straightforward but uninspired direction generates only paltry suspense while Joseph August's adequate but frequently static

Director: Roy William Neill; Associate Producer: Everett Riskin; Screenplay: Wells Root; Based on the 1933 Novel *Black Moon* by Clements Ripley; Photography: Joseph August; Camera Operator: Dave Ragin; Assistant Cameramen: Marcel Grand and Jack Andersen; Film Editor: Richard Cahoon; Dance Director: Max Scheck; Sound Engineering: Edward Bernds; Technical Advisor: Don Taylor; Props: Sanley Dunn; Released June 1934 by Columbia; 69 minutes

CAST: Jack Holt (Stephen Lane), Fay Wray (Gail), Dorothy Burgess (Juanita Lane), Cora Sue Collins (Nancy Lane), Arnold Korff (Dr. Perez), Clarence Muse (Lunch), Lumsden Hare (Macklin), Eleanor Wesselhoeft (Anna), Madame Sul-te-wan (Riva), Lawrence Criner (Kala), Henry Kolker (Doctor), Theresa Harris (Sacrificed Girl), Fred Walton (Butler), Billy McClain, Charles Moore, Robert Frazier, Ada Pen, Anna Lee Johnson (House Servants), Lillian West (Maid), Lillian Smith (Nurse), Grace Chapman (Welfare Worker), Edna Franklin (Girl Sacrificed by Mother), William H. Dunn (Langa), Pierre Lutere

Stephen Lane rescues his daughter (Cora Sue Collins) from the voodoo cult's clutches. His own wife raises the sacrificial knife in *Black Moon*.

CHLOE:
LOVE IS CALLING YOU
(1934)
Black Voodoo/White Racism

Wade: "What is all this voodoo, Colonel?"
Colonel: "Just a mixture of savagery, gin, mumbo-jumbo, and drum beats."

Like its fellow voodoo rediscovery *Black Moon* (released the same year), *Chloe: Love is Calling You* languished unseen for decades as another "lost" film until unearthed in 1997. If *Black Moon* disappoints as a rediscovery, *Chloe* becomes downright aggravating. Though a rather tepid thriller in its own right, *Black Moon* at least sports some decent acting (including a plucky turn from perennial screen favorite Fay Wray) and an occasional bit of action. *Chloe* can boast none of these—though it *can* lay claim to being the most overtly racist voodoo vision in cinema history.

Black mamaloi Mandy (Georgette Harvey), her half-white daughter Chloe (Olive Borden), and Mandy's (white) backwoods helper Jim (Philip Ober) paddle back to the old bayou community they left 15 years ago after Mandy's husband was lynched. Nursing a bitter hatred for the last decade-and-a-half, Mandy is intent upon finally revenging herself on those she deems responsible. "Here is your Mandy," she promises her dead husband, "come back to put curses on the cowardly white folk." By this she means Colonel Gordon (Frank Joyner), the local turpentine factory owner.

Jim, in love with Chloe, wants to marry her, but she'll have none of it. When Jim points out that her black blood separates her from the world of respectable whites, Chloe begins to cry and runs off toward the bayou, where she slips and falls in. Jim spies a large alligator entering the sluggish current, dives in with a knife, and dispatches the animal Tarzan-style before rescuing the flailing Chloe from the water.

Shortly thereafter, Chloe tries to fend off the lecherous advances of a thieving black turpentine worker named Mose (Gus Smith). Wade (Reed Howes), the new (white) factory foreman, beats Mose off. But as Wade comforts the girl, Mose rises and levels a pistol at the white man's back. Fortunately, Jim appears and tackles Mose, saving Wade's life (and rescuing Chloe yet again). After this (and despite the devoted Jim's heroism) Chloe has eyes only for Wade.

Mandy leaves a voodoo switch on the Colonel's doorstep. "Sombody puttin' the voodoo on you," the Colonel's servant, Ben (Richard Huey), tells the old gent. Mandy also runs into Mose, who invites Mandy to join him and "work voodoo together against that confound yank."

Jim, jealous of his rival for Chloe's affection, spills the beans and tells Wade that Chloe's mother "is an old voodoo negress." Also, being a decent fellow, Jim warns Wade that, "these blacks got it in for you plenty. You better be careful." Chloe, shamed by her "black blood"(after Jim points out to her that "You're not [white]—it isn't fair to *him*") realizes it's no use and breaks off with Wade.

Learning of Mandy's return and her antipathy toward him, Colonel Gordon goes to her cabin where he finds "an old voodoo bag" containing the clothes the Colonel's baby girl was wearing the day she drowned 15 years ago. Chloe appears at the cabin and mentions that these were *her* baby clothes. At this, the Colonel (who'd never seen her before now and instantly recognizes Chloe's resemblance to his deceased wife) realizes Chloe is actually his long-thought-dead daughter. "God be praised," he crows. "You're my little Betty-Ann."

After this astounding revelation, Chloe reconciles with Wade and the Colonel plans a huge party for his newfound daughter's "coming-out." At the party, however, Mandy shows up and proclaims that Chloe is indeed *her* daughter and not the Colonel's. Upset, Chloe runs off into the woods (again). There she falls into the clutches of Mose (again) who takes her to the voodoo ceremony where Mandy leads the voodooists in frenzied dancing.

The ever faithful, ever vigilant Jim follows the kidnappers but is shot by one of Mose's cronies for his troubles. With her secret about Chloe's true parentage now revealed, Mandy exhorts Mose to sacrifice the girl. Just as he raises his machete-like knife over Chloe's bound form, however, Wade arrives and attacks the would-be executioner. The voodooists scatter and Wade bests Mose. Off to the side, Mose's campadre raises his gun to shoot the unsuspecting Wade, but the injured Jim throws a knife into the coward's back, saving Wade's life yet again. Mortally wounded, Jim then falls into the bayou.

The Colonel, accompanied by the family physician, arrives after having dug up the grave of Mandy's real child (on a tip from his servant, Ben). "Its hair is kinky," pronounces the doctor about the little corpse they've uncovered, proving that Chloe/Betty-Ann was indeed a changeling. With Mandy in custody and her white parentage affirmed, Chloe and Wade are free to marry without a taint of miscegenation.

Dated and dull, the only thing more pervasive than *Chloe*'s racism is its lethargy. Little happens in

Chloe that doesn't involve prodigious jaw-flapping and static posing. Most of the film consists of actors standing stock still (to keep within the unmoving camera's range) and talking. The only moments of activity (aside from a few brief and unconvincing knocks on the chin when Jim or Wade "protect" Chloe) is Jim's (admittedly exciting) underwater battle with an alligator.

When Jim dives into the bayou to defend Chloe from the marauding menace, we're treated to an underwater display both thrilling and oddly graceful as the man grapples, twists, and twirls with the live alligator in the clear water (obviously a dressed-up studio tank rather than an actual murky estuary). It's also an extremely shocking scene, as the stuntman appears to really stab at the animal again and again with his knife—which perhaps he did. Since the filmmakers had no compunction about earlier showing actor Philip Ober brutally beat a real rattlesnake to death with a stick before our very eyes, killing a 'gator on-screen seems well within this movie's moral limits. (One won't be seeing the now *de rigueur* "No animals were hurt in the making of this film…" statement at the close of *Chloe*.)

Apart from this solitary scene, *Chloe* remains as lifeless as a reptile after meeting up with Jim. The camera rarely moves and the straight-on static medium shot seems to be the only option chosen by director Marshall Neilan. He holds on motionless scenes for so long that the proceedings appear more stageplay than photoplay. It's nine minutes in before there's a hint of camera motion—and this is merely an inconsequential introductory shot of the Colonel's Uncle Tom-like servant holding a tray of mint juleps before the camera pulls back slightly as his white masters retrieve the beverages from the platter.

While competently (if uninterestingly) lit by cinematographer Mack Stengler (most of it takes place in the bright illumination of sunlit afternoons), the film fails to generate any real atmosphere. No sinister shadows or twilight moments mar the sunny disposition of the picture's ambiance.

Cinematographer Mack Stengler's undistinguished screen career began in the silents and continued on through the late 1940s when he turned to television. Along the way he lent his mundane talents to such Poverty-Row productions as *Terror of Tiny Town* (1938), *Bowery at Midnight* (1942), *The Ape Man* (1943), and *Revenge of the Zombies* (1943). Though he does nothing exciting with *Chloe*, Stengler later gave slightly better service to another voodoo entry—*King of the Zombies*. Stengler died in 1962 at age 67. At the time, he was working on TV's *Leave it to Beaver*.

Director Marshall ("Mickey") Neilan, on the other hand, was a supremely powerful producer/director/actor in silent films (comparable to D.W. Griffith, who gave Neilan his first industry break in 1911—as his chauffeur!). At the height of his career in the 1920s Neilan commanded a fee of $100,000 per picture and lived (as one reporter termed it) "on the scale of an Indian prince." By the 1930s, however, Neilan could barely find a job (largely due to his alcoholism and unreliability) and was ultimately reduced to begging for bit parts in order to earn rent money. In 1939 he was arrested for passing bad checks. "I just couldn't make the grade," he told the court before being fined and placed on probation. In his heyday, Neilan worked with many of the top stars of the time. Among his over 70 directorial credits are *In Old Kentucky* (1920; with Mary Pickford) and *The Lotus Eater* (1921; with John Barrymore). As reported in *Variety*, "by 1933 there were no jobs available for him"—or at least no jobs of note, as evidenced by his accepting charge of an independent oddity like *Chloe*.

Obviously having lost his touch as well as his lofty reputation by this time, Neilan does as little with his actors as he does with his camera. The players emote with broad strokes that often cross the line from theatrical to ridiculous. As Mandy, Georgette Harvey plays her stereotypical part with ludicrous gusto, becoming an unintentionally comical caricature. When, eavesdropping, she realizes her secret's out. Harvey bares her teeth and shakes her fist up and down as if experiencing a toddler's temper tantrum. The rest of the cast do little better, including Olive Borden as Chloe, whose emotional outbursts are almost painful in their overblown melodramatics.

Like director Neilan, Olive Borden was a prominent figure in silent films whose career quickly evaporated with the coming of sound. One need look no further than her grossly theatrical emoting in *Chloe* to see why. *Variety*'s obituary related that "her last prominent part was in *The Social Lion* in 1930." (Apparently, that industry publication didn't feel *Chloe* held much prominence.) Her demise was even sadder than Neilan's (who at least lived to the ripe old age of 67); she died an alcoholic in a hotel for destitute women on Los Angeles' Skid Row—at 41 years of age.

Another of *Chloe*'s thespians was already a voodoo veteran. Actor Gus Smith, who plays the trouble-making Mose, is actually J. Augustus Smith, the black actor/playwright whose Broadway play *Louisiana* became the 1934 all-black film *Drums o' Voodoo* (in which Smith also starred).

Chloe is more of a (bigoted) love story than a voodoo tale—hoodoo remains secondary throughout much of the picture. From the very beginning, however, the frequent talk of voodoo sets the topic up as an important backdrop for playing out the drama. "Won't be long now, Sam," Mandy promises upon her return to their old shack, "'fore you can rest easy—'cause I'm gonna work my voodoo! The thunder's gonna *growl* and the lightning's gonna *rain*! The Devil's gonna walk on a white man's grave!" When Mose meets Mandy for the first time, he proudly pronounces, "I'm big Mose and I'm voodoo too. I'm papaloi!"

Despite all this hoodoo-oriented dialogue, nothing illustrative (nor even exciting) presents itself. Voodoo never rises above the white characters' perception as simply a stupid and savage superstition. In spite of Mandy's frequent talk of curses, nothing even remotely resembling a hex (nor any other supernatural manifestation—such as a zombie) appears. "Old Colonel Gordon," hisses Mandy in one scene as she jabs a wooden pin into a clay doll, "that's what I'm gonna do to ya for killin' my Sam!" Yet nothing happens to old Colonel Gordon. In the end, *Chloe* denies voodoo any magical or powerful qualities (much less any genuinely spiritual ones) while turning it into a simple excuse to dance about and "sometimes kills 'em on the alter and feed 'em to the 'gators" (as one character characterizes a voodoo "sacrifice party").

Voodoo finally takes center stage at the film's ceremonial conclusion. Sadly, there's nothing very climactic in the scenes of a group of black extras sitting around a large bonfire in the woods, waving their hands in the air or skipping and prancing around the fire. Amusingly, Mandy wears a black top hat and frock coat (perhaps in a visual nod to the voodoo god Baron Samedi—though nothing is made of it).

While voodoo stays mostly in the background, racism plays front and center throughout the film. (In fact, a more accurate title would have been *Chloe: Hate is Calling You*.) Apart from the obvious racially oriented story, such lines as "Don't you know no good come from mixin' white folks and black?!" and "You black as your blood, you is!" and "You think that because you got white blood some white man would have you? Yeah, he'd have you all right—but he wouldn't marry you!" Ideas like these hammer home the "horror" of miscegenation.

Such an abhorrent attitude comes not only from the plot and dialogue but from the very *appearance* of the characters as well. When Chloe (and the audience) are under the impression that she's part "Negro," actress Olive Borden appears rather frumpy, wearing unflattering makeup and a dowdy, sack-cloth dress. After it's confirmed she's all-white, however, Ms. Borden's natural assets come visibly to the fore,

enhanced by careful glamour makeup and revealing satin gowns. Only at this point does the viewer really see her as the great beauty she is—*after* she's been made "safe" by a clean bill of Caucasian health.

Apart from a few appealing locations (filmed in and around the moss-draped trees and sparkling water of Sun Haven Studios in St. Petersburg, Florida) and one rather brutal gator grapple, *Chloe: Love is Calling You* only offers the viewer a dreary hour of dull talk and insulting racism. After finally viewing this "lost" film, one can only wish it had stayed that way.

CREDITS: Director: Marshall Neilan; Photography: Mack Stengler; Film Editors: Helene Turner, Joseph Josephson; Art Director: Robert Stevens; Original Music: George Henninger; Musical Arrangement: Erno Rapee; Assistant Director: Jack Chapin; Produced at Sun Haven Studios; Released in 1934 by Pinnacle Productions; 64 minutes

CAST: Olive Borden (Chloe), Reed Howes (Wade Carson), Mollie O'Day (Joyce Gordon), Frank Joyner (Colonel Gordon), Georgette Harvey (Mandy), Jess Cavin (Hill), Gus Smith (Mose), Richard Huey (Ben), Philip Ober (Jim Strong)

OUANGA (1935)
Authentic Locales Are Not Enough

"I got the voodoo jitters!"
—nervous black servant

Ouanga was made as an independent production for Paramount's English distribution arm as a "British quota picture." (Great Britain would only import a limited number of American films [usually five] for each home-grown movie produced. Since Hollywood's prolific output exceeded many times that ratio, it behooved the major studios to occasionally back a British-made picture that would fulfill the quota and allow them to export more American product.) Paramount deigned to release the film stateside, however, and *Ouanga* (the film's British release title) apparently was not shown in America until early 1942, when states-rights distributor J.H. Hoffberg exhibited it briefly under the new title of *The Love Wanga*.

This "story of voodoo filmed entirely in the West Indies" (as the film's title card heralds the production) centers on Clelie Gordon (Fredi Washington), a plantation owner [1] and voodoo priestess on Paradise Island in the West Indies. When her neighbor, Adam Maynard (Philip Brandon), spurns her advances and becomes engaged to Eve Langley (Marie Paxton), Clelie sends a charm called an "ouanga" (pronounced "wang-guh") to cast a death spell over Eve. When this plan is thwarted, she sends two zombies to kidnap Eve and bring her to a voodoo ceremony for sacrifice. Maynard's foreman, Le Strange (Sheldon Leonard), whose love Clelie has rejected, tries to rescue Eve. Clelie shoots Le Strange, but the wounded man manages to snatch Clelie's protective ouanga from around her neck before the evil priestess takes Eve off to the ceremony. As Clelie lifts the sacrificial knife above Eve's prostrate form, Le Strange staggers into the clearing and sets Clelie's charm on fire. Terrified at losing her protective ouanga, Clelie races off into the jungle with Le Strange in pursuit. Cornering her by a huge tree, Le Strange strangles Clelie before he dies of his own wound, while Maynard shows up with the local gendarmes to rescue Eve from the voodoo cult's clutches.

On September 28, 1933, director/producer/screenwriter George Terwilliger took his American cast to the West Indies to shoot his screenplay *Drums of the Night* in an authentic Haitian setting. Though he initially won the confidence of the locals, he quickly raised the ire of their religious leaders when the

A Story of Voodooism

FILMED ENTIRELY IN THE WEST INDIES

Directed by
GEORGE TERWILLIGER

Ronald V. Borst/Hollywood Movie Posters

director asked to film their actual ceremonies. After several warnings (including a ouanga in the front seat of his car), Terwilliger had to move his production to Jamaica, shooting in the hills and jungles around Kingston to complete his picture.

The production was plagued with problems (including several deaths) which, actor Sheldon Leonard intimates, *may* have been related to some less-than-honest dealings with the voodoo faithful. "Our first port of call was Port-au-Prince, Haiti," wrote Leonard in his autobiography *And the Show Goes On*. "Our picture was to be about voodoo and Port-au-Prince was the voodoo capital of the world. Here, in the center of the voodoo religion, our company prop man expected to find many of the things with which to dress the sets so that they would look like authentic places of voodoo worship... In the case of the props he needed for *Drums in the Night* [the production's shooting title]—stuffed snake skins, goatskin drums, skulls, and other exotica—he couldn't buy them because they were sacred objects. Nor could he beg or borrow them, so there was nothing left but to steal them. Which he did." Terwilliger, who was reportedly an expert on voodoo, "was appalled when he learned how the props had been acquired. 'Bad luck will follow,' he said. 'Very bad luck.'"

Indeed, on the first day of shooting (with the scene set beneath a huge cottonwood tree), the cast and crew were attacked by a bunch of irate hornets whose hive they had disturbed. With several people hospitalized, the production went three days behind schedule before even getting a single shot in the can.

A week later, while setting up a light reflector for a beach shot, the company's key grip was attacked by something in the surf (probably a barracuda) which tore "a football-sized hunk of meat out of his thigh." The unfortunate died from loss of blood before help could arrive. In the third week of production, the film's makeup man, Jack Cameron, died of yellow fever. And in the last week of shooting, the assistant sound man fell from the sound boom and broke his neck.

Leonard himself didn't escape the "cursed" production completely unscathed. While shooting a chase scene, he fell and was impaled by a number of barbed cactus quills, which had to be cut out of his hide. The subsequent infection kept him out of action for four days.

The result of all these mishaps was that the film's six-week schedule (as reported by Leonard) turned into an 11-week nightmare (with the robust actor losing 18 pounds).

Unfortunately, the story of the film's production problems proved much more interesting than the finished product. *Variety* (January 1942) called it correctly when they asserted that "this quickie meller... is badly lighted, photographed, acted and directed."

Ouanga seems a very primitive production. Beyond the often grainy footage (of native workers and plantations) and poor lighting, the film even resorts to written narration to move the story rather than dialogue or visuals. Like a title card from a silent movie, words flash onto the screen to inform us "After a visit to New York, Adam Maynard starts back to his Haitian plantation."

The acting also harkens back to the silents. Heroine Marie Paxton's broad, unconvincing playing overflows with false smiles and vapid, transparent melodramatics, while the only expressions to cross hero

Philip Brandon's wooden features are gross parodies of emotion.

Though some references have claimed otherwise, *Ouanga* does indeed star *the* Sheldon Leonard, perennial screen gangster and later TV mogul who produced such hits as *The Dick Van Dyke Show*, *The Andy Griffith Show*, and *I Spy*. Leonard, who was at that time forging a career on Broadway, made his film debut in *Ouanga*. His broad, unconvincing mannerisms reflect his inexperience. (Leonard appeared in yet another voodoo film, 1945's *Zombies on Broadway*, where he gives a much more polished performance as a rather likable ex-gangster.)

George Terwilliger's awkward script doesn't help matters, as he fills his actors' mouths with dialogue that ranges from simply strained ("Your white skin doesn't change what's inside you; you're black, hear me, you're black!") to downright ridiculous ("So, the voodoo priestess has been out-voodooed").

As a director, Terwilliger makes little attempt to infuse atmosphere into his story, relying heavily on static medium shots with an occasional mundane close-up for visuals. He also spends too much time aboard well-lit ships or focusing on his screenplay's silly subplots (such as a flighty maid trying to slip a love ouanga to her dim-witted beau).

Though ads played up cinematographer Carl Berger's participation ("First Camera on *Bring 'Em Back Alive*"), the trumpeting rings hollow, for Berger's flat lighting is amateurish at best (garishly over-illuminating a scene so that all semblance of shadows or depth disappears) and downright unwatchable at worst (occasionally lighting so poorly that one can barely see through the muddy darkness). The film's British pressbook reported that, "Mr. Berger claims that *Ouanga* outdoes anything he has ever worked on." One can only hope that this was simply wishful thinking on the part of a publicist and not Mr. Berger's true opinion.

"You may laugh at superstition," begins a *Ouanga* ad-line, "but you feel that there may be 'something in it' when you see *Ouanga*, a tense and thrilling story

Bereft of her protective ouanga, voodoo sorceress Clelie (Fredi Washington) is about to meet her fate at the hands of a spurned lover (Sheldon Leonard).

of Black Magic in beautiful Paradise Island." Though the "tense and thrilling" claim rings hollow, the "something in it" notion proved real indeed—at least for one cast member.

"Superstition was rampant in the islands," wrote Sheldon Leonard of his views on voodoo. "People did get sick under the influence of a voodoo curse, but the curse didn't work unless the victim learned that it had been put in effect. Since the curse was powerless unless the victim knew about it, it is clear that the power of suggestion was a potent factor—that the power of voodoo was due, at least in part, to the credibility and profound beliefs of its practitioners." It's interesting to note that what Mr. Leonard labels the efficacy of voodoo curses ("the credibility and profound beliefs of its practitioners") is that very attribute, that *power*, which is behind *every* organized religion—the faith of its followers.

Leonard's recollections of Haiti, though reflecting the stereotyped—and exploitable—views of an outsider, still illuminate how important the Voudoun faith was to its Haitian people and how ingrained in everyday life it had become. For instance, Leonard relates how the maid at his hotel warned him to destroy his nail clippings and hair combings "lest some evil person get hold of them and put them in a voodoo doll, thus gaining the power of life or death over me." Leonard also tells of a party he attended which turned out to be a festive wake. "As we entered," remembered Leonard, "we were greeted by a young

lady who, after introductions, took us to meet the host. He was an elderly man seated at the head of a table loaded with fruits and meats. He was dead." Leonard explained that "they were not about to put his body in the ground until, after a couple of days in the tropical climate, it had deteriorated to the point where it was of no use to anyone who might have wanted to convert it into a zombie."

Unlike its contemporary voodoo entries *Drums o' Voodoo* (1934), *Black Moon* (1934), and *Chloe* (1934), *Ouanga* does at least sport a pair of zombies (two half-naked black men with no special makeup). Unfortunately, Terwilliger makes no attempt to make them the least bit frightening. He shoots the scene of Clelie supposedly raising them from the dead in brightly lit sunshine, and her frantic arm waving and intense stare look ridiculous in the full light of day. And Clelie herself subsequently refers to these creatures simply as "men." Apart from their kidnapping Eve, these zombies pose no menace whatsoever. In the end Maynard simply tells them to come with him back to the police and they readily comply. So much for terror.

The most entertaining part of this tepid voodoo vagary comes at the very beginning, when the off-screen narrator unwittingly provides a moment of high camp. Over the image of a silly-looking voodoo doll, he solemnly intones, "Wanga, wanga, that's *voodoo!*" *Ouanga, Ouanga*, that's awful!

Arthur Leonard (no relation to Sheldon) remade *Ouanga* in 1939 as *The Devil's Daughter*, again filming on Jamaica, though this time with an all-black cast.

---

[1] The film's British publicity exploited the theme of hero-worship when it emphasized the fact that, "the exterior of the house shown throughout the film is that of [Lord Admiral] Nelson's old home, now occupied by the Governor-General of Jamaica."

CREDITS: Alternate Title: *The Love Wanga*; Director/Producer/Screenwriter: George Terwilliger; Photography: Carl Berger; Released by British Paramount in 1935; 70 minutes (61 minutes as *The Love Wanga*)

CAST: Fredi Washington (Clelie Gordon), Philip Brandon (Adam Maynard), Marie Paxton (Eve Langley), Sheldon Leonard (Le Strange), Winifred Harris (Aunt Sarah), Sid Easton (Jackson, Adam's valet), Babe Joyce (Susie, Eve's maid), George Spink (Johnson)

THE DEVIL'S DAUGHTER (1939)
Ouanga Revisited (Though Not Improved)

"I'm gonna put that sweet sorority sister of mine in the Obeah sacrifice that's gonna make her so scared that she'll leave this island and never come back."
—Nina Mae McKinney as Isabelle

In early 1939, screenwriter George Terwilliger reworked the script he wrote, produced, and directed in 1935 as *Ouanga* for independent filmmaker Arthur Leonard. Leonard then took an all-black cast to Jamaica to film it as *The Devil's Daughter*. While this allows *The Devil's Daughter* the boast of being the only voodoo *remake* to date, that is the sole distinction this dull, amateurish anomaly can claim.

In a much altered (and much *softened*) version of Terwilliger's original tale of vengeful voodoo on a Haitian plantation, Nina Mae McKinney plays Isabelle, whose position of plantation head is usurped by her half-sister, Sylvia (Ida James), who returns from New York. Though Sylvia is willing to share the plantation with her sibling, Isabelle wants "all or nothing." While Isabelle really possesses no magical powers, she plans to frighten her sister off the island with Obeah (the Jamaican form of voodoo). "I only hope Miss Sylvia is superstitious," she says. "If our Obeah trickery is successful, she may go back to New York and then I'll have the plantation back again." To that effect Isabelle drugs Sylvia, takes her out into the jungle, and performs a mock voodoo death ceremony over her semi-conscious form. John Lowden (Emmett Wallace), a neighboring planter who loves Sylvia, arrives to put a stop to the malicious plot. Sylvia revives from the drug, agrees to marry John, and forgives Isabelle, turning over the family plantation to her.

The opening sequence of *The Devil's Daughter* proves an ill omen for the viewer. It begins with a horrendous scene of "local color," in which a group of islanders sing a "cute" song (if such toneless screeching can be called "singing") while performing a Jamaican jig around a mule. Although the dull sequence only lasts about three minutes, it seems never-ending. Sadly, this painful travelogue opening sets the lethargic tone that follows.

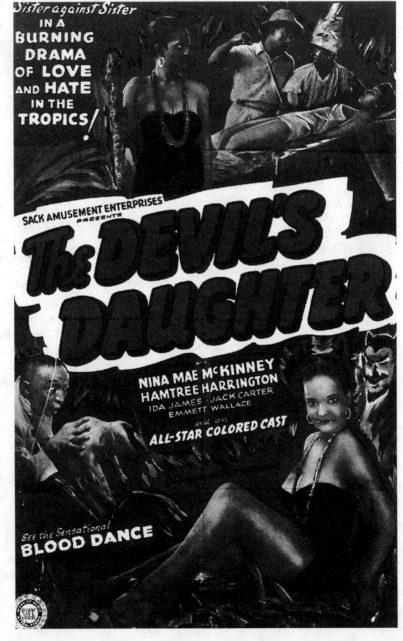

41

The authentic Jamaican plantation settings prove far more appealing than the bland hero (Emmett Wallace) and toneless heroine (Ida James) of *The Devil's Daughter.*

Taken as a voodoo film, *The Devil's Daughter* is even less successful than its indifferent model, *Ouanga*. Rather than a mystical force, *The Devil's Daughter* portrays voodoo as simply a fraudulent superstition. Nobody seemingly takes it seriously, including Isabelle, the supposed high priestess, who freely admits that she has no special powers and must drug and disorient her victim before conducting her sham ceremony. (While this lack of a supernatural element may be more true-to-life than most cinematic voodoo portrayals, the cavalier attitude Isabelle exhibits toward her sacred religion would make any self-respecting mamaloi cringe.)

The picture's main focus is on a romantic "square" involving Sylvia, Isabelle, John, and Philip (Sylvia's overseer). Looong scenes of tedious "native" dancing and a silly subplot about a gullible servant searching for a little pig which he believes houses his soul round out the proceedings. Everything takes place in bright sunshine, robbing the story of whatever sense of mystery or menace it might have generated. Director Arthur Leonard generally shoots in dull medium shot and rarely asks Jay Rescher to move his camera. Fortunately, the authentic jungle settings occasionally provide something interesting to look at.

Apart from Hamtree Harrington (as the pig-seeking servant) and Nina Mae McKinney, who sometimes manages to breathe a little fire into her performance,

the principals are as stiff and lifeless as zombies (which this film sorely lacks). The "comic relief" of Harrington, whose rolling eyes and "feets-do-your-stuff" portrayal is simply demeaning rather than funny, shows that even in all-black films such as this, it's difficult to get away from the pervasive stereotypes of the day.

Nina Mae McKinney was born in Lancaster, South Carolina. Her mother served as maid to the Springs family (Lancaster's wealthiest clan and founders of Springs Industries) while her grandmother worked as the household cook. Nina herself labored as an errand girl for the Springs. At about age 14 she went to New York with her mother where she began her singing/dancing career. After appearing at the famed Cotton Club, McKinney was brought to Hollywood to star in King Vidor's *Hallelujah* (1929). The MGM front office was so impressed by McKinney's sexy portrayal of the sassy vamp, Chick, that the studio signed her to a five-year contract. Unfortunately, they didn't know what to do with the screen's first black love goddess, and so used her in only two films—*Safe in Hell* (1931) and *Reckless* (1935) in which she appeared onscreen in only a small role (though she dubbed all of Jean Harlow's songs). McKinney left her stagnant film career to sing in nightclubs and cafes across Europe for a time, often billed as "the Black Garbo." Infrequent film roles and night-

This mild scene in which two voodooists restrain hero Emmett Wallace is about as much (non) action as *The Devil's Daughter* can muster. (Lobby cards courtesy Ronald V. Borst/Hollywood Movie Posters; Photos: Lynn Naron)

club appearances followed until her death from heart failure at age 54.

(White) Producer/Director Arthur Leonard was a former assistant director for Warner Bros. in New York. When the company closed its East Coast facilities, Leonard turned to the burgeoning low-budget black film industry. In explaining his career choice, the director's own words illustrate the white film establishment's attitude toward black films: "I figured there wasn't a chance in the Hollywood market and... the best thing I could do was to enter some freak field" (quoted in *From Sambo to Superspade*, by Daniel J. Leab). *The Devil's Daughter* was Leonard's directorial debut. He personally helmed only three more pictures (*Straight to Heaven*, 1939; *Boy! What a Girl!*, 1946; and *Sepia Cinderella*, 1947).

Devoid of suspense, excitement, or even a modicum of interest, *The Devil's Daughter* remains a celluloid voodoo "curiosity" that piques nobody's curiosity.

CREDITS: Alternate Title: *Pocomania*; Director/Producer: Arthur Leonard; Screenplay: George W. Terwilliger; Photography: Jay Rescher; Assistant Cameraman: Tom Priestley; Editor: Datlowe; Narrator: Leon Lee; Musical Score: John Killam; Sound:

Dean Cole; Location Manager: Syl Priestley; Makeup: Richard Willis; Wardrobe: Renee; Released December 1939 by Sack Amusement Enterprises; 65 minutes

CAST: Nina Mae McKinney (Isabelle Walton), Jack Carter (Philip Ramsay), Ida James (Sylvia Walton), Hamtree Harrington (Percy Jackson), Willa Mae Lane (Elvira), Emmett Wallace (John Lowden)

A worried Percy Jackson (comic Hamtree Herrington, left) thinks his soul has been lodged in the body of a pig via voodoo practiced by *The Devil's Daughter*.

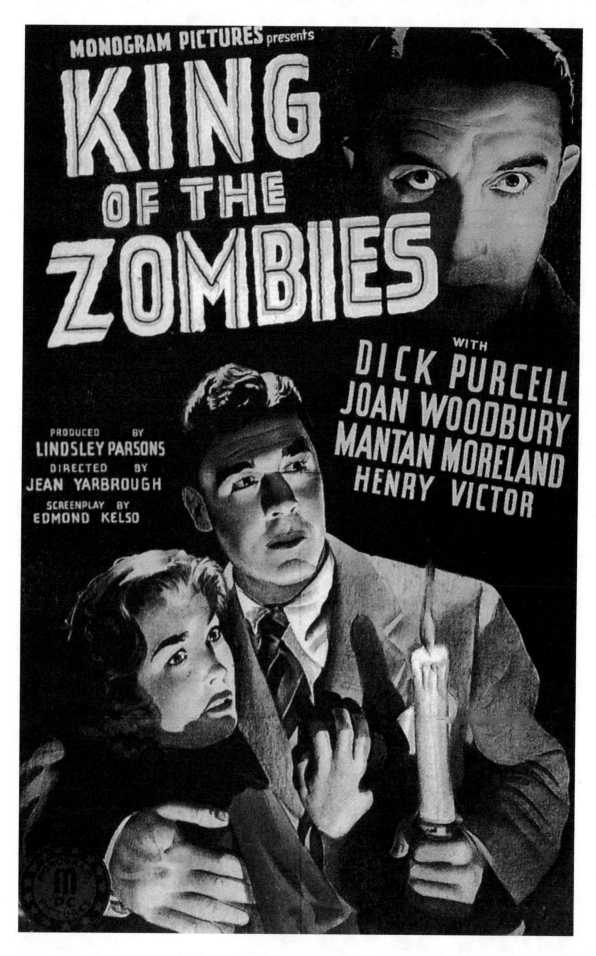

KING OF THE ZOMBIES
(1941)
Nazis, Zombies, and Harlem Humor

"If there's one thing I wouldn't want to be twice,
zombies is both of 'em."
—Mantan Moreland as Jeff

Of the seven voodoo films produced during the 1940s, four came from Poverty Row. Though far from the best of this questionable quartet, *King of the Zombies* can at least lay claim to being the *first*. Since it was concocted in 1941, it's only natural that scripter Edmond Kelso made his voodoo tale's bad guy an obviously Axis antagonist. Refreshingly, Kelso eschews the soon-to-be-clichéd madman-creating-a-zombie-army angle (introduced in the 1936 non-voodoo horror, *Revolt of the Zombies*) to utilize voodoo in a rather novel way. Here the notorious Nazi makes use of the local voodoo priestess' powers to try and elicit vital information from a captured American admiral—a voodoo version of the third degree! The evil warmonger also possesses a half-dozen or so zombies, but they don't really do much except provide frightening foils for comedian Mantan Moreland.

The story begins when our three patriotic protagonists, Bill (John Archer), Mac (Dick Purcell), and their valet Jeff (Mantan Moreland), crash their plane into a small West Indian island while on their way to undertake some vague mission for the Navy. On the island they find Dr. Sangre (literally "Dr. Blood," played by Henry Victor), his entranced wife (Patricia Stacey), his suspicious niece (Joan Woodbury), and a kitchenful of zombies. Though the doctor welcomes his unexpected guests, his hospitality proves false, as Sangre tries to hypnotize/zombify both Jeff and Mac. Sangre has captured an American admiral (Guy Usher) and plans to use the voodoo ceremony of "transmigration" (utilizing his own niece in some kind of soul transference) to wring vital war information out of him. Fortunately, during the climactic ceremony, Bill breaks through Sangre's hold over the zombified Mac and induces his entranced friend to lead the other zombies in an attack against the evil doctor. Sangre falls into a fire pit, Mac and Jeff recover, the admiral is saved, and all is well with the war effort.

When initially announced, *King of the Zombies* was to star Bela Lugosi under low-budget Western specialist Howard Bretherton's direction. As the production got closer to its start-time, however, both

Lugosi and Bretherton dropped from the project. Monogram sought Peter Lorre as replacement but finally settled on Henry Victor (and director Jean Yarbrough) by the time cameras rolled on March 31, 1941.

While Henry Victor does an adequate job as the Nazi-cum-zombie-master, he lacks the flamboyance necessary for this type of production—a trait which his two near-predecessors (Lugosi and Lorre) possessed in abundance. Relying on his imposing stature and straightforward manner, Victor brings little aplomb to a role that simply cried out for a touch of bombast. Victor, best remembered as the loutish Hercules from *Freaks* (1932), was born in London but raised in Germany. Beginning in the silents (he appeared in the 1916 versions of *She* and *The Picture of Dorian Gray*), Victor continued acting until his death in 1945 at the age of 52. Victor honed his Nazi-villain persona in films like *Confessions of a Nazi Spy* (1939) and *Sherlock Holmes and the Secret Weapon* (1942).

Jean Yarbrough's undistinguished directorial career stretched from 1936 to 1967 (ending—not inappropriately—with the dreadful *Hillbillys in a Haunted House*). He performed his usual dull service on *King of the Zombies*, which falls somewhere between his best (relatively speaking) genre efforts (*The Devil Bat*, 1940, and *House of Horrors*, 1946) and his worst (*The*

The zombies turn the tables on their evil Nazi master (Henry Victor) in *King of the Zombies*.

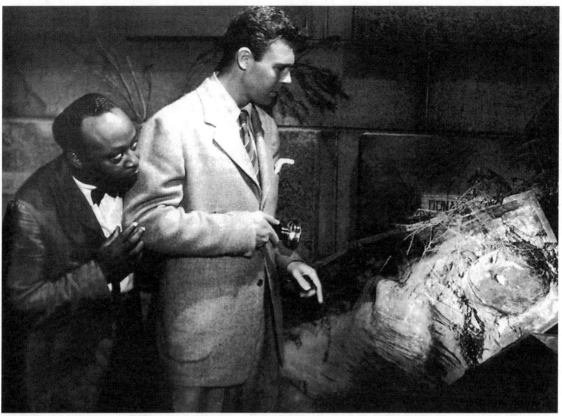

Jeff (Mantan Moreland, left) and Bill (John Archer) stumble upon a bit of atmospheric set dressing in Monogram's *King of the Zombies*.

Brute Man, 1946; *She-Wolf of London*, 1946; and *The Creeper*, 1948). Whatever visual interest the lethargically staged *King of the Zombies* holds comes from a few bits of atmospheric lighting (courtesy of Mack Stengler) and the fairly lush potted-plant jungle sets.

"Working at Monogram," explained *King of the Zombies* hero John Archer (in Tom Weaver's *They Fought in the Creature Features*), "the techniques were all the same [as at larger studios], except that they would just shoot a *lot* faster. They didn't rehearse as much, and they'd shoot the whole picture in a week. In a larger studio, it would take three or four weeks to do a B picture."

In the best of these just-get-it-done Poverty-Row traditions, the effects in *King of the Zombies* appear less than special. For instance, the wire holding up the model airplane is plainly visible as it makes a crash-landing on the miniature tabletop jungle. Also, the zombies receive no significant makeup treatment, and must make themselves menacing with blank stares, lurching gaits, and a few rips in their clothing. Fortunately, they're not asked to do much except put a few scares into Mantan Moreland's Jeff, who's seemingly frightened of his own shadow anyway.

Voodoo-wise, *King of the Zombies* proves far from regal. We occasionally hear voodoo drums in the background but never see any of the native practi-

tioners or ceremonies until the climax. Up to this point, voodoo is represented solely by an old crone (Dr. Sangre's cook) who occasionally cackles and spouts gibberish while trying to use her "powers" to make the entranced admiral talk. "Voodoo magic works slowly, but it is sure," she assures her impatient Nazi boss, but one begins to wonder since all her efforts yield little results. When the final "transmigration" ceremony arrives at the end, we're treated to some pathetically lethargic attempts at native dancing and the sight of the voodoo priestess wearing a silly feathered robe and headdress while Dr. Sangre sports a ridiculously oversized conehead mask with fangs. Sad.

The one true highlight of *King of the Zombies*, and the only real reason to watch, is Mantan Moreland. "I liked having Mantan Moreland to work with," remembered co-star John Archer. "He was a funny little guy who just cracked me up." Unlike his fellow black actor/comedians such as Stepin Fetchit or Willie Best (aka Sleep'n'Eat), Moreland could generally overcome the stereotypical attitudes of the day (encapsulated in his contemporaries' denigrating stage names) and bring a likable and self-possessed quality to his unprepossessing comedy characters, becoming a sort of pop-eyed, black Bob Hope. In *King of the Zombies*, Moreland was at his best—and he steals the show.

His natural delivery and impeccable timing as he throws out quips and asides left and right make the often suspect dialogue and self-deprecating lines seem downright funny. Moreland knows just when to go for the obvious and milk a line, such as when he hears the drums begin to beat like some bizarre jungle marching band and quips, "That's my cue for me to start parading outta here," or, when informed after the plane crash that he's not dead after all, he answers, "I thought I was a little off-color to be a ghost." Moreland also knows when to throw away a crack for a more subtle amusement, like when he tosses out, "If it was in me, I would be pale now," or, after Dr. Sangre assures him that, "You will be taken care of," Moreland shoots back, "That's what I'm afraid of."

Born in 1902 in Monroe, Louisiana, Mantan Moreland ran away from home at age 12. He subsequently worked in traveling minstrel shows as a barefoot dancer, joined the Hagenbeck Wallace circus, acted in Vaudeville, and worked in various nightclub acts and stage shows before breaking into films in 1937. Moreland appeared in over 125 movies from 1937 (*Spirit of Youth*) to 1973 (*The Young Nurses*). His popularity peaked in the 1940s when he made 103 films in only 10 years! (including two with his name in the title—*Mantan Messes Up* and *Mantan Runs for Mayor* [both 1946]). Moreland also acted on stage and even appeared on Broadway in a 1957 all-black revival of *Waiting for Godot*.

If looked upon as a Poverty-Row comedy, *King of the Zombies* fills the bill nicely; but seen as a voodoo horror film, this *King* wears only a paper crown. Amazingly, *King of the Zombies* proved to be the only voodoo film to date to receive an Academy Award nomination! Former dentist-turned-tunesmith Edward Kay saw his musical score join the ranks of Bernard Hermann's (*Citizen Kane* and *All That Money Can Buy*), Alfred Newman's (*How Green Was My Valley*), Max Steiner's (*Sergeant York*), and Franz Waxman's (*Suspicion*) in the race for best musical score. Not-so-amazingly, *King of the Zombies* did not win (Alfred Newman picked up the statuette for *How Green Was My Valley*).

CREDITS: Director: Jean Yarbrough; Producer: Lindsley Parsons; Screenplay: Edmond Kelso; Director of Photography: Mack Stengler, A.S.C.; Musical Score and Direction: Edward Kay; Production Manager: Mack Wright; Editor: Richard Currier; Settings: Dave Milton; Sound Directors: William Fox, Glen

Voodoo makes strange bedfellows in *King of the Zombies*.

Rominger; Art Director: Charles Clague; Released May 1941 by Monogram; 67 minutes

CAST: Dick Purcell (James "Mac" McCarthy), Joan Woodbury (Barbara Winslow), Mantan Moreland (Jefferson Jackson), Henry Victor (Dr. Miklos Sangre), John Archer (Bill Summers), Patricia Stacey (Madame Alyce Sangre), Guy Usher (Admiral Wainwright), Marguerite Whitten (Samantha), Leigh Whipper (Momba), Madame Sul-Te-Wan (Tahama), Lawrence Criner (Dr. Couillie), Jimmy Davis (Lazarus)

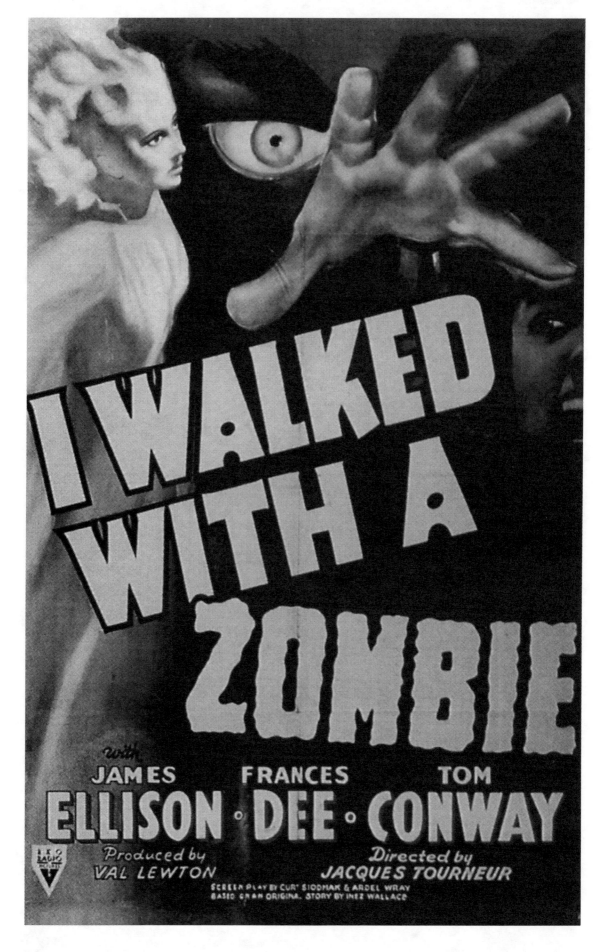

I WALKED WITH A ZOMBIE

with

JAMES **ELLISON** · FRANCES **DEE** · TOM **CONWAY**

Produced by
VAL LEWTON

Directed by
JACQUES TOURNEUR

SCREEN PLAY BY CURT SIODMAK & ARDEL WRAY
BASED ON AN ORIGINAL STORY BY INEZ WALLACE

I WALKED WITH A ZOMBIE (1943)
Drums of Poetry

"I walked with a zombie [laughs].
It does seem an odd thing to say."
—Frances Dee as Betsy
uttering the film's opening lines [1]

Over the years *I Walked with a Zombie* has (rightly) garnered much attention for its restrained atmosphere and near poetic tone. (Along with *White Zombie*, this is probably the best known—and the best—of all voodoo films.) Much of the film's literate quality can be put down to one man—producer Val Lewton. More than any other Hollywood producer, Lewton proved a hands-on supervisor whose touch pervaded every aspect of his productions (he nearly always re-wrote scripts, for instance, usually without taking credit). Lewton's RKO "horror unit" operated for three years (1942 to 1945) and generated nine low-budget (about $150,000 apiece) terror films, many of them—such as *Cat People* (1942), *The Body Snatcher* (1945), and this feature—the very best of the decade. Boris Karloff (whose 1940s horror pictures consisted mainly of repetitious mad doctor roles or juvenile entries like *The Ape* and *House of Frankenstein*) starred in three of the producer's intelligent pictures and dubbed Lewton as "the man who rescued me from the living dead and restored my soul."

Even before shooting began on the Lewton unit's first horror feature (*Cat People*), RKO executive Charles Koerner called Lewton into his office and gave him the title of his B-unit's second production: *I Walked with a Zombie* (to be based on a recent *American Weekly* article of the same name by Inez Wallace). To add insult to this titular injury, Koerner also told the dismayed producer that screenwriter Curt Siodmak would be penning the script. For the previous two years, Siodmak had toiled away on the more conventional horrors churned out by Universal: *Black Friday* (1940), *The Invisible Man Returns* (1940), *The Invisible Woman* (1940), *The Wolf Man* (1941), *Invisible Agent* (1942), etc. Granted, *The Wolf Man* turned out to be one of the decade's classics, but Lewton must have balked at having a writer thrust upon him whose last assignment was the Universal monster rally *Frankenstein Meets the Wolf Man* (1943). "[Editor] Mark Robson remembers," wrote Joel E. Siegel in *Val Lewton: The Reality of Terror*, "that Lewton's face was white and his manner impossibly gloomy when

he returned from that meeting with Koerner." The following day, however, Lewton showed up in an inexplicably exuberant mood and triumphantly told his staff that they would make "a West Indian version of *Jane Eyre*." (Before leaving his job as David O. Selznick's story editor for the RKO producer's post in early 1942, Lewton had helped prepare a film production of the Charlotte Brontë novel which was ultimately made by Orson Welles. Undoubtedly, Lewton had spent the night figuring out a way to make his ridiculously titled zombie project respectable and seized upon the Brontë classic as a literary out.)

Blessed with the sensibilities of a sensitive artiste rather than the crass traits of the typical Hollywood mogul, Lewton told his unit: "They may think I'm going to do the usual chiller stuff which will make a quick profit, be laughed at, and be forgotten, but I'm going to make the kind of suspense movie I like..." (quoted in *Cult Movies* by Danny Peary). To this end, Lewton brought in a second writer, Ardel Wray, and even rewrote the script's final draft himself (uncredited). Though it's difficult to pinpoint who contributed what to the finished screenplay, Curt Siodmak told *Filmfax*'s Dennis Fischer that, "[Lewton and Wray] made some changes. My idea was a little different. I started with the beautiful wife married to a plantation owner who every year went to Paris. He wants to keep her forever, so when he finds out that she wants to run away, he will not let her go. So he makes her into a zombie—then he can keep her, have her whenever he wants. But she has no reactions toward him. That's why she walks around. She was in a living death. But I don't know if he [Lewton] kept it this way. I never saw the picture afterwards." Obviously, Wray and Lewton heavily rewrote Siodmak's initial draft (which sounds very much like a reworking of *White Zombie*).

On October 26, 1942, cameras rolled on *I Walked with a Zombie* with Jacques Tourneur (who won the assignment on the strength of his excellent efforts on *Cat People*) twirling the director's baton. Like most facets of American life at the time, World War II also affected film production. Anticipating the necessity of cutting down on location trips because of the implementation of gas rationing, RKO eliminated five days of location shooting from the script. The changes necessitated the erection of three additional sets at the studio and added three days to the schedule. On November 19, a little over three weeks after principal photography began, the greatest voodoo film of all time was in the can.

Canadian nurse Betsy (Frances Dee) journeys to the West Indian island of St. Sebastian to care for the invalid wife of sugar planter Paul Holland (Tom Conway). Though Holland refers to his wife Jessica (Christine Gordon) as "a mental case," local legend

Moody lighting, low-key playing, and melancholy dialogue help make *I Walked With a Zombie* the most haunting and poetic of all voodoo films. Pictured: Tom Conway and Frances Dee

has it that she's been turned into a zombie, a creature "with no will of her own."

Soon Betsy learns the sordid story involving the Holland family—that Jessica fell in love with her husband's half-brother, Wesley Rand (James Ellison), and had planned to run away with him before succumbing to the fever that left her in this catatonic state. Betsy first hears of it when a melodious calypso singer (Sir Lancelot) captures the tale in musical verse:

"There was a family that lived on the isle,
Of St. Sebastian a long, long while.
The head of the family was a Holland man,
And the younger brother his name was Rand.

Ah woe, ah me, shame and sorrow for the family.

The Holland man he kept in a tower,
A wife as pretty as a big, white flower.
She saw the brother and she stole his heart,
And that's how the badness and the trouble start.

The wife and the brother they want to go,
But the Holland man he tell them no.
The wife fall down and the evil came,
And it burned her mind in the fever flame.

Ah woe, ah me, shame and sorrow for the family."

When drastic medical measures (insulin shock treatment) fail to alter Jessica's condition, Betsy, urged on by the family maid, Alma (Teresa Harris), determines to take her charge to the local voodoo houmfort (the voodooists' place of worship) to seek a cure. In her frightening nocturnal journey to the ceremony, Betsy encounters the gigantic, gaunt form of Carrefour (Darby Jones), "guardian of the crossroads," but the zombie lets them pass unmolested.

Once at the houmfort, Betsy is pulled inside by Mrs. Rand (Edith Barrett), Paul and Wesley's mother. The widow of a missionary, Mrs. Rand has been using the natives' belief in voodoo to proffer her medical and psychological advice, posing as the voice of Damballah.

All smiles now, Betsy doesn't yet know she's entered a world of mysterious voodoo and bitter family dynamics. Pictured: Frances Dee, James Ellison, Tom Conway

Jessica's presence disturbs the voodooists and, while Betsy talks with Mrs. Rand inside, they perform a ritual by which a man stabs a thin sword into Jessica's unflinching arm. "She doesn't bleed!" exclaims one. "Zombie!" pronounces another. (Note: This concept of imperviousness to pain and bloodshed is actually a trait of loa possession—the physical invulnerability a sign that the loa has indeed "mounted" his human "horse.")

Mrs. Rand urges Betsy to take Jessica back to Fort Holland, for Betsy's actions have stirred up the natives. "Seems those people up at the Houmfort won't stop drumming and dancing until they've got Jessica back and finished their ritual tests," one character later observes. To this end, the voodooists send Carrefour to retrieve Jessica, but a word from Mrs. Rand turns the zombie away before he can complete his mission.

Mrs. Rand breaks down and confesses that it was she who brought the zombie curse down upon Jessica. "I kept seeing her face, smiling because she was beautiful enough to take my family in her hands and tear it apart. The drums, the chanting, the dancing; I

heard a voice speaking in the sudden silence—my voice. I was speaking to the houngan. I *was* possessed. I told him the woman at Fort Holland was evil and asked him to make her a zombie."

The voodooists next utilize a voodoo doll which they pull forward on a string to summon Jessica to them. The zombie woman rises and goes toward the houmfort, but Betsy stops her by closing the gate. Wesley, who's still in love with Jessica and can no longer stand to see her this way ("She ought to be free," he laments), later opens the gate and follows Jessica out, pulling an arrow out of the garden's old figurehead statue of Saint Sebastian as he passes. When the bokor at the houmfort sticks a needle into the Jessica voodoo doll, we see Wesley rise from Jessica's body—having stabbed her with the arrow and ended her zombie existence.

With Carrefour following, Wesley carries Jessica's body in his arms and walks into the sea. That night local spear fishermen find their floating corpses and bring the bodies back to Fort Holland, leaving Paul and Betsy (who have fallen in love) free to pursue their own course.

I Walked with a Zombie is without a doubt the most haunting and poetic of voodoo films (and perhaps of horror films in general as well). From the moody lighting, death-oriented dialogue, and low-key, serious playing of the principals, an almost palpable air of tragedy hangs over the picture.

A meticulous attention to detail helped add to the richness of the film's tapestry. "The sets were beautifully dressed," observed director Jacques Tourneur to Joel E. Siegel in *Cinefantastique* magazine. "Val was very fussy about furnishings and it paid off. You don't know why you like a thing in a film. Every time you see a film that you like, somebody stayed up at night,

In *I Walked With a Zombie* the brave nurse leads her zombie-like charge on one of the most atmospheric nocturnal walks in cinema history.

somebody didn't sleep, somebody worried, somebody was fussy, somebody made enemies. Good pictures don't just happen... Val and I were both craftsmen. We were proud of our work."

About their working relations and various contributions, Tourneur had this to say: "Val was the dreamer and I was the materialist. I always had both feet on the ground. We complemented each other. By himself, Val might go off the deep end and I, by myself, might lose a certain poetry." Fortunately, the chemistry proved just right on *I Walked with a Zombie* to keep it afloat in "the deep end" with a series of poetically graceful strokes.

Among these are the elegant use of Sir Lancelot's calypso ballads to move the story along (acting like a musical Greek Chorus), the beautifully staged and lyrically tragic ending, and, most memorably, the pivotal "walk"—the picture's centerpiece.

Without a note of background music, the eerie sequence in which Betsy takes Jessica to the houmfort fills the ears with only those disturbing sounds heard by Betsy herself—the low howling of the wind, the eerie humming made by punctured ceremonial gourds, the mysterious rustling of the canebrake all around her, and the thundering silence when her light betrays the presence of the sentinel-like zombie, Carrefour.

For the eyes, the sequence becomes a veritable feast of menacing shadows and unseen presence as the two women (one fearfully alert and the other literally dead weight) pass. (Though accompanied by the zombified Jessica, Betsy is worse than alone on her nocturnal journey, her mute companion's unseeing, unknowing, and *unnatural* demeanor only intensifying Betsy's isolation and unease.) It begins with an eerie shot of Carrefour standing motionless in black silhouette to set the menacing tone. Then, the smooth camera motion and alternating viewpoints (following alongside, behind, in front of, and even shooting from Betsy's point of view) draw the viewer into this nocturnal trial of subdued terror as Betsy comes upon such disturbing sights as a human skull in a circle of stones (which Jessica's gown brushes over as she walks past—perhaps signifying the zombie-woman's closeness to death), a sacrificial goat suspended from a tree, and the zombie himself—first revealed as a pair of naked feet in the tiny pool of Betsy's flashlight which then shoots frantically upwards to illuminate his unearthly, staring countenance towering above her (and us). Thanks to the clever, sensitive, and evocative staging of director Jacques Tourneur, the atmospheric lighting and fluid visuals provided by cinematographer J. Roy Hunt, and the determined-yet-uneasy playing of Francis Dee, this three-minute sequence becomes one of the most effective and poetically moody moments in all of voodoo cinema (or any other celluloid branch, for that matter).

The uniformly naturalistic, even subdued acting by the principals does much to weave a thread of believability into the film's dark cloak of the mystical and supernatural. (Even as late as two weeks before filming, Anna Lee [*The Man Who Lived Again*, 1936; *Bedlam*, 1946] was set to play the role of Betsy, with Frances Dee stepping in only at the last minute. Though Ms. Lee showed herself time and again to be

Betsy (Frances Dee) and the entranced Jessica (Christine Gordon, left) encounter the zombie guard Carrefour (Darby Jones), one of voodoo cinema's most forbidding figures in *I Walked With a Zombie*.

an extremely capable actress, Ms. Dee's intelligent and sensitive portrayal proved a great asset.) The characters speak and act in normal tones and everyday inflections, with no trace of theatricality or melodrama—a rarity in horror films of the 1940s. But then nothing in *I Walked with a Zombie* (including its brooding, otherworldly atmosphere, highly literate dialogue, adult attitude towards both its story and characters, and its elegant visuals) indicates *any* close kinship with the Universal monsterfests or Poverty Row horrors proliferating at the time. Director Jacques Tourneur strove for such unaffectedness in his actors. "In [*I Walked with a Zombie*], as in others," explained Tourneur in Charles Higham and Joel Greenberg's *The Celluloid Muse*, "I made the people talk very low, as I think this indicates sincerity… it makes for the effect I want. I'll have an actor replay a whole scene as though he's just talking to me in a normal voice, and it's effective."

There's little doubt that *I Walked with a Zombie* is one of the most beautiful, graceful, and resonant horror films ever produced. But what of its voodoo element? Does this best-of-all-voodoo-films treat its subject any better than its schlocky contemporaries like *Voodoo Man* or *King of the Zombies*? Well, yes and no.

Lewton obviously strove for a modicum of authenticity. "We all plunged into research on Haitian voodoo, every book on the subject Val could find," remembered co-scripter Ardel Wray in Siegel's *The Reality of Terror*. "He was an addictive researcher, drawing out of it the overall feel, mood and quality he wanted, as well as details for actual production. He got hold of a real calypso singer, Sir Lancelot he was called—a charming, literate, articulate man. He, in turn found some genuine voodoo musicians. I remember they had a 'papa drum' and a 'mama drum,' that the crew on the set were fascinated by them, and by one particular scene in which a doll 'walks' in a voodoo ritual. They managed a concealed track for the doll, and it was effective. I particularly remember that doll because Val sent me out to find and buy one 'cheap.' Everything had to be cheap because we really were on a shoestring."

Lewton even employed a "technical advisor" versed in the ways of authentic Voudoun. On October 29, 1942, *The Hollywood Reporter* announced that, "LeRoy Antoine, who is one of the country's leading

Tragedy lies at the heart of this "West Indian version of *Jane Eyre*," as borne out by *I Walked with a Zombie*'s tragic conclusion.

authorities on Haiti and Haitian folk music and voodoo, will be the technical advisor on *I Walked with a Zombie*. Antoine will also teach the Negro actors Haitian rhythms for use in voodoo ceremony."

With such research incorporated into its literate and intelligent script, some sincerity couldn't help but penetrate the film's voodoo veneer. In fact, *I Walked with a Zombie* was the first feature to take a truly adult approach to voodoo. None of the usual human sacrifice business or diabolical sorcery mars its maturity. Instead, the picture focuses on showing the pervasiveness of this alternative religion in the lives of St. Sebastian's inhabitants. "[Voodoo] is part of everyday life here," states one character matter-of-factly, hinting at the normalcy of their voodoo worldview. The film also touches on the religion's cornerstone—possession. As Paul describes voodoo early on: "They sing and dance and carry on. And then as I understand it one of the gods comes down and speaks through one of the people." (Amusingly, Lewton applied his wry sense of humor to the topic by inserting this declaration among the fine print of the opening credits: "The characters and events depicted in this photoplay are fictional. Any similarity to actual persons, living, dead, or *possessed*, is purely coincidental.")

Utilizing authentic Voudoun terms, the dialogue also sometimes (slyly) emphasizes the strength of the voodoo faith (in this case flying in the face of the "whites'" ineffectualness):

> Betsy: "Doctors and nurses can only do so much, Alma. They can't cure everything."
> Alma: "Doctors that are *people* can't cure everything."
> Betsy: "What do you mean, 'doctors that are *people*'?"
> Alma: "There are other doctors; yes, other doctors—*better* doctors."
> Betsy: "Where?"
> Alma: "At the houmfort."
> Betsy: "That's nonsense, Alma."
> Alma: "They even cure nonsense, Miss Betsy... [Mama Rose] was mindless but the houngan cured her...

The houngan will speak to the Rada drums and the drums will speak to Legba and Damballah. *Better doctors.*"

Even the sensationalistic idea of zombies remains ambiguous and unexploited. The voodooists seem astonished when they realize Jessica is a true zombie, and Carrefour never attacks anyone; obviously, there is little real danger from these "zombies"—despite the white outsiders' fear.

The ceremonial dancing witnessed at the houmfort carries a note of genuineness and even a suggestion of possession in several of the participants' actions (though, admittedly, they're a bit too smoothly choreographed to appear entirely authentic). Unfortunately, this is where the voodoo verisimilitude abruptly ends, as a voice calls out from inside the hut, "Where are my people?...," and the voodooists step up one by one to place an ear near the perforated door and receive a few words from Damballah's oracle. No houngan or mamaloi would so sequester and segregate themselves (or the loa) from their flock. Nor would a voodoo priest actually seek possession for him or herself (though sometimes they have little choice in the matter and are mounted by the loa despite their reluctance) as this would interfere with their expected rites and duties. Houngans need their own full faculties during Voudoun worship and so leave possession to those members of the congregation favored by the gods.

Also, at this point *I Walked with a Zombie* seemingly turns the tables on its hitherto respected topic and (perhaps inadvertently) voices a somewhat more patronizing attitude. "These people are primitive," warns Mrs. Rand, mouthing the usual smug opinion of white interlopers. After revealing herself to Betsy at the Houmfort, Mrs. Rand explains, "Accidentally I discovered the secret of how to deal with [the natives]. There was a woman with a baby. Again and again I begged her to boil the drinking water. She wouldn't. Then I told her the god Shango would kill the evil spirits in the water if she boiled it [chuckles]. From then on she boiled the water… It seemed so simple to let the gods speak through me. I should have known there's no easy way to do good, Betsy." By faking possession, Mrs. Rand has turned the locals' worship into a sham in a misguided attempt "to do good." Such duping of the obviously simpleton believers becomes a tacit verification—and justification—of disdain for them and their religion. While far above its contemporary cinematic brethren in terms of voodoo attitude, *I Walked with a Zombie* still manages to dip its foot into those muddy waters of condescension that rage throughout most voodoo films of the period.

I Walked with a Zombie's rather lurid advertising captures little of this superior voodoo film's near-poetic tone. (Photo: Lynn Naron)

Director Jacques Tourneur considered *I Walked with a Zombie* "the best picture I've ever done. Very poetic." Indeed, not only is it among the greatest horror films of all time, it is, without a doubt, the most *elegant* voodoo picture to date. Despite a disparaging stumble here and there, it remains arguably the finest example of voodoo cinema ever set to celluloid.

[1] Producer Val Lewton's covert apology, perhaps, for the ludicrous title the RKO front office foisted upon his lyrical production.

CREDITS: Director: Jacques Tourneur; Producer: Val Lewton; Screenplay: Curt Siodmak, Ardel Wray; Based on an Original Story by Inez Wallace; Director of Photography: J. Roy Hunt; Music: Roy Webb; Musical Director: C. Bakaleinikoff; Art Directors: Albert S. D'Agostino, Walter E. Keller; Set Decorations: Darrell Silvera, Al Fields; Recorded by: John C. Grubb; Editor: Mark Robson; Assistant Director: William Dorfman; Released April 1943 by RKO-Radio; 68 minutes

CAST: James Ellison (Wesley Rand), Frances Dee (Betsy), Tom Conway (Paul Holland), Edith Barrett (Mrs. Rand), James Bell (Dr. Maxwell), Christine Gordon (Jessica Holland), Teresa Harris (Alma), Sir Lancelot (Calypso Singer), Darby Jones (Carrefour), Jeni LeGon (Dancer), Martin Wilkins (Houngan), Jieno Moxzer (Sabreur), Arthur Walker (Ti Joseph), Kathleen Hartfield (Dancer), Clinton Rosemond (Coachman), Alan Edmiston (Mr. Wilkens), Norman Mayes (Bayard), Melvin Williams (Baby), Vivian Dandridge (Melisse)

The Voodoo Man (Bela Lugosi) takes charge of yet another potential victim delivered by his two half-wit henchmen, Toby (John Carradine, center left) and Grego (Pat McKee, center right).

VOODOO MAN (1944)
More Monogram Madness

"The nation's number one horror film at the
moment is 'VOODOO MAN'!...
with the gruesome threesome,
BELA LUGOSI, JOHN CARRADINE... and
GEORGE ZUCCO! Lugosi, the King of Horror,
outdoes himself in 'VOODOO MAN'...
and with the help of two half-mad voodoo
villains, Carradine and Zucco,
you're assured a super thrill-chill show!

See 'VOODOO MAN'"
— (over)enthusiastic radio spot

Monogram, the most prolific of the "Poverty Row" outfits operating in the 1940s, churned out numerous no-budget supernatural potboilers to titillate the war-weary public. Included in this undistinguished group are three voodoo pictures, making Monogram the studio that went to the voodoo well most often. [1] *Voodoo*

Man, their second hoodoo horror (sandwiched between *King of the Zombies* and *The Face of Marble*) is certainly no classic and not even a good film even by "B" standards, though it *is* one of that bottom-of-the-barrel studio's best.

In June of 1943 Monogram announced that their new production of *The Voodoo Man* (which *may* have been based on the Andrew Colvin story "The Tiger Man" which the studio purchased in March—sources differ and Colvin receives no onscreen credit) would begin shooting in August. August came and went and the studio next announced a start date in October (after Lugosi had completed his current Hollywood stage engagement in *Arsenic and Old Lace*). William Nigh (*The Mysterious Mr. Wong*, 1935; Karloff's *Mr. Wong, Detective* series; *The Ape*, 1940; *Black Dragons*, 1942) was originally announced as the director, but he quickly gave way to Philip Rosen (*Spooks Run Wild*, 1941; numerous Charlie Chans). A change of plans put Rosen on Monogram's *Return of the Ape Man* which went into production first. When *Voodoo Man* finally began shooting on October 16, William "One Shot" Beaudine was waving the director's baton.

(Ironically, Beaudine had originally been slated to direct *Return of the Ape Man* (!); Monogram's behind-the-scenes planning was seemingly just as muddled as their movie plots!)

In *Voodoo Man*, Bela Lugosi plays Dr. Marlowe who, with the aid of gas station attendant Nicholas (George Zucco) and half-wit handyman Toby (John Carradine), kidnaps beautiful girls in an attempt to restore life to his zombie wife ("She's been dead for 22 years," Marlowe poignantly points out). The rather unorthodox method he employs to accomplish this feat is to first hypnotize the abducted girl and then, clasping the hand of his zombie wife, intone, "mind to mind... body to body... soul from body... emotion to emotion... life to death!" Of course everyone knows that this alone, even combined with Lugosi's powerfully hypnotic presence, would not be sufficient to transfer the life force from a young girl to a zombie. Consequently, Bela has John Carradine beat out a rhythm on a voodoo drum while George Zucco, decked out in an astrologer's robe and weird feathery headdress, does rope tricks and mutters unintelligibly to the great voodoo god "Ramboona." Even this doesn't seem to do the trick, since the basement is full of zombie-girls, results of previously unsuccessful attempts. Embroiled in this bizarre mess is a Hollywood scenario writer, Ralph (Michael Ames), and his fiancée, Betty (Wanda McKay), who just happens to possess "the perfect affinity" for Marlowe's life-transferring ceremony. After a sufficient running time has elapsed, the thick-witted Sheriff finally arrives at the Marlowe mansion to rescue the heroine (the hero having been knocked out), shoot the mad doctor (thus freeing the zombie girls from their trance), and presumably arrest the rest.

From the above scenario, it becomes painfully apparent that *Voodoo Man* is a long way from a voodoo classic. Well-paced at the beginning (with the wild get-up and bizarre ceremony grabbing one's attention), the script soon bogs down in seemingly endless running about by the hero and sheriff. "What I remember about *Voodoo Man*," recalled Louise Currie (who played Stella, an early victim) to Tom Weaver in *They Fought in the Creature Features*, "was walking around out in the woods with my eyes wide open, wandering around in a trance." Indeed, scene after repetitive scene of entranced subjects rambling about combined with frequent sequences in which the non-zombie characters drive endlessly to and fro almost brings the bizarre proceedings to a screeching halt.

Fortunately (as with all good "bad" movies) a few unintentionally choice lines provide periodic relief, such as Carradine's howlingly funny observation upon finding one of the zombie girls missing: "She's not there; she must be somewhere else." And the film does possess a (this time intentional) witty closing

Bela Lugosi as Richard Marlow, *Voodoo Man*!

scene: The screenwriter hero delivers a script to his producer based on the events he has just experienced, calling it "The Voodoo Man." When asked who he had in mind to play the title role, he replies, "Say, why don't you get that actor, uh—Bela Lugosi. It's right up his alley."

And right up his alley it was. With the story being so much hoke, the film's major asset becomes, of course, Bela Lugosi. Lugosi plays his role with a genuine relish that makes the film enjoyable to watch. *He* believes it and consequently so do *we* (that is, until John Carradine pops up with one of his "you've got pretty hair" lines). With Lugosi's commanding voice and powerful presence, one can almost give credence to Dr. Marlowe's much-touted hypnotic power.

In *Voodoo Man*, Lugosi gets to step beyond his usual "evil incarnate" persona and manages to slip in a bit of pathos—unusual in a Lugosi film. When Stella asks, "Is your wife ill?", Marlowe replies, "She's dead." Lugosi's voice, while in full control, betrays just a hint of sadness. Later, when Marlowe's procedure momentarily revives his zombie wife, the doctor exclaims, "I have brought you back to me my darling; now we are together again." Lugosi's heartfelt delivery carries an almost tremulous joy. Even at the end, as Marlowe lay dying, his last line (referring to his dead wife), "Soon we'll be together," is delivered with just the right amount of compassion to inspire a bit of pity for the old madman.

The result of Marlowe's voodoo vagaries?—A basement full of zombie-women.

Lugosi even occasionally adds a touch of (unintentional) humor to his role. When the Sheriff asks Marlowe if he's seen anything suspicious around Laurel Road, Lugosi answers, "No, not that I remember. I'm quite off—the road." Lugosi's brief pause after "I'm quite off" adds a humorous connotation to the innocuous line. "Yeah, that's right," the Sheriff agrees —and so do we.

Unfortunately, Lugosi doesn't always *look* as good as he acts. The production's (uncredited) makeup man fails to hide the ravages of age (and drugs), so that the frequent, intense close-ups of Lugosi's face show a visage marred by lined valleys and puffy hillocks. In the end it detracts from his otherworldly image.

It's amazing how much effort Lugosi put into his role of the single-minded doctor, considering *Voodoo Man* was his *ninth* film for Monogram in three years. One would think that he'd have tired of the ridiculous plots and threadbare productions. Then again, at least he was the "star" in these cheap features, whereas the major studios (when they cast him at all) generally offered him only cameos or supporting roles during

the 1940s. *Voodoo Man* proved to be Lugosi's final film for Monogram (though not the last one to be released—*Return of the Ape Man* was shot *before* but released after *Voodoo Man*).

"He was a charming man and a hell of an actor," remarked John Carradine about Bela Lugosi (in *Fangoria* #52). "He used to come on the set with a bottle of claret, which he sipped at a little bit all day long. He never got drunk, never lost a line, never lost his tempo or his accent, which was native to him. But Bela was a damn good performer and a charming gentleman." Indeed.

Sadly, Lugosi's horror veteran co-stars, John Carradine and George Zucco, don't fare nearly so well. Both these talented professionals are wasted in worthless roles (a fate these two actors suffered time and time again at the hands of cheap and unimaginative producers).

George Zucco, who can be such an elegant villain, mostly stays in the background muttering gibberish while sporting a silly feathered headdress. Still, Zucco's urbane presence and cultured tones always add a touch of class—even when playing a gas jockey-cum-voodoo master (complete with natty sweater vest by day and conjurer's robe by night). His sonorous voice and refined accent, along with a serious conviction that never rings false, nearly lifts such ridiculous dialogue as, "The failures we've had were due to the subjects—they were not the right ones; but remember, Ramboona is all-powerful," out of the dungheap and into the sublime. John Carradine commented that Zucco was "a *very* good actor"— while probably secretly thanking his lucky stars that *he* didn't have to wear that preposterous chapeau.

When asked by *Filmfax* interviewer Dennis Fischer if he had any particular interest in horror, Carradine replied, "No, I was just working. It was a job. I don't care what kind of role I play. I'm an actor." This anything-and-everything attitude was certainly in full swing for Carradine's stint in *Voodoo Man*. While *Voodoo Man* may not be his *worst* film (though the actor was at one time fond of saying so) when one considers such unwatchable dreck as *The Incredible Petrified World* (1957) and *Hillbillys in a Haunted House* (1967), it's without a doubt his most demeaning *role*.

Carradine once called his frequent co-star, Lon Chaney, Jr., "a big, good-natured slob." In *Voodoo Man*, Carradine seems to be trying to emulate that "good-natured slob" by playing a skinny version of Chaney's "Lennie" from *Of Mice and Men*. Trotting around like a demented puppy dog, Carradine, playing the mentally deficient henchman Toby, does little with his part and seems resigned to "building" his character with awful lines like, "You've got nice pretty hair," "Nobody ever talks to me," and "The master would be very mad if he knew you were out." It is a part far beneath the talented actor's ability (and a role which he no doubt accepted simply to fund his own Shakespearean theater company which was then the apple of his thespic eye). "Poor John Carradine," remembered co-star Louise Currie, "he played a half-wit in it. And may I say he played it very *well*—playing a half-wit is not the easiest thing to do when you're a good actor."

"I've done a lot of crap," admitted the actor himself in the book *Reel Characters* by Jordan R. Young. "I only did 'em for the money. I had five boys to raise." His role of Toby in *Voodoo Man* certainly fits *that* description.

Former airline hostess Wanda McKay (she was signed by Paramount after winning the title of Miss American Aviation at the Birmingham Air Show Beauty Pageant in 1938) does little with her admittedly thankless role, making Betty a pretty but rather toneless heroine. Happily, Louise Currie takes up the slack by showing some spunk (and even a little depth) as Stella, making one wish that the two actresses had switched roles and it was McKay who spent most of

the film in a zombie trance. Both actresses were veterans of Poverty Row horrors. McKay appeared in *Bowery at Midnight* (1942) with Lugosi, *The Black Raven* (1943) with Zucco, and *The Monster Maker* (1944), while Currie had previously starred opposite Lugosi in *The Ape Man* (1943).

"*Voodoo Man* was director William Beaudine's finest contribution to the horror genre," enthused Poverty Row aficionado Don Leifert in *Filmfax* magazine.[2] Considering Beaudine's track record (which includes *The Ape Man*, 1943; *Ghosts on the Loose*,

Good help is hard to find: The moronic Grego and Toby try to wrangle the zombified heroine (Wanda McKay) for their master.

1943; *Bela Lugosi Meets a Brooklyn Gorilla*, 1952; *Billy the Kid Versus Dracula*, 1965; and *Jesse James Meets Frankenstein's Daughter*, 1966), it's a tough point to argue. Even so, old "One Shot's" direction is plagued with dull staging, a heavy reliance on the medium shot, and an apparent aversion to interesting angles. It's no wonder that the director could spare little creativity on *Voodoo Man*, for the busy Beaudine made a total of *12* features in 1944! Though he may not have been good, Beaudine was certainly prolific, directing over 175 features, 325 one- and two-reelers, and 350 episodes for various television series. At the time of his death in 1970, he was the oldest active member of the Screen Directors Guild. Beaudine helmed (to better effect) one other voodoo movie, 1946's more-earnest-but-little-better *Face of Marble*.

What visual interest found in the film can be attributed to cinematographer Marcel Le Picard's evocative lighting. He fills the cramped settings with sinister shadows and weirdly flickering light (from voodoo torches, one assumes) that add some welcome atmosphere to the cheap sets. Le Picard lensed a num-

Through hypnotism and voodoo (and the life force of kidnapped women), Dr. Marlowe tries to restore his zombie wife. (At least his heart is in the right place.)

The late William K. Everson, in *More Classics of the Horror Film*, seemed to feel that *Voodoo Man* was an intentional parody: "In retrospect it can be seen as something of a forerunner of such send-up horror films as Roger Corman's *The Raven*." This particular thesis, however, seems a bit overgenerous, for nothing in the film's promotion (nor in the script or the principals' acting) indicates that *Voodoo Man* is anything *but* a straight horror picture. (In fact, the film's pressbook flatly states, "Unlike most horror films, *Voodoo Man* has no let-up of suspense, nor any comedy interludes to break the tension.") Intentional or not, the film does offer up a few laughs to go along with its fine performance from that charismatic master of Poverty Row horror, Bela Lugosi. To balance this, however, the picture seems intent on *embarrassing* its two other genre talents, John Carradine and George Zucco. For the viewer in the right frame of mind, this little voodoo cheapie can be a lot of fun. But take it seriously and one only laments the misuse of some of the horror genre's finest talents.

[1] The Katzman/Dietz production team at Monogram intended to make yet *another* voodoo movie called *Jungle Queen* (whose title quickly evolved into *Voodoo Queen*). Set to star Acquanetta, the proposed picture never made it off the drawing board. "At Monogram I had approval of my scripts," recalled Acquanetta, "and I *dis*approved of every one!"

[2] This same writer also claimed the film contains "one of [John Carradine's] finest performances in a horror film." (!)

ber of Lugosi movies, such as *Invisible Ghost* (1941), *Spooks Run Wild* (1941), *Return of the Ape Man* (1944), and *Scared to Death* (1947; Lugosi's only color film).

Voodoo Man's inappropriate music (by dentist-turned-composer Edward Kay), full of obvious cues and tinny strings (with an occasional harp arpeggio thrown into the mix), only cheapens the feel of this already threadbare production. Kay, who contributed (?) music to such horrors as *The Ape*, *The Ape Man*, *Return of the Ape Man* (do I detect a theme here?), *Revenge of the Zombies*, and *Ghosts on the Loose*, was an Academy Award nominee! He was nominated for his work on yet another voodoo voyage, *King of the Zombies*. He did *not* win.

Voodoo Man's voodoo element is no more convincing than the half-baked storyline. Nicholas seems to be in charge of the voodoo angle, but, apart from waving his arms about and muttering unintelligible gibberish (with the word "Ramboona" occasionally thrown in for emphasis), all he does is perform a conjure trick in which two pieces of rope tie themselves together into a knot (to what purpose one cannot say). In a more practical vein, Nicholas does employ his voodoo mutterings—er, powers—to summon a wandering zombie-girl back to the house and (using Betty's stolen glove) uses a long-distance spell to entrance the heroine and draw her to Marlowe's house (exiting the coffee shop she was in without even leaving a tip!).

Incredibly, *Voodoo Man* received the dreaded "H" certificate (adults-only) from the BBFC when released in Britain. The horror!

CREDITS: Director: William Beaudine; Producers: Sam Katzman and Jack Dietz; Associate Producer: Barney Sarecky; Screenplay: Robert Charles; Photography: Marcel Le Picard; Assistant Director: Art Hammond; Musical Director: Edward Kay; Film Editor: Carl Pierson; Set Designer: Dave Milton; Sound: Glen Glenn; Released February 1944 by Monogram; 62 minutes

CAST: Bela Lugosi (Dr. Richard Marlowe), John Carradine (Toby), George Zucco (Nicholas), Wanda McKay (Betty Benton), Louise Currie (Stella Saunders), Michael Ames [aka Tod Andrews] (Ralph Dawson), Ellen Hall (Evelyn Marlowe), Terry Walker (Alice), Mary Currier (Mrs. Benton), Henry Hall (Sheriff), Dan White (Elmer), Pat McKee (Grego), Mici Goty (Marie), Ralph Littlefield (Sam), Claire James, Ethelreda Leopold, Dorothy Bialer (Zombies); John Ince (S.K.)

Lon Chaney, Jr., struggles to fight SUPERSTITION with REASON and FACT in *Weird Woman*.

WEIRD WOMAN (1944)
Voodoo's Inner Sanctum

"Man's struggle upward from his dark past is the struggle of reason against superstition."
—Lon Chaney, Jr., as Professor Norman Reed

In June of 1943, Universal bought the rights to use the "Inner Sanctum" name from publishers Simon and Schuster, Inc. Under the guiding hand of low-end producer Ben Pivar, the studio planned to release two Inner Sanctum films a year, each starring their new golden boy of terror (and "Master Character Creator" as the studio PR department so grandiosely named him), Lon Chaney, Jr. What resulted were six more-or-less desultory pictures in a tiresome and disappointing series that stretched from December 1943 with the release of *Calling Dr. Death* to December 1945 with the final entry, *Pillow of Death*. In between, the studio crammed in four features: *Weird Woman, Dead Man's Eyes, The Frozen Ghost*, and *Strange Confession*.

The second in the series, *Weird Woman*, has traditionally been thought of as the best of the bunch (rather faint praise, actually). It's an appellation the film doesn't really deserve, however, since one of the entries (*Dead Man's Eyes*) is at least as good, and *two* others (*Strange Confession* and *Pillow of Death*) are decidedly better. Perhaps it's the fact that the film's predecessor, *Calling Dr. Death*, was simply so dull that anything that followed immediately after looked good by comparison. Or maybe *Weird Woman* has attained such a (modestly) elevated status because it is the sole Inner Sanctum film which carries a (semi)supernatural theme. God help those pictures which pass themselves off as "horror" (as the Inner Sanctum series did) but fail to present the devoted genre fan with some kind of monster or preternatural trick or two.

Professor Norman Reed (Lon Chaney, Jr.) returns to Monroe College from his research trip to "the islands" with a new book (entitled *Superstition Versus Reason and Fact*) *and* a new wife, Paula (Anne Gwynne). The daughter of a deceased archeologist, Paula has been raised by her native nurse, a voodoo high priestess. Norman's mundane small-town newlywed idyll is soon shattered, however, when he discovers his wife practicing her protective "white magic."

After forcing Paula to burn all her voodoo paraphernalia in an attempt to overcome her "silly superstitions," things begin to go horribly wrong for Norman. Ilona, an old flame (Evelyn Ankers) who's bitter over Norman's surprise marriage, uses deceit to induce a colleague (Ralph Morgan) to commit suicide and then intimates that Norman is responsible. Ilona also orchestrates a co-ed (Lois Collier) into accusing Norman of "taking advantage of her" while goading the girl's beau (Phil Brown—later Luke Skywalker's kindly uncle in *Star Wars*) into attacking Norman, resulting in the accidental death of the hotheaded boy. Ilona also begins terrorizing Paula with voodoo death chants played over the phone. Finally, the suicide's bitter widow, Evelyn (Elizabeth Russell), discovers that it was Ilona rather than Norman who was behind her husband's death. She and Norman formulate a plan to trap her. Showing Ilona a voodoo doll and telling her of a mysterious dream in which her dead husband claims "the woman who lied" will die in 13 days at exactly one minute past midnight, Evelyn plants the seed of fear in Ilona's mind. As the days go by, Ilona becomes more and more terrified until finally, just before midnight on the last day, she breaks down and confesses to Evelyn, pleading with her to destroy the evil doll. It's already been reduced to ashes, says Norman as he and several others step from the other room to confront the guilty woman. "You tricked me!" cries Ilona and dashes

Though frequently paired together onscreen, Lon Chaney, Jr., and Evelyn Ankers reportedly loathed each other off.

out the upper story window to make her escape across a vine-covered arbor. Racing across the top, the slats give way and she plunges through, only to end up swinging from a vine wrapped about her neck— dead. The time: one minute past midnight.

The film starts promisingly enough as Paula hurries fearfully down a dark, forbidding street while the wind blows violently and howls ominously. The production quickly becomes terribly set-bound, however, and on rather uninteresting sets at that. Most of the "action" (talk, actually) takes place in standard 1940s offices or living rooms. The only intriguing backdrop is a rather cramped graveyard set which Paula and Norman simply walk through on one occasion.

Reginald LeBorg's straightforward direction does little to augment the scenes, though he occasionally does come up with a minor flourish. For instance, after the suggestion has been planted with Ilona that she will die in 13 days, LeBorg (aided by editor Milton Carruth) utilizes a compact and effective montage sequence to show her mounting fear reflected in a series of seemingly ordinary events: A radio commercial announcing "remember only 8 more days left to get your…," a theater poster advertising the play "The Lady Lies" noting "LAST 7 DAYS," or Ilona opening up a package of yarn to find a card printed with "6 SKEINS YARN." For the most part, however, LeBorg makes do with the usual round of mundane angles and pedestrian staging. (To be fair, it must be noted that the director was allowed very little preparation time. According to LeBorg, he received the script on Friday and was told to start shooting a week from Monday.) Fortunately, cinematographer Virgil Miller provides effective lighting which at times generates some much-needed macabre mood, particularly with select low-key illumination at the proper moments.

For the voodoo fan, the main ceremonial sequence (a flashback to the island ritual at which Norman first met Paula) is a major disappointment, for it looks more like a genteel luau than a frenzied voodoo rite. Though Paula ominously labels it "the Dance of Death," sarong-wearing native girls pathetically stomp their feet and clap and wave their hands in an innocuously choreographed (and not choreographed very *well*, as several of these dancers can't seem to keep on the same rhythm) motion, making this "weird pagan ritual" look like low-rent nightclub-filler.

The *Weird Woman* scripters obviously failed to do their homework, for they cast their voodoo ceremony in a decidedly Polynesian slant (thinking, perhaps, that voodoo came from someplace "safe" like Hawaii rather than the seedier and more dangerous Caribbean). The drummers wear leis and flowers in their hair and worship the god "Kahuna-Anna-Anna" (a new one for the voodoo pantheon). Perhaps, as yet another stroke of Hollywood racism, the filmmakers chose to portray the voodoo homeland as populated by people no more exotic than well-tanned whites.

"I believe," stated Lon Chaney, Jr. in the *Weird Woman* pressbook, "that voodoo merely is the untutored savage's realization of the power of auto-suggestion." While such an articulate pronouncement from such an "untutored" actor like Chaney, Jr., seems unlikely (and probably leapt straight from the pen of a well-educated PR writer rather than from the actor's mouth), it accurately reflects the demeaning attitude commonly held by Americans toward the Voudoun religion and its practitioners (the "untutored savages").

> "I liked Lon in those Inner Sanctum mysteries. It's hard to act when you're covered with hair like a werewolf. But the Inner Sanctums gave him a chance to act and he proved he could do it." —Glenn Strange (frequent Chaney co-star)

Norman Reed disrupts an (oddly Polynesian-flavored) voodoo ceremony in *Weird Woman*. (Ronald V. Borst/Hollywood Movie Posters)

"An unexciting actor—a pall of dull sincerity hung over him—Chaney created characters that were more to be pitied than respected, more cringing than aggressive, more plebeian than aristocratic. If ever a star lacked charisma, it was Chaney, Jr."
—Arthur Lennig (author of *The Count*)

No matter to which camp one subscribes, it's dreadfully apparent that in *Weird Woman*, Lon Chaney, Jr. was woefully miscast. With his rather puffy face (looking just this side of jowly) and saddlebags under the eyes, no pencil-thin mustache can transform him into a B-grade Charles Boyer. But more important than Chaney's physical (mis)attributes are his less tangible traits. When a love-struck co-ed coos, "He's so brilliant... there's something so *dynamic* about him," the viewer can't help but give a sardonic snort. Chaney comes off as just the opposite of "dynamic," appear-

ing as a rather dull and pedantic pretender who's betrayed by his unsubtle mannerisms and blue collar speech patterns. Far from the "mental giant" one character labels him, Chaney's Norman only really seems to be in his element when he brutally manhandles an attacking student.

Chaney's (lost) cause isn't helped by the demands placed upon him by W. Scott Darling's unlikely script. Particularly awful is the hushed voice-over narration in which he shares his "thoughts" with the audience. *Sotto voce*, Chaney injects little inflection into the often obtuse and melodramatic dialogue (e.g., "The so-called phenomena of mysticism and sorcery are brought about by fear; fear, insulating countless millions, making them believe because they're afraid not to believe"). As Chaney's banal and toneless voice whispers its words on the soundtrack, his dramatic facial expressions (straining desperately to appear pensive and thoughtful) simply make it look as if he's battling a bout of intestinal trouble.

"When [Chaney] did the Inner Sanctum pictures," observed director Reginald LeBorg in *Cinemacabre*

The power of suggestion begins taking its toll on the villainous Ilona (Evelyn Ankers).

magazine, "he played them in very fine clothes... He didn't want to be a ghoul, but unfortunately he was typed and he wasn't suave enough for the Inner Sanctums. The pictures didn't cost much money [about $150,000 with a 10-12 day shooting schedule, according to LeBorg], so they made money, but if you had a William Powell doing them, it would have been a much better situation. But with Chaney, he never achieved that elegance that you had to have."

Chaney's co-star, Anne Gwynne, concurred: "He was wrong for the role in *Weird Woman*—In the picture, both Evelyn Ankers and Lois Collier are mad about him, but he's my husband. I think of Lon as a character heavy, like he was in *Frontier Badmen*, or as a monster. It seems strange that he would be in this type of part. I just didn't feel he was the leading-man type" (from *It Came From Weaver Five*, by Tom Weaver).

This is not to say that Lon Chaney, Jr., was a bad actor. Far from it, in the right role he performed admirably—even, at times, in this ill-fated Inner Sanctum series. Though for the most part Chaney failed to live up to the urbane characterizations handed him throughout most of the Inner Sanctums, he seemed to have finally hit his stride in the last two, giving rela-

tively good performances in both *Strange Confession* and *Pillow of Death*. (Of course, it helped that these two roles didn't require him to be impossibly suave, and that these pictures dropped the awful stream-of-consciousness narration which plagued the rest of the entries.)

In *Weird Woman*, however, Chaney's lack of charisma was such that his co-stars couldn't help but shine—simply out of contrast. In fact, apart from the lead, *Weird Woman* is a particularly well-acted film. Elisabeth Risdon (as Grace) brings to her part of Norman's friend and colleague a natural humor (commenting, "Ilona, there's something about your smile right now that makes me think of Jack the Ripper," with just the right touch of sardonic veracity), while Elizabeth Russell, as the ambitious and bitterly hateful widow, nearly drips with venom at the proper moments.

Anne Gwynne is quite good in the poorly written part of Paula. Her sincerity overcomes the condescending attitude the script and characters exhibit toward her (Norman thinking of her as a "superstitious child" or calling her [to her very *face*] a "poor, frightened, strange little child"). Gwynne brings a likable innocence to her role, and her almost hysterical fear

Lon Chaney, Jr., makes an unlikely college professor in *Weird Woman*. (Ronald V. Borst/Hollywood Movie Posters)

at hearing the "death chant" makes the viewer believe that *she* truly believes. Even when the screenplay forces her to pull that old chestnut—the fainting spell—we actually believe that she fainted out of fear.

In the pivotal role of Ilona, Evelyn Ankers makes a stylish villainess. Her natural poise and charm renders Ilona's vile machinations that much more heinous. Surprisingly (since most actors *love* playing the villain), Ankers was not pleased with her role. "*Weird Woman* was my first 'heavy' part," recalled the actress, "and not of my own choosing. This was a new field for me and I found it very difficult to feel comfortable or convincing. Reggie LeBorg, the director, sensed something was wrong, and on the first day, after each scene, asked 'Evie, what's the problem? It's not believable.' I answered, 'I know why—I'm miscast. I don't feel a bit mean and I don't want to hurt Anne [Gwynne] because she's my best girlfriend.' He answered, 'Well, this time forget all that. Think of something mean she must have said or done to you and try it again.' He then would say 'Action!' and I would sort of squint or narrow my eyes, even attempt to flare my nostrils in desperation—trying to work myself up to appearing evil—then turn my head and look Anne in the eye threateningly. Bang, we

would become hysterical with laughter, and so would the whole company watching us. This happened time and time again, until we were absolutely exhausted. It was not only ridiculous but also costly in time as well as money, not to mention poor Reggie's patience. We felt so sorry for him, even when he tried to get angry with us, which only made it worse. How we ever finished that picture, I'll never know. Universal got the message and never cast me as a villainess again." (Quoted in *Forties Film Talk*, by Doug McClelland.)

Ankers and Chaney, though paired together in a number of films (including *The Wolf Man*, 1941; *The Ghost of Frankenstein*, 1942; *Son of Dracula*, 1943; and *The Frozen Ghost*, 1945) apparently loathed one another. "He didn't like her," stated Patsy Chaney, the actor's second wife in, *Filmfax* magazine. "He called her 'Shankers'—Evelyn Shankers."

"I have nothing but glowing things to say about Boris Karloff," related Ankers' co-star and best friend, Anne Gwynne, "and only praise for Bela Lugosi, but Lon Chaney was something else, although we actually got along fine together. But... he would pull practical jokes on people—and they did become quite cruel. He never bothered me at all—it was Evelyn

Evelyn Sawtelle (Elizabeth Russell, right) helps turn the suggestive screw on Ilona.

who incurred his wrath. They worked together more often, and yet they couldn't stand each other, sort of like the way Jon Hall and Maria Montez never got along." (This mutual *detestation* society became so bad that at one time Chaney even picked a fight with Ankers' husband, Richard Denning, at a Universal press party.)

In her introduction to Doug McClelland's *The Golden Age of B Movies*, Evelyn Ankers herself recounts the genesis of Chaney's animosity toward her: "Just before I started [*The Wolf Man*], the front office called me in to tell me they liked my work and were rewarding me with a plush, new dressing room which I would share with Anne Gwynne, also under contract to Universal. Naturally I was thrilled. On the first day of shooting, Lon Chaney, Jr., my leading man, said to me, 'So you're the gal who swiped my dressing room. You took it away from Broderick Crawford and me—I think that was a hell of a thing to do!' Since I was going to have to work with this man (over and over again, as it turned out), I agreed. When I asked the front office about it, they told me Lon had been warned that this would happen if he didn't stop 'misbehaving.' Soon after, I found out just what 'misbehaving' meant. Someone told me that every Friday or Saturday night, Lon and Brod Crawford would take bottles into their dressing room, get loaded, and then somehow manage to hang the furniture from the ceiling and brawl. On Monday, the cleaning crew was treated to a sight resembling a World War II battlefield."

Surprisingly, *Weird Woman* garnered some rather favorable reviews at the time of release. *The New*

York Herald Tribune's Otis L. Guernsey, Jr. called it "A neat little murder tale all souped up with black magic... Universal has produced it with more taste and effort than is usual with a thriller of this type."

While *Variety*'s "Walt" labeled the film "a standard dual supporter and okay for the secondary and nabe houses," he went on to award it moderate praise: "Picture hits slow pace in early reels to establish characters and foundation for the series of mysterious events, after which it gains momentum and fairly fast clip through directorial efforts of Reginald LeBorg." Walt also felt that "Chaney, Miss Gwynne and Miss Ankers combine adequately for the three leads."

Not everyone liked the picture, however. *Harrison's Reports* observed that "Discriminating audiences will find it tiresome, and even the most ardent followers of this type of entertainment may find it but mildly interesting. Moreover, it is a slow-moving, moody entertainment." At *The New York Times*, Bosley Crowther merely exclaimed, "Boy, is it dull!"

Weird Woman is based on Fritz Leiber's novel *Conjure Wife*. The story was adapted twice more to the screen (plus once on television for the series *Moment of Fear*, which is Leiber's own personal favorite of the adaptations), first in 1961 as *Burn, Witch, Burn* and then in 1980 as an (uncredited) comic variation called *Witches' Brew*. Of all the versions, *Burn, Witch, Burn* stands head and shoulders above the rest. *Weird Woman* not only pales in comparison to the intelligent and enthralling *Burn, Witch, Burn*, but it turns absolutely transparent.

Even so, despite a horribly miscast lead, uneven scripting, and indifferent direction, *Weird Woman* still offers up a relatively painless 63-minute diversion— thanks mostly to the film's fine supporting cast.

CREDITS: Director: Reginald LeBorg; Associate Producer: Oliver Drake; Screenplay: Brenda Weisberg; From the novel *Conjure Wife* by Fritz Leiber, Jr.; Adaptation by W. Scott Darling; Director of Photography: Virgil Miller; Musical Director: Paul Sawtell; Art Directors: John B. Goodman and Richard Riedel; Director of Sound: Bernard B. Brown; Technician: William Hedgcock; Set Decorations: R.A. Gausman and A.J. Gilmore; Film Editor: Milton Carruth; Gowns: Vera West; Special Photography: John P. Fulton; An Inner Sanctum Mystery produced by arrangement with Simon and Schuster, Inc., Publishers; Released April 1944 by Universal; 63 minutes

CAST: Lon Chaney (Professor Norman Reed), Anne Gwynne (Paula Clayton Reed), Evelyn Ankers (Ilona Carr), Ralph Morgan (Professor Millard Sawtelle), Elisabeth Risdon (Grace Gunnison), Lois Collier (Margaret Mercer), Elizabeth Russell (Evelyn Sawtelle), Harry Hayden (Professor Septimus Carr)

A *voodoo* altar? Well, at least *Republic* thought so. Pictured: John Abbott as the vampiric Webb Fallon.

THE VAMPIRE'S GHOST
(1945)
Vampires and Voodoo
on the Dark Continent

"Africa! The dark land where voodoo drums
beat in the night, where the jungles are deep and
full of secrets, and the moon that lights
them is still a mystic moon. Africa,
where men have not forgotten the evil they
learned in the dawn of time. Always come back to
Africa. But even here there is no rest for me.
The path of time is curved upon itself
like a circle, without beginning, without end.
I must follow it forever.
I cannot die. I cannot rest… I cannot rest…
I cannot rest."
—opening narration
by John Abbott as the vampiric Webb Fallon

The Vampire's Ghost has long been dismissed as one
of the lesser Poverty-Row horrors (and not even a
Monogram or PRC product, but something from that
no-budget *Western* studio!) which can't even boast a
single Lugosi, Carradine, or Zucco. Yet despite its
lack of genre stars or Monogram-style wackiness, *The
Vampire's Ghost* is one of the best horrors to crawl
out from Gower Gulch—a unique Poverty-Row
sleeper possessing above-average intelligence (a rarity in its class) that remains both entertaining and potentially thought-provoking.

The West African plantation village of Bakunda
is plagued by several mysterious deaths in which the
victims are "partially drained of blood." The native
drums speak of vampires, but the local whites, led by
merchant Thomas Vance (Emmett Vogan), his daughter Julie (Peggy Stewart), her fiancé Roy (Charles
Gordon), and missionary Father Gilchrist (Grant Withers), scoff at the notion.

Seeking to solve the mystery, Roy visits waterfront saloon owner Webb Fallon (John Abbott) because the surprisingly cultured and erudite Fallon has
"come to know more about Bakunda's underworld

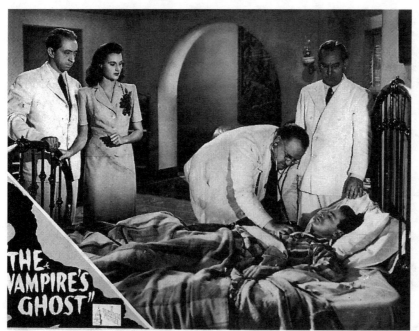

Unbeknownst to Julie (Peggy Stewart) and her father (Emmett Vogan), the doctor's (Frank Jacquet) diagnosis of Roy's (Charles Gordon) fever is way off the mark.

than most of the natives." Fallon can shed no light upon the mysterious murders, however.

When Fallon is invited to the Vance home for dinner that night, a servant, Simon Peter (Martin Wilkins), notices that the man casts no reflection in a mirror! (This special effect was accomplished in the best tradition of the "Invisible Man" movies. "They bandaged my head and hands up in black and photographed me up against a black background," related John Abbott in Donald F. Glut's *The Dracula Book*. "Then I held up a wine glass [actually a cup and saucer] and drank. You could see the glass being held up by an invisible hand. There was no head. Then I suppose they superimposed the actual background on top of it. You looked invisible except for the material things—coats and collars and wine glasses.") Simon inexplicably says nothing of what he's seen (or, more accurately, *hasn't* seen), perhaps knowing that the bwanas would not listen to a lowly, drum-beating, "heathen" native. The scene concludes with an effective shock: After Fallon notices the mirror and Simon's stunned expression, the looking glass spontaneously shatters in a startling moment of supernatural power.

Roy decides to journey to the back country village of Molongo to continue his investigation, and Fallon comes along. When they're attacked by hostile tribesmen, Simon Peter takes the opportunity to throw a silver-tipped spear into Fallon's chest.

Tending to the wounded Fallon, Roy is amazed to find no blood on the spear or on the man's body. Fallon entrances Roy with his gaze and explains that 400 years ago he was cursed with vampirism when

he caused a young woman's death. The vampire then forces Roy to take his injured body to the top of the mountain to be bathed in the restorative rays of the moon. Fallon also orders Roy not to reveal what he knows.

Back at Bakunda, Roy has fallen ill. Though the local doctor talks of jungle fever, Roy is actually suffering the malaise of the vampire's spell. Fallon spends much of his time attending to Roy—not out of altruism but to be near Roy's fiancée, Julie, whom Fallon has fallen for.

The murders continue while Roy struggles mightily against the vampire's enslavement—to no avail. The natives know the truth, however, and leave threatening voodoo charms on Fallon's door while their drums relay their information to all who will listen.

With Father Gilchrist's spiritual help, Roy finally breaks the vampire's spell and they go to confront Fallon. But the vampire has taken Julie and fled into the jungle. The men, accompanied by Simon Peter, pursue the fiend into the back country, guided by the native drums which track Fallon's whereabouts.

At the taboo "Temple of Death" in a deserted village, Fallon prepares to transform Julie into his undead bride. Just as he's about to exsanguinate the girl, his pursuers arrive. Father Gilchrist's cross forces the bloodsucker back while Roy lances him with the silver spear. They whisk Julie away, and Simon Peter finishes the job by setting the temple alight. As the flames rise higher, the forbidding four-armed altar statue topples onto the wounded Fallon and the flames consume his undead body.

Technically, *The Vampire's Ghost* is one of the better-looking, low-budget horrors of the 1940s. Director Lesley Selander and co-cinematographers Bud Thackery and Robert Pittack provide plenty of camera movement and effective set-pieces that raise the film above its Poverty-Row contemporaries.

The opening sequence, for instance, proves particularly strong. As John Abbott intones his melancholy narration, the scene dissolves from a primitive map of Africa to the darkened town of Bakunda. The camera moves through the village and, as Abbott concludes, "I cannot rest… I cannot rest… I cannot rest," closes in on a dim doorway. A hand enters the frame to stealthily push open the portal. Inside, a beautiful native girl awakens, and as a shadow passes over her prone form, she screams. This carefully constructed and fluidly effective opening sets a wonderfully macabre and somber tone.

In another scene, Fallon stalks his victim. An unsavory ship captain (Roy Barcroft) walks home through the darkened streets after cheating Fallon at cards. We see a pair of white-trousered legs follow slowly. The man looks nervously behind him and quickens his pace while the pursuing legs continue following. Finally, the man is cornered against a locked gate. He turns and a man-shaped shadow rises up to fall across his body, growing larger while simultaneously the camera glides in closer. The terrified captain drops his raised knife and the shadow's hands move up toward the victim's throat. Throughout the sequence we never see the pursuer, even though we know who—and what—he is. The close shots of the pursuing legs, the menacing shadow, and the claustrophobic camera movement (effectively *pinning* the victim to the wall like a trapped insect) add potent mystery and impact to the sequence.

Though it turned out he did a fine job, director Lesley Selander seemed an unlikely candidate to pilot a vampire movie, having made something of a name for himself as a low-budget *Western* specialist. Born in turn-of-the-century Los Angeles, Selander entered the film industry right out of high school as a lab technician. Becoming an assistant cameraman in 1920, he graduated to full cameraman two years later, and assistant director two years after that. After directing a series of comedy shorts, he went to MGM where he served as assistant director on films like *The Thin Man* (1934) and *A Night at the Opera* (1935). With the backing of his friend Buck Jones, Selander finally got his chance to direct features in 1936. Over the next 31 years, he helmed over 150 films, most of them oaters (often starring Jones, Tim Holt, or William Boyd—Selander directed 25 "Hopalong Cassidy" features!). Selander also worked extensively in television. Between 1954 and 1958 he supervised 60 *Lassie* episodes and was also a regular fixture on *Laramie* and *Cannonball*. Though he rarely left the cinematic saddle, Selander did hitch up to the horror/sci-fi post on two other occasions—for *The Catman of Paris* (1946) and *Flight to Mars* (1951). He died in 1979 at age 79.

Not to argue too strongly against the notion that *The Vampire's Ghost* is really nothing more than a low-budget, mildly entertaining potboiler, but... the film *does* explore (no doubt purely by accident) significant issues of religious efficacy and conflict. In the film, the white colonialists are left to their largely impotent Christianity, [1] while the natives possess their more accessible—and effective—voodoo. From the beginning, the "superstitious" natives know the cause of the mysterious plague of murders and quickly identify its source, whereas the whites haven't got a clue. Also, it is a voodoo-embroiled native that initially takes up arms against the vampire, and it is the voodoo drums that finally inform Father Gilchrist (Christianity's representative) of the truth and ultimately lead him to the unholy fiend.

The vampire himself laughs at the local religion—much to his eventual regret. When Fallon finds a voodoo doll pinned to his door with a knife, he shrugs

Though the "whites" may be in the dark, Simon Peter (Martin Wilkins, right) and the native voodooists know what must be done to stop *The Vampire's Ghost*.

the warning off with, "It's a lot of hocus-pocus; I don't let it bother *me*." Yet this dismissal of the sacred religion turns and bites him in the end, for it is the voodoo drums which lead his enemies to him and a native believer who sets the fire that destroys the vampire.

This religious dichotomy in a grade-B Hollywood screenplay inadvertently demonstrates one of the great

combination of voodoo and Christianity that defeats the vampire: The crucifix stops the fiend from consummating his unholy bloodlust on the entranced heroine, while Roy (a Christian) takes up a native voodoo spear dipped in silver to incapacitate the vampire. And it's Simon Peter, a native voodoo drumbeater (though friendly to Father Gilchrist and the Christian faith), who sets the temple ablaze and finally kills the undead monster (for only fire can truly destroy the vampire). Okay, so *The Vampire's Ghost* may not be the ideal Unitarian Leftist's treatise on religious tolerance, but it does offer some (inexpensive) food for thought to those hungry enough to look.

Despite *The Vampire's Ghost*'s backhanded support of the voodoo concept, on the surface it still took the expected condescending and stereotypical attitude toward the religion (character-

The Vampire's Ghost: A dark parable espousing religious tolerance—or just another B-horror flick?

differences between Christianity and the Voudoun faith: The Christian sees the supernatural as something distant and largely unaffecting (Heaven, angels, etc.); whereas the Voudounist sees the preternatural world of gods and spirits as a tangible force permeating his daily life.

Though it's doubtful that Butler and Brackett intended to say any such thing, *The Vampire's Ghost* subliminally argues for tolerance and even cooperation between disparate religions. In the end, it's a

izing the voodooists as "superstitious savages"). Regarding the age-old institution of vampirism, however, the picture proved much more liberal. Webb Fallon can move about in daylight (though he wears dark glasses to protect his eyes from the sun); he sleeps in a bed rather than a coffin (albeit with a small box of his native soil on the nightstand); he is *injured* by silver-tipped spears (rather than the traditional wooden stake) but *killed* only by fire; and he is healed by the restorative powers of moonlight. Like the more standard bloodsucker, however, Fallon *does* drain his victims of blood via two puncture marks in the neck; he shies away from crosses; he casts no reflection in mirrors; and his victims *do* turn into vampires themselves (though, disappointingly, this fact is revealed only through dialogue rather than visuals). Thanks to these rather innovative alterations, *The Vampire's Ghost* becomes an intriguing addition to the cinematic vampire canon (unless, that is, the viewer tolerates variation less well than Fallon tolerates the sun). NOTE: This whole notion of the "right" rules of conduct and attributes of a vampire seems both artificial and absurd to this author. One of the most intriguing aspects of the horror genre is the presentation and exploration of The Unexpected. If these supernatural creatures always conform to what's expected of them from film to film, they become much less intriguing. And why *should* they be the same in movie after movie? As long as a vampire doesn't violate the reality built into its own particular film, clever variations can only add interest. I've never understood the vehemence of vampire-loving pedants in their insistence that *all* Creatures-Of-The-Night conform to some arbitrarily concocted set of supernatural rules. And let us not forget that, thanks to Mr. Stoker himself, the most famous vampire of all could—and did—move about in broad daylight! (Please send all missives and complaints to the author, care of the publisher, at the Vampire Variation League.)

Another frequent complaint by vampire purists is the casting of John Abbott as the bloodsucker. Though pop-eyed and slightly built (and lacking the *de rigueur* penguin suit and cape), Abbott's deep voice, cultured tones, forceful delivery, and confident physical movements make him an imposing figure nonetheless. Abbott's natural assuredness adds a much-needed efficacy to some of the suspect dialogue, bringing to life even potentially trite passages like, "Sometimes things drive a man, regardless of his will, things that may even tear his soul."

Abbott was no stranger to the role of vampire, having played *Dracula* himself in a London stage production. "In *The Vampire's Ghost*," recalled the actor to *Movie Club*'s Don Leifert, "I tried to make my character pass for a human being as near as I could and yet keep the undercurrent of the vampire's special propensities." He succeeded admirably.

"You're one of the nicest people I've ever met," the naïve Julie tells Fallon at one point. It's an amusingly ironic moment, but one possessing a grain of truth, for Abbott's vampire is one of the most sympathetic of the decade. Thanks to the actor's soulful eyes, deep baritone, and subtle, almost wistful expressions, an aura of sadness and tragedy hangs on Fallon like a shroud. When Fallon expounds upon the impending devastation of those around him, he states,

"This has all happened before and it'll all happen again—until the end of time." Though Abbott speaks rapidly and matter-of-factly, his face and inflection betray a great sadness. "I enjoyed playing the role," enthused Abbott, and the discerning viewer enjoys *watching* him.

Born in 1905 to a London stockbroker, John Abbott was headed for a career in commercial art before the lure of the footlights swept him into the world of theater—ultimately landing him a position at the prestigious Old Vic (where he acted opposite the likes of Laurence Olivier and Alec Guinness). Abbott entered films in 1936, making half a dozen movies in England before coming to Hollywood in 1941 where he made over 80 more during the next five decades, including such prestige pictures as *Jane Eyre* (1944), *The Woman in White* (1948), *The Greatest Story Ever Told* (1965), and Disney's *The Jungle Book* (1967; as the voice of the Wolf Leader). For genre fans, Abbott's (all-too brief) presence livened up the otherwise dull

Voodoo and Christianity combine to defeat vampirism as Father Gilchrist (Grant Withers), Simon Peter (Martin Wilkins), and Roy confront the vampire.

Columbia effort, *Cry of the Werewolf* (1944), and he added some much needed élan to Curtis Harrington's 1973 TV terror, *The Cat Creature*. One of the actor's final film appearances before his death in 1996 (at age 90) was in the witty *Four Weddings and a Funeral* (1994).

The Vampire's Ghost is not, however, an undiscovered classic, for it admittedly carries its fair share of foibles. When things move indoors, for example, the expected Poverty-Row lethargy sets in, replete with statically-shot, talky dialogue scenes on cramped, underdressed sets. Adele Mara (under the guidance of "Dance Director" Jerry Jarrette) provides a truly awful and inappropriate gypsy-style (on the west coast of Africa?!) dance sequence that goes on for an embarrassingly long time. Apart from Abbott, the cast proves adequate but unremarkable—with the painful exception of Martin Wilkins as Simon Peter, who turns

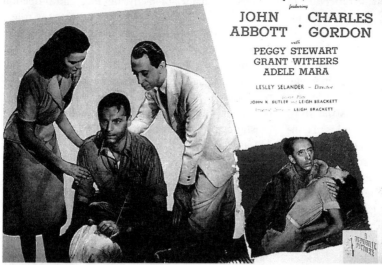

"THE VAMPIRE'S GHOST"

featuring

JOHN · CHARLES
ABBOTT · GORDON

with

PEGGY STEWART
GRANT WITHERS
ADELE MARA

LESLEY SELANDER – *Director*

Screen Play
JOHN K. BUTLER and LEIGH BRACKETT

Original Story – LEIGH BRACKETT

Though Julie (Peggy Stewart) thinks he's contracted jungle fever, Roy (Charles Gordon) is actually under the spell of the vampire.

Ryder' Westerns, at which task he had been gainfully employed." Phil Hardy's *Encyclopedia of Horror Movies* called it "a real shoestring shocker which is quite unable to make anything out of a potentially intriguing story"—before going on to get several key plot points (including the climax) completely wrong. (Do "critics" simply forget to *watch* these films before they write about them, or do they just fail to pay attention?)

To add insult to injury, just like *Voodoo Man* before it, *The Vampire's Ghost* was slapped with the restrictive "H" certificate (adults-only) by the BBFC when released in England.

Still, when one considers its Gower Gulch contemporaries (the amusing but puerile *King of the Zombies*, the entertaining but ridiculous *Voodoo Man*, and even the earnest but somewhat stodgy *The Face of Marble*), *The Vampire's Ghost* remains the best and most thought-provoking voodoo entry Poverty Row had to offer.

in an amazingly stilted and amateurish performance, even by low-budget standards. As the icing on the (fallen) cake, Grant Withers (playing Father Gilchrist) wearing a floor-length clerical smock in the middle of the African jungle topped by a *pith helmet* can't fail but induce derisive sniggers in the viewer.

The Rodney Dangerfield of vampire movies, *The Vampire's Ghost* simply "gets no respect." *Variety*'s "Sten," for instance, was singularly unimpressed: "John Abbott, as the vampire, along with Charles Gordon, Grant Withers and Peggy Stewart, go through their paces in stilted fashion. Script, settings and camerawork are just so-so."

The Hollywood Reporter complained that "there is little quality to the routine production, and Lesley Selander's direction reflects the confusion of the shabbily constructed screenplay." The reviewer did single out John Abbott, however, noting that "[Abbott's] own competence as an actor almost succeeds in making plausible the poorly-defined vampire story."

The Vampire's Ghost lacks even one champion among modern-day critics. The usually undiscriminating Michael Weldon called it "slow horror" in his *Psychotronic Encyclopedia of Film*. In *Poverty Row HORRORS!*, Tom Weaver labeled it "bleak and silly" and concluded that "*The Vampire's Ghost*'s mix of vampire, voodoo and jungle film elements is offbeat enough to be almost appealing, but the film generates so few thrills and so little atmosphere that even at a scant 59 minutes, it nearly succeeds in wearing out its welcome." In *B Movies*, Don Miller complained of the film's "cheap production values, uninspired performances and a director (Lesley Selander) who obviously preferred the more outgoing pleasures of 'Red

[1] There is one point where Christianity *does* become effective—when Roy, with the aid of Father Gilchrist, finally breaks free of Fallon's spell. This illuminates another intriguing tenet: A religion's power only works on the faithful of that religion. While the natives know what ails Roy, their voodoo magic cannot help him directly, for he is not of their faith. It finally takes Father Gilchrist and "the house of God" to overcome the evil spell placed upon Roy, demonstrating that each religion takes care of its own.

CREDITS: Director: Lesley Selander; Associate Producer: Rudolph E. Abel; Executive Producer: Armand Schaefer; Screenplay: John K. Butler and Leigh Brackett; Original Story: Leigh Brackett; Photography: Bud Thackery and Robert Pittack; Film Editor: Tony Martinelli; Sound: Dick Tyler; Art Director: Russell Kimball; Musical Director: Richard Cherwin; Set Decorations: Earl Wooden; Dance Director: Jerry Jarrette; Released May 1945 by Republic; 59 minutes

CAST: John Abbott (Webb Fallon), Charles Gordon (Roy), Peggy Stewart (Julie Vance), Grant Withers (Father Gilchrist), Emmett Vogan (Thomas Vance), Adele Mara (Lisa), Roy Barcroft (Jim Barrat), Martin Wilkins (Simon Peter), Frank Jacquet (The Doctor), Jimmy Aubrey (The Bum)

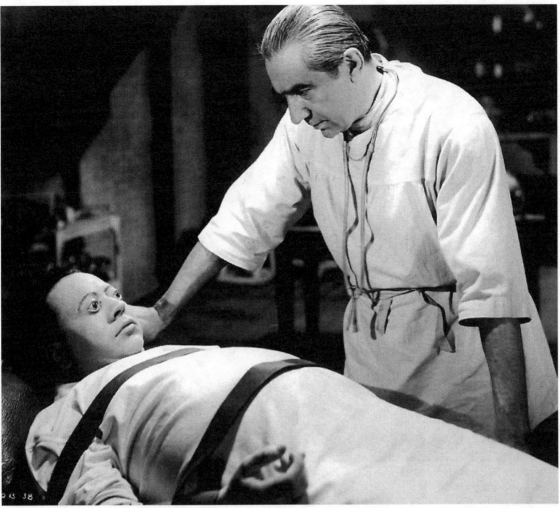

Dr. Renault (Bela Lugosi) temporarily turns the hapless (and halfwit) Mike (Alan Carney) into a zombie in *Zombies on Broadway*. **(Ronald V. Borst/Hollywood Movie Posters)**

ZOMBIES ON BROADWAY (1945)
I Walked With a Zombie's Comedic Offspring

"But the visitors would not so happy be,
If they could see what's behind the tree.
If they could see the eyes which are watching them,
They would leave this island of evil men.
But if they wait 'til the full moon comes,
To shine on the hands on the voodoo drums,
The chance to leave may come too late,
And blood on the ground will mark their fate."
—Calypso singer Sir Lancelot's "welcome" song

After producer Val Lewton's *I Walked With a Zombie* proved a critical and (more importantly) financial success, one can just imagine the RKO executives rub-bing their hands and trying to come up with a way to create a lucrative franchise out of their zombie hit (*à la* rival studio Universal's stable of returning monsters). They'd been burned before, however, when the head office tried foisting a sequel to the success-ful *Cat People* (1942) onto Lewton. But instead of making *The Curse of the Cat People* (1944) into the expected riotous monster-flick, the sensitive and lit-erate producer/writer came up with a compassionate and thoughtful tale of childhood loneliness. Though praised by the critics, *Curse* lived up to its name at the box office and failed to even approach the original's receipts. Obviously, Lewton could not be trusted with a zombie sequel, so what to do... what to do...

In June 1944 (three months after the studio brass examined *Curse of the Cat People*'s disappointing returns), *The Hollywood Reporter* announced that RKO had purchased a property called *Zombies on Broadway* from MGM as a vehicle for Wally Brown and Alan Carney. Perhaps comedy was the answer to their zombie dilemma, and the zombie follow-up be-

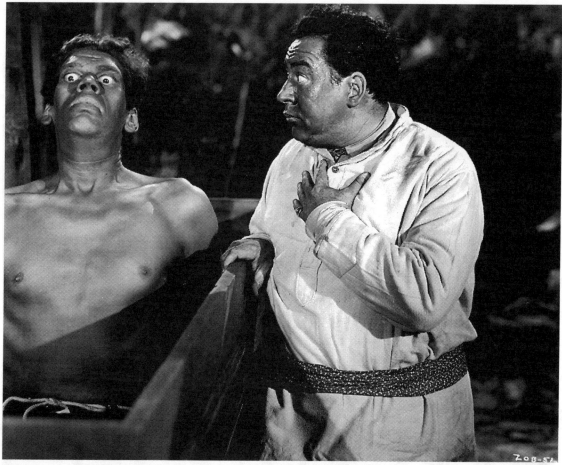

"Disguised" in blackface, Mike (Alan Carney, right) encounters the supernatural subject of the voodooists' zombie-making ceremony.

came a fright-fest/laugh-riot tailored for their torpid team of Abbott and Costello wannabes.

Zombies on Broadway proved to be a bastard child of *I Walked With a Zombie*. A parody rather than a direct sequel, the film borrowed Lewton's island setting (San Sebastian), its calypso singer (Sir Lancelot—who fashioned new lyrics for his old "Fort Holland" tune), and even the earlier film's zombie (Darby Jones), though his name metamorphosed from Carrefour into "Kolaga" (paralleling Universal's Mummy moniker switching). One of the film's comedy stars, Wally Brown, was even a Lewton alumnus, having previously appeared (*sans* Alan Carney) in *The Seventh Victim* (1943).

Shooting on *Zombies on Broadway* began around September 10, 1944 and wrapped on October 7. At one point during its final week of filming, director Gordon Douglas was bed-ridden with the flu and producer Ben Stoloff had to briefly step in to cover and keep the project on schedule.

In promoting "notorious ex-gangster" Ace Miller's (Sheldon Leonard) new night club called "The Zombie Hut," press agents Jerry and Mike (Wally Brown and Alan Carney) promise potential patrons a "real zombie." When Ace starts feeling the heat from an antagonistic radio personality ridiculing the audacious claim, the irate racketeer threatens the pair with all manner of bodily harm unless they come up with the genuine article (the ex-boxer the boys had picked to play a phony zombie fooled nobody).

Knowing nothing about real zombies, Jerry and Mike go to see Professor Hopkins (Ian Wolfe) at "The International Museum." Hopkins tells them of an old classmate of his, Dr. Renault (Bela Lugosi), who "over 25 years ago went to the only place where zombies were known to exist—on the island of San Sebastian, one of the smaller Virgin Islands."

Spooked by the whole subject (and by the rather odd Hopkins himself), Jerry and Mike decide to blow town, but with a little "persuasion" from Ace Miller's goons, they reluctantly board the next ship for San Sebastian.

Upon arriving, the pair go to the local café, where their talk of zombies attracts the attention of the beautiful saloon singer, Jean (Anne Jeffreys), currently stranded on San Sebastian. She agrees to help the boys with their quest of finding a zombie if they will take her back to New York with them.

Meanwhile, at Dr. Renault's castle home, the good doctor is trying to perfect a zombie formula. On hand as both model and obedient slave is Kolaga (Darby Jones), a real zombie. "Nearly 20 years ago I took him from the natives," states Renault, "and still no sign of disintegration. What they can do *I* can do." Unfortunately, to date Renault's scientific zombie serum has only resulted in his subjects' *temporary* zombification (and sometimes death). To test his new, revised formula, he needs another guinea pig and sends Kolaga out to procure one.

That night, Jean leads Jerry and Mike through the jungle toward the sound of the drums ("Those voodoo drums," Jean tells them, "that's the *death beat* you hear."). Unbeknownst to them, they are trailed by Kolaga, who has set his zombie sights on Jean for his master's next subject. When the trio become separated, the zombie comes upon Jean (who conveniently faints) and carries her back to his master.

The boys, however, finally arrive at the voodoo ceremony (a zombie-making rite, no less). Knowing

Though effectively sinister when present, Bela Lugosi's screen time only adds up to a paltry 10 minutes.

that, "If we were caught watchin' 'em make voodoo it means death for all of us," they hide in a nearby hut. By virtue of their own ineptness, however, they are soon discovered and chased through the jungle by the irate voodooists. (This rather atmospheric voodoo ceremonial sequence, in which half-naked natives whirl and dance with torches and knives around a crude coffin and bonfire surrounded by skulls stuck on poles, is sadly marred by the comedy team's inept "antics"—hiding in ceremonial baskets, running into monkeys, donning blackface as a disguise, etc.)

In their flight through the jungle, Jerry and Mike run into (literally) Renault's castle. The doctor and his henchman, Joseph (Joseph Vitale), welcome them. When the boys ask Renault about zombies, Renault puts them off, but offers his hospitality (for the doc has decided to experiment on them first, rather than the captive girl).

Renault sends Kolaga to fetch Mike from his room, and, via his new, improved serum, transforms the dimwitted PR man into a zombie. Intending to follow up with the same treatment for Jerry, his plans are thwarted when Jean escapes and (aided by a kleptomaniacal monkey who steals the hypo filled with the zombie fluid) helps Jerry overpower Renault.

Renault soon recovers, however, and sends for Kolaga. When the zombie arrives (carrying a shovel from his task of digging a grave), Renault orders him to "Kill, Kolaga, Kill." Kolaga does just that—by lifting up the shovel and bringing it squarely down on Renault himself! (A word to the wise—always be *very specific* in your instructions to zombies.) Kolaga dumps his ex-master into the newly dug grave while Jean and Jerry grab the zombified Mike and high-tail it back to the boat.

Back in New York on opening night, Jerry produces his promised zombie in the form of the entranced Mike. Unfortunately, just before Ace comes to examine his prize, the formula wears off and Mike reverts to normal. Ace is understandably disappointed, but in the ensuing melee is stabbed with the stolen syringe of zombie serum (the monkey having stowed away and followed the trio to New York) and so becomes his own main attraction. All's well that end's well... until Jerry accidentally sits on the syringe and promptly sports that tell-tale sign of pop-eyes and blank expression.

As an ersatz Abbott and Costello comedy team, Wally Brown and Alan Carney made eight pictures together between 1943 and 1946. Though each man had worked extensively in vaudeville, they had never worked *together* until RKO, eyeing the hefty profits Abbott and Costello were bringing to Universal, decided they needed their own comedy team and thrust the two independent comics (both RKO contract players) together in *Adventures of a Rookie* (1943).

As a comedy team, Brown and Carney simply don't possess the chemistry necessary to carry a feature, especially one as poorly written as *Zombies on Broadway*. They proved a singularly unremarkable—and, consequently, *unmemorable*—duo. After watching one of their pictures, the viewer finds it difficult even to recall what the innocuous pair look like, much less any of their supposedly funny shtick. Brown accurately reflects his name by remaining thoroughly bland, and Carney only succeeds in occasionally becoming annoying, his dimwit routine remaining undistinguished until he goes into Lou Costello's patented terror-stricken voiceless spluttering which ends in him yelling for Abbott—er—Brown.

Fortunately, "Brown & Carney" was not the be-all and end-all for the two comics, and both men continued their successful careers after their short-lived cinematic duo died from lack of interest following the release of their last starring vehicle, the tepid *Genius at Work* (1946).

After serving out his RKO tenure, Alan Carney later went under contract to Disney. Among his subsequent films are *The Pretender* (1947), *The Comancheros* (1961), and *It's A Mad, Mad, Mad, Mad World* (1963). Carney even returned to his roots briefly in 1952 when he created a new vaudeville act with Little Jack Little. On May 2, 1973, Alan Carney died of a heart attack at the Hollywood Park racetrack after winning the daily double. He was 63.

After their impromptu partnership dissolved, Wally Brown went on to appear in such films as *Notorious* (1946), *The Joker is Wild* (1957), and *The Left Handed Gun* (1958). Brown and Carney experienced a reunion of sorts in 1961 when they both appeared in Disney's *The Absent-Minded Professor* (Brown as the ecstatic Coach Elkins and Carney as the dumbfounded referee). Sadly, this proved to be Brown's last film, for he died on November 13, 1961 at age 57.

For *Zombies on Broadway*, scripter Lawrence Kimble provides little wisdom and even less wit, relying on standard devices like having Mike repeatedly see the menacing zombie while Jerry always seems to miss him. Time after time this happens, with the viewer's patience wearing more thin with each repetitive instance. It culminates in a ridiculously unfunny incident wherein Mike and Jerry are (stupidly) digging grave-sized holes for Dr. Renault. Mike falls through a trap door at the bottom of his hole, which drops him into an underground catacomb. There he spies Kolaga rising from his coffin, runs up some stairs and through a door which opens onto nothing and pitches him headlong back into his hole. Of course, Jerry refuses to believe his addled sidekick. Sigh.

Kimble's "amusing" dialogue doesn't help either, as evidenced by this pathetic attempt at humor when the duo order drinks in a bar:

> Mike: "I think I'll have something tripical."
> Jerry: "You mean 'tropical.'"
> Mike: "No, I mean *tripical*. (Holds up three fingers) I'll have a tripical rum punch—I'm thirsty."

When Mike timidly asks the ship captain, "Is [San Sebastian] a nice place?" the old salt answers, "To an undertaker a cemetery's a nice place," and laughs heartily. The viewer, however, does not.

Fortunately, *Zombies on Broadway* at least *looks* good, possessing a higher gloss than most Bs of the time, thanks to some expansive studio sets (including the convincing jungles seen in the Tarzan series), solid direction from Gordon Douglas (who later helmed the seminal *Them!* in 1954), and fluid camerawork and moody lighting courtesy of cinematographer Jack Mackenzie.

That *Zombies on Broadway* remains at all watchable and occasionally even mildly diverting can be put down to two reasons: Bela Lugosi's enthusiastic playing and director Gordon Douglas' deft handling of the fright factor (something few horror comedies can boast of). As in the best horror comedies (such as *The Ghost Breakers* and *Abbott and Costello Meet Frankenstein*), Douglas treats his "monster" (the zombie) with the proper respect, never lessening the creature's menace for the sake of a snicker. Darby Jones' zombie remains almost as eerily frightening as in *I Walked with a Zombie* (with his huge staring eyes, shuffling gait, unbending carriage, and long arms hanging loose at his sides until they reach out toward an intended victim...) thanks to Douglas' employment of sinister lighting, camerawork, shadows, and even appropriate mood music.

Kolaga's introduction shows just how committed Douglas was to keeping the *horror* in this "horror comedy." It begins when Renault opens a sliding panel in the wall of his laboratory to reveal a secret anteroom beyond. A small panel in the room's opposite wall rises slowly and out of the square of darkness a coffin noiselessly emerges. The rough-hewn casket's lid opens and Darby Jones, silent and staring, sits up stiffly, his naked torso looking emaciated yet oddly powerful. The zombie gets up and advances toward the camera until his disturbing round-eyed visage fills the frame.

Gangster-turned-nightclub-owner Ace Miller (Sheldon Leonard) inadvertently becomes his club's own star attraction at the "wacky" conclusion of *Zombies on Broadway*.

Thereafter, whenever Kolaga makes an appearance, titters take a back seat to shudders, culminating in the zombie's final frightening scene. When Renaults orders his living dead servant to "Kill, Kolaga, Kill!," the zombie obeys with impassive expression and literal immediacy by raising up his shovel and bringing it fatally down on Renault in a moment that is downright chilling—and one of the film's true shocks. The creature then lifts up his former master's body, slowly carries it outside, and drops it into the newly dug grave—an ironic and effective finale. (Too bad the film had to continue on for another 10 minutes to its unfunny conclusion.)

To be truthful, one of the scariest things (or at least the most amazing) is watching the rather thin Darby Jones heft the corpulent Alan Carney in his arms and carry him out of the room in the traditional captured heroine pose. Kolaga must indeed possess supernatural strength to lift the elephantine Mike like that. (And let's hope for Jones' sake that Douglas got the scene on the first take—herniated zombies can be a real liability.)

If *Zombies on Broadway* is remembered at all, it is solely because it proved to be one of Bela Lugosi's last major studio films. Unfortunately, as a Lugosi movie, it falls well short even of his frequently pathetic Monogram monstrosities—not because of the actor's performance (for Lugosi turns in an enthusiastic and energetic portrayal) but because he's onscreen for less than 10 minutes! The viewer must wade through 20 minutes of unfunny Brown and Carney before ever laying eyes on the perennial bogeyman who then, after one brief sequence, disappears for nearly *another* 20 minutes!

Thankfully, Lugosi is given a well-staged and dramatic intro: We follow Joseph as he goes down into a basement lab filled with bubbling beakers and smoking test tubes. "Dr. Renault?" he asks tentatively. The scene shifts to a lab table with a man in a white surgical smock standing behind it. The man's face, however, is totally obscured by a large smoking beaker. "Yes, what is it?" booms out a low, commanding voice with that unmistakable Hungarian accent. The man's head raises up from his work and the camera

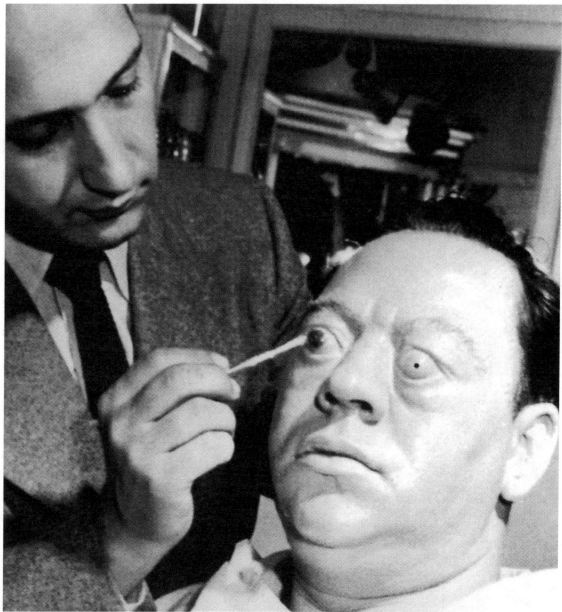

Alan Carney endures the application of the bulging, zombie eye makeup that will transform him into one of the *Zombies on Broadway*. (Note the small pinhole in the unpainted false eye through which the actor can see.)

dollies forward to reveal the concentrated countenance of Bela Lugosi.

For the most part, Lugosi (like Darby Jones) is treated with respect in regards to his sinister status, and the actor brings his trademark panache to his mad doctor persona. When he frustratedly asks, "How can the natives do with their silly voodoo what *I* cannot accomplish with scientific means?!," his voice and face come alive with the impatient anger and supreme arrogance of this madman's megalomania.

In his exchanges with Brown and Carney, Lugosi even gets in a few subtle zingers himself, handling the humor well—when given something effective to do or say. When Jerry offers, "Laboratory work—anything we can help you with?" Lugosi agrees,

"There may be something—," and after a pregnant pause accompanied by a slight, sardonic upturn at the corner of his mouth, adds, "—later." It's an uncharacteristically subtle and humorous touch which suggests that Lugosi could have handled comedy better than he was usually allowed. (Unfortunately, Lugosi quickly quashes that idea when, in an embarrassing scene of playing catch-the-monkey in a bureau, he reverts to the expected broad burlesque and exaggerated expressions when the simian keeps popping out of different drawers.) Worse was to come at the hands of Brown and Carney, however, for the aging actor popped up once again in the duo's final entry, *Genius at Work* (1946), in which he was wasted in an even briefer role.

Though showing both spunk and enthusiasm, the effervescent Anne Jeffreys could do little with her thankless role of female lead Jean La Danse. Apart from serving as some (admittedly lovely) window dressing, clinging nervously to Brown or fainting at the right moment, her "best" bits come when she brains first the villain and then (mistakenly) the hero. She does, however, get to display her pleasing voice in a brief café musical number.

Born Anne Carmichael in 1923 in Goldsboro, North Carolina, Anne Jeffreys worked as a model and an opera singer before becoming a leading lady in Hollywood Bs in the 1940s. From 1953-1956 she starred opposite her real-life husband Robert Sterling on television's *Topper*. Jeffreys appeared in two other Brown and Carney extravaganzas, 1944's *Step Lively* (in which she gave Frank Sinatra his first onscreen kiss) and the aforementioned final feature, *Genius at Work* (1946).

"The 'zombie' horror film swings over to the funny side with this picture," began *Variety*'s "Wear." "*Zombies on Broadway* turns out to be a ghost comedy, with about half of it punched hard for laughs, some of which fail to materialize." Feeling the film a rather mixed bag, the reviewer singled out Lugosi ("menacing as ever") and Anne Jeffreys ("lively"). He concludes, "Picture moves faster than previous entries in the 'zombie' cycle, with Gordon Douglas' direction mainly responsible. It's lots better than the script."

The New York Herald Tribune, however, succinctly labeled it "an appalling little film."

Modern consensus sees *Zombies on Broadway* as a sort of harmless but slightly embarrassing comedic Uncle. *Video Watchdog*'s Tim Lucas remarked that, "This short Carney and Brown programmer may be stale as comedy, but it has definite curiosity value as an appendage to Val Lewton's RKO horror series… Director Gordon Douglas presents [Darby] Jones' horrific appearances in a straight respectful manner which, combined with the none-too-original personalities of the comic duo, makes this oft-maligned quickie a virtual blueprint for the more successful *Abbott and Costello Meet Frankenstein*."

Ted Okuda of *Filmfax* gave the picture an ambivalent thumbs-sideways, denigrating the duo's work in general but giving guarded praise to this feature in particular, noting both Gordon Douglas' "efficient direction" and Bela Lugosi's presence, who "gives a much better performance than the slight material warrants." Okuda concludes, "Though hardly a cinematic milestone, *Zombies on Broadway* is a pleasant reminder of the kind of efficient little 'B' pictures Hollywood used to churn out so effortlessly. And throughout, Lugosi is so good that he makes the final result seem better than it actually is."

Roger Hurlburt was more blunt when he dismissed it in *Filmfax* as a "dismal comedy spooker," while Richard Bojarski (in *The Films of Bela Lugosi*) let it down easy with a "routine horror spoof." *Scarlet Street*'s Bob Madison gave the unkindest cut of all, however, when he maintained that both *Bela Lugosi Meets a Brooklyn Gorilla* and *Bride of the Monster* "are better than *Zombies on Broadway*"!

In Britain, which frowned upon horror films during the course of WWII (apparently real-life horrors were enough), the film's title was changed to *Loonies on Broadway* to make sure the English censors and public knew it was a *laugh*-fest rather than fright-fest. (They must have been dismayed to find that it's the sparse terror tidbits rather than the copious comedy that proved most effective.)

CREDITS: Alternate Title: *Loonies on Broadway* (United Kingdom); Director: Gordon Douglas; Producer: Ben Stoloff; Executive Producer: Sid Rogell; Screenplay: Lawrence Kimble; Story: Robert Faber and Charles Newman; Adaptation: Robert E. Kent; Photography: Jack Mackenzie; Art Direction: Albert S. D'Agostino, Walter E. Keller; Set Decoration: Darrell Silvera, Al Greenwood; Editor: Philip Martin, Jr.; Assistant Director: Sam Ruman; Gowns: Edward Stevenson; Music: Roy Webb; Music Director: C. Bakaleinikoff; Dance Director: Charles O'Curran; Released April 1945 by RKO; 68 minutes

CAST: Wally Brown (Jerry Miles), Alan Carney (Mike Strager), Bela Lugosi (Dr. Paul Renault), Anne Jeffreys (Jean La Danse), Sheldon Leonard (Ace Miller), Frank Jenks (Gus), Russell Hopton (Benny), Joseph Vitale (Joseph), Ian Wolfe (Prof. Hopkins), Louis Jean Heydt (Douglas Walker), Darby Jones (Kolaga), Sir Lancelot (Calypso Singer), Robert Clarke (Wimpy), Harold Herskind (Stenga [zombie]), Emory Parnell (Skipper), Carl Kent (Hot-foot Davis), Martin Wilkins (Sam), Nicodemus (Worthington), Walter Soderling (Dr. Robertson), Virginia Lyndon (Dancer), Betty Yeaton (Dancer), Norman Mayes (Bit), Bob St. Angelo (Steward), Jason Robards (Café Manager), Rosemary La Planche (Entertainer), Bill Williams (Jack [sailor]), Angie Gomez (Knife Thrower), Dick Botiller (Boss of Café), Max Wagner (Waiter), Rudolph Andrian (High Priest), Mathew Jones (Fat Warrior)

poraries, mixing voodoo and science with experiments to revive the dead. The pacing is just as slow, and the screenplay features the expected inanities ("Who can say where fact ends and superstition begins?" or "A hypo to relax the cranial nerves"). Despite its myriad shortcomings, however, *The Face of Marble* exudes an almost ethereal quality, as if striving to be something more than the sum of its cheap parts. There is a feeling of sorrow woven into the film's tapestry which draws one's attention, allowing the viewer to overlook the numerous flaws and simply enjoy the bizarre story being told.

Professor Randolph (John Carradine) is a kindly scientist working on a method to revive victims of drowning and suffocation for the betterment of mankind. With the help of his dedicated young assistant, Dr. David Cochran (Robert Shayne[1]), Randolph restores life to a drowned sailor who's fortuitously washed up on the beach. The process, however (involving a special serum and massive doses of electricity), turns the man's face a chalky white ("It's a face of marble!" exclaims David), and the unfortunate soon collapses again, dead (this time for good).

After improving the process, Randolph tries it out again—this time on his wife's pet Great Dane, Brutus. It works, and the huge dog revives, but he has the rather unusual (and unexplained) ability to walk through walls! Not only that, but Brutus goes about ripping out the throats of the local livestock and draining the animals of blood. (So here we have the screen's first vampire *dog*—and this a full 32 years before *Zoltan, Hound of Dracula* broke "new" canine ground.)

Creeping about in the background and listening at doors is the Haitian servant, Maria (Rosa Rey), who is devoted to Randolph's young wife, Elaine (Claudia

THE FACE OF MARBLE
(1946)
Vicious Voodoo, Sane Scientists, and Demonic Dogs

"Death, *violent* death, is the curse of Vidra
when the fetish is destroyed.
It is *you* who must pay the penalty—
you tried to destroy the magic of Vidra!"
—Rosa Rey as the voodoo practitioner, Maria

The Face of Marble is not the typical low-budget quickie churned out by the fistful at Monogram Studios in the 1940s. This one has something extra. The plot is certainly no better than its potboiler contem-

Drake). Elaine falls for David, but the feelings are not reciprocated because of the assistant's loyalty to the professor and the fact that David has a girl of his own, Linda (Maris Wrixon). When Linda arrives at the house for a visit, Maria, a practitioner of voodoo, places a toxic smoke pot "used in the voodoo death ceremony" in Linda's room. Due to a mix-up, however, the smoke kills Elaine instead. David and Randolph use their apparatus on Elaine and she is restored—apparently okay. Soon, however, she begins to walk through walls while keeping the vampiric dog company. Even worse, the warped Maria somehow uses her voodoo magic to maintain hypnotic control over Elaine. Maria forces her mistress to kill Randolph (who mistrusts Maria) and frames David for the crime. But Shadrach (Willie Best), the Randolphs' houseboy, has seen the whole thing and clears David. David rushes back to the house to save the imperiled Linda in the nick of time. The police find Maria dead from her own voodoo smoke, and a final shot reveals two sets of footprints on the beach leading off into the surf—one set human and the other set canine.

Way back in January of 1944, Monogram announced that they'd purchased the story for *The Face of Marble* from writers William Thiele and Edmund L. Hartmann and would soon put it into production under the supervision of producer Lindsley Parsons. Nothing further was heard of the project until almost two years later when, in September 1945, Monogram again announced the story's purchase, with the producer's chores going to Jeffrey Bernard. On Friday, October 5, 1945, the film began shooting under director William Beaudine (but whether Jeffrey Bernard *really* stood in the producer's shoes remains a question mark, since no producer's credit is listed on either the film print or in the publicity materials).

The Face of Marble possesses an engaging quality that most of its contemporaries lack—due mainly to the likable characters and the subdued performances of the actors, particularly John Carradine as Professor Randolph and Robert Shayne as his noble assistant, David. Carradine delivers a fine performance as the soft-spoken humanitarian, downplaying any opportunities the script provides for melodramatic histrionics and opting instead for a more realistic portrayal of a man driven by the best of motives. Even Boris Karloff could not have cut a more sympathetic figure. When Carradine kills his wife's dog in an experiment but then (initially) fails to revive him, Carradine shows real remorse, lamenting, "Poor Brutus, I'll never forgive myself." How can one fail to like an animal-loving mad scientist? And when an experiment fails on a human (resulting in the "face of marble" of the title—though it's never very clear as to what that means exactly except that the subject's countenance looks like it was dipped in flour), Shayne

warns, "In our experiments we've been walking a dangerous line." Carradine concurs and when Shayne decides to leave, discontinuing the work, Carradine admits, "Perhaps it's just as well, it'll keep us from making any more—mistakes." With *The Face of Marble*, Monogram finally offers us some *sane* science, since this is one particular "mad" scientist who keeps his head.

Speaking of heads… "FAMOUS HEAD OF HAIR IS CUT FOR MOTION PICTURE ROLE" read the headline of a Monogram publicity release. The "FAMOUS HEAD" to which the article refers belonged to John Carradine. According to Monogram, Carradine had sworn off all further mad doctor portrayals just weeks before that studio "lured him back to the klieg lights only after assuring the actor that the doctor which he portrays in *The Face of Marble* was completely sane." While it seems more likely that Carradine accepted the role because of financial con-

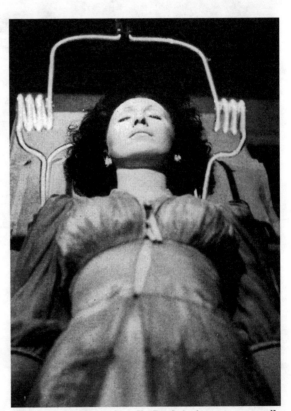

Elaine Randolph's (Claudia Drake) visage temporarily turns into a "face of marble" during treatment that revives her from death.

siderations (more cash for his beloved Shakespearean touring company), the more sympathetic and "normal" role might explain Carradine's uncharacteristically relaxed, low-key playing. Of the much-touted haircut, Carradine had grown his hair long for his various Shakespearean activities (including an extensive tour of *Hamlet* a few months before filming) and had to "cut off his Hamlet-like tresses to take the part."

A former household pet named Brutus (played by "General") menaces Linda (Maris Wrixon) after being transformed into a phantom canine during experiments to revive the dead in *The Face of Marble*.

While *The Face of Marble* is ostensibly a "mad science" movie (though both of the story's scientists are quite sane—for a change), the film's voodoo element remains considerable. (In fact, the picture's opening scene has Maria talking about the "great spirit, Tonga" while Elaine gently scoffs at her "voodoo magic.") Apart from placing voodoo "love charms" under David's pillow and in his pockets, Maria at times sits before a fire (in eerily lit and effectively shot scenes) to pray and commune with her voodoo gods or prepare a poisonous smoke concoction that employs "the root of the Tarishi plant used in the voodoo death ceremony." Indeed, if there's a "heavy" in the picture, it is Maria, who (in a misguided attempt to aid her love-smitten mistress) uses her voodoo magic and paraphernalia to commit two murders and bring tragedy to the household.

The Face of Marble rises above its Poverty Row contemporaries by possessing some above-average production values, including a better-dressed lab set than usual (with an abundance of glass tubing, beakers, coils, and tanks to give it a more cluttered, purposeful—and *authentic*—look than the expected token rack of test tubes on a bare workbench) and some wonderfully mobile camerawork. Harry Neumann's camera tracks smoothly along with the characters, moving not only from one side of a room to another but forward and back as well to add depth and involvement to the scene. (Most "Monogrammers" of-

fer up nothing more innovative than the occasional room pan, and relied on editing rather than motion to break up the monotony.) During the experiment on the sailor, for instance, the camera pans and dollies to stay near the two doctors as they move about preparing their subject and equipment. The close camera and movement effectively draws the viewer into the activity—something the standard static medium shots generally fail to do. Thanks to some careful work on Neumann's part, *The Face of Marble* becomes one of the more visually fluid of the Poverty Row horrors.

Director William "One Shot" Beaudine steps beyond his less-than-sterling reputation (and deserved nickname) to take some extra care in staging this production. His effective set-up of a dialogue scene between Maria and Elaine (doing her hair), for example, begins by shooting into a mirror. As the two women talk, Maria makes a rather mysterious and sinister comment, and Elaine stops. The camera then swings left away from the reflection to come to rest on the actual actresses just as Elaine turns to face Maria and demand, "What have you been up to?" The camera movement adds impact to the scene and punctuates the foreboding moment to catch the viewer's attention just as Maria's disturbing words have caught the attention of Elaine.

The Face of Marble is also blessed with a rather effective climax (something its two sister Monogram/voodoo productions, *King of the Zombies* and *Voo-*

doo Man, sorely lack). As David bursts into Linda's darkened room to find Brutus about to leap upon his fiancée, he attacks the menacing dog. Then, with David on the floor grappling with the hell hound, the ghostly Elaine bends over the unconscious Linda (having fainted) with her hands going towards the heroine's throat. Suddenly, the police inspector throws open the door and flips the light switch… and David is abruptly seen wrestling with thin air! Both the specters have vanished! It's a rather startling and unexpected moment (two qualities rarely found at the close of most Poverty-Row horrors). Then the final shot of the two sets of footprints leading into the ocean closes the film on a melancholy—and effective—note (a note which catches a touch of I *Walked with a Zombie*'s poetic tone—but only a *small* touch, mind you).

Of course, since it was a Monogrammer, *The Face of Marble* failed to completely escape its Poverty-Row roots. As expected, the film sports many, *many* talky scenes (talk is cheap, after all), usually revolving around the breakfast table (these people seemingly *love* their morning meal) or involving the visiting Inspector (who can't seem to stay away from his "old friend" Professor Randolph). Also, the typical wall-to-wall music, sounding cheap and inappropriate, becomes both intrusive and grating. But it's about what one can one expect from the redoubtable "musical director" Edward Kay, who scored (or is that "scarred"?) such films as *The Ape* (1940), *Ghosts on the Loose* (1943), and *Bomba on Panther Island* (1949), as well as all three of Monogram's voodoo entries.

Though his sincere and effective performance doesn't show it, Robert Shayne was not impressed with this particular voodoo vehicle. "It's undoubtedly the worst film I have ever done—," he stated years later. "It's deplorable." (These are pretty strong words coming from a man whose filmography includes such awful entries as *The Neanderthal Man*, 1953; *The Giant Claw*, 1957; and *Teenage Caveman*, 1958.)

Apparently, Shayne got off on the wrong foot with his famous co-star. "My relationship with the lead was no better [than the film itself]," remembered the actor. "One day I came onto the semi-darkened stage and Carradine was off somewhere on the set spouting

Shakespeare. I didn't know he was there, and I made some caustic remark. After that he wasn't very friendly to me."

According to *The Face of Marble* pressbook, being a dog-lover was mandatory to winning a role in the picture (since the dog, Brutus, plays such a major role in the film). "The producers figured that any fear or mistrust on the part of the human actors would reflect itself not only in their own performances, but also in the performance of the dog. So before each human actor was called in for an interview, he was first asked if he liked dogs. If not, he was eliminated." While doubtless horror star John Carradine's particu-

A drowned sailor (Clark Kuney) briefly restored to life frightens Professor Randolph (John Carradine) with his ghastly "face of marble."

lar canine proclivity figured into his casting not at all, Monogram's casting choices for the rest of the roles proved highly fortuitous (dog lovers or no).

In *The Face of Marble*, everyone plays it straight which makes all the weird goings-on *almost* believable. It helps, too, that the film is devoid of the usual goofy characters (grating sidekicks, inept assistants, dimwitted policemen) that plague most Poverty-Row productions. The closest this film comes to these stock caricatures is Shadrach, the timid black houseboy.

In the politically *in*correct era of the 1940s, people were not afraid to flaunt their racism. Even film studios promulgated such abhorrent attitudes in their advertising. "Utilize enough paint and hair stiffening," urged *The Face of Marble* pressbook in its "exploitation" section, "to give a street ballyhoo man, preferably a Negro, a really frightened look." Apparently, the feeling of the day was that "Negroes," along with having a natural rhythm and love of watermelon, made better scaredy-cats.

In this racist climate a few black actors worked within the system and managed to rise to (relative) prominence. Among them was Willie Best, who entered films at the age of 17 under the demeaning stage name of "Sleep 'n' Eat." (Fortunately, he soon abandoned that insulting moniker in favor of his own name.) Best made a career out of such stereotypical characters as the lazy sidekick or cowardly servant (which he again played in *The Face of Marble*). Though *The Face of Marble* doesn't really show it, Best was occasionally able to invest some warmth or spark into his nonsensical parts, as he did in *The Ghost Breakers* (1940). (Bob Hope once called Willie Best "the best actor I know.") Best continued working on into the 1950s, and often appeared in genre films like *The Monster Walks* (1932), *Mummy's Boys* (1936), *The Smiling Ghost* (1941), *The Body Disappears* (1941), and *A-Haunting We Will Go* (1942). He even turned up as a semi-regular on two television shows, *The Trouble with Father* and *My Little Margie*.

To promote *The Face of Marble*, Monogram suggested a contest, urging theater owners to run this ad in their local newspaper:

$25.00 REWARD
for sleeping
all night in the
COUNTY MORGUE
consult
"FACE OF MARBLE"
at the
MONOGRAM THEATRE

I'm sure that if there were any takers they must have slept like the proverbial dead.

The Face of Marble received more critical approval back in 1946 than it gets in 1996. *Variety* called it a "typical horror film [that] has a confusing story but a plausible, serious treatment to make it acceptable." The reviewer ("Bron") also noted "good camerawork, a well-chosen cast and a lot of pseudo-scientific and medical gadgets and palaver give pic more solid substance than it rates." *The Hollywood Reporter* felt it was "ok going in the chiller market. No work of art or beauty, the film nevertheless succeeds pretty well in achieving what it sets out to do— thrill and scare you." The reviewer also singled out John Carradine, praising his low-key performance: "Carradine proves the most competently restful character in the melee, underplaying and not once shaking his Shakespearean locks."

Today, the film gets little respect (and much less attention than the Lugosi Monograms). Tom Weaver,

in *Poverty Row HORRORS!*, labeled it "a dreadful film," complaining that its script made it "one of the unwieldiest films, horror or otherwise, of the 1940s." John Stanley's generally caustic *Revenge of the Creature Features Movie Guide* called it "barely watchable" while the usually less-critical Michael Weldon (in *The Psychotronic Encyclopedia of Film*) felt it was "bad as only a Monogram horror movie could be." At least *Castle of Frankenstein*'s Calvin T. Beck gave it a mild endorsement by noting that this "modest grade-B supernatural melodrama" was "quietly effective."

The Catholic Church definitely frowned on the film's subject matter. The Legion of Decency gave it their "B" rating, complaining, "Encourages credence in voodooism and superstitious practices" as well as citing "suicide in plot solution" as objectionable.

Monogram paired *The Face of Marble* with an Edmund Lowe/Jean Rogers hypnotist/mystery-type film called *The Strange Mr. Gregory* to create a "SUPER SHOCK SHOW!" with "This Twin Horror Smash!" (*The Strange Mr. Gregory* director Phil Rosen had *almost* directed a voodoo picture himself when he was at one time assigned to helm *Voodoo Man*, but was shifted to *Return of the Ape Man* instead.)

By no means a classic or even near-classic, *The Face of Marble* is still one of those happy accidents in which the elements came together to make something better than it should have been. And while it may not exactly be a *gem, it's better than most of the fool's* gold Monogram unearthed in the 1940s.

---

[1] Though often referred to as "the young doctor," Shayne was in his mid-40s at the time of filming (and looked even older). Carradine, who fr*equently* refers to Shayne as "my boy," was younger than his "young" assistant.

CREDITS: Director: William Beaudine; Screenplay: Michel Jacoby; Story: William Thiele and Edmund Hartmann; Director of Photography: Harry Neumann; Production Manager: Glenn Cook; Editor: William Austin; Assistant Director: Theodore Joos; Musical Director: Edward Kay; Technical Director: David Milton; Sound Recording: Tom Lambert; Set Decorations: Vin Taylor; Special Effects: Robert Clark; Released January 1946 by Monogram; 70 minutes

CAST: John Carradine (Prof. Randolph), Claudia Drake (Elaine Randolph), Robert Shayne (Dr. David Cochran), Maris Wrixon (Linda), Willie Best (Shadrach), Thomas E. Jackson (Police Inspector Norton), Rosa Rey (Maria), Neal Barns (Jeff), Donald Kern and Allan Ray (Photographers), Clark Kuney (Drowned Man), General and Captain (Brutus the dog)

ROUTING VOODOO VENGEANCE FROM HEADHUNTER VALLEY

JOHNNY WEISSMULLER

as JUNGLE JIM

VOODOO TIGER

with JEAN BYRON • JAMES SEAY • JEANNE DEAN and TAMBA (The Talented Chimp)

Story and Screen Play by SAMUEL NEWMAN • Based upon the famous Jungle Jim King Features Syndicate newspaper feature

Produced by SAM KATZMAN • Directed by SPENCER G. BENNET • A COLUMBIA PICTURE

Courtesy of Ronald V. Borst/Hollywood Movie Posters

VOODOO TIGER (1952)

Jungle Jim's Voodoo Insult

> "There's no sense talking to them—
> they're fanatics, blood crazy.
> One word from a witch doctor and
> they'd be up to their ears in voodoo again."
> —Rick Vallin as the condescending Sgt. Bono

"Standard Jungle Jim Adventure" read the headline for *Variety*'s review of *Voodoo Tiger*. Though it may be "standard" for the Jungle Jim series, *Voodoo Tiger* proved a decidedly *sub*standard voodoo film.

Somewhere in the African jungle, Jungle Jim (Johnny Weissmuller) and his two companions, Phyllis Bruce (Jean Byron) and Sergeant Bono (Rick Vallin), break up a voodoo sacrificial ceremony. (Miss Bruce is there on behalf of the British Museum searching for the source of the "voodoo tiger legend.") Jim knocks out the high priest, Wombulu (Charles Horvath), frees the intended victim, and sets fire to the practitioners' sacred "voodoo tiger god" statue. A trio of white men, led by Abel Peterson (James Seay), arrive and shoot the knife out of Wombulu's hand as he's about to stab Jim in the back. Jungle Jim sends

the native voodooists off with a scolding and heads back to his newfound friends' camp.

A message arrives asking Jim to come to the nearby Watusi airstrip. There they meet Commissioner Kingston (Richard Kipling) and Major Bill Green (Robert Bray) of the United States Army. Green and the Commissioner enlist Jungle Jim to take them to see a trader named Werner (Michael Fox). At the trading post, Green reveals that Werner is actually a former German war criminal named Colonel Schultz, who is the only one that knows the whereabouts of a two-million-dollar art collection stolen during WWII. Before they can take Schultz into custody, however (the U.S. government wants the treasures recovered), Peterson and his men arrive at the trading post. They're after Schultz too, since they're a band of art thieves. The two groups brawl and in the ruckus Schultz slips away.

Schultz makes his way to the airstrip and hijacks the waiting plane, whose passengers consist of a female dance troupe headed by Shalimar (Jeanne Dean, "the original Vargas girl") and her pet tiger. Forcing the pilot to fly inland, the plane crash lands (safely) right in the middle of voodoo tiger territory. The natives (headhunters, of course) rush to the site and menace the passengers, but when Shalimar's tiger

Former Tarzan Johnny Weissmuller played "Jungle Jim" 13 times in only six years.

promptly captured himself. But when the witch doctor raises his machete to sacrifice the intruding whites, Shalimar's tiger shows up again and Shalimar steps forward to order the whites spared.

Because of her tiger, Shalimar has so far been able to keep her companions (including Schultz) safe, but her influence is waning and they are all little more than prisoners.

The chief orders a "voodoo trial" for the next morning, which is "a fight to the death between a wild animal and an unarmed man." Placed in a bamboo enclosure with a lion, Jim kills the beast with a knife that his chimp, Tamba, had smuggled to him. Shalimar cuts loose the others and sics her tiger on the natives, who take refuge in a hut. During the spectacle, Peterson and his party (who'd been granted immunity by the headhunters because of their association with Wombulu) free Schultz and spirit him away.

The headhunters break out of the hut and pursue Jungle Jim and the girls. Jim and Green ambush Peterson and grab Schultz, leaving the art thieves to be killed by the now-angry headhunters. Jim uses the dynamite trap to stop his pursuers, Shalimar and the girls take off for Casablanca, and Major Green gets his man.

makes an appearance they fall to their knees to worship it.

Jungle Jim leads Green and company in a rescue mission/pursuit of Schultz, while Peterson enlists the evil Wombulu to guide *his* party into the voodoo tiger country. Peterson sets up a dynamite trap for Jungle Jim, but J.J. fights off several of Wombulu's lackeys and discovers the booby trap.

When Jim goes to scout ahead, the rest of his party are killed or captured by the hostile headhunting voodooists. With Major Green and Miss Bruce tied to stakes, Jim enters the headhunter village and is

When former Olympic swimming champion Johnny Weissmuller (born Peter John Weissmuller) first appeared as the Lord of the Jungle in the 1932 MGM epic, *Tarzan the Ape Man*, the success of this feature and its sequel, 1934's *Tarzan and His Mate* (which many consider to be the finest Tarzan film ever made), ensured that Weissmuller would be swinging on vines for a long time to come. Between 1932 and 1948 he starred in a dozen Tarzan features, first at MGM and then at RKO. When RKO producer Sol Lesser refused to grant him a percentage of the profits, Weissmuller abandoned his loincloth—but not the jungle, for low-end producer Sam Katzman immediately snapped him up for a series of "Jungle Jim" adventure films at Columbia. Though based on a comic book and radio program character, Jungle Jim was really a thinly disguised pants-and-shirt-wearing Tarzan. (It's just as well that Weissmuller's new character traipses about the jungle fully clothed, since the Tarzan loincloth was getting a bit snug for the 44-year-old ex-swimming champ.)

Weissmuller made 13 Jungle Jims (in only six years) and then three more films in which he played the same character but employed his real name rather than the (rather silly) J.J. moniker. Reportedly, he received $50,000 for each film plus a percentage of the profits. "He shot two Jungle Jims a year," recalled Weissmuller's *Voodoo Tiger* co-star Michael Fox (in Tom Weaver's *It Came from Weaver Five*). "They were shot in nine days, and he shot them virtually back to back. And that was all he worked! I think Johnny was living in Mexico at the time; he would come out here to Hollywood for a month to do the two pictures back-to-back, and there would be a break of maybe two days between."

A superb athlete (with five gold medals and 67 world records to prove it), Weissmuller was not much of an actor. As Tarzan, he was asked to deliver little dialogue—and *that* in broken English. In the Jungle Jim series, however, he spoke in complete sentences, and, while his scripters intentionally kept his speeches short, his inadequacies became more readily apparent. His flat, rather nasal voice injects little inflection into his lines, and he seldom changes expression. Even when he comes upon the corpses of his own men killed by the headhunters, all Weissmuller can do is look down at the bodies, look up at the chimp in his arms, and then back to the bodies again—with nary a twitch in his facial muscles. (Weissmuller even has trouble with names, referring to Wombulu first as "Wombul-*luh*," then as "Wombul-*lee*," and finally as "Wombul-*lo*.") Michael Fox (who was probably the best actor in *Voodoo Tiger*) agreed: "On the list of great actors, I don't think you'd find Johnny's name much before the number 4,000 [*laughs*], but he was a very nice man, and most enjoyable. We used to lunch together."

Voodoo Tiger looks and feels very much like a cheap serial, full of unconvincing fist fights, shallow characters, no-frills photography, and juvenile plotting. Considering the picture's director, this should come as no surprise. Spencer Gordon Bennet began in films in 1912 as an actor and stuntman for the

Jungle Jim (Johnny Weissmuller) prepares to protect his beautiful charges from the headhunters who worship the *Voodoo Tiger*. (Courtesy of Ronald V. Borst/Hollywood Movie Posters)

Edison company. He became a director in the early 1920s and made a (modest) name for himself as a serial specialist, directing 52 cinematic chapter-plays in all (including the popular *Batman and Robin*, 1949; *Atom Man vs. Superman*, 1950; and *Captain Video*, 1951). Among his non-serial features are several other Jungle Jims (*Killer Ape*, 1953; *Savage Mutiny*, 1953; and *Devil Goddess*, 1955) and the sci-fi entry *The Atomic Submarine* (1960).

Technically, *Voodoo Tiger* is adequate (i.e., in focus) but nothing more. Bennet and cinematographer William Whitley make no attempt to build anything resembling mood or atmosphere, lighting the cheap "jungle" sets (with the California hills standing in for the African veldt) as if everything takes place at high noon.

Editor Gene Havlick doesn't help. At one point during Jungle Jim's "dramatic" hand-to-paw battle with the lion, Havlick cuts to a shot of Tamba the chimp comically playing in a basket of flour and donning a silly headdress, spoiling what little tension and excitement the fight scene could muster.

The expected stock animal footage (tiger fighting an alligator; tiger mixing it up with a water buffalo; tiger battling a leopard) is both mismatched and repetitious. (The original release prints were tinted in sepia tone to try and mask the various sequences' uneven lighting. Michael Fox: "I once said to Spencer [Bennet], 'My God, some of these cuts, how are they gonna work?' And Spencer said, 'It's all right, we do the whole thing in sepia, so you don't notice.'" Unfortunately, without the sepia [as current prints

Jungle Jim and friend up a tree in *Voodoo Tiger*.

stand] you *do* notice.) The third tiger-vs.-animal match-up proves both comical and sickening in its one-sidedness and sadistic staging, since it consists of the large tiger simply holding down a much-smaller leopard with its huge paws while the leopard kicks frantically and ineffectually at the tiger's gigantic head, who in turn takes vicious bites out of its spotted opponent.

Even the live animal footage shot expressly for the film (involving the chimp's "cute" antics [1] and the battle between Jim and the lion) proves rather lackluster and unexciting. "There was a lion on *Voodoo Tiger*," recalled Michael Fox. "It was pathetic. It *looked* great, but it was so old, it could hardly stand up. And when you *got* him to stand up, *you-had-to-shoot-him-quick.* Of course, we had two lions, we had a lion who moved around, and then this one, who was more photogenic, but he was so old, poor fellow. Johnny was very good with him."

Not to be outdone by the big cats in the repetition department, screenwriter Samuel Newman includes round after round of human brawling: Jim slugging away at Wombulu; Jim and company pounding on Peterson and crew; Jim vs. a passel of natives at the booby trap site; Jim against another set of natives at the village; and yet again going at Peterson on the jungle trail. The fist fights are all so similar and generically staged that the ineffectual tussles (nobody ever really gets hurt) become a crashing bore.

"Voodoo vengeance in darkest Africa runs riot in *Voodoo Tiger*," lied a studio publicity piece. In actuality, the only thing that might "run riot" would be a disgruntled audience demanding their money back. As a voodoo picture, *Voodoo Tiger* would be better named *Voodoo Skunk*, for the topic is treated with condescension and indifference. In fact, voodoo is used simply as a label for the headhunters (who, by the way, are of the Hollywood cartoon variety—fat,

diaper-wearing, and obviously white—looking more like tanned Californians than "black savages"). There's nothing mystical or magical about it; voodoo is simply a peg used to hang this film's generic savages on. The theme of voodoo is left sadly unexplored—and even un*exploited*.

The film's tone (and level of sophistication) can be summed up in this exchange between Jungle Jim and Wombulu:

> Jim: "Stay away from voodoo. Voodoo bad medicine."
> Wombulu: "Wambulu high priest of Dombula [sic], tiger god of voodoo. Voodoo good, not bad medicine."

Ugh. *Voodoo Tiger* bad, not good movie.

Voodoo Tiger received rather lukewarm reviews (better than it deserved). *The Motion Picture Exhibitor* called it an "okeh [sic] series entry for the lower half." *Variety* also felt it "stacks up as okay program filler." The reviewer went on to note, however, that "actors meet a fate worse than Newman's script, with all thesping wooden... Weissmuller is virtually immobile... Spencer G. Bennett's [sic] direction is as mediocre as the acting."

---

[1] The chimpanzee was named "Peggy." Michael Fox told an amusing story about how when Jungle Jim producer Sam Katzman showed up on the set one day and sat next to Peggy the chimp ("who was wonderful, and certainly much brighter than Sam"), Johnny Weissmuller remarked, "Look! They're carrying on a conversation!" (Katzman was not what one would call an intellectual producer.)

CREDITS: Director: Spencer G. Bennet; Producer: Sam Katzman; Story and Screenplay: Samuel Newman; "Based on the newspaper feature Jungle Jim, owned and copyrighted by King Features Syndicate, and which appears regularly in the Comic Weekly"; Director of Photography: William Whitley; Art Director: Paul Palmentola; Film Editor: Gene Havlick; Set Decorator: Sidney Clifford; Assistant Director: Charles S. Gould; Musical Director: Mischa Bakaleinikoff; Unit Manager: Herbert Leonard; Released September 1952 by Columbia; 67 minutes

CAST: Johnny Weissmuller (Jungle Jim), Jean Byron (Phyllis Bruce), James Seay (Abel Peterson), Jeanne Dean (Shalimar), Charles Horvath (Wombulu), Robert Bray (Major Bill Green), Michael Fox (Carl Werner/Colonel Schultz), Rick Vallin (Sergeant Bono), John Cason (Jerry Masters), Paul Hoffman (Michael Kovacs), Richard Kipling (Commissioner Kingston), Fredric Berest (Native Chief), William R. Klein (Co-pilot), Alex Montoya (Native Leader)

VOODOO ISLAND (1957)

King Karloff, Killer Plants, and Polynesian (?) Voodoo

"[You intend] to prove that voodooism has no
religious significance,
but is only practiced to superimpose fear on
superstitious people."
—Sara (Beverly Tyler) to professional skeptic
Philip Knight (Boris Karloff)

In a recent movie magazine, a number of writers/critics/historians each submitted their "Top Ten Karloff Films"—and *Voodoo Island* made *none* of the 21 lists. Not surprising, since Boris Karloff's first foray into voodoo country proved to be a *serious* misstep. Sarong-wearing, light-skinned "natives" in birds' nest headdress, melodramatic acting that makes Madonna's hair-color seem natural, pedestrian photography so flat that the "garden island" of Kauai looks no more enticing than Bronson Canyon, and a where's-my-check? performance from an obviously already-on-vacation Boris Karloff all combine to make *Voodoo Island* about as appealing as Krakatoa. The single exciting aspect of this dull misfire is the monstrous man-eating (or woman-eating as it turns out) plants which pop up from time to time to liven up this dreary atoll.

The story follows writer/television host/professional debunker Philip Knight (Boris Karloff), who journeys to an unexplored Polynesian island at the behest of hotel magnate Howard Carlton (Owen Cunningham). Carlton had recently sent a four-man surveyor team to his remote holding to see if the island might be a prime spot for his newest resort. Of the four surveyors, only Mitchell (Glenn Dixon) returned—but he's in some kind of zombie-like trance. Knight intends to get to the bottom of it all and—accompanied by his assistant, Sara Adams (Beverly Tyler), two of Carlton's employees, Finch (Murvyn Vye) and Claire (Jean Engstrom), charter boat owner Martin Skyler (Elisha Cook), and Skyler's boat captain, Matthew Gunn (Rhodes Reason)—Knight heads for the mysterious island. Despite ominous warnings, including the appearance of a voodoo ouanga bag and some inexplicable engine trouble, the intrepid party finally land. Once there, they find the surveyors' equipment but no men. They also find three species of killer plants, one of which disposes of the skinny-dipping Claire. Then, after Finch witnesses a little native girl eaten alive by a giant artichoke-like bush, he too succumbs to the zombification process. The

Apparently *anything* can become a comic book. (Cover of a 1962 French photo/comic book adaptation of *Voodoo Island*; courtesy Lynn Naron.)

remaining members of Knight's party are soon surrounded by the local natives (all three of them) and brought before their chief, who tells the intruders that they want no truck with "modern" civilization and wish only to be left in peace. Knight tries to mollify them, but Skyler's greed outstrips his common sense and he begins an angry tirade about *his* slice of the development pie. Understandably, the natives take a dim view of this attitude and confine the intruders to a hut. In the morning, the party awakens to find Skyler gone and a wooden doll left in his place. Knight goes out to search for Skyler (the native guards now conspicuous by their absence) and finds him on a small suspension bridge acting very strangely—as if under a spell. Skyler sees the image of the doll appear before him, screams, and topples over the side to disappear into the water below. Knight then spies the Skyler doll at his feet with a wooden pin stuck into it—even though he'd left this very doll back at the hut with the others. "Now, I *do* believe," he tells the chief and promises to inform the outside world that "nothing can live on this island." Knight, the zombified Finch, Gunn, and Adams (who have conveniently fallen in love) walk off into the jungle after the chief wishes them a safe journey.

Boris Karloff made some incomparable pictures over his long career and turned in many undeniably brilliant performances. He is without a doubt the single most important onscreen contributor to the hor-

BORIS KARLOFF *Voodoo Island*

BEVERLY TYLER · MURVYN V
with ELISHA COOK · RHODES REA
JEAN ENGSTROM · FREDERICK LEDE
Written by RICHARD LANDAU · Music by LES BAX
Directed by REGINALD LE BORG · Produced by HOWARD W. KO
Executive Producer AUBREY SCHEN
A BEL-AIR Production · Released thru UNITED ARTIS

"Now I *do* believe," admits professional skeptic Philip Knight (Boris Karloff) when faced with the evidence of Voodoo magic on *Voodoo Island*.

ror genre. Who can forget his terrifying-yet-sympathetic Frankenstein Monster; his tragic, poetic turn as *The Mummy* (1932); his evil incarnate Satanist from *The Black Cat* (1934); or his subtly sinister portrayal of *The Body Snatcher* (1945)? Even at the very end of his life he was capable of remarkable work, as evidenced by his touchingly effective performance in *Targets* (1968). But the 1950s were not kind to King Karloff. The decade of alien antagonists and big bugs did not provide much in the way of worthy opportunities to a typecast Gothic-style horror star. So one can certainly forgive Boris Karloff for accepting such lucrative-yet-lowly assignments as *Frankenstein 1970* and *Voodoo Island* (at a cool $25,000 a pop, who could blame him?). Forgive—yes; forget—not so easy. Karloff's work in *Voodoo Island* is reminiscent of his later *Thriller* introductions—broad melodrama livened by a good-natured conspiratorial wink. Only his dialogue in *Voodoo Island* sorely lacks the dry humor which graced his later (and far superior) TV show. Consequently, in *Voodoo Island* the King of Horror comes across as an overripe piece of ham.

Karloff's (lost) cause isn't helped by the inappropriate props given him to wear and wield. First

off, he sports a goofy baseball-style cap with an absurdly large bill. One keeps looking for the cartoon eyes painted on top. Worse, the 69-year-old actor slashing through brush with a machete and later poking and waving the gigantic knife about like some obscene lectern pointer makes him appear downright ridiculous. You almost expect him to start using the deadly blade as a back-scratcher.

As might be expected, lines of nonsensical dialogue float by at regular intervals like rotten kelp beds in the *Voodoo Island* surf. "This stuff!" exclaims Gunn while slashing at some thick vegetation, "It grows while you look at it—like it was *alive!*" (Apparently biology was not this sea-biscuit's best subject.) After the first killer plant encounter, Knight pontificates that "these plants live in the water; they could also be on land—even *more* carnivorous." Come again? One is either carnivorous or *not* carnivorous; and why would simply living on land make something *even more* carnivorous anyway? Knight continues, "It might also mean that there's life on this island, *human* life." That's one mighty leap of inference that would have even Sherlock Holmes scratching his deerstalker. We just saw what this "less carnivorous" vegetation could do to a person. It seems to me that its presence ought to put a big *dent* in property values in terms of human habitation.

Richard Landau's (*Spaceways*, *The Creeping Unknown*,[1] *Frankenstein 1970*, *Pharaoh's Curse*) script sadly suffers from a lack of likable characters. Knight is an annoyingly arrogant and condescending know-it-all, full of smug smiles and dismissive comments. His assistant, Adams, is beautiful but cold, a "machine" rather than a woman (as Gunn puts it). Gunn's soused, hard-boiled Captain is another outwardly attractive but inwardly dreary type. The remaining characters are all unlikable ciphers (Skyler's weak, greedy island rat; Finch's money-wise lackey; Claire's world-weary party girl). This lack of a character anchor leaves the viewer drifting helplessly among the shoals of boredom and reefs of ennui, waiting only for the next killer plant episode to throw them a lifeline of interest.

The melodramatic acting only serves to sink the ship further as the players desperately try to make the audience believe in the banal human drama unfolding amidst a sea of clichés. The impromptu soul-redeeming romance going on between Adams and Gunn comes off as ludicrous and forced, with Gunn spouting such sink-like-a-stone dialogue as, "[You're] something so crammed full of facts and figures, names, dates, places, reports, typing up Knight's lectures, that you've no room left inside to be a woman, think like a woman, feel like one, to even *look* at a man much less ever learn to hate him—or *love* him."

Regarding voodoo, the film seems more concerned with the killer plant exploits than with exploring the (de)merits of the local religion (despite Knight's stated intention as quoted at this essay's beginning). Apart from the appearance of an "ouanga bag," the two (unexplained) catatonic casualties (supposed zombies?), and a few plastic-looking dolls stuck with slivers, voodoo as a concept remains as unexplored as the island. This superficial attitude includes a complete lack of ceremonials (but since only three adult natives appear in the film—*including* the chief—this island's religious rituals must be a rather lackluster affair anyway). Of course, *Voodoo Island* does represent the screen's first (and only) portrayal of *Polynesian* voodoo. Either screenwriter Richard Landau knows of some secret sect the rest of the world has yet to discover or he lives in an alternate universe in which the Caribbean lies in the Southern hemisphere.

Director Reginald LeBorg (*Calling Dr. Death*, *Dead Man's Eyes*, *Jungle Woman*, *The Mummy's Ghost*, *Weird Woman*, *The Black Sleep*, *Diary of a Madman*) obviously realized the picture's main focus when he bluntly told interviewer Bernie O'Heir (of *Cinemacabre* magazine), "The story was about man-

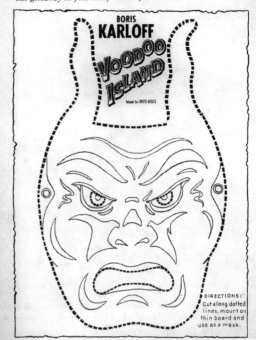

VOODOO MASK CUT-OUT GIVEAWAY

Make reprints of this art, adding theatre credits. Distribute in schools, clubs, in lobby and through cooperating local merchants. Announce this giveaway in your lobby and on your screen.

BORIS KARLOFF
VOODOO ISLAND

DIRECTIONS: Cut along dotted lines, mount on thin board and use as a mask.

Coloring and wearing this cheap cut-out mask probably gave the younger viewers of *Voodoo Island* more pleasure than watching the feeble film itself.

eating plants. The characters come to an island and they want to build the hotel. There are man-eating plants there and wherever they go, plants grab them and they are decimated, so to speak."

Actually, only one of their six-person party is "decimated" by killer plants, and her demise inspires more sniggers than shudders. When Claire (whose hard, hatchet face and angular body makes her an unlikely candidate for titillation) takes a nude swim in a lagoon, she drifts right into a batch of what look like giant floating pea pods and then proceeds to turn slow circles in the water while clutching the killer snow peas to her so as to wrap them about her body in a vain attempt to make these unwieldy props appear alive. Director Reginald LeBorg remembered (to Tom Weaver in *Interviews with B Science Fiction and Horror Movie Makers*) that "the special effects man showed us in a pool in Hollywood how these plants could wind themselves around the feet and legs of swimmers. It wasn't too good an effect, and I told him it had to be better. He said he knew then how they worked and that when we got to Hawaii it would be all fixed. They *never* worked very well at all." Indeed. What's more, though Knight labels the killer plant as carnivorous, this lackadaisical legume evinces no desire to actually eat its prey, since Knight and company stumble upon Claire's (uneaten) body on the

Vicious voodoo villagers are not the only dangers found on *Voodoo Island*. Here, Claire (Jean Engstrom) succumbs to some of the island's more active flora. (Rumor has it that a more revealing "European" version of this scene was shot for foreign distribution.)

bank packed into the giant leaves like some macabre cigar.

The second sinister shrub is no more convincing, consisting of a large thick stalk upon which is perched a roundish, flat "head" that sways forward and back while an oblivious Sara stands talking in front of it. (Milt Rice, who designed the plants, may have been "inspired" by *War of the Worlds* since his plant's head looks suspiciously similar to the Martian death ray devices from that 1953 classic.) This "cobra plant" (as the ads label it) teeters back and forth until finally toppling forward onto Sara's shoulder from its own inertia in a vegetable version of "tag-you're-it." Then, comically, it seems to fasten to her right breast as she holds its head and screams while Gunn impotently fires his pistol at its base. Finally, after the garden marauder gets a good grope, Gunn thinks to chop at the stalk with his machete. While this may not be the most realistic of scenes, it does provoke a smile.

The third and final plant attack is the one truly effective sequence in the whole picture, both for its (comparative) realism and alarming nature—the death of a little girl. When Finch, in a panic, runs through the jungle, he comes upon a clearing where two native children are playing. One of them steps on some unusual-looking fronds laid on the ground which suddenly rear up to close around her like some obscene giant artichoke. As the plant moves and undulates in its digestive dance, one tiny hand pokes through the

leaves only to be drawn back inside as the deadly bush completes its horrible meal.

About the vicious vegetation, director LeBorg was rather diplomatic, mildly stating that "the effects weren't the best ones. There were a few things that were all right" [perhaps referring to the solitary believable plant—the killer artichoke]. "The public accepted them, but they could have been so much better if they had spent money."

Producer Howard W. Koch (undoubtedly more concerned with the bottom line than better creatures) felt they filled the bill adequately enough. "We had a fellow named Milt Rice who did those plants," Koch told interviewer Tom Weaver. "He turned out to be one of the best special effects men in the business... But, again, *money*. He did the best he could with 'em, and I think they made the point." (Of course, Koch [whose credits include *The Black Sleep*, *Frankenstein 1970*, and *Pharaoh's Curse*] called *Voodoo Island* the favorite of all his horror films: "I *love* that picture, I think it's a classic!") That makes one of us.

Milt Rice's questionable creations graced several other 1950s genre outings as well, including the classic *Invasion of the Body Snatchers* (1956) and the not-so-classic *World Without End* (1956) and *Queen of Outer Space* (1958).

Executive producer Aubrey Schenck holds a different (and much more realistic) opinion of *Voodoo Island* than does Koch. "That picture didn't come through," admitted Schenck to Tom Weaver in *Fangoria* magazine. "You see, you can't put Karloff in a good-guy part—he has to be the heavy or it's wrong. That was a lost cause. Making those man-eating plants the heavy, that didn't make any sense. But, hell, you take a chance. With Karloff's name, we thought we had a good chance, but it didn't work out. I'm not proud of that picture at all."

United Artists played up their killer-plant angle in press releases and trade papers. One grandiose article (obviously taken straight from the PR man's typewriter) appearing in *The Hollywood Reporter* (October 26, 1956—the same day the picture began shooting) claimed, "special effects men have been studying every type of carnivorous plant known and have come up with some realistic beauts that will put scares into movie audiences equal to any monster thus far created for exploitation chillers."

If *Voodoo Island* can be called noteworthy at all, it's for introducing the cinematic world to TV's *Batman*—for it was Adam West's (uncredited) film debut. "I'd had a couple of jobs in Honolulu," recalled the actor in *Famous Monsters* magazine. "I was struggling along in television and I had a sideline flying people around the Islands. One day I played hooky from my jobs because I'd heard Boris Karloff was in the Islands to do a movie called *Voodoo Island*, and I said, 'Well, you know, I think maybe I should be in that movie... maybe that's a beginning.'" An inauspicious one, to be certain—playing a bit part (as a radio operator) in one of Karloff's worst films.

Contrary to the scathing commentary one might expect, *Voodoo Island* received surprisingly mild reviews upon its release on a double-bill with (the far superior) *Pharaoh's Curse*. *The Motion Picture Exhibitor* called *Voodoo Island* a "programmer with horrific overtones and undertones, one that may scare the kiddies and please the addicts of such entries... The cast is fair, the direction and production average, and the story of medium interest." *Variety* felt that "the thriller gimmicks come off with the desired impact under Reginald LeBorg's direction... William Margulies did satisfactory photography, while Les Baxter gives the melodramatics an appropriate musical backing." At least the reviewer ("Brog") came a little closer to reality when he noted that "none of the performances is more than stock." Perhaps critics of 1957 were so relieved to find a terror tale *without* an accompanying alien or giant insect that they became overly generous with their tolerance.

Voodoo Island was shot back-to-back with *Jungle Heat* (also with Rhodes Reason) on the Hawaiian island of Kauai. Director Reginald LeBorg claimed the budget was about $150,000—but given what appears onscreen, this seems to be a rather optimistic figure. In 1963, Cari Releasing Corporation reissued *Voodoo*

Retitled *Silent Death* for a 1963 re-release, *Voodoo Island* topped the bill with a re-named *The Black Sleep*. Here Karloff and company get their first sight of the dreaded Voodoo Island. (Courtesy Lynn Naron)

Island under the new title *Silent Death*, double-billing it with yet another (far superior) Bel-Air production, *Dr. Cadman's Secret* (a retitled *The Black Sleep*). With regards to *Voodoo Island*, manure by any other name smells just as rank.

[1] According to director/co-screenwriter Val Guest (as related by interviewer Tom Weaver), Landau's scripting credit for *The Creeping Unknown* was unmerited, and all Landau really did was Americanize a few lines of dialogue.

CREDITS: Director: Reginald LeBorg; Producer: Howard W. Koch; Executive Producer: Aubrey Schenck; Screenplay: Richard Landau; Photography: William Margulies; Music: Les Baxter; Editor: John F. Schreyer; Assistant Director: Paul Wurtzel; Production Designer: Jack T. Collis; Script Supervisor: Kathleen Fagan; Wardrobe: Wesley V. Jefferies and Angela Alexander; Property Master: Arden Cripe; Lighting Technician: Joe Edesa; Operative Cameraman: Ben Colman; Makeup Artist: Ted Coodley; Hair Styles: Mary Westmoreland; Sound Mixer: Joe Edmondson; Sound Editor: Charles G. Schelling; Music Editor: Carlo Lodato; Re-recording: Charles Cooper; Special Photographic Effects: Jack Rabin and Lewis DeWitt; A Bel-Air Production; released February 1957 by United Artists; 77 minutes

CAST: Boris Karloff (Phillip Knight), Beverly Tyler (Sara Adams), Murvyn Vye (Barney Finch), Elisha Cook (Martin Skyler), Rhodes Reason (Matthew Gunn), Jean Engstrom (Claire Winter), Frederick Ledebur (The Ruler), Glenn Dixon (Mitchell), Owen Cunningham (Howard Carlton), Herbert Patterson (Dr. Wilding), Jerry Frank (Vickers), Adam West (Radio Operator)

"Native" drummers set the appropriate mood in *Voodoo Woman*.

VOODOO WOMAN (1957)
Voodoo and Science
Spawn a Monster

"Black Voodoo, hear the drums beat.
I'm consumed with desire.
With the spell that you weave,
My whole life is afire
With Black Voodoo."
—lyrics to the song "Black Voodoo" sung by
Giselle D'Arc as Yvette

"Not since the days of *Dracula* and *White Zombie* has there been a horror picture so packed with weird and unusual thrills as American-International's *Voodoo Woman*," announced an AIP publicity blurb. Comparative delusions of grandeur aside, *Voodoo Woman* turned out to be a generally ludicrous yet occasionally entertaining voodoo voyage that can at least boast of being the best voodoo movie of the decade (small praise actually, considering its competition of *Voodoo Tiger*, *Voodoo Island*, and *The Disembodied*).

Shot in six days for $80,000, according to producer Alex Gordon (though some sources put the figure at $65,000 and Gordon himself has previously used the even lower number of $60,000!), *Voodoo Woman* begins promisingly enough at an African jungle voodoo ceremony. As the natives dance and twirl about the clearing, two men (one white, the other black) perform a bizarre ritual/experiment on a beautiful native girl, Saranda (Jean Davis). "We're doing it, Chaka—," says the white man, Dr. Roland Gerard (Tom Conway), "—white man's science and the black voodoo." What they're "doing" is transforming the girl into a huge scaly creature via Chaka's (Martin Wilkins) sorcery and a special serum injected by Gerard.

Gerard intends to "create a new being—not man, not beast, but a combination of the best of each." His "new being" proves nearly indestructible, its armor-like hide withstanding the onslaught of bullets, fire, and even acid. What Gerard *really* wants, though, is an indestructible creature that will do his bidding without question or hesitation. To this end, he tests the transformed Saranda by ordering her to attack her village and kill her own people. But Saranda, being kindly by nature, will not do anything as the monster that she wouldn't do ordinarily and so awakens from the spell when commanded to do so. The disappointed Gerard sends her home.

Enter Marla English as Marilyn Blanchard ("we thought up the name," revealed Alex Gordon, "from a combination of Marilyn Monroe and Mari Blanchard"), a conniving tramp who murders a man for his treasure map and sets out for the dreaded voodoo country beyond Bantalaya with her equally despicable toady of a boyfriend, Rick (Lance Fuller), and an unwitting jungle guide, Ted (Touch Connors).

Needless to say, Marilyn and Gerard's paths soon cross, and Marilyn's killer instinct (she calmly shoots her boyfriend in cold blood when the natives demand his death) proves to be just what the doctor ordered. Gerard tricks Marilyn into submitting to his voodoo/science ceremony (promising access to the voodoo cult's gold once she's been initiated) and turns her into his new, improved killer monster.

Meanwhile, Gerard's terrified wife, Susan (Mary Ellen Kaye), conspires with the imprisoned Ted to escape. Their plans are foiled when Gerard offers Susan as a sacrifice to appease the voodooists. Things get out of hand when Chaka and his followers decide that *all* the whites must die and seize Gerard as well. Gerard summons the monstrous Marilyn, who kills several natives and throws Chaka into a bubbling pit. Discovering that the native gold is really just painted clay, the enraged Marilyn Monster strangles Gerard. Reverting back to human form (Gerard's death breaks the spell), Marilyn stoops down to pick up a gold idol lying next to the crater and clumsily stumbles into the smoking pit. Ted and Susan free themselves, send the angry natives running with a few molotov cocktails, and head back to civilization.

The project, originally titled *Black Voodoo*, was literally dumped in Producer Alex Gordon's lap. "The Milner brothers, who made *Phantom From 10,000 Leagues*, were going to make it," Mr. Gordon told this author in 1995, "and then something happened between their setup and American International. So Sam Arkoff and James Nicholson took it over and virtually handed it to me to produce with about two weeks' notice."

This last-minute hand-off had Gordon scrambling to find a star for his impromptu picture. Gordon's first choice for the mad scientist role was Peter Lorre. "Unfortunately, we had a very bad experience with his situation on *The She-Creature*, which I also produced at AIP. Although the Jaffe Agency had committed him to [*The She-Creature*], when he saw the script he refused to do it. Frankly, I don't really blame him. But, there was a big to-do about it. *Voodoo Woman* was supposed to be an additional project for him. So of course he never saw it and never got to the point of serious discussion about it, but I was thinking about him."

Gordon next tried to tap the talent of veteran villain George Zucco, perennial mad scientist and horror star of the previous decade (who hadn't done a film in over five years). Sadly, Gordon found the actor in poor health. "His agent told me that unfortunately by that time Zucco was quite elderly [the actor was 71] and had problems remembering lines. In fact, he was on the senile side; but that he would like to bring him in anyway and have me meet him at the agent's office because it would sort of give Zucco a boost to think that he was still wanted. So I went over to the agent's office and I met Zucco who was with his wife, and they were very very nice people. And of course I started off talking about all his old pictures and he was thrilled that somebody would remember him and would remember all that work, especially the non-cheap horror pictures, the bigger things. And he said that much as he appreciated our offering him this picture, he didn't really want to do this kind of picture anymore. What he would like to do is go back to England and do some of the classics, like a picture based on a Dickens story, and not do any more of the low-budget horror type of things. So it was a nice conversation and everybody left happy, except of course I regretted that I was unable to get him. But I realized that he wouldn't have been able to do it even if he had decided that he would consider it." (Zucco had suffered a stroke on the set of *The Desert Fox* in 1951 and had to be replaced. With his subsequent memory difficulties, he never made another picture. Zucco remained at home under the care of his wife for two years before he entered a nursing home. He died of pneumonia in 1960.)

The producer considered a few others for the pivotal role of the mad Dr. Gerard, including John Carradine. "But Carradine had thrown a fit when we offered him *The She-Creature*, because he had just done *The Ten Commandments* with DeMille and he was now back to his big picture and Shakespearean stage appearance mode and refused to do any more low-budget horror films. Of course later he did, but at that time he didn't want to do any more."

With time running out, Gordon turned to one of his favorite actors to work with, Tom Conway. "We had a commitment with Tom Conway. He had really rescued us twice. Once by coming into *The She-Creature*—we had a lot of problems there, not only with Peter Lorre but also Edward Arnold, who was supposed to co-star with him in that and died a couple of days before the picture was due to start. The point is, Tom Conway and AIP sort of owed each other, so I thought even though this was *reaching* a little bit to get Tom Conway to do the mad scientist there…"

"Not since he starred in the *Cat People* and *I Walked with a Zombie* pictures," stated a *Voodoo Woman* publicity piece, "has Tom [Conway] had a role like his current one." And I'm sure Mr. Conway thanked his *un*lucky stars that this was true, for *Voo-doo Woman* may very well be his worst feature. Conway, brother of George Sanders, gained popularity in the long running "Falcon" detective series of the 1940s and, while mostly eclipsed by his brother's career, is a fine actor in his own right. Here, playing a mad doctor mixing voodoo with science, he's a long way from his notable appearances in those two Val Lewton classics. Conway looks awfully silly wearing a birds' nest headdress (almost identical to the one worn by George Zucco in 1944's *Voodoo Man*) and injecting a girl with a mysterious serum while a back-lot native intones a pidgin voodoo chant. The actor obviously needed the $2,500 he was paid for the week's work. Sadly, Conway would die a decade later, alcoholic and penniless.

Not surprisingly, in *Voodoo Woman* Conway's performance is not among his best, with the usually unflappable actor proving wildly unsteady. At times he projects a cold and callous detachment, such as when, unmoved by his wife's tears, he unfeelingly thrusts her away and states matter-of-factly, "If you try to leave—I'll kill you." But when speaking of his work, Conway's eyes gleam and take on a faraway look as if viewing some wondrous sight only *he* can see. Add to his enraptured gaze an excited animation to his voice, and Conway completes the picture of a zealous near-insanity.

Unfortunately, at other times the actor seems unsure of just what he's supposed to be doing or saying, speaking his lines disjointedly and without conviction: "If they—kill me so much—evil will come to them; my—magic will curse them forever," he tells Chaka haltingly. Conway's unsteadiness and flat delivery rob the scene of whatever impact it could have mustered.

As the picture progresses, Conway seemingly can't speak without constantly casting his eyes about (searching for cue cards?). Perhaps he's simply trying too hard to appear "shifty," with his frequent sideways glances and bobbling eyes becoming a much-too-obvious and theatrical gesture of insincerity.

Though it has been intimated that Conway had difficulty with his lines (his distracted performance and misplaced pauses seem to bear this out), Alex Gordon remembers no such problems. While Conway *had* become ill on *Runaway Daughters* (suffering a cerebral hemorrhage), necessitating his replacement on that previous picture, Gordon reported that "he had no trouble on *Voodoo Woman* whatsoever; he was in very good shape."

And the producer had nothing but praise for Conway: "He's just a terrific person," enthused Gordon. "It was a real pleasure to work with him. He had a great sense of humor and we were always kidding around about his brother, George Sanders, and his escapades with Zsa Zsa Gabor and all this kind of

Trouble in paradise as Chaka and Gerard have a falling out over what to do with a *Voodoo Woman* monster.

stuff, how Tom had to pull him out of various scrapes and things. But he was a very serious actor."

"It was a nice little group of professionals, cast *and* crew," continued Gordon. "They didn't look down on it because it was a six-day picture. They took pride in their work and worked as hard as if they were on a bigger picture."

Among these professionals was an up-and-coming leading man who went by the name of Touch (later Mike) Connors. Alex Gordon characterized Connors as "a very nice guy, really a pleasure to work with. He hadn't yet done *Tightrope!* and *Mannix*, so he was still struggling and so was agreeable to being in that."

In *Voodoo Woman*, he did indeed make an agreeable hero, his rugged good looks and straightforward delivery filling the bill nicely. Though the part is not what one would call dramatically demanding, and his sudden romantic interest in the doctor's imprisoned wife seems forced and abrupt, Connors' sincerity and obvious good-guy demeanor make his character Ted Bronson *almost* believable.

Born Krekor Ohanian (no wonder he changed his name—twice) in Fresno, California in 1925 to poor

Armenian immigrants, Connors earned a B.A. from UCLA after serving in the Air Force during WWII. He began studying law, but dropped out when bit by the acting bug. (Ironically, he played a *lawyer* in his stage debut.) Making his screen debut in 1952, he subsequently worked for AIP in two Roger Corman Westerns, *Five Guns West* and *The Oklahoma Woman*, then acted for producer Alex Gordon in *Day the World Ended*, *Shake Rattle and Rock*, and *Flesh and the Spur*.

About his time at AIP, Mike "Touch" Connors speaks warmly, calling them "wonderful days when anything and everything went"—with the possible exception of a decent paycheck. "I think the highest price I got to star in a picture was $400," the actor/producer confided to *Fangoria*'s David Everitt, "but I look back on it with great fondness and affection." Connors later became a TV star on the series *Tightrope* and *Mannix*, and appeared in a number of (generally undistinguished) films throughout the 1960s and 1970s.

Connors' co-star, however, did not do so well with her (better-written) part. Though the ruthless Marilyn proves much more interesting than Connors' white-

Understandably, Saranda (Jean Davis) balks at being transformed into a scaley monster in *Voodoo Woman*.

washed hero, Marla English turns her treasure-hungry character into a ridiculous caricature. Ms. English is easy on the eyes but hard on the ears, for she can't seem to say her lines without spitting and looking like she'd just love to bite the head off a chicken. (Even so, turning into a hulking Paul Blaisdell wearing a second-hand monster suit is too terrible a punishment for any actress, no matter how bad.)

San Diego native Marleine Gaile English began her career as a professional photographer's model. She entered films in 1954 with *Shield for Murder*, playing the girlfriend of lead Edmond O'Brien. After a few more pictures like *Desert Sands* and *Three Bad Sisters*, this "top glamour queen" (as AIP publicity labeled her) worked almost exclusively for American-International throughout the mid-1950s, appearing in films like *Runaway Daughters*, *The She-Creature*, and *Flesh and the Spur*. "Marla English had a multiple deal with us and was a delight to work with," remembered Alex Gordon. "She really wanted to make Westerns, so she wanted to do things like *Flesh and*

the Spur, which I also produced there. But she agreed to do [*Voodoo Woman*] and she was quite content with it." Ms. English never followed through on her yearning "to make Westerns," for, after *Flesh and the Spur*, she retired from acting reportedly to marry a San Diego businessman who owned a group of parking lots. San Diego's gain was *not* Hollywood's loss.

Two of the film's better performances come from Lance Fuller as Rick and Paul Dubov as Marcel, a shifty tavern owner. Each player brings a convincing seediness to his character—Fuller as the henpecked sub-villain houndoggedly following his female superior; Dubov as the unscrupulous yet likable Marcel, offering fake handguns and worldly witticisms (in a convincing gutter-French accent) in equal measure.

Apparently, Lance Fuller sometimes took his work a bit too seriously (especially considering just *what* he was working on). "Lance was always a bit of a problem," remembered Alex Gordon. "He was a very nice guy personally, although a bit strange—but he was nice. But he wanted to really be a good actor, almost like a method actor type of thing. He would think up more gimmicks—he always wanted to have some kind of little bit of business to do and he would dream up all kinds of things. It was difficult to keep him on the straight and narrow and have him just remember his lines. He maybe felt a little uncomfortable just standing there delivering the lines, and wanted to *do* things. He was always fiddling around with stuff, wanted to pick things up and put them down and that sort of thing…He took up a lot of time discussing the motivation of his role (laughs)." Fuller appeared in several other genre outings, including *This Island Earth* (1955), *The She-Creature* (1956), the Ed Wood-scripted *The Bride and the Beast* (1958), and *Whatever Happened to Aunt Alice?* (1969). Always "a bit strange," Fuller experimented with LSD and, in 1968, was arrested when he went on a drug-induced rampage in which he smashed car windows and reportedly ranted and raved that he was Christ. After recovering, he resumed his sporadic and unspectacular acting career.

"Paul Dubov was a *very* good actor," opined Alex Gordon. "He started with us in the *Day the World Ended* and he was in virtually every picture that I made and a lot of Roger Corman's as well at AIP. He was very reliable and never held us up or anything—a very useful actor." Dubov was also a writer. With his wife, he wrote the 1968 Doris Day film *With Six You Get Eggroll*, inspired by their own domestic situation— they had six children between them.

"The reason James Nicholson brought [director Edward L. Cahn] in there," explained producer Alex Gordon, "was because he knew he could bring in pictures on time and on budget. But I hit it off with him tremendously. We really just loved talking about the old days and all that. And we respected each other for our mutual knowledge, he with the craft and I with the casting. I immediately won him over with my attempts to use the old-timers in the pictures so we got on very well and he directed virtually everything I did over at AIP."

Beginning his career in the days of silent film, Cahn became head editor at Universal in 1926. "His first big thing came along when he reedited *All Quiet on the Western Front*," remarked Gordon. After a few test screenings of *Voodoo Woman*, studio brass decide that they needed to replace comedienne Zazu Pitts with Beryl Mercer. "But the opening of the picture had been set for New York and Eddie Cahn had to re-edit the picture, take out the Zasu Pitts and insert the Beryl Mercer scenes on a *train* going from Los Angeles to New York. So he was editing on this train and he got it done in time so Universal gave him a chance. And he directed a highly acclaimed picture called *Law and Order* with Walter Huston and Harry Carey. But he wanted to be a producer as well as a director and

he wanted the independence rather than just working under the studio system...I think that's what hurt his career, because he went to England to make pictures."

Cahn helped fill AIP coffers by directing seven low-budget pictures for the company, none of which were very good and all of which made money: *Girls in Prison*, *The She-Creature*, *Voodoo Woman*, *Shake Rattle and Rock*, *Jet Attack*, *Runaway Daughters*, and *Invasion of the Saucer Men* (arguably the most enjoyable of the bunch).

"I resent the fact that people, so-called self-styled critics, that know nothing about [Edward Cahn] denigrate and write nasty things about him in these publications," complained Gordon. "They don't realize that the pictures he had to do at the end of his career, these small things were under tremendous budget restrictions and he always brought them in on time and budget. He was very loyal to the producer."

Indeed, despite *Voodoo Woman*'s minuscule budget and unreasonably short shooting schedule, Cahn took care to wring as much quality as he could out of the sorry scenario. Under his careful direction, Frederick E. West's camera moves more often and with greater purpose than in most similar productions. In one scene, it glides in close-up from one voodoo object to the next (skull, snake, symbol, doll, etc.) in a fluid motion to build an ominous ambiance. In another, it creates impact when Susan approaches her bamboo-barred window only to have the camera track back to suddenly reveal the hitherto unseen spear-wielding guard standing outside. Later, when Susan moves toward the door, the camera moves with her, finally stopping to zoom in on a frightening voodoo mask hanging on the wall as she bolts out the door. The carefully choreographed and revelatory camera movements augment and intensify Susan's helplessness and feeling of imprisonment. In addition, the native drumming and chanting heard in the background, Susan's obvious unease, and the camera movement ending on the intimidating mask all serve to create a tense atmosphere tying the voodoo motif into the malevolent milieu.

Cahn even manages to slip in an effective transition on occasion. As Gerard lifts a glass of liquid (undoubtedly blood) to his lips during "the blood ritual" at the voodoo ceremony, the scene dissolves to a close-up of a man casually drinking from a glass as the camera pulls back to reveal a low-rent dive (in which we meet Marilyn and company). The fluid motion and near-identical transition shot visually ties the two disparate plot threads together in a foreshadowing of the meeting to come.

Cahn also does the best he can with the ridiculous monster. Rather than exposing the silly-looking creature to full daylight (and disastrous scrutiny), Cahn limits its display to brief glimpses of a leg, arm, back, etc. To heighten its mystery (and further avoid full-view derision), he makes effective use of shadows (showing the monster's menacing shadow stretching out before it and growing larger as it approaches a native hut, for instance). Sadly, one can't keep a determined *Voodoo Woman* in the dark forever, and when we finally do get a more substantial sight of the monster, we can only applaud the director's previous obfuscating techniques.

Though most fans (and reviewers) scoff at *Voodoo Woman*'s crude creature costume, there's no doubt that without it the film would be even less memorable than it is. It's little wonder that the monster turned out so disappointingly, for it was constructed by two different makeup artists working separately— and who each derided the other's contribution! The body was monster-maker Paul (*It Conquered the World*, 1956; *Invasion of the Saucer Men*, 1957; *It! The Terror from Beyond Space*, 1958; et al.) Blaisdell's recycled *She-Creature* (1956) costume which AIP asked Blaisdell to strip down and modify. (Blaisdell originally presented the studio with a production illustration of a more traditional "zombie-woman," but AIP was "determined to produce *Voodoo Woman* in record time" and so talked him into revamping the existing creature suit.)

To construct the monster's head, AIP engaged makeup man Harry Thomas (*The Neanderthal Man*, 1953; *The Unearthly*, 1957; *Frankenstein's Daughter*, 1958; etc.). "According to the AIP folks," Blaisdell's assistant, Bob Burns, told *Filmfax*'s Ted Okuda, "[Thomas] went down to the Hollywood Magic Shop and bought a skeleton mask, then put a woman's white wig on it. That's about all he did. When the AIP people saw this thing, they said, 'Holy... we can't use this!' So they called Paul [Blaisdell] and asked him, 'Is there anything you can do to save it? We can't afford to put much more money into it.' Paul took liquid rubber and built up the cheekbones. That gave some form and definition to the inexpensive rubber mask. Then he added some big eyes and fangs. It was a terrible thing, but at least Paul managed to give it a little bit of class considering what he had started with. He only had a few days to work on it."

Not surprisingly, Harry Thomas puts a slightly different spin on the monstrous tale. "I made the skull head, and laid the hair on it," Thomas related to Tom Weaver in *Interviews with B Science Fiction and Horror Movie Makers*. "When I took it over to [AIP executive] Sam Arkoff, he liked it, and we made a deal right there. I asked Arkoff, 'Now, what have you got for the body?' I suggested at that time that they should put a scary, Inner Sanctum shroud on it, and make the hands up, sort of skeletal. Then, they could put a bit under the mouth so that whoever was in the mask could bear down on the bit and the mouth would open. Arkoff said, 'Oh, we've got something already made up.'... I was very surprised when I later saw pictures of it, with this hideous costume they had used in another movie. They had every opportunity not to *use* the mask—they could have gotten something that would have been more befitting to the horrible suit, which looked like a butcher who had meat cleavings all over his gown!"

In this writer's humble opinion, both the suit *and* the head are pretty pathetic (but then I never liked the original cumbersome foam-rubber *She-Creature* to begin with).

Voodoo Woman's less-than-creative creature wasn't treated too well either, for she receives one of the most pitiful anticlimactic ends to any screen monster. After all her complicated conniving, manipulating and rampaging, the Marilyn Monster deserves better than just an awkward trip and a splash. But wait, is that a rubbery arm rising up from the pit in the closing shot?! As one character said when informed of Marilyn's death, "I have a feeling that one still lives." Luckily for us, we were never given the opportunity to find out in a sequel.

Though no sequel materialized, AIP *still* wasn't finished with this monster. After its stint in *Voodoo Woman*, the suit's original head turned up as a wall-plaque in *How to Make a Monster* (1958) and the entire costume made a cameo appearance in *Ghost of Dragstrip Hollow* (1959). The overworked outfit finally ended up as an impromptu home for several generations of raccoons nesting in Paul Blaisdell's attic.

In *Voodoo Woman*, Blaisdell wore his own monster suit (just as he had in *The She-Creature*) and, just as in the previous picture,[1] met with a dangerous accident (the dreaded "Curse of *The She-Creature* Suit" strikes again?). "I suffered an acid burn on my left leg," Blaisdell reported to Randy Palmer in *Fangoria* magazine, "the remnants of which are still there to this day! What happened was, as you may recall if you saw the movie, Tom Conway poured acid on me [as the monster], and it went up in a cloud of smoke on my leg, just to prove I was 'acid-proof,' which was in accordance with the script. I asked the special effects man if it was a kind of chemical smoke we used to make in chemistry class in high school (using hydrochloric acid and ammonia). This'll give out a beautiful cloud of smoke—as long as you don't pour it on living tissue! He assured me it was a new type of chemical called 'Brett Smoke' that caused no harm whatsoever. The only mistake Tom and I made was taking his word for it! Well, the smoke poured out of my leg beautifully when Tom poured it on me, and I was completely invulnerable; but inside the suit I was feeling the warmth collecting on my leg, which is

Scientist Gerard (Tom Conway, left) and voodooist Chaka (Martin Wilkins) prepare to combine their talents and make a monster. Note the painted backdrop and scaffolding in the background. (Photos for *Voodoo Woman* courtesy Eric Hoffman.)

significant of an acid burn. When that particular scene was over and Eddie Cahn yelled 'Cut!,' *I* started yelling for help. It was a real hard-luck picture!"

Apart from a ludicrous monster and Marla English's equally unconvincing lead villainess (and not forgetting Tom Conway's pitifully erratic mad doctor), *Voodoo Woman* also suffers from an over-abundance of the expected slapdash silliness that often accompanies low-budget horror. For instance, the principals all wear clean, freshly-starched white shirts in the middle of the steamy African jungle. Then there's the usual quota of pathetically mismatched stock animal footage; Conway's ridiculous headdress with its feathery fringe hanging down over his eyes that makes him look like some over-the-hill moppet; the angered Africans comically hopping from foot to

foot while shaking their spears in a visual parody of the old "restless natives" routine; Marilyn's colorful patterned sarong inexplicably transforming into plain burlap sackcloth when she becomes the monster; undisguised lion roars unconvincingly dubbed in for the bulky creature's "voice"; and a uniformed native houseboy named... "Bobo." (Bobo was played by Otis Green, whom Alex Gordon characterized as "a young black actor who was very ambitious. He was really making quite a lot of noise trying to get better working conditions for blacks and getting going with decent black roles and things." "Bobo" was *not* a step in the right direction.)

Along those same lines, Martin Wilkins, who played the native witch doctor Chaka, fools absolutely no one with his huge beer belly, cartoonish facial ex-

Neither Martin Wilkins nor Tom Conway look particularly happy in this posed publicity shot for *Voodoo Woman*.

pressions, and pitiful pidgin speech ("She good," he booms out when speaking of Saranda. "She no do nothing under spell she not do when awake.") According to Alex Gordon, Frank Lackteen (*Tarzan the Fearless* serial, 1933; *Mummy's Boys*, 1936; *The Sea Wolf*, 1941; et al.) was originally set to play the role of Chaka, but when the elderly Lackteen became ill, his agent suggested Martin Wilkins. "I was very reluctant when I saw his credits—Shakespearean roles and stage stuff," recalled Gordon. "To offer him a role like that, I thought it would be very demeaning to him. Although at that time we were not yet that race conscious, of course, as we were later, showing the blacks like that. Anyway, I guess he needed the money or whatever; he wanted to do it and he appreciated my attitude. I said if you want to do it, of course we'd be delighted to have you, but I don't want you to think we're trying to insult you by offering you a role like this when you have these kind of credits, you know. So anyway he worked out very nicely and that was fine." Not so fine for the viewer, however, for Wilkins makes one sorry Voodoo Ambassador.

After about an hour or so watching *Voodoo Woman*, it all begins to wear a bit thin. Fortunately, there's less than 20 minutes to go before the Voodoo Woman takes that big splash. "I realize that seeing it again leaves a lot to be desired," admitted Gordon, who quickly added, "but I like it because of the players in it." As a voodoo film, *Voodoo Woman* is rather silly (in fact, as a plain old *film* it's *very* silly). Still, it contains enough bizarre occurrences, occasionally effective ambiance, and wacky monsters to make it a mildly entertaining (in the Poverty-Row vein of a *Voodoo Man*, for instance) 60 minutes. Too bad it actually runs 77 minutes.

Perhaps not inappropriately, *Voodoo Woman* nearly cost producer Alex Gordon his fiancée. He was engaged to a woman named Ruth Succop, who had never seen any of his films. "I wanted to impress her with one of my pictures so I took her to the sneak preview of *Voodoo Woman* in the Cornell Theater in Burbank. And when we came out of there, she gave me back the ring. She said, 'If this is the kind of picture you make, I don't think this is going to work out.'"

It had a happy ending, however. "She gave me back the ring and she flew to New York and fell into the clutches of my brother [producer Richard Gordon] who, of course, had been alerted by me. And over a three-hour lunch he explained to her the difference of doing something like *The Red Shoes* and being in the category that *I* was in. So anyway, she sort of bought it. But then she noticed that two of my pictures, *The She-Creature* and *Runaway Daughters,* were playing at a theater together up in Queens, so she took a bus up there and went to see them—and that didn't make her feel much happier!" The experience must not have been too traumatic, for she eventually turned to screenwriting (using the pen name Ruth Alexander), and scripted films like *The Bounty Killer* and *Requiem for a Gunfighter.* But more importantly, laughed Gordon, "we worked it out and we've been married for 37 years."

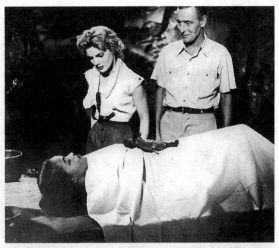

In his hidden cave/laboratory, Dr. Gerard shows his fearful wife Susan (Mary Ellen Kaye) the *Voodoo Woman.*

Critically, *Voodoo Woman* received thumbs down on a roughly two-to-one ratio. *Box-office* predicted that "Customers… probably will experience more laughs—of the wrong variety—than chills… The screenplay, in its fruitless attempt to be horrific, departs on more tangents than Euclid ever dreamed of." *The Motion Picture Exhibitor* also complained about this "nonsensical yarn that may get by and scare the kiddies," while observing "acting, direction, and production are routine." The reviewer warned, "Don't expect too much and you won't be disappointed." Across the pond, Britain's *Kinematograph Weekly* gave the picture one of its few favorable reviews, citing its "exciting story, tireless cast, and eerie thrills… The leading players take the hocus pocus seriously and bring conviction to its serial-like thrills… Marla English scores as the comely, though wicked, Marilyn. Tom Conway does wonders in the unrewarding role of the mad Roland, and Touch Connors cuts a manly figure as Ted."

Modern critics have continued the pattern, with (at least) two dissenters for every proponent. *Cult Movies'* Buddy Barnett called it "AIP's version of a Bela Lugosi Monogram film" that's "lots of cheezy fun." On the other hand, *Filmfax's* David J. Hogan labeled it "one of the dreariest films ever to be released by American International Pictures," citing its "lugubrious pace; the illogical, cluttered script; and the embarrassing air of cheapness (literal and figurative) that hangs over everything." Calling it "a most routine B-movie," *Fangoria's* Dr. Cyclops complained, "under director Edward L. Cahn's heavy hand, you'll feel every last one of the film's 77 minutes."

Voodoo Woman was released on a double-bill with Roger Corman's bizarre (and far superior) tale of witchcraft, *The Undead,* to create a supernaturally charged schlock—er—*shock* show. Financially, "it did okay," related Alex Gordon, who added, "of course those things were so cheap. By that time AIP had pretty good relations with exhibitors of drive-in theaters, so it did all right. Not as big as *Day the World Ended* and *Phantom From 10,000 Leagues.* But all those combinations played a lot of drive-ins and they all returned their costs within about a year or so."

[1] During filming of *The She-Creature,* Blaisdell was nearly drowned in the California surf when the bulky suit became waterlogged.

CREDITS: Director: Edward L. Cahn; Producer: Alex Gordon; Executive Producers: Samuel Z. Arkoff and James H. Nicholson; Story and Screenplay: Russell Bender and V.I. Voss; Director of Photography: Frederick E. West; Production Supervisor/Assistant Director: Bart Carre; Film Editor: Ronald Sinclair; Music Composed and Conducted by: Darrell Calker; Song "Black Voodoo": lyrics by John Blackburn, music by Darrell Calker; Art Director: Don Ament; Set Decorator: Harry Reif; Properties: Karl Brainard and Richard M. Rubin; Wardrobe: Bob Olivas; Makeup: Carlie Taylor; Special Makeup: Harry Thomas; Sound: Bob Post; Script Supervisor: Judith Hart; A Carmel Production released by American-International February 1957; 77 minutes

CAST: Marla English (Marilyn Blanchard); Tom Conway (Dr. Roland Gerard); Touch [later Mike] Connors (Ted Bronson); Mary Ellen Kaye (Susan Gerard); Lance Fuller (Rick Brady); Paul Dubov (Marcel Chateau); Martin Wilkins (Chaka); Norman Willis (Harry West); Otis Greene (Bobo); Emmett E. Smith (Gandor); Paul Blaisdell (Monster); Giselle D'Arc (Yvette); Jean Davis (Saranda), Dale Van Sickel

Tonda (Allison Hayes) uses her feminine wiles on hero Tom (Paul Burke) in *The Disembodied*.

THE DISEMBODIED
(1957)
"The Big Safari of Voodoo Terror!"

"In Africa there exists remote islands
of savagery where the ancient rites
of Voodoo are still practiced.
The African Witch Doctor does not know
the meaning of 'psychology,' yet he has
mastered its art for centuries. It is an
established fact that with primitive peoples,
a native can die by power of
'suggestion.' White men, as a rule, are not
susceptible to Voodoo. Yet there are
recorded instances of lost travelers 'losing
their minds' to the 'Black Magic.'
Our story is concerned with such events."
—opening written narration

The 1950s proved to be a difficult decade for screen voodoo. (In fact, if you weren't an Alien or Big Bug you had a pretty tough row to hoe.) None of the four voodoo movies released during the decade (*Voodoo Tiger*, *Voodoo Island*, *Voodoo Woman*, and this sorry feature) proved to be anything more than lower-berth filler. *The Disembodied* is the worst of the lot—and that's saying something.

Not quite the "Big Safari of Voodoo Terror" the ads promised, this voodoo Peyton Place begins in the jungles of Africa as the beautiful Tonda (Allison Hayes) ties a noose around the neck of a voodoo doll, causing her husband, Dr. Metz (John E. Wengraf), to gasp for breath. She releases the cord before the diabolical operation is completed, and then goes to him as the dutifully sympathetic wife.

Three white strangers arrive, Tom (Paul Burke), Norman (Joel Marston), and Joe (Robert Christopher), members of a motion picture company (who apparently were filming in the jungle, though no elaboration is forthcoming). Joe lies near death, having been critically mauled by a lion. That night Tonda, who is the natives' white voodoo queen, presides over a voodoo ceremony in which she cuts out the heart of her native servant, Suba (offscreen, of course), in order to heal the wounded white man. As an odd side effect, the now-restored Joe is in some sort of trance and there's talk of "personality transference."

Tonda comes on to the handsome Tom, but when she exhorts him to kill her husband so they can leave together, the enamored filmmaker balks. After numerous scenes of romantic friction between Tonda,

Tom, and Dr. Metz, Tom and Norman decide to leave (*without* Joe, for he's disappeared—whisked away by Suba's widow who seemingly sees her dead husband in the entranced man). Dr. Metz (who for the whole time has been rather hostile to the intruders) now decides to go with them, leaving the conniving Tonda to her jungle worshippers.

In a rage Tonda suddenly stabs her husband. As Metz hovers near death, Tonda uses a voodoo doll to kill the servant Kabar (Otis Greene), a witness to the crime. With this done, she intends to pin the murder on Tom and Norman. (Metz is not yet dead, but will die without a doctor's care, and Tonda even tries to finish the job by smothering him with a pillow before she's interrupted by Tom.)

The two filmmakers fool Tonda by propping up Kabar's body in a jeep as if he were alive and having Norman drive off to get the magistrate. Now the frantic Tonda wants her husband to *live* (so she won't be hanged for murder). To this end, her native followers seize Tom and take him to the sacrificial altar. There she intends to perform the same wound-healing ceremony for her husband as she did for Joe—this time with Tom as the victim. Through her voodoo powers she summons Joe, and the entranced man readies a knife to strike at his friend's heart. Out of the shadows steps Lara (Eugenie Paul), Suba's widow, who thrusts a dagger into Tonda's chest as revenge for killing her husband. At this, the spell over Joe is broken, he releases Tom, and the natives, lost without their voodoo queen, flee into the jungle. Soon after, Tom, Norman, and Joe bid good-bye to the recovering Dr. Metz and drive off toward civilization.

The Disembodied simply wallows in dime-store voodoo. The only element more prevalent than jungle sorcery is the grade-B soap opera ambiance. Beginning with the very first scene we have strangulation by voodoo doll (interrupted); exotic voodoo rumba; wound-healing via human sacrifice; ditto personality transference; voodoo funeral; zombie-like roaming from entranced victim; a second strangulation via doll (this one completed); a second healing ceremony (interrupted); and zombie-victim recovery at death of sorceress. Too bad all this hoodoo excitement is negated by scene after dull scene of jungle soap opera as wife makes eyes at stranger; husband berates wife; wife scorns husband; wife kisses native; wife placates husband; wife kisses stranger; husband confronts stranger; *ad infinitum*, *ad nauseam*. Though only 65 minutes long, *The Disembodied* seems muuuuch longer.

The convolutions pile atop one another like cord wood with everything becoming so entangled that sorting through the various plot points becomes not only tedious but pointless as well—since little of it makes any sense. First Tonda seems to be killing her

105

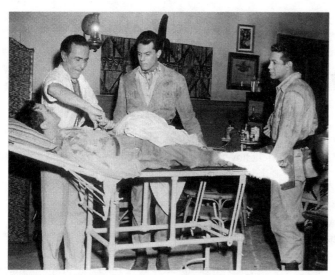

Joe (Robert Christopher) lies near death after being mauled by a lion. Dr. Metz (John E. Wengraf, left) can't save him—but voodoo can...

husband with the voodoo doll—then inexplicably puts it away and lets him recover (even making nice with him on the porch). Next, she sacrifices her willing native servant, Suba, in order to heal the wounded Joe for no discernible reason. Also, Tonda's magic seemingly transfers Suba's personality into Joe's body, and Suba's widow takes her new/old husband into her care. Though Tom had witnessed said sacrificial ceremony with Tonda presiding as the undulating voodoo priestess, the next day he makes no mention of it. (It seems incredible that he didn't recognize her as the priestess, especially with her beautiful face and unmistakable figure—not to mention the fact that she's the only white woman around for miles.) Tonda, on the other hand, becomes a frightened kitten and asks Tom to take her away ("Tom, it's all so weird," she asserts, illustrating scripter Jack Townley's level of scintillating dialogue). Tonda then exhorts Tom to kill her husband so they can get away (when, in fact, she obviously possesses the power to do so cleanly, neatly, and at a distance, so that no one would be the wiser). Tonda finally does try to kill her husband herself—with a knife. She does this in front of three witnesses when she could have simply used her deadly doll in private and got off scot-free (as she subsequently does with Kabar, one of the witnesses). Then, realizing she'll be convicted of murder if her husband dies of his stab wound, she plans another healing ceremony to keep him alive (apparently unconcerned with an *attempted* murder charge). Finally, Joe somehow loses Suba's personality when Tonda is stabbed at the end to become plain old likable Joe again.

Even the film's title makes no sense: *Disembodied* what—spirit? voodoo gods? head? (*that* at least would have been moderately interesting as evidenced by the far more entertaining dead-head features *The*

Thing That Couldn't Die and *The Brain That Wouldn't Die*). When originally announced, the project was called by the more illuminating title of *Voodoo Girl*, though that handle quickly gave way to the totally inappropriate *Vampire Girl* (!) before finally evolving into *The Disembodied*. In the end, a more accurate moniker for *The Disembodied* would have been *The Disenchanted* because that's exactly how the viewer feels after the 65 minutes are up.

Despite the quantity of voodoo present, the quality of its presentation leaves much to be desired. The studio-bound sets possess as much authenticity as *Gilligan's Island* on an off day. Coupled with the sparse, dingy interiors of Dr. Metz's jungle house, the cramped jungle sets give the film a decidedly small-scale cast. Director Walter Grauman (who obtained a leave of absence from his regular work on NBC's *Matinee Theatre* to do the film) shows off his shoddy sets to worst advantage when, as hero and friends depart in the final scene, the camera is carelessly placed so that the viewer can clearly see the tops of the painted scenery flats, with the jungle ending several feet below the frame! Oops. And this seems to be about the level of care taken with the film, as DP Harry Neumann's camera rarely moves and Grauman stages his scenes in a straightforward and mundane manner devoid of any originality or atmosphere.

While the script is short on believable motivation and even a modicum of intelligence, it's definitely long on dialogue. The characters talk, talk, and talk, and, apart from the occasional vague comment about voodoo, all the chatter generally leads nowhere. About the best dialogue Jack Townley could come up with is a statement made by Tonda that, "The natives are a very strange people; they believe what they want to believe and distrust what they do not understand," answered by Tom with, "Isn't that about the same with all mankind." And this obvious, slightly awkward platitude is the *best* he could offer.

The Disembodied's one saving grace comes in the statuesque form of Allison Hayes, a 50-foot—er, 5-foot-6-inch beauty who became a perennial favorite in '50s low-budget fantasy. Her gorgeous presence enlivened such films as *The Unearthly* (1957), *The Undead* (1957), *Zombies of Mora Tau* (1957; a borderline voodoo flick), *Attack of the 50 Foot Woman* (1958), *The Hypnotic Eye* (1960), and *The Crawling Hand* (1963).

Born Mary Jane Hayes in 1930, Allison entered show business as a symphony musician. Appearing as Miss Washington in the 1949 Miss America pageant, she soon began modeling which ultimately led

As Tonda the voodoo queen, Allison Hayes works her jungle magic in *The Disembodied*.

to a motion picture contract (and name change) with Universal-International in 1954. After appearing in nearly a score of films over the decade, she turned her energies toward television, appearing on shows like *77 Sunset Strip*, *Hawaiian Eye*, and *Perry Mason*, and even co-starring in the short-lived series *Acapulco* (February to April 1961) and (briefly) on *General Hospital*. She semi-retired from acting in the early 1970s when her health began to fail. She died on February 27, 1977, at the age of 47. Though she'd been receiving treatments for leukemia, the cause of death remains conjectural, as the actress herself claimed that she was suffering from lead poisoning.

Hayes' large eyes and expressive mouth created an image of vulnerability while her voluptuous figure and swaying hips shouted "female predator." Besides this, she also happened to be a decent actress, which meant that she could exploit this dichotomy to her (and the film's) advantage as the script required. In *The Disembodied*, Hayes runs the gamut from feline seductress to frightened innocent to enraged she-cat. Her astute playing makes what as written as a rather schizophrenic character into a believably "bad woman" (as the doomed Suba labels her) who uses whatever wiles the situation calls for to get what she wants—be it sultry seduction, timid vulnerability, or murderous voodoo. Thanks to her conviction and intensity, Hayes is a joy to watch (and not *just* for the obvious reasons).

Sadly, the same cannot be said for the rest of the players. As the heroic Tom, Paul Burke (later a regular on various TV series such as *Naked City*, *Twelve O'Clock High*, and *Dynasty*) is square-jawed and square-dealing and about as deep as a cardboard cutout. What Tonda sees in him (apart from a carefully coiffed ruggedness) is anybody's guess. But then, when one considers his competition in the form of John E. Wengraf playing her husband, I suppose we can forgive Tonda's shallowness. Wengraf plays the doctor as a snippy, bad-tempered whiner, making one almost appreciate Tonda's impulsive knife thrust toward film's end. The remainder of the characters are all stock, though Robert Christopher as the wounded Joe looks pretty good walking about bare-chested in a trance, sporting a neat array of scars from his lion attack. Despite the fact that he has no dialogue at all, this victim of Tonda's personality transfer spell makes more impact than the remaining cast members.

Variety gave *The Disembodied* a rather indifferent review (much better than it deserves), calling it an "okay meller which generally sustains interest and

In *The Disembodied*, hero Tom (Paul Burke) finds himself not only at the mercy of gun-toting native servants, but of a conniving (and lascivious) voodoo queen as well.

should please the young 'uns… Cast members all perform adequately under okay direction of Walter Grauman."

Few modern reviewers even bothered with the film, and those who did either disliked it or felt it something of a guilty pleasure. Incredibly, *Filmfax*'s Bruce Dettman called *The Disembodied* "an unabashed foray into the realm of jungle cliché and voodoo hokum that rarely has been bettered."(!) (Tellingly, Mr. Dettman also got his brief synopsis quite wrong.) David Hogan, however, writing in a later issue of the same magazine, had obviously recently *seen* the film when he succinctly labeled it "awful" while going on to say that "Allison [Hayes] brought enthusiasm and the full force of her beauty to her role [and] for this reason *The Disembodied* deserves to be seen." Phil Hardy's *Encyclopedia of Horror Movies* dismissed it as a "silly jungle saga" whereas Michael Weldon called it "fun jungle nonsense" in his *Psychotronic Encyclopedia of Film*.

The Disembodied was released on a double-bill with another jungle horror, *From Hell It Came* (in which a native spirit inhabits a walking tree stump). The Killer Tree movie proved the less wooden of the two productions.

For voodoo fans, the 1950s brought us voodoo cinema's worst collective gathering—with *The Disembodied* as the scruffy, three-legged member trailing the pathetic pack.

CREDITS: Director: Walter Grauman; Producer: Ben Schwalb; Screenplay: Jack Townley; Director of Photography: Harry Neumann; Art Director: David Milton; Film Editor: William Austin; Production Manager: Allen K. Wood; Assistant Director: Austen Jewell; Sound Editor: Del Harris; Music: Marlin Skiles; Set Decorator: Joseph Kish; Set Continuity: Richard Michaels; Recorded by: Ralph Butler; Wardrobe: Bert Henrikson; Makeup Artist: Emile LaVigne; Construction Supervisor: James West; Property: Sam Gordon; Released August 1957 by Allied Artists; 65 minutes

CAST: Paul Burke (Tom), Allison Hayes (Tonda), John E. Wengraf (Dr. Metz), Eugenia Paul (Lara), Joel Marston (Norman), Robert Christopher (Joe), Norman Frederic (Suba), A.E. Ukoni (Voodoo Drum Leader), Paul Thompson (Gogi), Otis Greene (Kabar)

Macumba Love begins promisingly enough with this impressively staged nighttime voodoo ceremony, but (like the sequence itself—which drags on for a full *seven* minutes) the film quickly overstays its welcome.

MACUMBA LOVE (1960)
Surf, Sand, and Ceremony

"This is the twentieth century,
the age of science and enlightenment.
There should be no corner of the world
where such things are permitted to exist."
—Walter Reed as writer/skeptic J. Peter Weils

"Advance reports have it that we've a real 'sleeper' in our town over at the _____ Theatre," began a prepared UA publicity piece, "where the United Artists scary mystery drama, *Macumba Love*, is playing. In case you're not up on motion picture parlance, a 'Sleeper' is a film that unexpectedly turns out to be unusual." In *Macumba Love*'s case, the film proved a "Sleeper" only in the *literal* sense, for that's exactly what it induces in its viewers.

Macumba Love was filmed in Brazil, making it the sole English-language voodoo movie to bear that distinction. However, unless you're a fan of Brazilian beaches (upon which this picture spends an inter-

minable amount of time) or June Wilkinson's talents (both of them), the film's glacial pacing and dull dramatics leave little to recommend to the discerning viewer.

On an island off the Brazilian coast, American "novelist, lecturer, and general debunker of mankind" J. Peter Weils (Walter Reed) frolics on the beach with his sometime girlfriend, local heiress Venus de Vaisa (Ziva Rodann). While playing in the surf they find a dead body with a six-inch hatpin stuck in its abdomen—the victim of a ritual voodoo murder.

Peter intends to write a book on the subject ("voodoo cultists don't frighten me, I'll expose them as well"). To this end he takes the hatpin to the local "voodoo queen," Mama Rataloy (Ruth de Souza). When he confronts her, she simply labels him a disbeliever and an enemy. Despite her veiled threats, Peter remains unafraid and undeterred, later stating, "I propose to trace these murders right to their source—to Mama Rataloy."

Peter's daughter Sara (June Wilkinson) and her new husband Warren (William Wellman, Jr.) arrive on their honeymoon. Venus promptly begins to flirt

The only voodoo film shot entirely in Brazil. (Courtesy Ronald V. Borst/Hollywood Movie Posters)

with the young bridegroom, rousing Sara's jealousy, but Warren ultimately rebuffs her advances.

Meanwhile, Mama Rataloy sends Peter a skull with a hatpin imbedded in its forehead as a warning. Later, he finds yet another voodoo victim on his beach. Looking on from behind some rocks, Mama Rataloy stabs a pin into a doll and Peter grabs his arm in pain.

The voodoo priestess comes to Peter's house to deliver another warning to stay out of their voodoo affairs and "give more thought to your loved ones." Upon leaving, she slips something into his coffee. By chance, however, he becomes distracted and fails to drink it.

That evening he goes to see Venus and discovers that her liquor has been tampered with and that a ring given to her by Mama Rataloy has made a tiny prick in her finger. "Venus, you're being drugged," he tells her. Becoming distraught, Venus confesses to lately experiencing confusion and blackouts. Peter advises Venus to stay home and take a sleeping pill while he goes to confront Mama Rataloy. After he leaves, however, Venus (apparently under some hypnotic influence) places the ring back on her finger and drinks a mysterious potion.

Back at Peter's house, Sara sees a sinister and frightening woman, whose face "was like a snake," lurking in the garden. While she talks with the police, the voodooists kidnap Warren and take him to their ceremonial clearing. They also capture Peter and force him to watch the proceedings. Drugged and under Mama Rataloy's hypnotic control, Venus approaches the prostrate Warren with a poisoned hatpin. Just as she lifts the deadly needle, the police arrive with Sara, scattering the voodooists in all directions. In the ensuing fracas, Venus collapses and Mama Rataloy is killed (though *how* is unclear, since she simply falls to the ground—dead). As Peter and the Inspector look on, the voodoo queen's face changes into that of a scaly creature before suddenly bursting into flame. Peter comforts Venus, who has no memory of the diabolical events, and Warren and Sara are reunited.

Though voodoo is the main focus of *Macumba Love*, scripter Norman Graham and director Douglas Fowley do little to either explore or exploit the topic. Time after time, when issues arise the filmmakers back off before they can fully develop. For instance, at one point Mama Rataloy uses a voodoo doll to cause a sharp pain in Peter's arm, but this remains an isolated incident and nothing further comes of it. (If she indeed had such power, why doesn't she simply stab her pin into the talisman's heart and be done with the troublesome writer?) With this, Graham and Fowler miss a prime opportunity to examine the power of faith vs. the power of supernatural magic, for Peter has felt himself immune to the ill-will of the voodooists because, "only the superstitious are in danger; I don't believe in fixes [hexes]." Peter also opines that, "the whole concept of voodoo is a sort of auto-suggestion, a self-hypnosis, a disease that preys on an ignorant mind." Yet Mama Rataloy's "fix" with the doll seems to work quite effectively on him, even though he "doesn't believe in fixes" and claims to possess a "learned" mind. This brings up many questions—that simply go begging.

A voodoo victim about to meet Mama Rataloy's dreaded hatpin.

Then there's the intriguing concept of the "serpent goddess" who "has been known to slay thousands" and is destroyed "only by seeing her reflection." Legend has it that once every 10 years the spirit of Damballah enters the body of a woman, who becomes a "half-woman, half-reptile" vengeance-seeking monster. (While, of course, no legend like this exists in real Voudou, the idea nevertheless offers a terrifying and highly cinematic potential.) The film even intimates that *Venus* could be this bloodthirsty creature (a heroine-as-unwitting-monster concept that was later fully explored in Hammer's *The Gorgon*, 1964). After several characters bring it up, however, this engaging idea simply fades into the background (until the final—and hopelessly unconvincing—shot of Mama Rataloy's face transforming in death into that of a scaly creature).

Norman Graham's script briefly opens the door on voodoo as a legitimate form of worship—then promptly lets the wind of ennui blow it shut again. At one time Venus defends the voodooists by pointing out that "Voodoo is a religious ritual. They're expressing a desire to worship, a desire to appease the unknown. You do the same thing in your more *re-fined* societies.*" While, again, this idea carries potential for further exploration, the script simply has Peter ignore such a notion and continue with brash statements like, "the black art of voodoo has been preying on the Western mind for almost 200 years," and, "voodoo is a very dangerous and ignorant practice."

According to star Walter Reed, "There were real voodoo people in the movie! One guy came up to me and gave me this little figure that he'd carved out of soapstone, and somebody said, 'Oh, that's good luck.' I said, 'But it's *voodoo*!' And they said, 'Look, there's good voodoo and bad voodoo.' They *like* you!' I said, 'Good! I'm gonna have them keep *on* liking me!'" (quoted in Tom Weaver's *It Came From Weaver Five*).

While it's not unusual for a voodoo film to go light on the exploration of its sensationalistic subject (even with "real voodoo people" involved), the typical hoodoo horror at least manages some level of entertaining *exploitation*. Not so *Macumba Love*, whose leaden pace and endless filler leave little room for excitement. The film opens on a promising note with a night-time ceremony in which drums beat rapidly,

Israeli actress Ziva Rodann—*Macumba Love*'s one bright spot.

Caribbean calypso inexplicably emigrated to rural Brazil remains unexplained); another musical interlude at the open air marketplace (with a new calypso tune, "To Market"); a tedious sequence of (a barely visible) Peter creeping along a darkened path for several minutes; and the two newlyweds dancing on the patio or frolicking in the ocean. (Yet another sign of the film's bargain basement roots shows through when the film repeats the *same* shot of Warren diving into a wave and then taking a silly bow.)

Star Walter Reed admitted that the film was "corny and also slow-paced. The first part of the picture, all that voodoo music and dancing—I thought they'd never get through with that! It went on and on and on! They got involved with the beauty of the dancing girls and things like that, they got carried away and forgot about the story sometimes. Actually, what

participants chant, and dancers twirl about a bubbling cauldron. A corpulent mamaloi stabs a cloth doll with a pin and then drops it into the smoking pot. (When a huge cloud of smoke subsequently shoots up, the actress jumps back with a bewildered look on her face and looks questioningly into the camera, obviously startled and taken unawares. The fact that this gaffe remained in the final print rather than being excised or reshot amusingly exposes the film's level of [in]competency.) While initially impressive in its frenetic energy, the ceremonial sequence goes on far too long (seven full minutes!) and so ultimately inspires more boredom than interest.

The film then immediately segues into another long (five-minute) sequence (and this one lacks any sort of energy at all) as Peter and Venus engage in awkward, tepid banter on the beach ("You are the most exciting woman in the world," etc.).

Further time-filler consists of a long nightclub sequence in which Venus flirts with Warren and then sings a calypso ditty called "Dance Calinda" (just *how*

they probably were really doing, if you really want to know, was purposely dragging it out, because you can't sell a picture that's too short."

In only two isolated instances does the film generate any excitement, and these are moments of pure visceral shock rather than of any thematic or artistic merit. The first comes as Peter and Venus play in the surf. When Peter playfully lifts Venus up and tosses her into the gently rolling waves, he ducks under the water for a moment and then comes up holding not the beautiful Venus as expected but the rigid corpse of a dead man, its eyes open and staring. Director Fowley hammers the shock home with an abrupt zoom into the face of the cadaver while Venus (now having surfaced herself) screams in horror. (Walter Reed recalled how "the guy that did that [played the corpse] didn't know how to do it, and finally the director, Fowley, took his shirt off and his pants off and jumped in the water and said, '*This* is the way to do it!'")

The second memorable moment comes when Mama Rataloy takes a hatpin and approaches a suffering captive tied to the back wall of her shack. "To disbelieve is to die," she tells him and abruptly jabs the long needle into his eye. The man screams and the screen then cuts to a literal victim's-eye-view as bright red blood suddenly gushes over the camera lens—as if we're seeing from behind the punctured orb itself. It's a gruesomely inventive (though arguably tasteless) bit of camerawork that remains one of the few memorable things in the picture.

Not surprisingly, the film's level of acting perfectly matches its technical (un)proficiencies. Though easy on the eyes, the two young leads, June Wilkinson as Sara and William Wellman, Jr. (son of famed director William A. Wellman, creator of such classics as *The Public Enemy* [1931], *A Star is Born* [1937], and *The Ox-Bow Incident* [1943]) as Warren, are excruciatingly bland. Even after finding himself staked out on the ground as a sacrifice, Wellman, Jr., never loses his blank expression. Ironically, the film's pressbook noted that "In *Macumba Love*, Wellman has his most challenging role to date, calling for a full display of dramatic emotion." The young actor must have simply forgotten to *answer* that call.

While one could never accuse June Wilkinson's 44-20-36 figure of being flat, the same can not be said of her *acting*, for she perfectly complements the non-presence of her onscreen partner via her vapid demeanor and vacuous expressions. "June was a nice girl," remembered co-star Walter Reed. "She had the big body on her and all that kind of stuff [*laughs*], but she was a sweet young 19-year-old kid. She was an English girl, not a highly educated woman, but attractive." This full-figured "19-year-old kid" (known as "the most photographed nude in America" and, more amusingly, as simply "The Bosom" in the pages of *Playboy* magazine) enjoyed her moviemaking adventure in Brazil. "That was great fun," she told *Psychotronic*'s Ian Johnston. "I did have a wonderful time shooting that." Too bad the viewer can't say the same about *watching* it. Ms. Wilkinson herself has no illusions about the film: "It ain't much of a movie, but what a time… I fell madly in love with a Brazilian and hey, I had my nineteenth birthday down there and it was this exotic country and Latins love blondes." After a few more minor pictures (often requiring her to appear sans apparel), Wilkinson achieved her greatest recognition in the hit play *Pajama Tops*, a bedroom farce that she's toured with off and on for the last three decades. (Two versions of *Macumba Love* were shot. In the European version, Wilkinson went topless in one scene whereas in the U.S. release—the only one currently available—she wears a one-piece bathing suit.)

Walter Reed agreed that the month-and-a-half experience of "making that picture was a lot of fun," despite the occasional near-mishap. "The guy who was handling the snakes was named Jooveneel—I called him 'Juvenile' [*laughs*]! One day a little tiny snake jumped out from a tree so I stepped on him, killed him—it was only about a foot long. And Jooveneel said, 'If that snake had hit you, you would be dead within 30 seconds.' It was one of the deadliest, most dangerous snakes down there!"

Reed also commented on the production's international flavor, with an American director, English, Israeli, American, and Brazilian leads, and "a Hungarian cameraman, a Russian makeup guy (who was also an actor), and the crew was Brazilian."

Though veteran character actor Walter Reed may be the most experienced professional in the cast, his performance fails to reflect it. As Peter, he takes a smug, high-handed tone that makes him sound more like a conceited *caricature* than a concerned character. Reed doesn't speak his dialogue, he *announces* it. His harsh voice and strident manner rarely change, nor does his self-satisfied expression.

The film's one bright spot comes in the form of Israeli actress Ziva Rodann (whom the film's pressbook labels "the world's most glamorous army veteran—having served for a year in the Israeli army"). Not only is she sexier than the grossly pulchritudinous June Wilkinson, she out-acts her (and everyone else in the picture). In reviewing *Macumba Love*, *Variety*'s "Holl" (who had little good to say about the production) praised Ms. Rodann's "outstanding performance" and called her "an attractive and fiery performer who has a chance to make an important impact in future films." Sadly, such a chance never materialized, for, after half a dozen more unimportant and gimmicky pictures like *Giants of Thessaly* (1961) and *Three Nuts in Search of a Bolt* (1964; her last), she dropped from sight. Rodann's presence also enlivened one other exotic horror, *Pharaoh's Curse* (1957).

According to Walter Reed, Ms. Rodann was not the easiest of actresses to work with, and they got off to a bad start. "While we were shooting that first scene on the beach," Reed told Tom Weaver, "she turned her head a certain way and upstaged me. I just turned to the director and I said, 'Cut it!' And I said to her, 'If you ever do that again, you'll be in blackface for the rest of the picture.' I'd just get in her keylight, *that's* all I had to do [*laughs*], and she'd be in blackface for the *whole* rest of the picture. She said, 'I don't know what you mean!' and I said, 'Come on, honey, you know what you're doin'. Now knock it off.' She got the message real fast and we got along fine after that, and I got so I *liked* her after a while."

Macumba Love was the directorial debut of actor Douglas Fowley. As such, it proved a very inauspicious one, as Fowley fails in his pacing, staging (apart from the two aforementioned shocks), and direction

According to Walter Reed, *Macumba Love* cleaned up at the box office. "Early on, they said I could have a salary or I could take five percent of the picture," the actor regretfully recalled. "I said, 'You must be out of your mind! I don't want five percent of this thing!' And it made $3,000,000 in this country—that wasn't including the foreign rights. I would have made a *lot* of money on that show."

Perhaps the reason the film did so well financially was due to savvy promotion. United Artists exhorted their exhibitors to perpetrate all sorts of promotional ploys to lure in unsuspecting potential patrons. Among them were suggestions of staging a "Voodoo Queen Funeral: A hearse bannered with copy and carrying a Calypso Band toured city for two days before opening. Voodoo queen in coffin waved to crowds." Another was to "Invite a local dance group—including both Negros and whites—to stage a realistic Voodoo Ritual Dance in town square or shopping center mall. Hoke it up for good-natured fun by planting effigies (small rag dolls) on poles so that dancers can stick pins into them. Dolls can be labeled 'Poor Schools,' 'Slow Transportation,' 'High Taxes,' etc." Imagine, politically oriented exploitation! Now *that's* innovative.

Sadly, the film itself was not innovative. In fact, *Macumba Love*'s final sequence epitomizes the picture's level of ineptitude. It begins when Mama Rataloy's face dissolves into an obviously papier-mache mask with wrinkled skin and misshapen cardboard lips in one of the most amateurish makeup jobs ever seen in 35mm. Then, after an awkward (and very noticeable) jump cut, the fake head bursts into flame—just as the viewer bursts out laughing.

CREDITS: Director/Producer: Douglas V. Fowley; Executive Producers: M.A. Ripps, Steve Barclay; Original Story and Screenplay: Norman Graham; Photography: Rudolph Icsey; Choreography: Solano Trinidade; Musical Score: Enrico Simonetti; Art Director: Pitrino Massenzi; Supervising Editor: Herbert R. Hoffman; Production Manager: Camno Campaio; Camera Operator: George Pfister; Sound: Ernst Masassy; Film Editor: Mauro Alice; Assistant Director: Wladimir Lundgren; Second Assistant Director: Henry Kupty; Makeup: Victor Merinow; Wardrobe: Pia Garazzi; Script: Olga Chart Vlarianos; An Allied Enterprises/Brinter-Brasil Internacional Filmes/Barclay Films International co-production released in May 1960 by United Artists; 86 minutes

CAST: Walter Reed (J. Peter Weils), Ziva Rodann (Venus de Vaisa), William Wellman, Jr. (Warren), June Wilkinson (Sara), Pedro Paulo Hatheyer (Insp. Escoberto), Ruth de Souza (Mama Rataloy), Clea Simões, Jean Thuret, Ricardo Campos

of actors. It's little wonder that he was never entrusted with the director's baton again and for the remainder of his career worked only in front of rather than behind the camera.

Born Daniel Vincent Fowley in 1911, he began acting in films in the 1930s and went on to play in over 200 pictures. While *Macumba Love* was his first (and only) job as a director, he had previously *acted* the part of one (to hilarious effect) in *Singin' in the Rain* (1952). Among his acting credits are the genre entries *One Body Too Many* (1944; with Bela Lugosi), *Mighty Joe Young* (1949), *Cat Women of the Moon* (1953), *7 Faces of Dr. Lao* (1964), and *Homebodies* (1974).

Neil Hamilton (soon to attain TV immortality as *Batman*'s Commissioner Gordon) plays the "High Executioner" wielding *The Devil's Hand*.

THE DEVIL'S HAND
(1962)
The Good (Looking),
the Bad (Acting),
and the Ugly (Production)

"Oh great Gamba, highest executioner, supreme
devil-god of evil, make your decision;
shall the maiden live—or *die*?"
—Neil Hamilton as Lamont

The Devil's Hand is a deservedly obscure entry in the voodoo sweepstakes whose only real point of interest lay in the astounding beauty of its star, Linda Christian. Christian plays Bianca Milan, an enticing temptress who sets her sights on Rick Turner (Robert Alda). Bianca, a prominent member of a modern-day voodoo cult that worships "Gamba, the devil-god of evil," uses her powers of thought transference to invade Rick's dreams. Though Rick is engaged to be married to Donna (Ariadne Welter), he is enticed by Bianca's vision of loveliness to visit a small doll shop, run by a rather sinister man named Francis Lamont

(Neil Hamilton). There he sees a doll with Bianca's face and another one that looks like his fiancée, Donna.

Lamont turns out to be the leader and "high executioner" of the cult, and by sticking a long pin into the Donna doll, causes her to wind up in the hospital with a heart condition. With Donna laid up, Bianca ensnares Rick with her captivating beauty. He agrees to join the cult so that they can be together, and so "renounces goodness and virtue."

At his initiation, Rick sees the cult's sacrificial wheel which hangs from the ceiling at work. "It's like Russian roulette," explains Bianca, "except the odds are greater. In our ceremony we use a sword, concealed in one of the covers hanging from the wheel. The wheel is spun and Gamba makes his decision. The cover is lowered upon the heart of the subject. If the sword is in the cover, it *pierces* the heart. If Gamba decides to spare the subject, the cover bends harmlessly."

After swearing allegiance to Gamba, Rick is amazed at his subsequent financial success. Under Bianca's guidance, Rick plays the ponies and the stock market with astounding ease.

But Rick has not completely forgotten the hospitalized Donna. While he cannot escape his bewitching Bianca, he *can* alleviate Donna's suffering. Rick sneaks into the doll shop and removes the pin from

Bianca (Linda Christian) initiates her newfound beau Rick (Robert Alda) into the voodoo cult of Gamba.

the Donna doll, releasing his former fiancée from her torment.

When Bianca and Lamont discover Rick's "treachery," Bianca uses the Donna doll to place the girl within her power. At the next coven meeting, they bring out the sacrifice for the test. It's Donna and they wish Rick to prove his loyalty by spinning the wheel of swords himself. He rebels and in the ensuing fray knocks Lamont onto the altar and sets the curtains ablaze. The wheel drops and the sword impales Lamont while the rest of the cultists go up in flames. But when Rick tells Donna that they're truly free of the horrible cult as they drive away from the conflagration, Bianca's ethereal image appears and intones, "That's what *he* thinks." It is THE END.

As a voodoo film, *The Devil's Hand* ultimately gives its audience the finger. While it sports the stereotypical voodoo doll concept, the scenes involving the manipulation of the dolls and subsequent result to the victims are handled in such a pedestrian and banal manner that they lose whatever interest the potentially terrifying moments contain. And apart from the dolls, the only other voodoo variants come in the form of a black bongo drummer beating out his rhythms while a fully clothed black couple does a tame Eisenhower-era version of "dirty dancing." The blandness extends to the remaining coven members (all white), who give the impression of middle-aged bohemian-wannabes (in suits and cocktail dresses!) rather than evil devil worshipers.

This obviously threadbare production sports only cramped and minimalist sets. Even the critical altar room is nothing more than a small chamber hung with thick curtains, with a table for an altar, a lectern behind which Lamont stands, a couple of tiki-type braziers (standing ready for that climactic conflagration), and a few throw pillows for the cultists to sit on.

William J. Hole, Jr.'s direction is adequate, but only just, with a heavy reliance on the master shot and nothing extra in the way of evocative angles or mood-enhancing photography. It's about what you would expect from the director of *The Ghost of Dragstrip Hollow*. Hole, after helming a handful of low-budget J.D. films like *Speed Crazy* (1959) and *Twist All Night* (1961), turned to television, directing episodes of *Peyton Place*, *Highway Patrol*, *77 Sunset Strip*, and *Hawaiian Eye*. He died in 1990 of respiratory failure.

Jo Heims' rambling screenplay offers absolutely no depth of character anywhere, ignoring whatever tortured reasons caused these people to seek out this "devil-god of evil." And, apart from sticking it to the Donna doll and playing a swashbuckler's version of Russian roulette, the script fails to provide any real manifestation of their "renouncing goodness and virtue." Nobody, even Lamont the "high executioner," really comes off as evil—though that's what they profess to be (methinks thou dost *profess* too much!). None of the bland characters seems to have lost their souls (they don't appear interesting enough to have even had one in the first place), and the coven comes across as nothing more than a silly and rather dull after-hours club.

As the "high executioner," Neil Hamilton makes a truly one-dimensional (or, more precisely, *non*-dimensional) and uninteresting villain. His smug, one-note performance, in which his tone never changes and he never even gets excited, makes one long for a bit of his Commissioner Gordon histrionics to liven things up. (Hamilton later achieved TV fame as the perpetually surprised and sputtering police commissioner on the *Batman* television series.)

Robert Alda is just as toneless and lacking in charisma as he was in *The Beast With Five Fingers* (1947), and it's hard to fathom what Bianca sees in this rather seedy middle-aged man. (This was the last American film the former Broadway star and father of Alan Alda made before abandoning Hollywood for the sunny climes of Rome and 15 years of European productions.) Fortunately, Linda Christian as Bianca, with her sultry, come-hither looks and breathy, sexy voice, makes Rick's impetuous decision to devote his life to a devil-god cult just to get laid seem *almost* credible. Lounging provocatively in nearly see-through negligees, Christian creates a heady air of seething sensuality. Of course, her acting can't match her looks, and her character, apart from a rather appealing and focused nymphomania, seems no more evil than your typical spoiled fashion model.

Born Blanca Rosa Welter in Mexico, Linda Christian, daughter of a Dutch oil man, grew up in exotic locales such as Venezuela, South Africa, and Palestine (where, for a time, she attended medical school). She entered movies in the mid-1940s in films like *Holiday in Mexico* (1946), *Green Dolphin Street* (1947), and *Tarzan and the Mermaids* (1948) but never really made it as a leading lady. She was better known for her numerous offscreen romances (involving such luminaries as Hugh O'Brion, Errol Flynn, and Turhan Bey) than for her onscreen performances. Among her husbands were actors Tyrone Power and Edmund Purdom. She eventually moved to Spain where she continued her romantic pursuits among the European aristocracy.

The best performance in *The Devil's Hand* comes from Roger Corman (and, later, Jerry Warren) regular, Bruno VeSota, who plays a terrified cultist about to be punished by Lamont via voodoo doll. (Of course, the scene abruptly ends *before* we see what form this punishment takes—*that* might have actually been interesting.) Unfortunately (since he seems to be the only cast member who can actually rise above a monotone), VeSota only has this one scene.

Amazingly, the legendary Jack P. Pierce provided the makeup—a colossal waste of talent since, lacking any zombies or horrific scenes whatsoever (not even a solitary burn victim at the rushed and confusingly shot climax), he had little to do except keep the shine off Linda Christian's nose. Pierce had fallen on hard times after his callous dismissal from Universal, where for 25 years he created such memorable creatures as the Frankenstein Monster, the Mummy, and the Wolf Man. Forced to freelance, he basically took whatever job he could get (usually no-budget productions like *Teenage Monster* [1957] and *Giant from the Unknown* [1958])—as evidenced by his involvement on this unworthy project. On *The Devil's Hand*, Pierce was a *looong* way from the remarkable makeup he provided for *White Zombie* (1932).

Though completed in 1959, *The Devil's Hand* wasn't released until 1962; unsurprising, since it is a

Playing the high executioner of the voodoo cult of Gamba, Neil Hamilton subjects one cultist to the ordeal of the hanging wheel.

singularly unremarkable—and unmemorable—production save for the sultry presence of Linda Christian. Instead of a firm grip on horror, *The Devil's Hand* offers only a limp wrist.

CREDITS: Alternate Titles: *Devil's Doll*; *Live to Love*; *The Naked Goddess*; *Witchcraft*; Director: William J. Hole, Jr.; Producer: Alvin K. Bubis; Screenplay: Jo Heims; Director of Photography: Meredith Nicholson; Executive Producer and Production Supervisor: Jack Miles; Associate Producers: Pierre Groleau, Harris Gilbert, Dave Carney; Assistant to the Producer: Carl Carn; Music Director: Manuel Francisco; Compositions and Orchestrations: Allyn Ferguseon and Mischa Terr; Dance Theme: Baker Knight; Special Arrangements: Rene Hall; Film Editor: Howard Epstein; Associate Producer: Rick Newberry; Assistant Director: Raoul Pagel; Second Assistant Director: Bill D'Arcy; Technical Advisors: Richard Glavin, J. Steven Blowner; Art Director: Sherm Lautermilk; Camera Operator: Jack McCoskey; Sound Mixer: Phil Mitchel; Makeup: Jack Pierce; Wardrobe Woman: Marge Corso; Script Supervisor: Frank Remsden; A Bubis-Katz Production; Released in 1962 by Crown International Pictures; 71 minutes

CAST: Linda Christian (Bianca), Robert Alda (Rick), Ariadna Welter (Donna), Neil Hamilton (Francis Lamont), Gene Craft, Jeannie Carmen [Julia Thayer], Julie Scott, Diana Spears, Gertrude Astor, Bruno VeSota, Dick Lee, Jim Knight, Coleen Vico, Roy Wright, Ramona Ravez, Tony Rock

The *Curse of the Voodoo* follows Mike Stacey (Bryant Haliday) to London as demonic visions of Simbaza warriors.

CURSE OF THE VOODOO (1965)

African Sorcery in Regent's Park

"Africa! Where primitive tribes still practice evil
religions which weave a dark web of death
around all who sin against their gods."
—offscreen narrator

After tackling such terrifying topics as body-snatching (*Corridors of Blood*, 1958), bloodsucking astronauts (*First Man Into Space*, 1959), *brain*sucking thought-monsters (*Fiend Without a Face*, 1958), and possessed ventriloquist dolls (*Devil Doll*, 1963), executive producer Richard Gordon felt the time was right to try his hand at voodoo. What resulted was an earnest but rather sluggish low-budget tale of African "black magic" (with London-area woodlands standing in for the Dark Continent).

"We had finished *Devil Doll*, which had turned out pretty well in my opinion," Richard Gordon related to this author about the genesis of the project, "and Ken Rive [head of England's Gala Films], who was my partner in the film, decided we'd like to find

a follow-up vehicle for Bryant Haliday [star of *Devil Doll*]. And it seemed logical to also have Lindsay Shonteff [director of *Devil Doll*] direct it again. So we were looking around for properties and there was a script that was brought to us by a man named Tony O'Grady, who had written it on speculation, called *The Lion Man*. We thought it would make a pretty good vehicle, and that despite the fact the setting of the story was mostly in Africa, we felt it could be done very well in England with a little bit of luck in finding the right locations. So we acquired the rights to it and did some little rewriting on the screenplay to fit the locations we'd selected and went right ahead with it.

"Unfortunately," continued Gordon, "there were a lot of problems because the weather was very bad. When we were shooting on location, which was really Regent's Park near the London Zoo which was simulating the plains of Africa, we ran into continuous rain and there was no cover available immediately. So there were a lot of problems and the picture went somewhat over budget. But eventually it got finished—though it didn't really turn out the way we'd hoped that it would."

In Africa, big-game hunter and safari guide Mike Stacey (Bryant Haliday) breaks taboo by following a wounded lion (the result of his client's inept shooting) into the dreaded Simbaza territory. "The Simbaza," relates colleague Major Lomas (Dennis Price), "are a tribe that worship lions. They also practice a very potent form of black magic." Accompanied only by his loyal native bearer, Saidi (Dennis Alaba Peters), Stacey ultimately kills the wounded beast, but not before receiving a minor mauling in the process.

Later that day, a Simbaza witch doctor (Danny Daniels) and several tribesmen walk into Stacey's camp and symbolically throw a spear into the ground at his feet. Then, on the way back from the safari, Saidi, under the influence of the Simbaza magic, tries to knife Stacey before being fought off by Major Lomas.

When he gets back to his home in Johannesburg, Stacey finds that his wife, Janet (Lisa Daniely), has left him (due to his inattention and heavy drinking), taking his young son and returning to her mother's estate in England. Stacey flies to London to attempt a reconciliation. When Janet stands him up for their meeting, Stacey picks up a woman in a bar (Valli Newby) who takes him back to her place. Once there, he passes out.

Back in Africa, the Simbaza have Saidi stretched out and tied to a pole. They perform some sort of ritual, paint his face with white powder, and stab a spear into his shoulder. At that very moment, Stacey awakens with a stabbing pain in *his* shoulder—the lion-inflicted wound has reopened. Walking through the park on the way back to his hotel, Stacey hears a lion growl and imagines something stalking him through the bushes.

When Janet finally does meet him later that day, Stacey suddenly hears jungle drums and sees a black man (in hat and trenchcoat) staring at him through the door. Pursuing the man, he boards a bus—but the man is not there. Stacey sits down to catch his breath, and when he glances around he sees the man sitting behind him, staring. Stacey turns away, looks again, and the man is gone.

That night Stacey fires off four pistol shots through his hotel room door when he sees the painted face of a Simbaza warrior there. When the police arrive, of course, there's no tribesman, and the inspector looks pointedly at the empty whisky bottle on Stacey's nightstand. The hauntings/hallucinations worsen, for the next day Stacey flees through the park, pursued by two spear-carrying tribesmen. He col-

lapses and we next see him back in his hotel room with a doctor (Ronald Leigh Hunt) in attendance. His wife is also there, for she feels that in his weakened condition he needs her help. The doctor puts Stacey's hallucinations down to "delirium caused by that infected arm."

Three days of treatment and sedation fail to bring the infection and attendant delirium under control. "I've never seen a basically healthy man deteriorate so rapidly," declares the concerned doctor.

Janet goes to see an expert on African tribes and customs (Louis Mahoney), who tells her that the Simbaza penalty for killing a sacred lion would be "a curse, seeking out across continents, hounding and haunting a man no matter where he might hide—the gradual destruction of mind and body and spirit…

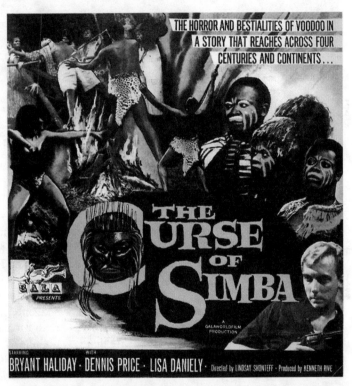

Curse of the Voodoo was titled *The Curse of Simba* in Great Britian. (Photos courtesy Richard Gordon)

Some might call it the psychology of the guilt-ridden; others might call it praying a man to death." Stacey's only hope, he tells her, "is to return to the scene of his crime, seek out the man who cursed him, and slay him."

Janet relates this to her husband and, despite his weakness, he returns to Africa. When he gets to the Simbaza land, Stacey finds the witch doctor and another tribesman beating Saidi. Stacey shoots the tribesman, but the witch doctor runs off into the bush. The two men then play a deadly game of cat-and-

Dancer Beryl Cunningham contributes some vigorous voodoo vibrations to the Simbazas' ceremony.

mouse until Stacey has exhausted his ammunition. Now the hunter becomes the hunted and Stacey makes a run for his Jeep. The tables turn yet again when he reaches the vehicle; Stacey uses the Jeep as a weapon and runs down the witch doctor. "The curse is broken," concludes the narrator as Stacey limps out of the bush with Saidi, "broken as the gods demand—by *death*."

The picture's shooting schedule was four weeks, "but it went over [by one week]," recalled Richard Gordon, "because of the weather and because things had to be reshot, and certain days we couldn't work and we really didn't have any cover prepared." Largely due to these delays, the meager £35,000 budget (less than $100,000) escalated to £50,000 by the time it was completed.

These weather problems can clearly be seen in the finished film. "In fact," Gordon points out, "you can see in the sequence where the two natives are chasing Bryant that it's pouring with rain. And progressively he's getting more and more drenched. It's not as apparent in black and white as it would be in color, but it's definitely there."

It's difficult to dislike *Curse of the Voodoo*, mostly because of its sheer earnestness. It is a deadly serious film with no touch of whimsy or camp about it (unlike so many voodoo pictures—either through intent or accident). The participants play their parts and treat their subject with a grim solemnity (whose somber tone is only enhanced by the gray skies and dark photography)—no doubt due, in part, to the lousy weather and uncomfortable conditions that prevailed during shooting. ("It was the weather that really botched up things and also sort of depressed everybody," recounted Richard Gordon, "because there's nothing worse when you're shooting a film than when you suddenly find yourself in a situation where for one reason or another you have to stand around doing nothing.")

Yet it's also nearly just as difficult to *like Curse of the Voodoo*, for its slow pace and cranky characters possess little appeal. Though he provides an intense yet effectively low-keyed performance, Bryant Haliday makes for a rather unlikable protagonist as the alcoholic, self-pitying Stacey. Humorless and continually scowling, Stacey's condescension and arrogant attitude inspires little sympathy in the viewer—a pathos vital in order to make the "curse" scenario come to life for the audience. When Stacey treats Saidi (the only man possessing enough courage and loyalty to follow him into the taboo territory) with disdain and indifference, or when he sneers, "the Simbaza are just a backwards tribe that would come and carry your bags for two cents a day like all the rest," the viewer comes to think that perhaps this horrible curse is somewhat deserved.

Saidi (Dennis Alba Peters) at the mercy of the lion worshipping voodooists.

Not only does the picture sport seemingly endless scenes of Stacey lying in bed suffering nightmares or of his dysfunctional attempts to reconcile with his wife, director Lindsay Shonteff includes numerous filler sequences that do nothing to advance the story or mood. One such is a long and dull nightclub scene (shot on a cheap and cramped set) in which a native woman (Beryl Cunningham) in bikini top and gold lame hotpants (!) does a silly gyrating dance to a drums and wah-wah trumpet tune, concluding with her lying on the floor and simply bobbing her head up and down for the "big finish." Ridiculous.

Even some of the (disappointingly few) "action" sequences drag on far too long. For instance, the two tribesmen chase Stacey over the well-groomed expanses of Regent's Park for what seems an interminable amount of time. (The image of two half-naked, face-painted, spear-wielding natives pursuing a man wearing a suit and raincoat across a vast well-manicured lawn looks more than slightly ludicrous.) Even worse, the long sequence provides no payoff. Stacey simply collapses on the ground and the film cuts to show him lying in his bed with the doctor in attendance.

Other filler scenes include a drawn-out sequence of "establishing" stock shots showing various neon signs (to let us know we're now in the big city) and lengthy generic airport/airplane-in-flight shots (so we know that we're actually going somewhere).

Brian Fahey's driving musical score, full of blaring horns and pounding drums, doesn't help matters. Such a "rousing" score sounds very out of place here, since *Curse of the Voodoo* is definitely *not* an action-oriented film. The loud music comes on too often and frequently destroys the mood of a scene (even during Stacey's Lewtonesque walk home through the park, trumpets blare and the music marches on [1]).

Fortunately, the film is saved by its effective cast, whose solid, no-nonsense playing ground the events in reality and bring the various characters to life (if not quite to likability). Though playing a rather cold fish, Bryant Haliday brings an intense assuredness to the role of Stacey that adds efficacy and (some) poignancy to the plight of a man bedeviled by forces beyond his control.

Bryant Haliday originally had no designs on the entertainment industry, having first studied for the priesthood (even winning several scholastic prizes in theology) and then international law at Harvard (at the same time John F. Kennedy was a student there). After working as a teacher of Latin and Greek, he was bit by the acting bug and helped form the prestigious Brattle Theater Company in Cambridge, Massachusetts as well as ultimately co-founding Janus

The Simbaza utilizes Saidi (Dennis Alaba Peters) as a living voodoo doll to inflict their *Curse of the Voodoo* on big-game hunter Mike Stacey.

Films, which distributed many foreign movies (such as the early work of Ingmar Bergman). While on a business trip in France, Haliday was asked by a French producer to star in a gangster film. This began a long association with French cinema and television (Haliday speaks fluent French), resulting in his permanent relocation to Paris.

Gordon met him through his association with Janus. "One time when we were at the Cannes Film Festival together," recalled the producer, "I saw two films that he made in France, both of which he had villainous, sinister roles, and I was very impressed with what he did. He always wanted to do an English- speaking film and he hadn't done any. I thought physically he was very much the type for *Devil Doll* and I think it worked out very well. I did four films with him altogether. After *Devil Doll* and *Curse of the Voodoo*, we did *The Projected Man*, which I thought he also did very well. And then we did *Tower of Evil*, which wasn't really what I would call a Bryant Haliday role, but I wanted to fit him in because I wanted to work with him again."

Retired and living in Paris, Haliday died in 1996. "The four films he made with me," continued Gordon, "were his only English-speaking films. He did, over the years, quite a lot of television in France. He was completely bilingual and spoke French as well as he speaks English. He liked working in France. He did English dubbing for French films and television series that were coming to the United States. He also dubbed his own voice in French for the French-dubbed versions of *Projected Man* and *Tower of Evil*."

Though he only made four English-language pictures, Haliday always had a particular "dream part" in mind. "He always wanted to play in a remake of *The Most Dangerous Game*," recalled Gordon. "He saw himself very much as Count Zaroff, the Leslie Banks role." It's a pity that Gordon was never able to bring this proposed project together, for Haliday would have been ideal as the calculating, half-mad hunter.

Allied Artists misspelled Haliday's name (as Halliday) on the American prints. Fortunately, Mr. Haliday didn't notice. "I don't think he ever knew it," stated Gordon. Lisa Daniely suffered the same fate (a superfluous "l").

Dennis Price, as Stacey's friend and colleague Major Lomas, lends credence to the proceedings with his naturalness and sincerity. He tosses off lines like, "the Simbaza believe that the lion is a god and that anyone who kills one is instantly avenged," with such casual aplomb that the viewer has little doubt that he knows of what he speaks.

"We had Dennis Price," enthused Gordon, "who then was still in good health and able to undertake a role at that time. He was always a pleasure to work with. He had a great sense of humor, a very very nice man. Unfortunately he ruined his career with drinking. He was one of the big stars at the Rank Studios and they were building him up, and his career deteriorated because he had a drinking problem. At the time I had him in *Tower of Evil* [1972] and *Horror Hospital* [1973], he was only taking cameo roles because he couldn't sustain a full-length role in a feature film any longer."

Shonteff and company occasionally had to adjust their schedule to accommodate the alcoholic Price. "There was always a problem keeping an eye on him and shooting when he was at his best rather than late in the day," recalled Gordon. "He wasn't drinking to the point where he'd show up drunk on the set, but he liked to drink at lunch time and he—wouldn't be at his best, let's put it that way." Price's penchant for tippling, however, never caused any major problems, explained Gordon. "It was just a matter of being aware of the fact. He really had a *cameo* role; he's not in the major bulk of the picture. It was an easy situation to handle."

Often a suave leading man or an aristocratic villain in British films of the 1940s and 1950s, Price's age and drinking relegated him to briefer and briefer roles (frequently in low-budget horror movies) in the 1960s and 1970s. Among his many genre ventures are *Witchcraft* (1964), *The Earth Dies Screaming* (1964), *Venus in Furs* (1969) and *Vampyros Lesbos* (1970; two horror/sex films from the notorious Jesus Franco), *The Horror of Frankenstein* (1970), *Twins of Evil* (1971), and *Theater of Blood* (1973). Price died in 1973 at the age of 58.

Though given the rather thankless role of Stacey's estranged wife, Lisa Daniely's sincerity adds substance to the poorly-drawn character. "Lisa Daniely had a very big success in England in a film called *Lilli Marlene*," recalled Richard Gordon about why they hired her for the role. "She did a lot of pictures. Mostly she was the leading lady in second features or a supporting player in bigger pictures. She had quite a long career and was well-known in England."

Though Ms. Daniely was subsequently quite active on British television and has remained so in the theater as well, her career never really flourished. As of this writing, she currently works in a bookshop in north London. Her most recent theatrical venture, a one-woman show called *Snakes About Her Cradle*, presented in Edinburgh, "was not a success" (in the words of the play's director, David McGillivray). According to Daniely's latest bio, "she has recently recorded a video on *The Joy of Sex*. She gets to keep her clothes on."

Ms. Daniely has seemingly disavowed her film work, claiming not to remember anything about it. "Money" was her terse reply when asked what attracted her to *Curse of the Voodoo* and "crap" her evaluation of it.

Visually, *Curse of the Voodoo* looks like all of its (meager) production dollars ended up on the screen, thanks in no small part to the clever use of some impressive stock footage. "We got some pretty good black and white stock footage to pump up the African scenes," remembered Richard Gordon. Indeed they did, and the well-integrated shots of African animals add a bit of verisimilitude lacking in the closer jungle scenes (with English forests standing in for the African bush).

Though pacing was obviously not his strong suit, director Lindsay Shonteff, with the aid of cinematographer Gerald Gibbs (who lensed such early Hammer sci-fi entries as *X—the Unknown* and [the over-rated] *Enemy from Space*, as well as Bryant Haliday's earlier feature, *Devil Doll*), does manage to create some effective scenes.

The sequence in which Stacey stalks the wounded lion, for instance, is a marvel of creative staging, camerawork, and editing. When the (stock footage) lion charges him, the film cuts to a shot of the camera rushing through the brush in a lion's-eye-view shot. Then, in quick cuts, Stacey raises his rifle, the camera seemingly leaps upon his chest, and we see a momentary extreme close-up of the beast's face. This ingenious sequence displays how inventive individuals can overcome a lack of money to create an exciting something out of nothing. (Too bad these occasionally effective moments are buried under a morass of drawn-out *in*effective ones.)

Voodoo-wise, this *Curse* proves disappointing. Despite the voodoo curse theme running like a thread throughout the film's tapestry, too many side-pockets filled with scenes involving Stacey's dysfunctional marriage clutter up this cinematic vestment. "I thought the voodoo scenes probably worked better than anything else in the picture," opined Gordon. "And I wished we'd devoted more time to the whole idea of the voodoo and less to some of the other things. Because the picture is sort of slow and it has a number of dead spots where you're really waiting for something more interesting to happen. I wished we'd had more voodoo-type footage. If it hadn't gone over budget to begin with, we might have decided to shoot some additional stuff. As it was, the finances were already rather strained."

Unfortunately, even the "voodoo-type footage" is not all that impressive, consisting primarily of shots of a few natives, their faces painted with streaks of white, yelling and beating on drums. Apart from sticking a spear into Saidi's shoulder (discretely offscreen, of course), these voodooists do little except examine their trussed-up captive from time to time. The scenario does include one full-blown ceremonial sequence, however; shots of which are interspersed throughout the film. Sadly, even this proves rather lackluster, as a half-dozen dressed-down natives shake spears and beat on drums while a woman (Beryl Cunningham again) dances about. It serves little purpose except to provide some much-needed activity in the rather plodding plot.

Bryant Haliday recalled (to *Midnight Marquee*'s John R. Duvoli) the delays caused by the grueling weather, and how crew members began bringing liquor to the location shoot in an effort to keep warm (at least on the inside). After a time, the (now thoroughly "warm") native dancers got a little too lively, causing some concern when they "really started getting into the spirit, as it were, and waving their spears around."

In hiring actors to play the voodoo-practicing natives, Richard Gordon inadvertently added a dose of near-authenticity: "They were actually mostly West Indians, Jamaicans, from the West Indies, Barbados."

Curse of the Voodoo contains one particularly intriguing (and original) voodoo variation—the idea of one man becoming a living voodoo doll (the Simbaza using their magic to somehow link Saidi to Stacey so that when they stab Saidi's shoulder, it re-opens Stacey's own wound). The script makes little use of this unique device, for the Simbaza do nothing further with Saidi besides periodically turning his face from side to side to make sure their captive is still alive.

Originally announced as *The Lion Man* (the script's original title), the film became *Curse of Simba* in the U.K. and *Curse of the Voodoo* in the U.S., where it was double-billed with *Frankenstein Meets the Spacemonster*. The American distributor, Allied Art-

Curse of the Voodoo executive producer Kenneth Rive, director Lindsay Shonteff, actress Lisa Daniely, executive producer Richard Gordon, and actor Dennis Price.

"Rino" was wrong in at least one case, however, for *Castle of Frankenstein*'s editor (and avowed horror-suspense patron) Calvin T. Beck felt that this "trim, crisp little voodoo chiller gives freshness to familiar idea of hunter haunted by jungle curse after killing sacred lion. Imaginatively made in restrained Val Lewton tradition, with excellent photography and many fine sequences. Well acted by Bryant Halliday, Lisa Daniely, Dennis Price, Ronald Leigh-Hunt."

[1] According to Richard Gordon, this low-key, fear-of-the-unseen approach was purely intentional. "The idea was to do a kind of Val Lewton type of picture," related Gordon. "We had hoped that the sequence when he hears the lion roaring and it turns out to be from the zoo would play a little bit like the *Cat People* sequence and things like that." Hope springs eternal.

ists, decided that the original title of *Curse of Simba* wouldn't sell well as a horror picture and so changed the moniker to make no mistake about the voodoo element. "They felt that going along with *Frankenstein Meets the Spacemonster* and voodoo would make a good double-bill," recalled Gordon. (In England the picture was trimmed by 10 minutes in order to fit the distributor's need for a shorter supporting feature. Consequently, the retitled American version is the more complete—dare I say—director's cut.)

Too weak a picture to stand on its own or topline a double-bill, *Curse of the Voodoo* made fortunes for no one. "Over a period of time it was financially successful because of television and video but not really on its initial release," admitted Gordon. "Yes, it did all right because it was such a low-budget film, but it didn't lend itself to being exploited separately—like *Devil Doll* which we released as a single feature in the United States and did extremely well with."

Gordon has no illusions about the film's quality. "In terms of how it turned out as opposed to the original concept I would say it was my least favorite of the pictures I worked on." Still, though rather somber and leaning toward the dull side, *Curse of the Voodoo* stands as an offbeat, occasionally intriguing entry for the fan of voodoo cinema.

Curse of the Voodoo was also the "least favorite" of the critics. Typical was *Variety*'s "Rino" calling it a "substandard programmer" possessing "few real horror or suspense jolts, a cliché story, and only occasional action… For horror-suspense patrons, this kind of mild fare has low lure."

CREDITS: Alternate Titles: *Curse of Simba* (British); *Voodoo Blood Death*; Director: Lindsay Shonteff; Executive Producers: Kenneth Rive, Richard Gordon (uncredited); In Charge of Production: Fred Slark; Screenplay: Tony O'Grady; Additional Scenes and Dialogue: Leigh Vance; Photography: Gerald Gibbs; Music Composed and Conducted by: Brian Fahey; Nightclub Music by: The Bobby Breen Quintet; Art Director: Tony Inglis; Editor: Barrie Vince; Camera Operator: Brian Elvin; Assistant Director: Bill Snaith; Sound Recordist: Jock May; Casting Director: Ronnie Curtis; Makeup: Gerry Fletcher; Wardrobe: Mary Gibson; A British Galaworldfilm and Gordon Films production released by Allied Artists in December 1965; 82 minutes (66 minutes for the British print)

CAST: Bryant Haliday (Mike Stacey), Dennis Price (Major Lomas), Lisa Daniely (Janet Stacey), Ronald Leigh Hunt (Doctor), Mary Kerridge (Janet's Mother), John Witty (Police Inspector), Jean Lodge (Mrs. Lomas), Beryl Cunningham (Night Club Dancer), Danny Daniels (Simbaza), Dennis Alaba Peters (Saidi), Tony Thawnton (Radlett), Michael Nightingale (Second Hunter), Louis Mahoney (African Expert), Valli Newby (Girl in Bar), Andy Myers (Tommy Stacey), Jimmy Felgate (Barman), Nigel Feyisetan (Simbaza in London), Bobby Breen Quintet (Night Club Band)

DR. TERROR'S HOUSE OF HORRORS (1965)

Voodoo Anthologized

"Do not jest at the image of
a god, the powerful and
malign god of voodoo!"
—Thomas Baptiste as the
voodoo priest

"I had always admired *Dead of Night* (1945)," stated producer/screenwriter Milton Subotsky in *Little Shoppe of Horrors*, "and thought the time was ripe for another film like it." Indeed, *Dr. Terror's House of Horrors* proved to be the first (though not the best) in a long line of Amicus anthology films which included *Torture Garden* (1967; also directed by Freddie Francis), *The House that Dripped Blood* (1971), *Tales from the Crypt* (1972; written by Subotsky and directed by Francis), *Asylum* (1972), *The Vault of Horror* (1973; again scripted by Subotsky), and *From Beyond the Grave* (1973). Headed by Subotsky and his partner Max J. Rosenberg, Amicus

The German pressbook for *Dr. Terror's House of Horrors*. (Courtesy Eric Hoffman)

(whose company name originated because, "we just tried to think of something nice, and 'Amicus' means 'friendly'") proved to be Hammer's biggest competitor in the British horror arena.

Amicus' first anthology feature was originally going to be shot in 1962 with financial backing from Columbia Pictures. Unfortunately, a little matter of £4,000 derailed the project for over two years. "I had a deal with Columbia to do *Dr. Terror's House of Horrors*," related Subotsky to *Midnight Marquee*'s John R. Duvoli. "The budget was £90,000 in black and white. So, they had the chap who checks out the budgets for the Hammer films check out our budget. After going through the budget he said, 'No, it'll cost you £94,000' and Columbia dropped the deal!"

It took another two years to obtain alternate financing for the (now-color) project, and even after production finally got underway, the difficult dollar (or, more accurately, problematic pound) reared its ugly head yet again. "Max [Rosenberg] had a dreadful time obtaining financing," reported Subtosky in Deborah Del Vecchio and Tom Johnson's book *Peter Cushing: The Gentle Man of Horror and His 91 Films*, "and we nearly stopped shooting the film after the first two weeks. Our British co-financier, Joe Vegoda, came to the rescue with additional investment after part of the American financing was withdrawn." As a result of this temporary set-back, Rosenberg (the money man in the Amicus Rosenberg-Subotsky partnership) had to scramble for cash. "I was three weeks into shooting," remembered Subotsky (in *Midnight Marquee*), "before we got the money. I would go to the cast and crew and say 'Look, the money is coming through. What do you need to live on?' I paid the rest off later." ("[Subotsky and Rosenberg] were never able to raise the proper amount of money for their films," complained frequent Amicus director Freddie Francis to this author, adding with a laugh, "but they were good guys and I liked the films we made anyway.")

Dr. Terror's House of Horrors relates five tales of the supernatural, tying the disparate stories together via Dr. Schreck (Peter Cushing), a mysterious "doctor of metaphysics" who, with a deck of tarot cards

"The god Damballah is a jealous god," the voodoo priest tells trumpeter Biff Baily (Roy Castle) who's been cribbing the voodooists' sacred ceremonial music. "If you steal from him, he will be revenged."

("I call it my House of Horrors" he says with a twinkle), tells the futures of the five men sharing his train compartment. "There is within each of us a twin destiny," explains Schreck, "the natural and the supernatural. The cards are attracted to the supernatural part of our destiny as one pole of a magnet attracts an opposite part." (Subotsky had originally written the five stories back in 1948 as scripts for a planned TV series that never materialized. He later dusted them off and added the clever wrap-around involving Dr. Schreck and his five ill-fated travel companions.)

The first story, entitled "Werewolf," is a rather muddled lycanthrope tale (complete with poorly lit manor house, skulking servants, and easily whipped-up clip of silver bullets), while the second yarn, called "Creeping Vine," has an intelligent mobile plant inexplicably cut phone wires, put out fires, strangle people, and trap a family inside their house.

The third tale is named "Voodoo" (which, according to some sources, is a thinly disguised, uncredited version of Cornell Woolrich's story "Papa Benjamin"). A London jazz band headed by fun-loving trumpeter Biff Baily (Roy Castle) gets a gig at a nightclub in the West Indies. On his first night in the islands, Biff notices that everyone at the club wears voodoo amulets and rings. "Voodoo is the one thing you don't mess with around here," warns singer Sammy Coin (Kenny Lynch). Later Biff sneaks out into the jungle

to witness the "frenzied dancing" of a secret voodoo ceremony. Captivated by the rhythmic drumbeats, Baily steals the "sacred music of the great god Damballah." Despite dire warnings from the imposing voodoo priest ("The god Damballah is a *jealous* god; if you steal from him he will be revenged!"), Biff incorporates the sacred tune into a jazz arrangement. Back in London, Biff and his band perform the voodoo number in his old club. As they play, a mysterious wind rises up *inside* the nightclub, scattering tables and chairs and sending the patrons scurrying for the exits. Despite this supernatural warning, Biff is still not convinced of voodoo's power and decides to take the arrangement home to rework it. After a rather harrowing walk through the deserted, windy streets, Biff arrives at his flat. There windows and doors slam shut, the lights go out, and he's confronted by a huge black man wearing menacing face paint— Damballah's messenger (or the deity himself?). The figure advances and extends his hands toward the terrified Biff's throat. Biff faints and the intruder simply reaches into the musician's jacket pocket and retrieves the sacred music. With Biff lying prone on the floor, the door opens of its own accord and the apparition exits.

The fourth (and best) segment has pompous art critic Franklin Marsh (Christopher Lee) humiliated by artist Eric Landor (Michael Gough). The spiteful

critic then runs over Landor with his car, causing the artist to lose his hand. After the despondent Landor commits suicide, his disembodied hand haunts Marsh, leading to the critic's demise in a bit of poetic justice.

In the fifth and final story, Donald Sutherland plays a small-town doctor whose new French bride turns out to be a vampire.

As the *piece de resistance*, the film ends with the train pulling into the station. Schreck has disappeared and the platform is dark and deserted. A newspaper wafts down to the confused travelers which reads "5 dead in train wreck." They see the figure of Dr. Schreck across the platform, but his gaunt bearded countenance has transformed into that of a grinning skull. The Grim Reaper leads his five "guests" away.

"I like anthology films," opined Subotsky in *Fangoria* magazine, "because I feel that in SF and horror the short story format works better than either the novel or novelette." Subotsky's preference notwithstanding, the down-side of the anthology format is that there's very little time to develop characters or build and sustain mood—two key components in successful horror films. It's very difficult to fashion a believable milieu or create intriguing characters in less than half-an-hour. When given only about 15 minutes (as with all but one of *Dr. Terror's* segments), it's

nearly impossible. The five stories plus the rather lengthy wrap-around in *Dr. Terror's* allows for very little build-up in any of the segments, so that the tales' bizarre events seem to spring out of nowhere. The fantastical notions are too abrupt as characters seemingly take these unlikely happenings as a matter of course (since there's no *time* for any doubt), allowing for no real credibility.

Fortunately, Subotsky and Rosenberg gathered together a cadre of fine actors who, in an exceedingly brief time, managed to invest some realism in their often stereotypical roles. Peter Cushing, Christopher Lee, Michael Gough, Neil McCallum, and Donald Sutherland in particular all bring a believable quality to the unbelievable situations.

At 25 minutes, "Voodoo" is by far the longest of the five segments in the film. As such, there's (slightly) more room for character development and build-up. Unfortunately, the extra time is eaten up by musical numbers. While the club scenes are well-mounted and the tunes admittedly catchy, they add little to the story or ambiance (supernatural wind sequence excepted).

In talking of his various anthology movies, director Freddie Francis explained that "my approach to these films is that no one is really going to believe

While "Voodoo" is this anthology film's longest segment, it's not the best. That honor goes to the "Disembodied Hand" vignette starring Michael Gough (left) and Christopher Lee.

that these sort of things happen… so I believe that though people may find it horrid for a while, they find it horrid in a *giggly* sort of way."

Of all the segments, "Voodoo" possesses the most of this "giggly" quality. Unfortunately, the mix of humor and horror doesn't sit easily here. Roy Castle's likable but goofy demeanor (complete with cavalier quips and amusing pratfalls) make it clear that the voodoo issue is a less-than-weighty matter. ("To my mind," admitted Francis, "it was a *fun* thing, obviously not to be taken seriously.") The fact that Damballah's "revenge" consists of nothing more than frightening Biff into fainting only bears this out. (This also results in a rather unsatisfying ending which, in effect, pulls Damballah's teeth by making him all bluster—*literally*, when one considers the supernatural winds—and no bite.)

The frequent Bob Hope-style asides reinforce this notion. Consequently, the scare factor becomes negligible (even during Biff's Lewtonesque walk of terror, he takes a pratfall over some garbage cans). Some of these quips *are* funny, however, thanks to Roy Castle's amiable attitude and low-key delivery. When the forbidding voodoo priest tells Biff that "[The music] belongs to the god Damballah, known only to his own people for centuries—" Biff happily inter-

rupts with "Oh well, if it's that old it's out of copyright."

Just before the band performs their new voodoo number back in London, singer Sammy Coin and Biff have this exchange:

> Sammy: "You still gonna do that voodoo thing, man?"
> Biff: "Sure, why not."
> Sammy: "I'll tell you one thing, you've got guts. We'll probably see 'em before the night's out—spread *all over* the floor."
> Biff: "They'll eat anything here."

The physical humor often proves effective as well. When warned by Sammy about stealing the voodoo tune, Biff scoffs, "What can a voodoo god do to me?"— just before the second-story railing he's leaning on gives way, unceremoniously dumping him into the fountain below.

Dr. Terror's was entertainer/singer Roy Castle's third film. The next year Castle appeared opposite Peter Cushing again in another Amicus production, *Dr. Who and Daleks* (1966), and yet again in 1975's *Legend of the Werewolf* (also directed by Freddie

128

Francis). "I quite enjoyed *Dr. Terror*'s," reported Francis in Wheeler Winston Dixon's *The Films of Freddie Francis*, "because I knew I could get various friends of mine for it, such as Roy Castle. He longed to be an actor." According to Francis, "Roy can play any instrument—he's multitalented—but he wasn't playing the trumpet in this film because it was prerecorded."

"Roy was a lovely guy," added Francis when interviewed by this author. "We became great friends; in fact, he became my daughter's godfather." About Castle's performance Francis remarked, "He's very good, a very funny guy."

On the plus side, the voodoo dance ceremony proves more visually exciting than most (thanks to effective staging by Francis and cinematographer Alan Hume, along with some energetic choreography by Boscoe Holder). In the flickering firelight the dancers whirl and twist frenetically to the rapid drumbeats and staccato chanting. One dancer even appears to be possessed by a loa, falling and writhing on the ground in a nod to authenticity not often found in voodoo movies. Low-angle shots of the participants' legs intercut with close-ups of faces and overhead shots of their frenzied motion give the scene an effective kinetic energy.

The voodoo priest (Thomas Baptiste) doesn't fare quite so well, however. "You wrote down the sacred music of the great god Damballah," thunders the forbidding bald-headed houngan, who then lets go with an angry growl that's an uncanny impersonation of Karloff's Frankenstein Monster—an amusing rather than frightening effect. Also, during the tense exchange the voodoo priest's voice seems to emanate from inside an echo chamber—a distracting and unconvincing technical touch.

So while "Voodoo" remains a musically and comedically effective segment (with the added bonus of a more energetic and authentic-looking voodoo ceremony than most), it fails to generate any real scares by undercutting its potential.

Of the four other segments, only the "Disembodied Hand" episode really works well. "Werewolf" is rather dull (not to mention poorly lit), while the "Creeping Vine" remains ridiculously unconvincing (it's tough to make a plant menacing—triffids included) with a poor build-up leading to a weak (anti)climax.

Despite the ever-quirky presence of a young Donald Sutherland (in only his third film), "Vampire" also fails to satisfy thanks to its perfunctory plotting and all-too-ready staking (though it does possess an unexpected and effectively amusing final twist).

Fortunately, the film's wrap-around is a creepy, suspenseful, well-constructed story unto itself, with the passengers becoming more and more uneasy as Dr. Schreck relates their horrific fates one by one. Of the omnibus format, director Freddie Francis opined, "The only thing one has to do is to make sure you have a good link. And I think the link has to be able to stand on its own. I think the link we had with Peter Cushing in *Dr. Terror* was one of the best." Indeed it was.

"I believe you make pictures in two places: in the script and in the cutting room," opined Milton Subotsky in *Midnight Marquee*. "What happens in between isn't always that important." This rather reactionary (and unrealistic) *anti*-auteur theory rises from Subotsky's own background in filmmaking, since he worked both as an editor (of Army training films) and screenwriter. By his own account, Subotsky himself often recuts the films he produces (usually

Peter Cushing as the mysterious Dr. Schreck (Dr. Terror) in *Dr. Terror's House of Horrors*. (Courtesy Lynn Naron)

"saving" them, according to the immodest writer/producer/editor).

"If Milton was walking down the street and saw two pieces of film on the ground," laughed Freddie Francis, "he'd pick them up and try to join them together! Milton always used to like being in the cutting room, so I used to have to shoot the film in such a way that Milton couldn't touch it."

For the film's director, Subotsky made a fortunate choice in Hammer veteran Freddie Francis, who

Dr. Terror's House of Horrors **features one of voodoo cinema's more effectively staged dance ceremonials.**

(Subotsky's postulations aside) made "what happened in between" *very* important. "I was looking around for a good horror director," recalled Subotsky to *Filmfax*'s Dennis Fischer. "I saw some of Freddie's work for Hammer, and particularly liked his black-and-white films, not the color films he made later. He did three in black-and-white (*Paranoiac, Nightmare,* and *Hysteria*) and they were nicely done. So I thought yes, Freddie Francis will do. I was looking for a cinematic director really."

Francis, an Academy Award-winning cinematographer-turned-director, brought a strong visual sense to *Dr. Terror's*. He turns Biff Baily's walk home, for instance, into a frightening Val Lewton-style excursion that highlights the fear of the unknown. As Biff scurries nervously through the dark windy streets, a phone booth door suddenly swings open, startling both Biff and the viewer. Then, as he grows more and more afraid, a car abruptly enters the camera frame and squeals to a stop just in front of him. Fisher deftly handles these Lewton "buses" to generate maximum unease. Too bad Francis also includes a comical trip over some garbage cans that serves to partially dispel the mood: Val Lewton meets the Three Stooges. (Despite its "Lewtonesque" tone, this sequence was definitely *not* an intentional Lewton homage, for the director admitted that he'd never even *seen* a Lewton film.)

Dr. Terror's House of Horrors did very well for Amicus, resulting in a long string of subsequent hor-

ror anthologies. As well as scoring at the box office, the picture garnered some fairly favorable reviews. *Variety* (March 3, 1965) stated, "Five short horror episodes, thinly linked, provide a usefully chilly package deal which will offer audiences several mild shudders and quite a lot of amusement… The cast… sensibly play it straight… The film has good production values and several imaginative directing touches."

The New York Herald Tribune's Robert Salmaggi remarked (June 17, 1965), "that each scary adventure will keep you watching, sitting on the edge of your seats one second, laughing the next (there are some deft touches of humor) and all in all, nicely entertained."

Ann Guarino of *The New York Daily News* (June 19, 1965) enthused, "Horror fans are in for a treat in the English Technicolor production of *Dr. Terror's House of Horrors*… Skillful direction by Freddie Francis keeps suspense high throughout and though the stories are only predictions, the results are scary. Acting is tops."

The Monthly Film Bulletin's reviewer, however, singled out the "Voodoo" episode as the lamest of the lot, feeling the film "lapses into crudity in the weakest, Voodoo story, with too many brash comedy asides from Roy Castle and others. Yet four of the stories are undeniably compulsive, thanks to ironic variations played on familiar routines, and to several strong performances." Alexander Walker of the *Evening Standard* also complained about the ill-placed comedy:

"The mood is horror-comic, and the film would be all right if it showed it realized this. But too many of the laughs come in the wrong places."

Dr. Terror's has stood the test of time (and criticism), since most recent assessments come out on the positive side. *Fangoria's* Dr. Cyclops felt that, "Although the plots of the episodes are mostly familiar, Freddie Francis' strong direction makes the most of the stories' well-timed twists. Next to *Asylum*, this may be Subotsky's best anthology." In *Peter Cushing*, Del Vecchio and Johnson felt that it was "rich in atmosphere" and proclaimed it "a very well-produced film on all levels and cast performances were uniformly good." Author Mark Miller (in *Christopher Lee and Peter Cushing and Horror Cinema*) called it "solidly entertaining," while The Phantom of the Movies labeled it a "fun fright anthology" worth three (out of a possible four) stars. Even Leonard Maltin used terms like "intelligent episodic thriller" and "enjoyable horror-fantasy" in his *Movie and Video Guide 1995 Edition*.

Dr. Terror's is Milton Subotsky's personal favorite of all the horror/fantasy films he's produced. "It had a lot of variety," said the filmmaker. "It had a nice little musical story in the middle of it with four musical numbers, and the last story, the vampire story, was very funny."

Thanks to a clever connecting device, the superbly acted and genuinely scary "Disembodied Hand" segment, and (to a lesser extent) the flawed but still entertaining "Voodoo" story, *Dr. Terror's House of Horrors* remains a fairly solid entry in the notoriously uneven anthology subset.

NOTE: The Amicus film should not be confused with the 1943 road show pastiche similarly titled *Dr. Terror's House of Horrors*, which consisted of scenes lifted from *Vampyr* (1932), *White Zombie* (1932), *The Golem* (1936), and others. Also, the discriminating viewer should definitely steer clear of yet another anthology film, released only two years after Amicus' *Dr. Terror's*, called *Dr. Terror's **Gallery** of Horrors*, an execrable, amateurish production that somehow wrangled the services of both Lon Chaney, Jr., and John Carradine. *Caveat Emptor.*

CREDITS: Director: Freddie Francis; Producers: Milton Subotsky and Max J. Rosenberg; Screenplay: Milton Subotsky; Photography: Alan Hume; Production Manager: Ted Wallis; Art Director: Bill Constable; Film Editor: Thelma Connell; Special Effects: Ted Samuels; Assistant Director: Bert Batt; Camera Operator: Godfrey Godar; Sound Recordist: Buster Ambler; Continuity: Pauline Harlow; Dubbing Editor: Roy Hyde; Makeup: Roy Ashton; Hairdresser: Frieda Steiger; Wardrobe Supervisor: Bridget Sellers; Director of Sound: John Cox; Music Composed by:

Plagued by a vengeful disembodied hand, Christopher Lee tries to send the marauding member (neatly boxed and wrapped) to a watery grave.

Elizabeth Lutyens; Conducted by: Philip Martell; Songs by: Kenny Lynch; Jazz Music: Tubby Hayes; Choreography: Boscoe Holder; A British production released March 1965 (U.S.), February 1965 (U.K.) by Amicus; 98 minutes

CAST: "WEREWOLF": Neil McCallum (Jim Dawson), Ursula Howells (Deirdre), Peter Madden (Caleb), Katy Wild (Valda), Tauros (Werewolf); "CREEPING VINE": Bernard Lee (Hopkins), Jeremy Kemp (Drake), Alan Freeman (Bill Rogers), Ann Bell (Ann Rogers), Sarah Nicholls (Carol Rogers); "VOODOO": Roy Castle (Biff Bailey), Kenny Lynch (Sammy Coin), Harold Lang (Shine), Thomas Baptiste (Dambala [sic]), Tubby Hayes Quintet (Bailey's Band), Russ Henderson Steel Band (Themselves); "DISEMBODIED HAND": Christopher Lee (Franklyn Marsh), Michael Gough (Eric Landor), Isla Blair (Pretty Girl), Judy Cornwell (Nurse), Faith Kent (Lady in Art Gallery), Frank Forsyth (Toastmaster), James (Simian Artist); "VAMPIRE": Donald Sutherland (Dr. Bob Carroll), Max Adrian (Dr. Blake), Jennifer Jayne (Nicolle Carroll), Irene Richmond (Mrs. Ellis), Frank Berry (Johnny Ellis); "DR. TERROR": Peter Cushing (Dr. Schreck)

In *The Plague of the Zombies* corpses rise from their graves in what is perhaps the most chilling moment in any Hammer horror.

THE PLAGUE OF THE ZOMBIES (1966)
Voodoo Hammered Home

"I find all types of witchcraft slightly
nauseating, and this [voodoo]
I find absolutely *disgusting*!"
—Andre Morell as Sir James Forbes

When someone mentions Hammer movies, one's thoughts naturally turn to monsters. In the annals of Hammer horror, the classic figures of Frankenstein and Dracula loom large. With seven entries each (not to mention a passel of vampire variations, including the Karnstein trilogy), these two figures have proved to be the monstrous cornerstones of Britain's Hammer Films. But these were not the only film franchises staked out by the studio. Hammer continued in its "series" mentality with the Mummy theme (four features to its bandaged credit), a prehistoric subset (consisting of *One Million Years B.C.* [1966], *When Dinosaurs Ruled the Earth* [1970], and *Creatures the World Forgot* [1971]), the Quatermass triad, and innumerable post-*Psycho* "psychological thrillers" (such as *Taste of Fear* [1961], *Maniac* [1963], *Nightmare* [1964], ad infinitim, ad nauseam). Hammer was nothing if not repetitious.

Over the years, however, the studio occasionally left off beating their stable of (un)dead horses to venture outside the fiscal safety of its popular monster corral. Unique one-shot productions such as *The Abominable Snowman* (1957), *The Devil Rides Out* (1968), and *Countess Dracula* (1970; a "Dracula" in name only) are worthy efforts that have largely been overshadowed by the studio's various series, remakes, and clusterings. Among Hammer's originals are the two "Cornwall Classics" (as some devotees have overzealously labeled them), *The Reptile* and *The Plague of the Zombies*. The two were filmed back-to-back (*Plague* first and then, with only a week's break, *The Reptile*) utilizing many of the same sets and much of the same personnel (both in front of and behind the camera). Though similarly themed (exotic foreign deviltry invades a rural English village to spawn monsters that decimate the xenophobic locals), the two pictures are miles apart in efficacy. *The Reptile* is a slow-moving, predictable, sleep-inducing misfire while *The Plague of the Zombies* stands as a visually exciting, occasionally frightening, and thoroughly entertaining horror yarn.

In turn-of-the-century England, medical professor Sir James Forbes (Andre Morell) receives a distressing letter from his former pupil, Dr. Peter Tompson (Brook Williams), whose Cornish village has been "beset by a mysterious and fatal malady." Accompanied by his daughter Sylvia (Diane Clare), Sir James journeys to the remote hamlet to see if he can help.

Upon arriving, they find the young doctor in a despondent state, for he has been unable to diagnose, much less stop, the rash of unexplained wasting deaths that have plagued the village over the last year. To make matters worse, Peter's wife, Alice (Jacqueline Pearce), is exhibiting some of the fatal symptoms herself. The local squire and magistrate, Clive Hamilton (John Carson), has not allowed Peter to perform any postmortems, so Sir John and Peter determine to turn grave-robber in order to examine the latest victim.

That night, Sylvia sees Alice leave the house and follows her through the woods past an old tin mine. In the forest, however, Sylvia is accosted by a band of aristocratic ruffians who spirit her away to the Squire's manor house, intent upon a bit of "sport" at her expense. Their fun (and Sylvia's terror) is interrupted by the appearance of Squire Hamilton, who orders the brutal young hedonists away. Sylvia rebuffs Hamilton's conciliatory gestures, however, and insists on making her own way home. As she passes the tin mine, she's confronted by a horrible sight—a grinning corpse holding Alice's dead body. When the creature dumps Alice's cadaver at her feet, Sylvia flees in terror.

Meanwhile, the doctors have discovered that the latest victim's coffin is empty. This fact, along with Sylvia's story, induces Sir James to spend the afternoon reading books on voodoo in the vicar's library. That night, Sir James, Peter, and the vicar (Roy Royston) keep a vigil at the recently buried Alice's graveside. When she rises as a zombie, Sir James cuts off her head with a shovel. At this, Peter faints and dreams that all the dead of the cemetery rise up and attack him.

Squire Hamilton pays a visit to Sylvia to once again apologize for the actions of his underlings and to express his condolences over the death of her friend, Alice. He contrives to cut Alice's finger when he clumsily drops a glass, and then surreptitiously secrets a few drops of her blood in a vial. Alice had been wearing a bandage to cover a cut—just before she had died...

Learning that Hamilton had spent time in Haiti and had been the last one to see the latest victim alive, Sir James connects the aristocrat with the zombies. He goes to the Squire's manor and confronts the man,

133

Alice's decapitated zombie corpse during the frightful dream sequence from *The Plague of the Zombies*.

happen in this picture, and happen frequently. We have a sinister pre-credit sequence, then a scene in which the riding ruffians callously knock a funeral procession off a bridge to expose the shocking sight of the coffin spilled open in the ravine below. Next comes Alice's nighttime walk and Sylvia's attack and abduction by the self-same riders. Then there's the horrific moment when a living corpse dumps Alice's dead body at Sylvia's feet.

Sadly (though perhaps not unexpectedly), at this point the film enters into a lengthy dull stretch (a seemingly inevitable occurrence in a Hammer production) in which the police question a suspect, Sir James questions the suspect, the two doctors talk and plan, Sir James pays a visit to the vicar's library, Hamilton visits Sylvia and, through a complex subterfuge (lasting a full five minutes), acquires a few drops of her blood, and the principals attend Alice's funeral. These scenes add little to the film and simply allow the characters to discover what the viewer already knows—as well as eating up a significant portion (about 30 minutes) of the running time.

Fortunately, while *The Plague of the Zombies* did not entirely escape The Plague of Hammer, the film picks up again with the graveyard sequence and from then on it maintains a shuddery and relatively fast pace to the end.

"Horror, as we at Hammer films know the word," pontificated producer Anthony Nelson-Keys in *The Plague of the Zombies* pressbook, "has nothing to do with nastiness or cruelty or sadism for its own sake… We try to make horror films with a sense of taste and style, but whether we did or didn't, audiences still recognize that a horror film in period costumes is pure, honest-to-goodness fantasy."

Filming for a mere 28 days in late July/early August 1965, Keys and company did indeed succeed in infusing *The Plague of the Zombies* with "a sense of taste and style." Director John Gilling, working with cinematographer Arthur Grant (whose steady hand and artful eye enhanced such Hammer productions as *The Abominable Snowman*, 1957; *The Curse of the Werewolf*, 1960; *The Phantom of the Opera*, 1962; *Frankenstein Created Woman*, 1967; *Dracula has Risen from the Grave*, 1968; and *Frankenstein Must*

who, of course, denies any knowledge of it. Later, Sir James sneaks back into Hamilton's house and finds a number of miniature coffins and dolls. When one of the Squire's lackeys discovers Sir James in the study, the resulting melee sets the room alight.

Down in the old mine, Hamilton and his cohorts use the zombies as slave labor. Via voodoo magic, Hamilton summons Sylvia who, in some sort of trance, comes to him at the mine. There he prepares to sacrifice her on the altar and make of her another undead slave. Just as Hamilton raises the knife over Sylvia's prostrate form, Peter, having followed her, rushes into the mine and stops him. The zombies quickly begin to close in upon him, but then suddenly burst into flame—the coffins and dolls in the room above have caught fire, which has magically set their undead counterparts aflame. In the ensuing chaos, Sir James, Sylvia, and Peter escape while the remaining zombies turn on their former masters and the entire mine goes up in flames.

One of the things that sets *Plague* apart from (and above) many a Hammer horror is the fact that things

A pair of the infamous "Zombie Eyes" given away to female patrons brave enough to attend the *Dracula—Prince of Darkness* and *The Plague of the Zombies* double bill. (Photo: Lynn Naron)

be Destroyed, 1969) stages and films scenes with an eye toward composition, movement, and atmosphere. When Alice comes upon the old tin mine during her fateful nocturnal walk, for instance, the camera shoots her through a huge disused gear-wheel, enclosing her image so that she looks small and trapped within the confines of the massive metal structure. The next moment she steps past the apparatus and moves closer to the camera. She stops, obviously seeing something, and her head turns aside just slightly as if she wants to look away (or scream) but cannot. Suddenly, the shadow of a hand rises up from the bottom of the frame. As the unseen figure advances toward her, the silhouette moves steadily up Alice's body before the shadow's bulk finally blots our her whole image with its ominous darkness. The staging and camera position, combined with the use of the sinister and intrusive shadow (further augmented by Jacqueline Pearce's uneasy demeanor) creates a moment ripe with dread—a dread that is realized fully a few minutes later.

In the next sequence, the vicious riders converge on Sylvia in the woods. Gilling takes the time and effort to shift the camera back and forth from the attackers' perspective to the victim's, creating an involving—and harrowing—ambiance. First the camera is mounted high and appears unsteady, as if riding one of the horses that surrounds Sylvia. Then low-angled shots of the whirling and snorting beasts show us Sylvia's terrified viewpoint. Back and forth the perspective goes for several seconds until one of the toughs finally grabs Sylvia up and rides off. The camerawork and varied perspectives create an energetic immediacy and excitement that would have been completely lacking had we simply seen the ruffians chase her down and carry her off in the standard medium shot.

In the following sequence, the men have Sylvia inside the manor house. Here Gilling continues the motif from the previous scene (both thematically and visually) as she's roughly thrown from captor to captor and finally falls to the floor, hemmed in by the legs of the laughing men (just as she had been trapped by the charging horses). Low-angle shots looking up at the forbidding enclosure of limbs as she desperately moves this way and that, seeking an opening, alternate between high-angle shots that look down upon her from her attackers' vantage point.

Gilling stages the first appearance of a zombie (obviously a pivotal moment in something called *The Plague of the Zombies*) for maximum impact. It begins when Sylvia passes the same giant gear-wheel that Alice had come by earlier (with Sylvia's image momentarily framed behind it just as the doomed Alice had been). She rounds it and advances toward the camera (just like Alice) so that her worried face is backed by the dark sky and forbidding mine silhouetted behind. Then she suddenly whirls around and the scene cuts so that the camera is now above and looking down upon her now-shocked visage. The next shot has the camera start from behind her and swiftly zoom past, tilting upward to reveal what she sees hovering on the rise above her—the horrible figure of the walking corpse holding Alice's lifeless body in its arms. A rapid zoom reveals the hideous grinning countenance in all its ghastly glory. Then, after a quick reaction shot of Alice cringing behind the gear-wheel, we see the creature gleefully dump its burden, which falls out of the frame seemingly at our very feet. Enhanced by careful positioning and camera movement, this scene, both shocking and terrifying, becomes one that, once seen, is not soon forgotten.

"The director that I got on with extremely well was John Gilling," recalled perennial Hammer favorite Michael Ripper (who plays a no-nonsense constable in *The Plague of the Zombies*) to interviewer Bruce G. Hallenbeck. "He was very good—and he thought a lot of me, I know that. He was very good as far as I was concerned, because I'm one of those actors who 'dies soon.' By that I mean, give me a few rehearsals and get to take three. After that I was dead, you know? If he saw me dying, he'd lean forward and say, 'Oh, Michael, when such and such a thing happens, say something like…'—which inspired me, you see, got me working again."

John Gilling entered the British film industry in 1933 as an assistant director. He turned his hand to writing in 1938, but didn't score a breakthrough until

Roy Ashton's horrific makeup make this *Plague*'s zombies some of the most frightening in the voodoo canon.

nearly a decade later with his screenplay for *Black Memory* (1947). After penning several more produced screenplays, he turned director on *Escape from Broadmoor* (1948), which he also scripted. Over the next two decades he directed nearly 40 more features (many of which he wrote) as well as periodically working in English television (including the series *The Saint*, *Gideon*, and *Department S*). His first foray into the horror genre came in the pathetic form of *Old Mother Riley Meets the Vampire* (1952), which he directed but did not write. Fortunately, his opportunities soon improved, and he moved on to (somewhat) worthier projects like *The Gamma People* (1956), *Shadow of the Cat* (1961), *The Reptile* (1966), *Night Caller from Outer Space* (1966), and *The Mummy's Shroud* (1967). In 1959 he wrote and directed what proved to be the most effective and atmospheric Burke and Hare picture made to date, *Mania* (aka *The Flesh and the Fiends*). In 1970, Gilling relocated to Spain, but only made one more feature there, *La Cruz de Diablo* (*The Devil's Cross*; released in 1974) before retiring from films to devote himself to painting. Gilling died in 1984 in Madrid. After the underrated classic *Mania*, *The Plague of the Zombies* (which Gilling claimed he rewrote extensively as he shot) re-

mains his best horror film. If one looks upon Gilling's directorial outings as a body of work, it doesn't really add up to much; but on at least two occasions (with *Mania* and *Plague*) he managed to construct that proverbial silk purse.

As with most Hammer productions, the acting in *The Plague of the Zombies* is first-rate. Andre Morell is simply a joy to watch, playing the elegant, no-nonsense Sir James with a twinkle in his eye and a droll half-smile on his lips. "I don't know why I put up with you at all," he offhandedly tells his daughter when she interrupts him, "I should have drowned you at birth." At this, Morell gives the hint of a soft smile at his feigned annoyance and gruff joke. When Hamilton angrily demands of Sir James, "Are you mad?!," Morell answers, "I almost wish I was, this business is so appalling," with just the right mix of throw-away glibness and introspective sincerity to make the rather unlikely line work.

Morell adds further depth to his character by making Sir James' assured, take-charge facade human enough to give way during the odd unguarded moment. Cleaning up after dinner, he tells Peter of his plans to illegally exhume a corpse. When the shocked Peter voices his objection, Sir James answers, "Why not? It's a full moon, couldn't be better. We'll start about midnight." Morell then promptly fumbles and drops the plate he'd been drying, his unsteady action and the slightly vexed look on his face belying his nonchalant words.

Born André Mesritz in London in 1909, Morell turned to amateur acting in 1930 and made his professional debut in 1934. Four years later he joined the illustrious Old Vic company and simultaneously started his screen career. After serving as a Major in the Royal Welsh Fusiliers during WWII, his stage and screen career flourished. Among Morell's 70-plus film credits (which span 40 years— right up until his death in 1978) are such prestige pictures as *Bridge on the River Kwai* (1957), *Ben Hur* (1959), *Julius Caesar* (1970), *QB VII* (1974), *Barry Lyndon* (1975), and *The Great Train Robbery* (1978). Morell's presence graced a number of genre features as well, including *1984* (1956), *The Hound of the Baskervilles* (1959; in which he created what some consider to be the screen's definitive Dr. Watson), *The Giant Behemoth* (1959), *Mysterious Island* (1961), *Shadow of the Cat* (1961), *She* (1965), *The Mummy's Shroud* (1967), and *The Vengeance of She* (1968). Of special note to Hammer fans is his marvelous turn in the little-seen crime thriller *Cash on Demand*. In this 1962 film Morell plays a perfect foil to Peter Cushing, who gives one the finest performances of his long career.

The walking dead make their first shocking appearance in *The Plague of the Zombies*.

As *The Plague of the Zombies'* head villain, John Carson possesses the appropriately aristocratic bearing and cool charm of a James Mason (he even sounds like Mason), adding both weight and dignity to the rather ill-defined roll. (Sadly, the character of Squire Hamilton remains both one-dimensional and underdeveloped, and we're left simply to wonder at the motivations and root of his heinous actions.) Carson went on to appear in two other Hammer horrors, *Taste the Blood of Dracula* (1970) and *Captain Kronos, Vampire Hunter* (1973).

Of the female leads, Jacqueline Pearce (who essayed the title role in *The Reptile*) is the more effective of the two, for she is both attractive and affecting. In her introductory scene, her obvious relief at seeing her old school friend Sylvia seems subtly tempered by a guilty nervousness. She appears skittish and secretive, refusing to let Sir James look under her

bandage (as if somehow knowing it's an unholy wound yet at the same time feeling protective of it). Pearce speaks rapidly, her eyes and head often downcast, though she frequently glances up as she talks in a furtive, almost pleading manner. The actress' demeanor immediately pulls the viewer in and arouses sympathy. "She was fine to work with," remembered Michael Ripper, "very good."

Diane Clare, though possessing a larger role, makes less of an impression. She appears rather stilted and never quite convinces, even in her potential showcase scenes of fear or anger. (No doubt the fact that Hammer dubbed her voice with that of another actress didn't help her cause any.) In any case, next to Pearce, the chubby-cheeked Clare looks girlish and passionless.

The Plague of the Zombies carries a significant (and effective) voodoo quotient. From the picture's opening scene, one knows that this is a full-fledged and unapologetic voodoo movie. It begins with a trio of (black) drummers beating out a rapid rhythm in what looks like an underground cavern while a white-robed (and white-skinned) man in a weird mask opens a miniature wooden coffin to reveal a clay doll covered in bright red blood. [1] We next see a young woman tossing in her bed as the voodooist performs his ritual. The man drips more blood onto the voodoo doll and the woman suddenly sits bolt upright in bed shrieking "noooo!"

"The authentic and thoroughly researched sequences of voodoo practices shown in the film are said to follow the actual rituals performed in Haiti,"

Squire Hamilton (John Carson, left) prepares to transform Sylvia (Diane Clare) into one of his undead slaves and so spread *The Plague of the Zombies*.

proclaimed a studio publicity article. This was undoubtedly "said" *only* by the studio's PR writers, for the "voodoo practices shown in the film" are about as authentic as a mail-order voodoo doll. Delusions of authenticity aside, the ceremonial scenes are well handled by Gilling and his crew to infuse a sense of danger and excitement into the proceedings. While far from convincing (thanks to some outlandish "heathen" headgear and bone necklaces sported by the trio of dark-skinned drummers, as well as the out-of-place white clerical-style robes and druidical masks worn by Hamilton and his cronies), these sequences possess an oppressive yet lively air due to the cave-like mine setting and the rapid, incessant drum rhythms. With the mine's overhanging rock ceiling and walls pressing in upon the scene, the drummers pound frantically in the foreground while (in contrast) the white-robed practitioners move slowly and deliberately about the paraphernalia-laden altar stone to pour vials of blood over dolls in miniature coffins. It makes for an atmospheric and disturbing spectacle.

At one point Sir James tells Peter that, "I spent the afternoon reading up on the subject [of zombies] in the vicar's library. And it's all there. It's all *clearly, scientifically* stated." Sir James must have found some amazing books, for until Wade Davis' 1985 book *The Serpent and the Rainbow*, there had been no clear, scientific investigation into the phenomenon of zombies, and the concept had been chronicled only as unsubstantiated stories, legends, and hearsay.

Regarding zombies, *Plague* features some of the most effective in the voodoo subgenre. Dressed in sackcloth shrouds, these walking dead are quite frightening with their dead-gray pallor, flaking skin, wide-staring filmy eyes, and evil grins and smirks (admittedly a ridiculous trait for a creature with no will of its own—but a visually chilling one nonetheless).

The film's horrific highlights center on these "undead" creatures (as Sir James labels them). The famed dream sequence, in which mottled hands thrust up through the newly dug graves as the zombies rise from their earthen tombs to close upon the frightened Peter (who stands motionless, seemingly rooted to the spot), may well be one of the most memorable (and chilling) scenes in the Hammer canon. The off-kilter camera angles, eerie flowing mist, gruesome makeup, and the inherent terror of death (symbolically represented by these perambulating corpses) make this shuddery sequence a justifiably revered one among horror enthusiasts in general and Hammer fans in particular. Macabre details, such as the rainwater lying on the raw, red earth looking like puddles of blood, combine with the horrific appearance and slow-but-inexorable movements of the hideous host to make the hackles stand on end. It's a brief, relentless, and frightening scene, and one that probably inspired George Romero in filming his *Night of the Living Dead* (and surely served as a blueprint for Bob Kelljan's effectively creepy opening for *The Return of Count Yorga*). (Note: This sequence is *not* tinted green as some uninformed writers have erroneously claimed, but features an effective use of *full* color—as exemplified by the blood-red puddles.)

Zombies rise from their earthen tombs in a relentless and frightening scene that may have served as inspiration for George Romero's *Night of the Living Dead.*

Castle of Frankenstein's Russ Jones visited Hammer's Bray Studios during the filming of *The Plague of the Zombies* and related how quickly and efficiently the production team worked. Lunching with Tony Keys, Jones wrote that, "across the room sat Andre Morell and the rest of the cast of *Plague of the Zombies*, deeply engrossed in discussing the afternoon shooting schedule. After our meal, Reg [Williams, who worked in the publicity department] was to take us to an interior set for a fight scene in which Andre Morell battled one of the zombie leaders. We walked to the set. Here an astonishing thing occurred. In the room were nothing but four walls and a bare floor. Within 20 minutes it was an English pub with a bar, bookcase, chairs, tables, carpets, pictures and various bric-a-brac. The cameras and crew came in, and the scene was put in the can after three takes."

The Plague of the Zombies was placed on the bottom half of a double-bill with *Dracula—Prince of Darkness* (which is rather unfair because *Plague* certainly moves faster and is arguably the more entertaining of the two). In the United States, the films were ballyhooed as "The Greatest All New Fright Show in Town!" and patrons were blessed with promotional giveaways: "Boys! Fight back… Bite back with Dracula Fangs! Girls! Defend Yourself with Zombie Eyes!" (cheap cardboard cutouts with small eyeholes).

Poor pairings and grotesque giveaways aside, *The Plague of the Zombies* stands near the top of voodoo's cinematic ladder and, indeed, if not on the top *Hammer* rung as well, then at least solidly positioned on its second step.

[1] Here the credits begin abruptly, complete with a discordant brass section blaring on the soundtrack. This interruption before anything truly happens seems an arbitrary and ill-conceived decision. It would have been better if Gilling had followed the scene to its conclusion and *then* cut to the credits. Fortunately, the film quickly and easily recovers from this initial misstep.

CREDITS: Director: John Gilling; Producer: Anthony Nelson-Keys; Screenplay: Peter Bryan; Director of Photography: Arthur Grant; Music Composed by: James Bernard; Musical Supervision: Philip Martell; Production Designer: Bernard Robinson; Editor: Chris Barnes; Supervising Editor: James Needs; Production Manager: George Fowler; Assistant Director: Bert Batt; Camera Operator: Morry Grant; Art Director: Don Minghye; Sound Recordist: Ken Hawkins; Sound Editor: Roy Baker; Continuity: Lorna Selwyn; Makeup: Roy Ashton; Wardrobe: Rosemary Burrows; Special Effects: Bowie Films, Ltd; A British Hammer Films production released January 1966 by 20th Century-Fox; 90 minutes

CAST: Andre Morell (Sir James Forbes), Diane Clare (Sylvia), John Carson (Clive Hamilton), Alex Davion (Denver), Jacqueline Pearce (Alice), Brook Williams (Dr. Peter Tompson), Michael Ripper (Sergeant Swift), Marcus Hammond (Martinus), Dennis Chinnery (Constable Christian), Louis Mahoney (Coloured Servant), Roy Royston (Vicar), Ben Aris (John Martinus), Tim Condon (Young Blood no. 1), Bernard Egan (Young Blood no. 2), Norman Mann (Young Blood no. 3), Francis Willey (Young Blood no. 4), Jerry Verno (Landlord), Jolyan Booth (Coachman)

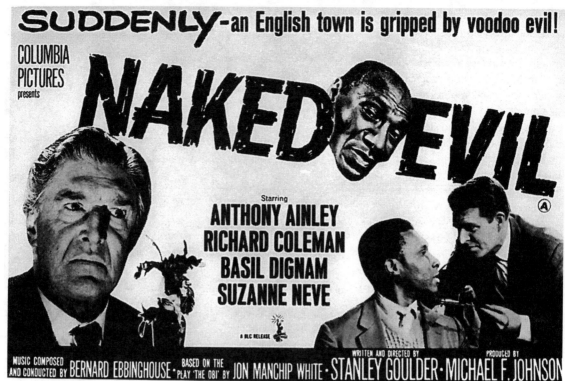

SUDDENLY—an English town is gripped by voodoo evil!

COLUMBIA PICTURES presents

NAKED EVIL

Starring
ANTHONY AINLEY
RICHARD COLEMAN
BASIL DIGNAM
SUZANNE NEVE

A BLC RELEASE

MUSIC COMPOSED AND CONDUCTED BY BERNARD EBBINGHOUSE · BASED ON THE PLAY 'THE OBI' BY JON MANCHIP WHITE · WRITTEN AND DIRECTED BY STANLEY GOULDER · PRODUCED BY MICHAEL F. JOHNSON

"We were looking for something that would give it a little bit of flair," commented executive producer Richard Gordon on the titling of his voodoo property then known as *The Obi*. Gordon's partner came up with the appropriate "flair" and the film became *Naked Evil*.

NAKED EVIL (1966)
Jamaican Obeah vs. British Gangsters

"This idea of one gang putting the fear of
the Lord into the other with the aid of Obeah
is quite inspired, isn't it?"
—Father Goodman

Less than a year after producer Richard Gordon's initial, disappointing foray into voodoo territory with *Curse of the Voodoo*, Gordon took another chance on the subject and co-executive produced his second hoodoo horror. Though it proved no more successful financially than *Curse*, aesthetically speaking *Naked Evil* far surpasses its dull predecessor.

While *Curse of the Voodoo* is a difficult enough picture to see these days, *Naked Evil* is nearly impossible. (This author first saw it only when Gordon himself generously supplied a print.) This is a great pity, for the film is a unique, engrossing, and suspenseful addition to voodoo's cinematic subset.

The project began when Steven Pallos (a well-known producer in England and former business partner of Alexander Korda) brought the proposed pro-

duction to Richard Gordon's attention. "I had been representing [Pallos] in the United States for many years on the sale of his pictures here through Gordon Films," recalled Gordon. "We had talked about doing something together in production, and he sent me this play by Jon Manchip White which had been done on the BBC called *The Obi*. I read and liked it and thought it would make a very good genre movie. He suggested we do it together and I said fine."

The film was designed as a low-budget (about £60,000 according to Gordon—which at that time was less than $150,000) British program filler. "This was made as a quota picture," explained Gordon, "to fulfill a certain requirement by Columbia to fill a certain slot because they needed to have a certain amount of British product in distribution, and the theaters needed to play a certain amount of British product. It wasn't intended to be anything more than that. That's all that happened to it in England. If it had been the genre picture that I'd *hoped* it would be, it might have gone on a double-bill with another English X-rated movie as a horror bill [the British "X" certificate signified horror rather than sex]; it might have done a lot more. But it really didn't lend itself to that."

Even though intended as a low-budget feature, Gordon and Pallos still wanted to make the most of their upcoming production. To this end they approached Columbia with the idea of filming it in color (since at that time color was becoming more and more crucial to film distribution). Columbia didn't bite. "When the subject came up just before shooting started of doing it in color, because everything was switching to color at that particular moment," recalled Gordon, "Columbia wouldn't go along with the idea. Even if Steven and I had put up the extra money, Columbia didn't want it because their distribution expenses would have been much higher because they would have had to make color prints instead of black and white prints. In those days that involved a substantial difference in costs. For the slot for which they had figured *Naked Evil*, they didn't think it was warranted."

The shooting schedule was four weeks and (unlike Gordon's previous voodoo picture, *Curse of the Voodoo*) *Naked Evil did* come in on-schedule and on-budget.

Though based on a play called *The Obi*, Pallos and Gordon didn't feel that rather non-threatening moniker lent itself well to exploitation. "*The Obi* didn't seem like a title that would be practical to use," remembered Gordon, "and we were looking for something that would give it a little bit of *flair*, and Steve [Pallos] came up with *Naked Evil*. I thought it was a very good title." Indeed it was, for as well as being mildly titillating, it captured the tone of the film very well—the idea of a raw, overpowering force of malignancy.

In the black section of an English town, two rival drug-dealing gangs engage in street warfare. One of the groups (headed by a gangster named Lloyd [Dan Jackson]) is using Jamaican Obeah (a variation of voodoo) to decimate their competitor's ranks. To accomplish this, Lloyd sends his intended victims a dreaded obi (a bottle filled with graveyard dirt and "muck" topped with feathers). "With an obi, smash the bottle and you unleash the devil," explains one character. Three of Spadey's (the rival gangster [Bari Jonson]) men have succumbed to the evil magic already ("a fall from a window of a locked room, a frightened man dashing in front of a bus, and yet another found in the canal," delineates the police inspector assigned to the case).

Meanwhile, Inspector Hollis (Richard Coleman) investigates a churchyard desecration after the priest, Father Goodman (Olaf Pooley), interrupts someone stealing grave dirt. This leads the inspector to a nearby university hostel "for colored students" run by Mr. Benson (Basil Dignam), an expert on Jamaica and its customs.

While Hollis is there, Benson collapses during lunch, though he soon recovers. Later, in his study, Benson pulls an obi from his desk drawer. Dick Alderson (Anthony Ainley), Benson's assistant, destroys it, but soon after another obi shows up in Benson's liquor cabinet. Benson grows more and more ill as the the dreaded obis play on his mind.

It comes to light that the mysterious "obi-man" is Amazan (Brylo Forde), the hostel's unsavory Jamaican caretaker, who's been selling his magic to Lloyd (and applying it to Benson as well, since he knows the headmaster is about to fire him). One of the Jamaican students from the hostel, Danny (George A. Saunders), has been playing delivery boy for Amazan "in order to support his pregnant girlfriend."

One evening, Spadie sees Danny delivering an obi to Lloyd and chases Danny back to his girlfriend's apartment. Brandishing a knife, Spadie tries to force entry but fails. The inspector then takes Danny home to the hostel, where Benson calls him into his study. Before the headmaster can "give him a good talking to," however, Danny becomes hysterical, shouting "there's evil here," and Benson subsequently finds a third obi bottle hidden in the room. In anger, Benson dashes the evil object to the floor and Danny runs from the room in terror.

The next morning, Janet (Suzanne Neve), Benson's secretary and Dick's fiancée, finds the headmaster dead in his study, stabbed repeatedly with a ceremonial spear taken from a display on the wall. The inspector comes to investigate and finds Danny cowering in his room with the bloody spear on the floor in front of him. Danny tells them that someone—or some*thing*—had pushed the horrid weapon under his door during the night. When the inspector asks, "Who would do such a thing?," Danny shouts "Amazan!" and rushes down to the basement where the old man lives. There Danny finds Amazan pinned to the door—dead. The inspector places the body on some boards in the cellar to await the coroner.

Meanwhile, Dick (who, along with Danny, was also present when Benson smashed the obi in his study) has fallen into a lethargy, a "ritualistic trance" as Father Goodman (who has written a book on Jamaican voodoo) describes it.

With the help of another Jamaican student, the priest takes Danny (who now also seems to be in a trance-like state) down to the cellar. As Goodman and the student set about burning all of Amazan's paraphernalia, a storm rises outside. The padre finds a box of obis and tosses them into the boiler's fire, then reads an exorcism over them. When he finishes the exorcism rite and drops the last obi into the flames, Danny screams and a wind rushes through the cellar, lifting the sheet covering Amazan's body—revealing that it has disappeared!

The supernatural wind moves upstairs. When it reaches Dick's room, the catatonic man suddenly grabs his throat as if choked by an unseen attacker. Father Goodman and company rush upstairs, where they discover Dick has seemingly become possessed by the spirit of Amazan. The priest brandishes a cross and demands, "Come out of the man thou unclean spirit." Dick screams and the window explodes outwards.

Meanwhile, the inspector returns with Janet and Beverly (Danny's girlfriend), and they see a shadowy figure by the road that seems to be Amazan—though they know that the obi-man is dead. Rushing into the house, they find Dick in an almost hypnotic state. Father Goodman has Dick relate what happened the night of Benson's death. Apparently, Benson had finally realized that Amazan was responsible for the obis and went looking for him. Before Benson located the Jamaican villain, however, he collapsed (Amazan, the inspector had learned from the autopsy, had been poisoning the man's whisky). While Dick went for the first aid kit, Amazan stabbed the helpless Benson with the spear. Dick then cornered Amazan in his basement shack and strangled him, only, "it wasn't my voice I could hear," relates Dick, "it was Benson. It was Benson strangling Amazan. Since then I've been walking down a long tunnel, straining for light and sanity."

While the inspector tries to provide a rational explanation for the mysterious events ("maybe Amazan wasn't dead after all..."), Father Goodman pronounces, "Whatever it was, the evil in this house has left with it, and that evil will surely drag it down to hell." As we see a shadowy figure move off through the woods, the priest concludes, "Those that do the Devil's work forfeit their souls to the Devil—and his torments."

The 1960s was one of the more successful decades for voodoo cinema, producing such diverse and effective entries as *Dr. Terror's House of Horrors*, *The Plague of the Zombies*, and *The Oblong Box*. *Naked Evil* fits into this company quite nicely and, while perhaps not as well-crafted as say *The Plague of the Zombies*, it remains one of the more atmospheric and thought-provoking of its contemporaries.

Naked Evil is one of the few films to effectively juxtapose Christianity and voodoo (though, naturally, it shows a bias toward the former) by pitting the power of the Christian faith (in the person of the rather obviously named Father Goodman) against the power of voodoo sorcery (in the form of the obi-man Amazan). When Benson finds a ring of headless cockerels encircling the school, he calls in Father Goodman to perform an exorcism and "cleanse the grounds of whatever filthy spell was intended." The priest motions to the bloody talismans and comments, "You still believe in the power of these things, don't you," to which Benson replies, "I believe *your* magic is stronger." The padre also performs a benediction of sorts over the obi found in Benson's study and then concludes with a brisk, "Right, you can get rid of this

now,"—confident that his Christian evocation has neutralized the power of the voodoo sorcery. At the film's end, it is Father Goodman's exorcism over Dick (with the priest thrusting a cross at the possessed man, who cringes from the sacred relic) that sends the voodoo demon packing.

These events lead to two possible lines of thought, each an intriguing interpretation. First, that voodoo magic relies primarily on the power of suggestion ("an obi only works on you if you're suggestible," states Benson at one point). Consequently, when a victim feels he's gained sanctuary from another source (the Christian church), he basically heals himself. The second possibility is that Christian magic is indeed inherently "stronger" than the evil voodoo sorcery. Either way, it makes for a fascinating conflict.

Though obviously low-budget and occasionally crude, *Naked Evil* often succeeds on a cinematic level. Stanley Goulder's clever staging and Geoffrey Faithful's atmospheric lighting and camerawork weave a palpable spell of evil around the sinister events.

"Steve Pallos had a director, Stanley Goulder," explained Richard Gordon as to why Goulder was chosen to helm their voodoo project, "who had just done a film for him called *Silent Playground*, which was a very exceptional no-budget movie about a child molester. It was extremely well done and received a lot of critical attention in England. Steve suggested that Stanley would direct the picture and it seemed a perfectly valid suggestion to me." And a *fortunate* one. Gordon characterized Goulder as "a very pleasant and talented guy, a guy who knew exactly what he wanted." Indeed he did.

Goulder sets the tone at the very beginning, during the pre-credits sequence. It begins as a man, obviously frightened, races up the stairs to his third-floor room in a cheap boardinghouse. As he runs up the steps, his corpulent landlady (no doubt after her rent money) hounds his fleeing heels. He dashes into his apartment and locks the door. When he turns around, he freezes, for on his cramped kitchen table sits a sinister dirt-filled bottle topped with tatty feathers. A strange wind moves like fingers through the feathers as the man hugs the wall while sliding past the fearful object. Grabbing the edge of the table, he gingerly pushes it away from him until it stands against the door. Then, in horror, he watches the bottle slide toward him on the table, moved by the landlady's persistent pounding on the door—or perhaps by some unholy force. As the object moves ever closer to the table's edge, the man's face registers near-terror until the bottle falls and shatters on the floor. At this, the man lunges backward through the closed window— though it appears as if he's somehow *pulled* through it. Quick cuts from the advancing bottle to the man's face, whose expression becomes more and more terrified with each passing moment, add both suspense and immediacy to the scene.

Then, impressively, the camera seems to fly out the window *with* the man, and we briefly see the open sky before the camera tips toward the street and plummets downward in a victim's-eye-view shot as the man screams. While the camera falls, we glimpse a clothesline hung with washing, and the scene cuts to a shot of a woman hanging

The film's first victim of Jamican voodoo backs away from a dreaded obi bottle ("with an obi, smash the bottle and you unleash the devil").

out her laundry on the line just before it's suddenly jerked from her grasp. Then, as the man's scream abruptly stops and we hear a sickening thud, two boys working on a bicycle look up, startled. They walk out of the shot and after a quick view of the shattered bottle up in the apartment, we see the lads standing by the man's crumpled body—the clothesline and scattered laundry lying underneath his broken form. It's a wonderfully cinematic sequence that draws the viewer into the film at the very outset.

Goulder fills *Naked Evil* with eerie touches. When Dick drops the first obi bottle into the basement furnace, for instance, the cellar door suddenly slams shut and the dangling light begins swinging as if pushed by an unseen force. Even the credits sequence builds a macabre atmosphere when, as the credits roll, the camera silently prowls through a church graveyard at night, coming to rest at a graveside where we see a mysterious hand placing fistfuls of grave dirt into a shoebox.

The climax (or what *should* have been the climax) presents a collage of chilling and effective images that blend together to form a terrifying whole. In close-up, we see the profile of Amazan's dead face under the sheet, backlit so that all we can see is a dark

silhouette. The scene then cuts to a shot of Dick's shadowy profile upstairs, with the silhouettes of bushes whipping outside the window and rattling against the glass with skeletal fingers. Next, as the priest finishes his exorcism in the cellar, the wind howls and the sheet covering Amazan's body suddenly whips upward to momentarily obscure the camera, only to drop down again and reveal an empty table. With the preternatural wind continuing to rage through the cellar, the camera cuts to a long shot of the stairway and we see the dark outline of a man at the top. The camera zooms in and we see that it *could* be the shadowy form of Amazan. Then, when Dick gives a strangled cry and collapses as Father Goodman thrusts a cross in his face and demands that the "unclean spirit" depart, the camera whirls violently to the right to show the window suddenly explode outward as if smashed by some invisible escaping force.

Rather than ending on such an atmospheric and exciting sequence, however, the picture continues on for several minutes as the various characters talk about what happened and what they saw (though we *do* get the explanatory flashback from Dick). Sadly, it makes for a rather anti-climactic ending which closes the eerie proceedings on a mundane and unsatisfactory note.

Even during this talky denouement though, the camera plays a vital role in setting the tone. As Dick concludes, "I've been walking down a long tunnel, straining for light and sanity," the camera gradually pulls back away from the speaker—as if *it* were moving down a long tunnel—to emphasize Dick's feeling of isolation.

Unfortunately, the picture's rather schizophrenic construction tends to weaken the film's overall impact and undermines Goulder and Faithful's careful staging. The more mundane gangster scenes and subplot (with the black wiseguys complaining about their "business" troubles on cheap nightclub sets) seem dull and out-of-place next to the more fantastical Obeah angle. Even a frantic chase scene in which Spadie pursues Danny through the streets generates little excitement when transposed with the terrors of the obi.

"You can see what it might have been if there'd been more emphasis on that aspect of the story rather than on the kid's romance with the girl and being chased by the gangsters and the gang warfare and all that," observed Richard Gordon. "I'd thought it would be a real horror picture, and that there would be much more use made of the voodoo stuff and less of the gangsterism and all that. It's not what I would really call a genre picture in its present form. It's sort of neither fish nor fowl." Despite Gordon's regrets, it's still a fairly tasty bird.

British films from this period are generally very well acted and *Naked Evil* is no exception. (There seems to be much less stigma attached to low-budget productions in general and horror pictures in particular in England. Consequently, competent British actors, even stars, are more likely to appear in them.) Worthy of note is Basil Dignam as Benson. His natural and authoritative delivery does much to lend conviction to the strange events. Dignam is quite believable as a man becoming more and more unnerved. His skepticism and stiff-upper-lipped demeanor slowly crumble under the weight of a mounting fearfulness. A rational man, he knows his fear is ridiculous, but he cannot help it (labeling a shot of whisky "Dutch courage" or ridiculing his unreasoning fear one moment yet asking Dick to stay "until I calm down" in the next).

"Basil Dignam was an extremely well-known stage and screen actor in England," remembered Richard Gordon. "He made literally dozens if not hundreds of movies. You'll find him repeatedly playing Scotland Yard inspectors, school heads, Members of Parliament, those kinds of roles. He is a very, very familiar face in British films." Dignam's familiar face and steady presence added to such pictures as *The Quatermass Xperiment* (1955; aka *The Creeping Unknown*), *Corridors of Blood* (1958), *Gorgo* (1961), and *Lawrence of Arabia* (1962).

In England, Columbia released *Naked Evil* as intended (as a supporting feature in black and white). In the United States, however, things didn't go quite according to plan. "First we tried to release it as *Naked Evil* with a distributor that Alex [Gordon, Richard's Hollywood-based brother] knew and was working with in California," explained Richard Gordon. "His name was Robert Saxton [of Hampton International]. He, unfortunately, was not able to do much with it. It had *some* play as *Naked Evil*, but he didn't do anything much with it and then he had to fold his company because he didn't have enough product to keep it going."

While this spotty distribution was bad enough, Saxton took the film and *tinted* it, coloring scenes variously red, green, blue, and amber. "Saxton and [my brother] Alex," recalled Gordon, "arranged the original tinting of the picture. In fact Saxton's release publicity said it was in 'Evil Color' [laughs], which I thought was a nice gimmick. It promised a lot but didn't guarantee anything." Nor did this unfortunate and unnecessary tinting *deliver* anything—except occasional confusion and eyestrain (not to mention washing out some of the picture detail by upping the contrast too high).

Naked Evil's trials and tribulations didn't end there. In the mid-1970s, Gordon made a deal with Sam Sherman and his Independent International company which allowed Sherman to put the film out on drive-in triple features along with other former Hampton International properties. "It had no value theatrically," Sherman told this author. "It was basically triple-billed just to load up a show at drive-ins."

In the late 1970s, Sherman was putting together a package of horror films to sell to television. "I was just looking to assemble what was available easily," related the enterprising producer/distributor. "I thought of *Naked Evil*." On December 1, 1978, Richard Gordon licensed Sherman the rights to distribute the film to television. Sherman couldn't sell the film as is, however, because "it was tinted senselessly. I'd have to be able to add some color footage to it. Basically, my idea was to create a framing story for the original film, and have the tinting be in some way explained—though I don't know if it explained it very well." To this end, Sherman wrote the "new" script "in one evening" and hired Steve Jacobson to shoot it all in a single day (on a budget of "about $5,000"). Using up more than a few favors, Sherman obtained permission to shoot at a hospital on Roosevelt Island in New York and induced Lawrence Tierney (as well as several other actor friends) to act in this new mini-movie.[1] Tierney plays Dr. Fuller, a psychiatrist who treats a disturbed young black man (portrayed by an actor who did *not* appear in *Naked Evil*) who supposedly witnessed the events seen in the original film. By using an experimental laser device that projects different colors, Fuller is able to bring out the man's memories (the original footage) and so (sort of) explain the various color tintings in these scenes. ("We found the color amber suggests restful scenes," clarifies Fuller. "Blue evokes scenes dimly recalled in memory, things that may have occurred at night, where red evokes scenes that may have tended to upset or frighten the patient. We use the various colors as we question him to draw out his thoughts." Right.)

Sherman used nearly the entire original picture for the flashback story. The few scenes the frugal Independent International decided to discard include an intimate (but G-rated) character-development sequence between Danny and his pregnant girlfriend and (surprisingly) an atmospheric shot of a shadowy figure—Amazan's spirit (?)—after the climax.

Sherman's added footage looks garish and sounds cheap, jarring painfully with the original *Naked Evil* sequences. Tierney is terribly miscast. Even Sherman laughingly observed that, "he always acts like he's John Dillinger and *we* make him a doctor!" Sherman retitled his "new" movie the nonsensical *Exorcism at Midnight* and sent it out through the airwaves.

Naked Evil/Exorcism at Midnight currently resides in distribution limbo. Sherman still owns the rights to the new footage he shot but not to the original *Naked Evil* footage. On December 1, 1993, those rights reverted to the estate of Raymond Rohauer, as Rohauer had meanwhile bought all the rights to the film from Richard Gordon. "Unless we can get together," stated Sherman, "which over the years has seemed to be impossible, my version will never be seen again." (No great loss, really.) "I'm willing to sell them *my* part of it, but nobody seems to want it," laughed the producer. Of his *Exorcism at Midnight* bastardization, Sherman bluntly labeled it "just a way of getting another pressing out of the grapes."

Richard Gordon was disappointed with his second voodoo voyage (just as he was with *Curse of the Voodoo*). "It didn't quite work. I think the budget was too low, and it was hampered by the deal with Columbia Pictures [and their insistence on keeping it black and white]. It just didn't come out the way we hoped it would. That's why we had a problem with it in the States and I eventually made the deal with Sam [Sherman]—for purely financial considerations."

Sherman himself was more kind to the feature: "It was a good film, a small film well-made. It's a small black and white British film with suspense that had no market in the U.S. because by that time we had pretty much effected a complete changeover to color; people were not making films in black and white over here, and you could not dispose of them."

Despite its flaws, *Naked Evil* is an original, suspenseful, and effective voodoo movie, one that holds the viewer's interest with its intelligent handling and atmospheric staging. It's a pity that at present it is not readily available, for (unlike so many of its more accessible brethren) it deserves to be seen.

[1] Unbeknownst to him at the time, Sherman *could* have gotten actor George A. Saunders (who played Danny in *Naked Evil*) for his "patient" role and thus created some much-needed continuity between the new and old footage. "He called me up because someone had seen this on television or taped it or something," recalled Sherman, "and he was in Hollywood. He's a very nice fellow. Funny, if we'd have known it then, we could have tied it in so much better. He was in *Room 222* on television. He'd been in England and came here. He originally *was* from Jamaica."

CREDITS: Alternate Title: *Exorcism at Midnight* (includes additional scenes shot for its American television release); Director/Screenplay: Stanley Goulder; Based on the play *The Obi* by Jon Manchip White; Producer: M.F. Johnson; Executive Producers: Steven Pallos, Richard Gordon (uncredited); Director of Photography: Geoffrey Faithful; Music Composed and Conducted by: Bernard Ebbinghouse; Editor: Peter Musgrave; Art Directors: George Provis, Denys Pavitt; Production Manager: Denis Johnson; Assistant Director: Malcolm M. Johnson; Camera Operator: Len Harris; Sound Recordist: Clive Winter; Makeup: Stella Morris; Continuity: Lorna Selwyn; Hairdresser: Mervyn Medalie; A British Gibraltar Films production released in 1966 by Columbia (in the U.K.) and Hampton International (in the U.S.); 79 minutes

CAST: Basil Dignam (Benson), Anthony Ainley (Dick Alderson), Suzanne Neve (Janet), Richard Coleman (Hollis), Olaf Pooley (Goodman), George A. Saunders (Danny), Carmen Monroe (Beverley), Brylo Forde (Amazan), Bari Jonson (Spadey), Dan Jackson (Lloyd), Oscar James (Dupree), Ronald Bridges (Wilkins). NOTE: As *Exorcism at Midnight*, the cast also includes Lawrence Tierney, Bob Allen, Catherine Erhardt, Nuba Stuart, and Addison Greene

THE LIVING DEAD

Whimpers an Unspeakable Curse and Claws with Bony Hands To Free its Evil From ---

THE OBLONG BOX

NOW, FOR THE FIRST TIME...
EDGAR ALLAN POE'S
HORROR CLASSIC!

IN COLOR BY
BERKEY PATHE

STARRING
Vincent PRICE
Christopher LEE

M Suggested for MATURE audiences
(parental discretion advised)

AN AMERICAN INTERNATIONAL PICTURE

PRODUCED AND DIRECTED BY
GORDON HESSLER · LAWRENCE HUNTINGDON · CHRISTOPHER WICKING · EDGAR ALLAN POE

SCREENPLAY BY   ADDITIONAL DIALOG BY   BASED ON THE STORY BY

THE OBLONG BOX
(1969)
Voodoo Meets Poe (Sort of)

"[I am] a man turned inside-out through sorcery
by a handful of powders and obscure drugs.
My mind's been unhinged, my face destroyed.
I've been killed and then brought
miraculously back to life.
I am a very remarkable creature, doctor."
—Alister Williamson as the cursed Edward

When originally announced, *The Oblong Box* was to be shot in Spain as a Spanish/Anglo co-production. The project was subsequently rescheduled for filming in Ireland under *wunderkind* director Michael Reeves (*The She Beast*, *The Sorcerers*, *Conqueror Worm*). When Reeves, who was having severe mental problems at the time (he died of an overdose of alcohol and barbiturates shortly thereafter), dropped out during pre-production,[1] producer Gordon Hessler took over the directorial reins himself at the last moment (with "maybe two days' notice" according to executive producer Louis M. Heyward). With the project now moved to the more familiar environment of England's Shepperton Studios, the three-week shoot (with a budget of about $175,000) began on November 20, 1968.

Executive producer Louis M. Heyward remembered (to Tom Weaver in *Science Fiction Stars and Horror Heroes*), "In trying to get this picture in on budget and on schedule, knowing Gordon [Hessler] as a quick director, I propositioned him to do it for an infinitely small sum. He accepted it. But Gordon is a little more than a director, he also happens to be a tremendous producer and a tremendous respecter of budgets. Once you tell him a budget, he will keep it inviolate. Gordon saved my ass on that picture, because we didn't have the money to do it. Gordon pulled that picture through."

The story begins in nineteenth-century Ghana, where the natives perform a horrible voodoo rite which disfigures the face and unhinges the mind of white plantation owner Edward Markham (Alister Williamson). When he returns to England, Edward's brother Julian (Vincent Price) keeps his unbalanced sibling chained in a room. Meanwhile, the family lawyer, Trench (Peter Arne), conspires with Edward and friend Norton (Carl Rigg) to secure the afflicted man's escape from Julian's imprisonment. To accomplish this, Trench bribes a witch doctor to prepare a capsule that will make Edward appear dead.

Upon his brother's "death," the unwitting Julian has Edward's body immediately sealed in a coffin and forces Trench to find a substitute body which can lie in state in place of his sibling's disfigured corpse. To this end Trench commits murder to secure the desired cadaver substitute and then abandons the real Edward to his horrible fate of being buried alive.

Lying in an unmarked grave, Edward is freed when body snatchers fortuitously bring his coffin to anatomist Dr. Newhartt (Christopher Lee). Edward revives and blackmails the body-snatching doctor into housing him while he plots his revenge on those who had betrayed him. After dispatching Norton, Trent, Newhartt, and several others, he finally confronts his brother Julian. In the confrontation, we learn that it was Julian, not Edward, who had perpetrated the deed (callously trampling a native child) which had brought down the horrible voodoo curse upon Edward's head.

Forced to shoot Edward, Julian tries to comfort his brother as he lay dying, but Edward only bites Julian's hand. Several days later, Julian's wife (Hilary Dwyer) finds him brooding in Edward's old room. When Julian turns toward her, we see that half his face has become hideously disfigured—Edward has passed the curse on to its rightful victim.

Conventional fan "wisdom" has it that *The Oblong Box* is a dull, weak, disappointing entry in AIP's Poe series. Nothing could be further from the truth. Thanks to excellent acting, a lively storyline, convincing period settings and costumes, and some involving direction from Hessler, it remains one of AIP's better non-Corman films from the 1960s—and definitely Gordon Hessler's best directorial effort.

Many fans feel that of Hessler's four genre films from this period (*The Oblong Box*, *Scream and Scream Again*, *Cry of the Banshee*, and *Murders in the Rue Morgue*), the sci-fi/horror amalgam *Scream and Scream Again* is the strongest entry. But *Scream* sinks beneath the weight of a hopelessly uncertain and confusing screenplay (a charge which is, ironically, often unfairly leveled at *The Oblong Box*), and neither *Banshee* nor *Rue Morgue* possesses near the verisimilitude or intensity of *The Oblong Box*.

The two faults most commonly attributed to *The Oblong Box* are its story ("convoluted" and "sloppy"—Tom Weaver, *Cult Movies*) and its gruesomeness ("gratuitous exploitation of gore" and "nauseating atmosphere"—Calvin Beck, *Castle of Frankenstein*). Both these baseless complaints seem incredible. The storyline is actually rather straightforward and unfolds (with one flashback—which is appropriately denoted as such) in a smooth, linear fashion. Granted, an occasional subplot (the artist who finds the discarded substitute body making an incriminat-

This lady of the evening (Uta Levka) learns the hard way not to solicit custom from men wearing masks.

ing sketch; a maid dallying with the masked Edward) branches out from the story's main trunk, but these only add further interest to the film and ultimately tie together quite nicely.

When interviewer Tom Weaver led his witness by asking Gordon Hessler if he felt the film's story was "hard to follow," Hessler (amazingly) concurred. "The story was sent to us from America," stated the producer/director, "written by an American, and we had to try to re-adapt and save it." NOTE: This statement brings Hessler's memory (in addition to his critical judgment) into question, for in this Hessler was sorely mistaken; original screenwriter Lawrence Huntington was actually born and raised in England. [2]

"Chris Wicking," continued Hessler, "who is an absolute horror buff, rewrote the script." Wicking told *Fangoria*'s Philip Nutman that, "I got a call from [Hessler] on Monday asking for more scenes for Vincent Price. They also needed scenes with more production value, scenes of extras in taverns, whatever. Vincent often felt like Christopher Lee in the *Dracula* pictures, that he was just being used as a name, wasn't being given enough to do."

In actuality, these "production value" scenes proved to be one of the picture's main flaws, for Hessler spends too much time in the tavern lingering on shots of tame "debauchery" (necking). These pad-

ding sequences add nothing to the story and quickly become tiresome.

What Wicking *did* add to the film was some effective subtext revolving around the voodoo angle. "[The voodoo curse theme] was already in the story," recounted Wicking about his last-minute rewrite, "but wasn't being used to any real effect. I made the theme of imperial exploitation of the natives the subtext, the cause of the curse."

Of the film's "excessive gore" complaint, one can only suppose that those offended are referring to the opening sequence, which is indeed rather shocking: Natives brutally nail a man's hands to a crude cross. Yet, apart from this particular shot (which serves its purpose by grabbing the viewer's attention), Hessler employs no further "gratuitous gore," wisely revealing the revenging natives' further mutilation only to the mind's eye—which can invariably conjure up things more terrifying than any FX artist. (In fact, once Edward's face is finally revealed at film's end, the oversized pig-nose and few patches of bubbly skin prove a serious disappointment.) Hessler even coyly cuts away when the voodoo priest uses his knife on a sacrificial goat. (It's interesting to note how filmmakers will display in unflinching close-up a spike being driven through a man's hand, but will shy away from showing a dagger driven into a goat. Does this say something about the human animal's self-hating sensibilities?—it's okay to mutilate and torture humans, but one does *not* show the death of an animal!) In any case, the impalement scene is no more shocking than the copious torture and death sequences found in the same year's *Conqueror Worm*, a film universally praised for its tough, hard-hitting approach.

"*The Oblong Box* is the fifth Edgar Allan Poe subject to be made by AIP in England," reported the film's pressbook (with the other four being *The Masque of the Red Death*, 1964; *The Tomb of Ligia*, 1964; *War-Gods of the Deep*, 1965; and *Conqueror Worm*, 1968). Like its two latter sister productions, *The Oblong Box* takes nothing from Poe but the name. Still, as AIP publicity takes such pains to point out, "It is typical of Edgar Allan Poe terror-territory, where the atmosphere is one of impending doom, where every awful happening is the harbinger of something worse." While not as good as its Anglo predecessors (the muddled misfire *War-Gods of the Deep* excepted), *The Oblong Box* manages to generate a substantial and melancholic atmosphere which does conjure up the mood of America's greatest terror scribe.

Director Gordon Hessler, along with cinematographer John Coquillon, creates an atmosphere of macabre claustrophobia, as if the characters are trapped within an ever tightening noose (or confining space—such as a certain "oblong box"). Even during the pre-credit sequence, the frantic hand-held camera, distorting close-ups of painted natives, and moody flickering lighting create a terrifying scene of voodoo ritual as the natives chant and dance and shout to the relentless drumbeats, culminating in a man's crucifixion.

For the scene in which the vengeful Edward confronts his betrayer, Trench, Hessler's direction augments the script's excellent dialogue (which effectively captures the *tone* if not the exact words of Poe). "Waking up in that horrible oblong box," begins Edward as he advances toward the frightened Trench, "no air to breathe, trapped and no escape; the earth raining down on the lid, every shovelful burying you more *deeply*!" As he speaks, the camera holds on Edward while he advances toward it—toward the viewer—then switches to show the horrified Trent. The camera continues to move toward Trent while

The brutal vengeful voodoo rite at film's beginning starts *The Oblong Box* off on an exciting (and unflinching) note. (Courtesy Ronald V. Borst/Hollywood Movie Posters)

Edward delivers his sinister soliloquy. The switching of perspective and the hand-held camera movements add a jarring, claustrophobic impact to the dialogue, complimenting and intensifying the sheer horror of the idea of being buried alive.

Vincent Price himself felt that "Gordon [Hessler] did a very good job with it, because he only took on the film a couple of days before we started shooting" (quoted in *The Complete Films of Vincent Price*, by Lucy Chase Williams).

Gordon Hessler was born in Germany to a Danish mother and English father. Raised in England, he came to the United States while in his teens. After working for Alfred Hitchcock on the master of suspense's two television shows (first as a story reader and finally as a director and full-fledged producer), he turned to the big screen in 1964. After *The Oblong Box*, Hessler helmed a string of horror films, including *Scream and Scream Again* (1970), *Cry of the Banshee* (1970), *Murders in the Rue Morgue* (1971), *The Golden Voyage of Sinbad* (1973), and the eerie *The Girl in a Swing* (1989), as well as the TV terrors *Scream, Pretty Peggy* (1973), *The Strange Possession of Mrs. Oliver* (1977), and *KISS Meets the Phantom of the Park* (1978).

One of the more intriguing aspects of *The Oblong Box* is the fact that none of the main characters are completely villainous—and none are completely pure either. Edward, of course, is as much sinned

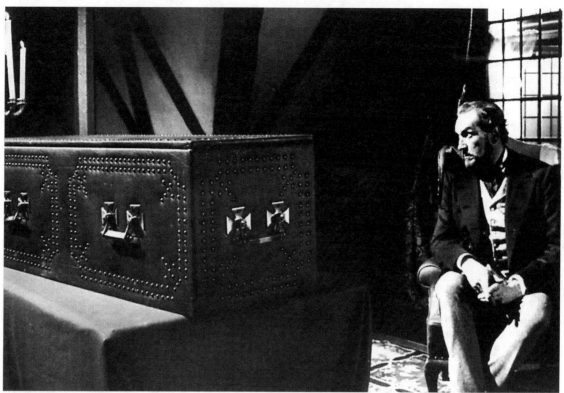

As Julian, Vincent Price gazes at *The Oblong Box* of the film's title in a shot evocative of Edgar Allan Poe. (Courtesy Ronald V. Borst/Hollywood Movie Posters)

against as he is sinner, murdering those who have betrayed him. Thanks to Alister Williamson's cool delivery and steady, articulate speech, Edward doesn't *sound* like a raving madman, and his obvious pain at his affliction even inspires sympathy at times. Dr. Newhartt is cast in the vein of Dr. Knox, and Christopher Lee effectively characterizes him as a man driven by his work to overlook his own morality.

Even the film's ostensible hero, Julian, turns out to be the real villain of the piece, having perpetrated the thoughtless crime that instigated the curse and resulting horror. Vincent Price (dubbed "The Merchant of Menace" in the film's pressbook) plays Julian as a man tortured by conscience yet too weak to act upon it. "Sin and retribution," he observes sadly. "We sinned out there in Africa all right, plundering their land. And we're still stealing their wealth, though they're too innocent to know it." Julian knows what is right and what is wrong but cannot break free of the comfortable status quo. In the end he pays the ultimate price for his amoral complacency.

Price brings a welcome dimension and subtlety to his character, whose hard surface practicality hides a tortured sensitivity underneath. Upon finding Edward dead (or so he thinks), Julian asks, "Oh Edward, can your soul ever forgive me?" While Price's voice is strong and hard-edged, it carries a hint of sadness and remorse that reveals the humanity under the stony exterior.

In promoting *The Oblong Box*, AIP used ad-lines like, "Edgar Allan Poe's classic tale of the restless dead and their subterranean world of horror and the unspeakable!" and "Where beatless hearts still hunger and dead hands twitch and tremble with desire." Though such enticing ravings point ("with bony hands"—another ad-line) in the direction of the walking dead, there are no zombies to be found in this voodoo tale. Even so, the opening ceremonial sequence and the few scenes with the "witch doctor" (played with a calm menace by Danny Daniels[3]) sitting before his bubbling cauldron create a terrifying voodoo ambiance that permeates the rest of the picture.

At the time of release, the film's critical reception could charitably be described as mixed. A.H. Weiler of *The New York Times* opined that *The Oblong Box* merely "illustrate[s] once again that horror can be made to be quaint, laughable and unconvincing." *The Monthly Film Bulletin*'s reviewer, however, felt that "[It] is firmly stamped with the vigour and assurance that one is coming to associate with the horror films of Gordon Hessler."

"*The Oblong Box* is a sort of chiller," wrote *Variety*'s "Whit," "if the audience isn't too demanding in a clear-cut story line... Price as usual overacts, but it is an art here to fit the mood and piece and as usual Price is good in his part. Alister Williamson acquits himself well and Christopher Lee likewise scores."

Today's Cinema (an English trade publication) felt that "played straight and, on the whole, very well acted, the film's impact is lessened by a banal script and a negative story line which flits from sub-plot to sub-plot, from character to character, with the inevitable loss of suspense... Quite exciting at times but generally rather slow and never particularly horrific."

More recent re-assessments also remain divided. *Cult Movies'* Tom Weaver called it "sick rather than scary." Dennis Fischer, in *Horror Film Directors*, wrote that "the results were not particularly horrific but rather routine, though John Coquillon's cinematography gives a nice sheen." (Of course, Fischer also got several significant plot points wrong in his obligatory synopsis.) Even "Special Guest Star" Christopher Lee dismissed *The Oblong Box* as "really only important as the first film I ever made with Vincent Price" (*The Films of Christopher Lee*).

The Phantom of the Movies (in *The Phantom's Ultimate Video Guide*), on the other hand, gave it three out of a possible four stars, labeling it "a well-mounted period piece," while *Halliwell's Film Guide* called it a "nastily effective horror film with a frail story but good background detail." In *The Edgar Allan Poe Scrapbook*, Ron Haydock felt it "a very entertaining film."

Despite the critics' (and participants') complaints, *The Oblong Box* did well at the box office, earning AIP just over a million dollars in film rentals. Long thought of as the "poor relation" to AIP's Poe family, *The Oblong Box* deserves respect from both Poe lovers and voodoo fans alike.

Producer/director Gordon Hessler's own opinion: "We made it imaginatively as we could, given the material we had, given the three weeks we had to shoot it in." In the end, the material and those three weeks were enough.

[1] "That poor boy," lamented Vincent Price of Reeves in *Cinefantastique* magazine. "He was so talented and had such a bright future, but he was a deeply troubled young man. I realized only after I saw [*Conqueror Worm*] finished how talented he was. He was brilliant, but he had a lot of problems; really mixed-up problems, one of them being dope, another being an unhappy romance."

According to script-doctor Christopher Wicking, however, Reeves withdrew from *The Oblong Box* more because of aesthetic than mental health reasons. "Michael only agreed to do the picture because AIP used it as a carrot on a stick," Wicking told *Fangoria*. "They said he could do his pet project, a film about Jesus returning in modern times, if he did this one first... In all the meetings we had, Michael was clearly uncomfortable with the material. He had allowed himself to be railroaded into making it. There was no way it was going to be as good as the other [films] he'd

made. He knew this and his perfectionism prevented him from doing the film."

[2] Lawrence Huntington (who was initially scheduled to produce and direct the film as well before he died in 1968 and Michael Reeves entered the picture) was a veteran writer/director whose career stretched all the way back to 1929. He helmed over 30 (mostly British "B") pictures (many of which he also wrote), with his last being *The Vulture* (1966).

[3] Danny Daniels was a veteran at this type of role, having previously played an African witchdoctor in *Curse of the Voodoo* (1965).

Star Vincent Price chats with "Special Guest Star" Christopher Lee between takes on *The Oblong Box*.

CREDITS: Director/Producer: Gordon Hessler; Screenplay: Laurence Huntington (Additional Dialogue: Christopher Wicking); Cinematographer: John Coquillon; Executive Producer: Louis M. Heyward; Associate Producer: Pat Green; Art Director: George Provis; Editor: Max Benedict; Production Manager: Bryan Coates; First Assistant Director: Derek Wittehurst; Continuity: Barbara Rowland; Camera Operator: Les Young; Sound Recordist: Bob Peck; Sound Editor and Mixer: Bob James; Sound Editor: Michael Redbourn; Wardrobe: Kay Gilbert; Makeup: Jimmy Evans; Set Dresser: Terence Morgan; Released in June 1969 by American International Pictures; an American/British co-production; 101 minutes

CAST: Vincent Price (Julian), Christopher Lee (Dr. Newhartt), Rupert Davies (Kemp), Uta Levka (Heidi), Sally Geeson (Sally), Peter Arne (Trench), Alister Williamson (Edward), Hilary Dwyer (Elizabeth), Maxwell Shaw (Hackett), Carl Rigg (Norton), Harry Baird (N'Galo), James Mellor (Holt), Ivor Dean (Hawthorne), Danny Daniels (Witchdoctor), John Barrie (Franklin), Michael Balfour (Ruddock)

This Mexican/American co-production's Spanish language title translated to *The Living Dead*. (Photos courtesy Ronald V. Borst/Hollywood Movie Posters)

ISLE OF THE SNAKE PEOPLE (1971)
Karloff's Mexican Horror

"During many centuries in various parts of the
world, various diabolical rites
and ceremonies have been practiced in
homage to various sinister gods who
are believed to have supernatural powers.
These rites are generally known
as voodoo, which consists mostly of
black magic and the cult of death."
—"*various*" lines from the opening narration

In early 1968, Mexican producer Luis Enrique Vergara made a deal with Boris Karloff to appear in four horror films to be shot back to back in Mexico. Vergara then hired Roger Corman alumnus Jack Hill to write the four screenplays. With partial financial backing provided by Columbia (in exchange for the U.S. distribution rights), Vergara learned that the ailing Karloff could not fly to Azteca's Mexico City studio due to health reasons (his emphysema prevented him from working in higher altitudes). Plans were then drawn up to shoot all of Karloff's scenes in Hollywood for all four films in only three weeks. To this end, Vergara flew the pertinent Mexican actors and crew to Los Angeles and rented the Hollywood Stages (a cheap film studio that provided shooting facilities for such schlock as *The Incredible Two-Headed Transplant* and *Dracula vs. Frankenstein*). It didn't prove quite so simple, however, for the guilds dictated that for every Mexican crewmember, an American also had to be employed. Scripter Jack Hill directed the Hollywood scenes in four weeks in April and May of 1968, going a week over schedule "due mostly to poor organization and planning on the part of the Mexican producer," according to Hill. (In addition, the $300,000 allocated for the three-week stint ballooned to a cost of nearly $400,000.) According to the director, "Vergara brought the actors in from Mexico, and it was total chaos. The actors were not the actors who were supposed to come, they were not showing up on time, and we had to keep changing the schedule all the time. Everybody was just freaking out. It was tough because I couldn't get the kind of coverage that I like to get. And the producer was off at Disneyland when he should have been on the set."[1] With the chaos ended and the Karloff footage in the can, the Mexican cast and crew then returned south of the border to finish the films in their more economical homeland under Juan Ibanez' direction.

Arguably the best of the four productions, *Isle of the Snake People* takes place on the (supposedly French) Pacific island of Koabia. There the natives engage in profane voodoo ceremonies that include raising up a zombie girl to satisfy a lustful overseer and indulging in human sacrifices. Captain Labiche (Ralph Bertran) comes to the island to clean up the corrupt police department and "reestablish law and order." Also arriving on the island is Annabelle Vandenberg (Julissa), a young and enthusiastic temperance worker there to visit her uncle, Carl Van Molder (Boris Karloff), "who owns almost half the island."

Labiche, along with the world-weary Lieutenant Wilhelm (Charles East), seeks Van Molder's aid in his attempt to stamp out the voodoo practices. Van Molder, however, laughs at the Captain's intentions and instead talks of "a vast untapped power that has lain dormant for thousands of years." Showing the newcomer his laboratory, he demonstrates this power by moving a mirror slightly with his mind and then ordering his servant woman, Kalea (Tongolele), to set a bowl of leaves on fire using just her thoughts.

That night, the Captain and his men break up a voodoo service by beating up one of the practitioners and ordering the rest to disperse. Later, the voodooists return to the sacred site, kill the three guards Labiche had left there, and resume their ceremony (which consists of a black-clad dwarf [Santanon] whipping an apparently willing woman to death).

Labiche is understandably outraged, and sets his sights on bringing to justice the mysterious figure of Damballah who is "their religious symbol, their leader." Damballah serves as the voodoo high priest. "Tradition says," Van Molder explains to the Captain, "that Damballah, who is the servant of Baron Samedi, must produce a human sacrifice. Then Baron Samedi will appear." Despite all of Labiche's efforts (including torturing one of the voodooists), he cannot discover the identity of this mysterious leader, who presides over the ceremonies covered from head to foot in black cloth.

At Van Molder's plantation, Kalea (who frequently dances with a sacred snake at the voodoo rites), accompanied by the unsavory dwarf (Damballah's right-hand man), creeps into Annabelle's room and, via a smoking bowl, invades her dreams. ("Offer your dreams to Damballah," intones Kalea.) Apparently, Annabelle has been chosen for the sacrifice that will manifest Baron Samedi.

Meanwhile, a group of cannibal women (!) have been decimating the local police force. With the rest of their men fled, Labiche and Wilhelm are left alone to combat the evil voodooists. Wilhelm still finds time to romance Annabelle, however.

Van Molder catches his overseer, Klinsor (Quintin Bulnes), playing with his zombie-girl mistress and beats the man for "defiling a daughter of a god with your brutal lust." Van Molder then calls in Kalea who, through the power of her mind, causes Klinsor's beloved zombie girl to crumble to dust.

In a fit of pique, Klinsor goes to Captain Labiche and tells him that the invocation of Baron Samedi is to occur that very evening. "If you do exactly as I tell you, you will be able to capture the voodoo leaders in an act of murder."

That night, two zombies kidnap Annabelle, while Damballah comes upon Klinsor preparing to flee and sics the cannibal women on him. Inexplicably, the

A bit of slithery sexual suggestion from an *Isle of the Snake People* dream sequence. Pictured is Julissa.

dwarf (up to then a key player in the voodoo ceremonies) is also killed by an unseen attacker while Damballah looks on.

In disguise and armed with explosives, Labiche and Wilhelm attend the ceremony. Damballah arrives and a man carries in the unconscious Annabelle. Kalea dances and then runs her snake over the prostrate girl's body.

Labiche pulls a pistol and confronts Damballah, addressing him as Van Molder. (We now see it *is* Van Molder, since Damballah's previously impenetrable black hood has amazingly turned into a transparent veil which clearly reveals the visage of Boris Karloff underneath.)

Kalea sidles up the Captain and has her snake bite his pistol hand. The gun goes off and the bullet hits Damballah/Van Molder. "I am dying, Kalea," intones Van Molder. "Offer my blood and the blood of my niece Annabelle to Baron Samedi... so that they can start a new empire on earth."

Wilhelm grabs Annabelle and spirits her away. The Captain, dying from the snake bite, staggers forward and topples into the ceremonial fire, setting off the dynamite he'd hidden under his robes and blowing up the voodoo cult.

The reason producer Luis Vergara hired Boris Karloff to star and Jack Hill to script (and co-direct)

Even in failing health at the very end of his life (and in a less-than-sterling production), Boris Karloff gave his all.

tion. Vergara, for some reason, wanted *four* pictures."

Isle of the Snake People proved substandard in all departments. A confused storyline, strained acting (not helped by bad dubbing), poor pacing, inadequate direction, and the fact that the film's star, Boris Karloff (name above the title, no less), is onscreen for only 10 minutes makes this *Isle* a deserted one as far as entertainment goes.

The film's direction ranges from indifferent to downright annoying. Jack Hill's footage (involving Karloff) is straightforward and pedestrian, with the director simply relying on Karloff's presence to carry the show rather than evocative angles, lighting, or camerawork. Mexican director Juan Ibanez, on the other hand, alternates between banal staging (the dull dialogue stretches which make up the bulk of the film) and bizarre camera tricks (during the ceremonial sequences). At times, Ibanez seemingly can't control his camera as it zooms in and out on faces, skeletons, dancers, etc. at a dizzying and irritating rate. He occasionally even resorts to a fish-eye lens, whose distortion only exposes an obvious (and desperate) attempt to create a "weird" atmosphere. It doesn't work and serves only to remove the viewer from the immediacy of what should be the film's most intense moments, becoming a visual annoyance.

was to make *Isle of the Snake People* and his three other features more palatable to non-Mexican audiences. "They wanted these films to have an international flavor," related Hill, "like an American picture would, rather than have it look like a Mexican film which would have a very limited audience." The ploy failed, for the only flavor "international" viewers come away with is a bad taste in the mouth.

Hill opined that Azteca and Vergara had second thoughts about Americanizing the pictures. "The only one I ever saw anything of was *Isle of the Snake People*, and it seemed to me as though they'd changed a few things in it from what we'd shot. They hired me, as an American, to do this job. But then when the Mexican producers saw what we had done, perhaps it didn't look right to them and they changed things to look better to a Mexican audience."

Not surprisingly, Hill blames the awful results on the Mexican contingent and their tampering with his scripts and footage, along with the financial pressures imposed upon him. Though Hill readily accepted the assignment to write four scripts for Vergara, he felt it was a mistake.[2] "I thought it was a crazy idea. I think he should've done one, maybe two, and we would've had a chance to do a real good produc-

Reportedly, Boris Karloff was to be paid $400,000 for his efforts on these four films. The actor had little time to enjoy the monetary benefits for, sadly, he died in February 1969 (without collecting the money owed him). Also sadly, the experience offered him very little in the way of *artistic* benefits. (Thankfully, the pictures weren't released until two years after his death, sparing him at least *that* indignity.) Still, these four terrible features provided work for the venerable veteran who simply refused to retire, helping to grant his wish to "die with my boots on."

Karloff, ever the trouper, rose above his failing health during shooting. "When we made these four films," remembered Jack Hill, "[Karloff] had emphysema and was dying. We had to keep him in a chair most of the time. But he was able to get up and do short scenes. There was one scene [in *Snake People*] where he had to get up and beat someone with his cane, and I was worried that we might have some problems doing that one. But when it came time for Karloff to do the scene he flew out of that chair and did the action—he appeared to really beat the hell out of the other actor! Then he had to sit down and take his oxygen. But he really loved to work. And under seemingly any conditions he was a tremendous actor."

Julissa fondles a snake in this publicity shot from *La Muerte Viviente* (aka *Isle of the Snake People*).

Karloff does indeed attack the scene (and the actor) with vigor. (The sequence in question occurs when the enraged Van Molder finds Klinsor profaning the sacred voodoo by dallying with his zombie mistress.) Thanks to the dying actor's professionalism and dedication to his craft, Karloff gives what must have been a Herculean physical effort in order to turn what could have been a feeble and laughable moment into an effective and believable one.

Onscreen for only 10 minutes, Karloff still manages to bring some believability to his underwritten and confusing part. Asked to ramble on about "vast untapped power that has lain dormant for thousands of years" or of "a new world of Baron Samedi," the actor's wonderfully expressive voice (thankfully he was allowed to loop his dialogue himself) and charming demeanor at least hold the viewer's interest.

In fact, the film is not *all* bad. Apart from showing Boris Karloff in his final screen appearance, *Snake People* offers a few effective moments. The pre-credit sequence at the graveyard, for instance, definitely holds one's attention. It begins when a black-clad dwarf leads the seedy-looking Klinsor into a graveyard at night. The narrator tells us that "unscrupulous adventurers take advantage of these superstitions to put docile native girls under their power, transform-ing them into zombies so that they will submit to their primitive instincts." The unholy duo then dig up a coffin, and the dwarf throws down a voodoo doll (complete with pins), cuts the head off a chicken, and drips the blood onto the coffin. The box's lid rises to reveal the shrouded figure of a shapely girl. Klinsor gets down into the grave and begins fondling and kissing the now-animated corpse ("primitive instincts" indeed). Though shocking and more than a little distasteful, this opening scene surely is a "grabber."

The dwarf (played by Santanon), in black coat, top-hat, and dark glasses, laughs creepily and never says a word, making for an effective (if pint-sized) degenerate sorcerer. He even clutches the chicken corpse to his face and rubs the dead feet across his cheek in a sick caress as he watches his "client" kiss the cadaver.

This unsavory sexuality continues when Kalea and the dwarf later use a magical smoke to induce bizarre dreams in Annabelle's sleep. In her dream, Annabelle opens a coffin only to find her own body with a live snake stretched out along its thinly covered form. The doppelganger rises and pursues her, using the snake as an obvious phallic symbol (caressing it suggestively and even putting the head inside her mouth). The double teases Annabelle with

Director Jack Hill (left) goes over the script (such as it was) with Boris Karloff (in full "Damballah" gear) on the set of *Isle of the Snake People*.

pounding out his muddled screenplay, for even the expected voodoo clichés are hopelessly addled. Oddly, Hill claims that he "did indeed do considerable research into the literature and lore of zombies and such matters, and obviously made use of much of that information in the screenplay." The only thing "obvious" is that either Hill made the *wrong* use of such information or his script and footage was hopelessly mangled when the production was completed and cobbled together in Mexico—an admittedly likely scenario. Hill states that he's never been able to watch any of the four features in their entirety because "what I saw of what had been done to them by the Mexicans was enough so that I haven't had the heart to look at them any further."

First off, simple geography seems to be a problem. As the offscreen narrator drones on at the film's beginning, the camera roams about a map of the world (undoubtedly taken from an issue of *National Geographic*—the fold lines are clearly visible!). Instead of coming to rest on the Caribbean, however, the camera continues panning across the Mexican peninsula to the middle of the Pacific (!) where it zooms in on an (obviously hand-drawn) island crudely lettered "Island of the Snakes." Voodoo in the Pacific... Hill must have seen Karloff's previous voodoo venture, *Voodoo Island*, once too often.

Second, the narrator tells us that "the practice of voodoo invokes the supreme god, Baron Samedi, who is supposed to be able to revive the dead." While in the Voudoun religion Baron Samedi is indeed seen as the guardian of the spirit world, he is just one of dozens of loas, not the "supreme god" (*Bon Dieu*, the creator of all things, for whom the various loas act as intermediaries). The narrator further expounds that "this rite is presided over by Damballah, a kind of supreme priest to whom the witches or followers dedicate their diabolical ceremonies, the same as the snake priestess." Even casual voodoo-bashers know that Damballah is actually a loa, especially since he is the voodoo deity most commonly played up by Hollywood screenwriters. Hill ignores this and simply reduces Damballah to an evil human priest.

Third, the film can make neither fish nor fowl out of its zombies. Van Molder ("Damballah" himself, remember) explains that a zombie is the result of a venomous snake bite and antidote application which "slows down the metabolism and the heartbeat so much that the person appears to be dead." This process keeps the body alive but destroys the brain, "so

a violently passionate kiss on the lips in a visual explosion of sexual narcissism. Though blatantly obvious, this Freudian dream remains unsettling nonetheless.

The film's sets, particularly the eerie graveyard full of tilted tombstones and half-exposed skeletons, are well-dressed and generally effective. Unfortunately, they're often overlit. Mexican cameraman Bagdon Mondaugis turns his red flood lights up high on the cemetery set, for instance, creating a garish quality that looks more artificial than eerie.

When asked why he chose voodoo as a subject for one of his four scripts, Jack Hill explained, "I was required to generate four horror screenplays within a period of only a few months, and so a zombie picture was sort of an obvious quick choice, particularly as the subject matter offered an exotic locale as well as an interesting role for Boris Karloff."

As a voodoo film, however, *Snake People* ranks among the most confused and inaccurate ever made—and that's saying something. As the movie stands, Hill seemngly did little background research before the victim becomes a sort of walking vegetable." But if the zombies are nothing more than drugged people with burnt-out brains, then why do they take on a ghastly gray pallor, and how does Kalea cause one to decay and crumble like a decomposing corpse?

In addition, these zombies (according to the narrator) join the ranks of the brainless *willingly*. "They gladly go to their death in the hope that they'll be accepted into the legion of the zombies, winning the favor of Baron Samedi and in this way enjoy the privilege of the living death." The terms "enjoy" and "privilege" seem a bit optimistic when one sees the blank stare and complete lack of will in these pathetic creatures. Besides, in Haiti the Voudoun believer fears not the zombie but rather that he/she may *become* one.

Beyond the various voodoo errata, *Snake People* seems confused about its nationalities as well. Captain LaBiche (the representative of the "colonial government") speaks with a Spanish accent, yet he refers to Annabelle as "mademoiselle" (and one of the policeman answers a question with the French "oui"). Lt. Wilhelm, on the other hand (who possesses an American accent), addresses Karloff (who's British, of course) as "Herr" Van Molder. So we have Spanish, American, and English accents using French and German forms of address. *Snake People* has something for everybody.

The story's turn of events raise numerous practical issues as well, such as how does Van Molder miraculously lose his pronounced limp whenever he dons the disguising garb of Damballah? (Obviously, Karloff's Mexican double forgot to emulate that aged actor's gait.) Even more disturbing, why does Van Molder's voice change from one moment to the next at the film's climax? (Of course, the answer is obvious—Karloff had finished and gone home and they needed some additional dialogue and simply had another actor, who sounds nothing like Karloff, speak the lines.) Also, who kills the dwarf—and why? These questions (and much, much more) remain unaddressed at the perfunctory climax. It all serves to expose the production's slapdash roots and makes one wish that the venerable King of Horror was offered a more worthy final vehicle.

Upon completion, Columbia was less-than-thrilled with their new Karloff features. Though it's difficult to reconstruct just what happened (sources conflict), two of the films, *Isle of the Snake People* and *The Incredible Invasion* (aka *Sinister Invasion* and *Alien Terror*), may have enjoyed a brief and spotty regional theatrical release in 1971 before the studio washed their hands of them and sold the pair to television via a company called Horror International Films. Due to financial difficulties complicated by producer Luis Vergara's death from heart failure, the two other pictures, *The Fear Chamber* (aka *Torture Zone*) and *Macabre Serenade* (also known as either *House of Evil* or *Dance of the Damned*), were apparently never released to theaters at all in their English-language versions and only came to light via the video boom of the 1980s.

[1] All quotes attributed to Jack Hill are taken from interviews conducted by Michael Copner (*Cult Movies* magazine), Jeffery Frentzen (*Fangoria* magazine), and from personal correspondence with the author.

[2] Jack Hill was in no position to turn anything down at this point in his career, for, apart from directing fill-in footage for Roger Corman (on cobbled-together films like *Battle Beyond the Sun*, 1963; *The Terror*, 1963; and *Blood Bath*, 1966), Hill had only directed two full features on his own; and one of these, 1964's *Spider Baby* (ironically, Hill's best film), had yet to be released due to legal entanglements. Hill went on to make his mark (such as it was) in the exploitation field with features like *The Big Doll House* (1971) and *The Big Bird Cage* (1972; two women-in-prison flicks) and the self-explanatory *Swinging Cheerleaders* (1974) and *Switchblade Sisters* (1976). His last film to date was *Sorceress* (1982), on which Hill had his name removed from the credits as writer and director because of tampering by executive producer Roger Corman.

CREDITS: Alternate Titles: *Snake People* (television title), *Cult of the Damned* (video title); Director: Juan (misspelled as "Jhon" in the credits) Ibanez; Director of Hollywood Unit: Jack Hill; Producer: Henry Verg (Luis Enrique Vergara); Screenplay: Jack Hill; Director of Photography: Austin McKinney; First Cameraman: Frank Ruttencutter; Assistant Cameraman: Bagdon Mondaugis; Production Coordinator: Richard H. Dunlap; Music: Alice Urreta; Musical Director: Henry Caviatti; Makeup: Louis Lane; Dialogue Director: Stim Segar; Special Art Designer: Jo Anne Jordan; Production Manager: J.L. Cerad; Special Effects: Ross Hahn; Film Editor: John Mungea; Art Director: Ray Markham; Set Decorator: Bob O'Neil; A Mexican/American co-production by Azteca/Columbia; (probably) released March 1971; 90 minutes

CAST: Boris Karloff (Dr. Carl Van Molder), Julissa (Annabelle), Charles East (Lt. Wilhelm), Ralph [Rafael] Bertrand (Capt. Labiche), Tongolee (Kalea), Quintin Bulnes (Klinsor), Santanon (Dwarf), Martinique, July Marichael, Yol Duhalt

Compared to its mean-spirited co-feature, the cheesy *I Eat Your Skin* becomes downright enjoyable.

I EAT YOUR SKIN (1971)
Del Tenney's Science and Ceremony

"You actually contemplate taking that lovely,
voluptuous kook of a wife,
whom you claim to love, and me, your breadwinner,
whom you claim to be your
best friend, to an island overrun with dead people
practicing human sacrifices
and voodoo for the sake of a good book?!"
—writer/hero to his agent

Shot in 1964 but not released until 1971, *I Eat Your Skin* is actually a better film than its horrendous title would suggest. (Thankfully, no skin—or any other body part—is ever eaten.) Filmed in and around Miami and Key Biscayne, Florida as the nondescript *Caribbean Adventure* (to disguise its horror status from local merchants/investors, according to second unit director William Grefe [1]), the film's title metamorphosed into *Zombie* and then *Voodoo Blood Bath* before ultimately becoming *I Eat Your Skin* upon its much-delayed release.

"I always thought that voodoo was very interesting, an interesting kind of religious ceremonial, and

the whole thing of killing the chicken or whatever they did, was an interesting theatrical event and was kind of 'fun'—if you want to call it that," related writer/director Del Tenney to this author about why he chose to spice up his self-proclaimed "low-budget adventure film" with voodoo. "It had a certain sense of theatricality."

After producer/director/scripter Tenney's success with *Horror of Party Beach* and *Curse of the Living Corpse*, he was on a roll (these films, along with his *Psychomania* had made Tenney over a million-and-a-half dollars!). Unfortunately, with his new voodoo project, the momentum couldn't quite carry Tenney over that next distribution hill—for *Voodoo Blood Bath* remained unreleased for seven years. (Tenney had planned to make a ready-made double-feature consisting of a Frankenstein/Dracula film [succinctly titled *Frankenstein Meets Dracula*] and the voodoo picture. When *Voodoo Blood Bath* generated no distribution interest, however, the "Monsters Meet" project died on the celluloid vine.)

Even in 1964, shooting a low-budget horror film in black and white and expecting to find a decent (or *any*) distributor was an act of pure optimism. "What happened," Tenney recounted, "was that the bottom fell out of that kind of genre—grade-B black and white movies with no names—about that time. So I couldn't sell the package of *Frankenstein Meets Dracula* and *Voodoo Blood Bath*. I thought it was a good package but 20th Century-Fox said I don't think we're going to be able to take these pictures. So [*Voodoo Blood Bath*] was the last one I did." Tenney shelved his final feature and worked for the remainder of the 1960s as a television producer before ultimately returning to the legitimate theater, his first love. ("I'm a stage director, you know, and have always been sort of a 'priest of the theater.' I've directed probably 150 to 200 plays and have been involved with certainly over 300 plays. All this [movie work] was done sort of tongue in cheek, for the commerciality of it.") Tenney also began a very lucrative real estate business, which he supervises to this day. He never made another feature. [2]

Tenney's voodoo movie might still be moldering on the cinematic shelf today had it not been for producer Jerry Gross who, in 1971, needed a second feature for his rabid hippie opus *I Drink Your Blood*. Gross purchased *Voodoo Blood Bath* for about $40,000 dollars (only a third of its cost—"on *Voodoo Blood Bath* I took a bath," laughed Tenney) retitled it *I Eat Your Skin* and advertised the pair as "Two Great Blood Horrors To Rip Out Your Guts!" Compared to the mean-spirited *I Drink Your Blood*, Tenney's cheesy co-feature becomes downright enjoyable.

Writer/playboy Tom Harris (William Joyce) journeys with his agent (Dan Stapleton) to a small private island in the Caribbean (succinctly named "Voodoo Island") to research and write his next bestseller. Upon arriving, Tom is menaced by zombies, meets a scientist (Robert Stanton) combining snake venom and radiation to find a cure for cancer, and falls for the doctor's beautiful daughter, Jeanine (Heather Hewitt). The natives seem intent upon kidnapping Jeanine and sacrificing her to their voodoo gods, Jeanine being the only blonde virgin around for miles (though Tom's irresistible charm soon changes *that*). After more encounters with the oatmeal-faced zombies and escapes from the natives, Tom rescues Jeanine from under the sacrificial knife and makes his escape.

As their boat speeds away, the dying scientist (who'd taken a native knife in the back) makes his confession/explanation: "Instead of getting closer to a cure for cancer, the bombarded snake venom was setting up a curious reaction in the body tissues, making the subject devoid of will—a human vegetable" (as well as turning their faces into oatmeal and their eyes into what looks like fried eggs). The local plantation overseer (Walter Coy), posing as the voodoo high priest Papa Negro, had been blackmailing the misguided scientist into "creating an army of these unfortunate people." The island blows up (the scientist had set the equipment in his lab to explode) and Tom returns with Jeanine to civilization.

Principal photography was completed in three weeks (a luxurious schedule for Tenney, whose three previous features had all been shot in two). This longer schedule, however, was not the director's idea. "That was simply the way it worked. Union-wise you had a certain schedule. I even had to have union *drivers*; it suddenly became a whole different ball park." Had it been a non-union picture (like his other films), Tenney would probably have completed it in his usual fortnight time-frame.

"We had a lot of trouble," Tenney recalled about filming *I-Eat-Your-Caribbean-Zombie-Blood-Bath.* "First of all we had a hurricane which caused about a week's delay. Secondly, it was the first film that I did union. When 20th Century-Fox picked up *Curse of the Living Corpse* and *Horror of Party Beach* and played them at the drive-ins, being union, they insisted that the next film I did was union. So instead of costing the usual 40 or 50 thousand dollars which is what the others cost, this one cost me about a 120 thousand." Unused to union regulations and restrictions, Tenney tried to circumvent them whenever he could. "When I closed down the filming with actors, I did a lot of pick-up stuff. And I used my friends and my crew and whatever people I had that were not union people that I'd brought down—and myself and my brother and my wife (who's an actress) and so on."

Such nefarious (by union standards) activities turned around and bit him in the end. "They [the union] got wind of the fact that I was shooting off the cuff. And they did not like it at all. I threw a party at my house that we were renting on Key Biscayne for the whole cast and crew and everybody that was involved and catered it—quite a nice affair I thought. They set all the curtains on fire and ruined several sofas—they poured drinks on the sofas, the union guys—to get back at me. It cost me four or five thousand bucks in repairs and damages. So I'm not a very thankful person as far as the unions go [*laughs*]." Of course, Tenney went on to remark that he himself has belonged to several unions, including SAG, Equity, and AFRA, and is not anti-union *per se.* "I just thought that those *particular* [union] people down there treated the situation badly. And the fact that I was funding the thing myself was never taken into consideration."

Other (non-union) difficulties arose as well. "Half the crew was going to the hospital with snake bites or malaria or whatever the hell was going on," remembered Tenney. "Everybody was getting sick because they weren't used to being out in the jungle like that."

A few tropical bugs was not the only physical menace around, however, and, though ignorant of it at the time, one cast member narrowly escaped disaster. "You remember the sequence where the heroine was swimming out in the bay?" asked Tenney. "Well, the day after we shot that movie, we were talking to the Coast Guard and the Coast Guard told us that that particular bay was infested with sharks! I was like, aaargh, I can't believe that I would put her in jeopardy like that!"

Despite the contrary weather, unions, viruses, and just-missed predators, Tenney still found *I Eat Your Skin* "an enjoyable picture to shoot. It was a fun movie to make. The cast was terrific. Everybody was very cooperative. For a low-budget film we had a lot of special kind of stuff with the boats and the airplane and all the special effects, the makeup and the snakes and all that stuff. It was very interesting and fun to do. I enjoyed working on the film."

Though not as enjoyable to *watch* as Tenney's wacky *The Horror of Party Beach*, and not as slick as his *Psychomania* or *The Curse of the Living Corpse, I Eat Your Skin* still maintains that combination of hard-edged violence (shocking decapitation; gruesome zombie faces) and raw energy (ceremonial sequences and chase scenes) which makes Tenney's features as memorable as they are.

Technically, the film plays just slightly *below* the competency level. Most scenes had to be overdubbed, and the poor quality sound and (mis)matching shows ("I could never get good enough sound [on location]," commented Tenney. "We did a lot of looping.") Also, apart from the few ceremonial sequences (which admittedly make atmospheric use of sinister shadows and flickering firelight), the film is often poorly lit in

A voodoo priest prepares a ceremonial participant in *I Eat Your Skin*. **"We sort of had to make it up as we went along as to the ceremonies," remarked writer/director Del Tenney. "Actually, most of it was just our imagination."**

that dull, flat style common to black and white pictures of the 1950s and early 1960s. The trashy model of the island blowing up (with bits of papier mache flying into the air along with tiny gouts of flame) is about on a par with Ed Wood. The acting ranges from adequate (Walter Coy giving a fairly good Cameron Mitchell impersonation) to downright annoying (Betty Hyatt Linton's nasal interpretation of the agent's airheaded wife). Lon E. Norman's intrusive and often inappropriate jazz score (with trumpets blaring and drums pounding like a *Jonny Quest* episode) doesn't help.

Tenney's occasionally absurd script (combining the old mad-science-zombie and radiation chestnuts of the previous decade with large doses of cheese) does little to flesh out the characters, though he seemed to want to make his writer hero into a literary version of James Bond since he alternately jumps into action and jumps into the sack with equal aplomb. (In fact, Tenney told the locals that this was *exactly* what he was filming—a 007-style adventure film. "There was kind of a stigma about turning Caribbeans into zombies and so on," remarked the filmmaker, "and I thought they would be more receptive if they thought it was a James Bondish-type of thriller rather than a

zombie film. As I look back on it, it was stupid because, you know, they didn't really care [laughs].") Fortunately, Tenney keeps the story moving at a fairly brisk pace via the various zombie encounters and native chase scenes.

"It has been a long time since any [monsters] have come along as terrifying as the humanoids in *I Eat Your Skin*," (over)stated the film's pressbook. "These weird humanoids are enough to make one jump out of his skin, which, incidentally, is exactly what this horror-chiller is all about." Though the PR boys definitely exaggerated their merit, the movie's zombies do provide a few genuine shudders, and so fulfill the first rule of zombie cinema—dead people should be scary. With their cataract-covered eyes, flaking, wrinkled skin, and tall, gaunt frames, these "humanoids" (as the pressbook labels them) wield machetes (one decapitates a local fisherman) and take bullets to the chest (the holes appearing in the dead flesh one by one) without missing a step. Never mind that they're really a product of science rather than sorcery (and consequently *should* be stopped by bullets since they're actually live people transformed into "human vegetables"). It still makes for some startling moments. ("I had to hire two or three union makeup people, which was very expensive," complained Tenney, "but they did a good job.")

Apart from the zombie encounters, the film's highlights are the convincing voodoo ceremonial scenes. This is a rarity in voodoo cinema, since so often filmmakers stage their dancing/sacrifice/ ceremonials in such an ineffectual, lackluster, and trite manner that these supposedly sacred ceremonies become moments of voyeuristic derision. Fortunately, Tenney took care with his rituals, ensuring that the participants invest both enthusiasm and energy into their roles, their bodies writhing in ecstatic rhythms as shadowy lighting plays over their rapt forms. Consequently, one actually comes to believe in their beliefs—or at least in their earnestness—which carries the viewer beyond the sensationalism of the moment to feel some small measure of the *appeal* of Voudoun.

Tenney reported that he "read several books on voodoo," before writing the screenplay, but noted that at the time "there wasn't a lot actually, there's not a lot on it. So basically we sort of had to make it up as we went along as to the ceremonies and so on. Actually, most of it was just our imagination."

"We did have a kind of a [voodoo] expert as an advisor," continued Tenney. "And he told me basically that some of the story had a basis of truth in it—that snakes, of course, are always used in voodoo ceremonies, and chickens, and so on and so forth. Also, there *was* a cult of voodoo Caribbeans that did believe that snake venom was a *cure* actually for whatever particular thing they had down there at that point. So there was sort of a basis of truth in the storyline." Hmm. Perhaps a bit of wishful thinking?

Reviews were (and are) invariably harsh. *Castle of Frankenstein*'s Calvin T. Beck labeled it an "execrable zombie cheapie" in which "crusty-looking native monsters walk around amid endless tribal dancing and *Disembodied*-level dialogue. Even Mantan Moreland couldn't have saved this." *Fangoria*'s Dr. Cyclops called it "a feeble voodoo picture." Singling out the "horrible acting" and "terrible makeup," he concluded, "Certainly atrocious on every count, but not as laughably inane as *Horror of Party Beach*, Tenney's masterwork."

When asked what he thought of the finished film, Tenney laughingly admitted, "I didn't like it very much; I thought it was sort of silly." While definitely far from the best voodoo pictures of the 1960s and 1970s, *I Eat Your Skin* is not as bad as all that and still deserves a look for its effective zombies and involving voodoo sequences. Despite his sci-fi denouement, Del Tenney did Damballah proud.

[1] Second unit director William Grefe later made his own low-budget features, the most (in)famous of which is the dreadful *Death Curse of Tartu* (1967).

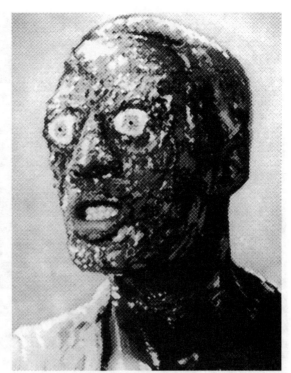

Despite the title, the fearsome-looking zombies of *I Eat Your Skin* are strictly vegetarians.

[2] "I am currently working on another film project," Tenney told this author in July of 1997. "I wrote an original treatment called *Infidelity Inn* which is kind of an Edgar Allan Poe turn-of-the-century murder mystery. So I'm still fooling around with it; it's still in my blood. I'd love nothing better than to work on motion pictures again."

CREDITS: Director/Producer/Screenwriter: Del Tenney; Associate Producers: Dan Stapleton, Jesse Hartman; Director of Photography: Francois Farka; Music Composed and Conducted by: Lon E. Norman; Art Director: Robert Verberkmoes; Second Unit Director: William Grefe; Production Manager: Mel Pape; Editor: Larry Keating; Assistant Editor: Monty Swartz; Camera Operator: Ed Gibson; Assistant Camera: Leonard DeMunde; Sound Recording: Edmund Wright; Makeup: Guy Del Russo; Casting Director: Doris Bernhar; Production Secretary: Frances Hidde; Costume Supervisor: Jane Hagerty. Released in 1971 by Cinemation Industries; 81 minutes

CAST: William Joyce (Tom Harris), Heather Hewitt (Jeanine Biladeau), Walter Coy (Charles Bentley), Dan Stapleton (Duncan Fairchild), Betty Hyatt Linton (Carol Fairchild), Robert Stanton (Dr. Biladeau), Vanoye Aikens, Rebecca Oliver, Matthew King, George-Ann Williamson, Don Strawn's Calypso Band

The Spanish pressbook for this Paul Naschy voodoo vehicle sports *Vengeance of the Zombies'* original language title (translated as "The Rebellion of the Dead"). (Courtesy Eric Hoffman)

VENGEANCE OF THE ZOMBIES (1972)
Paul Naschy's Voodoo Vagary

Kontaka, don't use [the zombies] again
for your personal ruinous plans.
You were given the maximum of power
to spread your sacred voodoo
all over this earth, *not* to wreak your
wretched vengeance on others."
—Pierre Besari as the zombie-master's
uppity (and long-winded) servant, Ti-Zachary

Spain's Paul Naschy, screenwriter and star of *Vengeance of the Zombies*, is the combined Christopher Lee and Peter Cushing of Continental cinema. In fact, to carry the Hammer analogy further, he's also the Terence Fischer (or at least Freddie Francis) of Eurohorror because, in addition to starring in over two-dozen terror films (in which he plays everything from werewolves and mummies to hunchbacks and vampires), he also directed over a dozen of the features himself.

A professed lover of Gothic horror in general and the Universal classics in particular ("all the marvelous films made by Universal Studios in the 1930s are the main source of inspiration for all my work"[1]), Naschy almost single-handedly began a Gothic revival in Spanish cinema in the late 1960s and 1970s with his scripting, acting in, and ultimately directing the Waldemar Daninsky/Werewolf series. Though few Americans know his name or have seen his films, the dedicated Eurohorror aficionado and offbeat cineaste have been seeking out his movies for years. (Whereas only a handful of his 60-odd pictures ever played in American theaters, many more of them have been released on video.) While the plots are sometimes trite, the production values often suspect, the acting usually bad, and the dubbing always awful, Naschy's films show an eccentric enthusiasm and appeal in a quirky, almost quaintly exploitative fashion that no American- or British-produced horror film of the same era can duplicate (though, admittedly, some might add "nor would they *want* to").

What sets Naschy's movies apart from (and *above*) the often mean-spirited and cynically exploitative product of his contemporary countrymen like Jess Franco and Amando De Ossorio is Naschy's respect of and outright affection for the cinematic horror tradition. Naschy's upbeat attitude and enthusi-asm often transferred itself to those around him as well. "I thoroughly enjoyed working with Paul," exclaimed Caroline Munro (who acted opposite Naschy in *Howl of the Devil*), "and would like to work with him again." Though Naschy's budget-conscious and often puerile journeys into Gothic fantasy are no better *cinematically* than most of the genre Eurotrash of the decade, their storylines possess an appealing dose of almost wistful nostalgia—spiced, of course, with the requisite dashes of sex and blood.

While Naschy is both prolific and sincere, he's not necessarily good. In fact, many of his films can generously be labeled "barely watchable." The writer/actor/director himself has no illusions about his movies or his talent, as this self-assessment shows: "I wouldn't say that Paul Naschy was marvelous nor that he was very good; but for any person who sits down to watch a film of mine on the big screen or on television, I believe it will communicate to him that what he is watching was made with love."

Having written and starred in movies about werewolves, vampires, mummies, the Frankenstein Monster, Dr. Jekyll, and even Jack the Ripper, it seems only natural that Naschy should eventually get around to zombies. In 1972 he faced the walking dead in *La Orgia de los Muertos* (aka *The Hanging Woman*), but Naschy worked solely as an actor on this film about corpses animated by mad science. When it came time for Naschy to write his own zombie movie, however, he turned to the creature's more traditional source—voodoo.

The film opens when a husband-and-wife grave-robbing team are locked in a tomb by a mysterious black-cloaked figure, who then pours blood over a wax doll, sets it aflame, and calls upon "the power of Baron Samedi" to raise the tomb's occupant (a young woman) from the dead. The newly created zombie strangles the husband and brains the wife with a candlestick (!) before following the shrouded voodooist out into the night.

The story then concentrates on Elvira (European fashion model-turned-actress Romy) who, along with her psychiatry professor friend, Dr. Lawrence Redgrave (Vic Winner), becomes embroiled with a Hindu guru named Krishna (Paul Naschy). First impressed by Krishna's spirituality, Elvira ultimately falls in love with the man. (Note: Screenwriter Naschy named his heroine "Elvira" after his real-life wife.)

Meanwhile, the black-cloaked figure has created several more zombie women and sends them to Elvira's house. The walking dead kill her father, but are frightened away by the police before they can get to Elvira.

Lawrence (who is an expert on the occult) has been helping Scotland Yard with this bizarre series of murders/body-snatchings. The police learn that the murdered girls belong to three English families that once lived in India. It soon comes out that these families were part of a nasty incident involving Krishna's deceased brother, Kontaka. Apparently, back in India Kontaka had raped an English girl ("which was the cause of her death"), and in retaliation the girl's relatives, aided by those three English families, burned the house in which Kontaka was hiding. "But my brother," Krishna ultimately explains to Elvira, "with his face monstrously disfigured, saved himself... Then he became a novice of voodoo in its most diabolic form. He had a fixed idea of destroying, using his occult powers, all the families that had wronged him." Krishna knows all this because Kontaka has entranced him. "My brother converted me to a slave, to serve as a medium in ceremonies of voodoo."

Now it just so happens that Elvira's last name is Irving—she belongs to the original family which sought revenge against Kontaka back in India. That night, Kontaka (Naschy again, with a burn scar on one side of his face) sends his zombie women to fetch Elvira, intending to use her as a sacrifice in a ceremony which will make him immortal. But when he orders the entranced Krishna to cut Elvira's throat, Krishna overcomes the spell. Kontaka then has his zombie women attack and kill his brother for his troubles.

Taking up the knife to finish Elvira himself, Kontaka is suddenly stabbed in the back—by Elsie (Maria Kosti), the household maid. "I'm the one who was sent to watch you," she tells the dying voodoo master. "*Traitor*! You have destroyed the voodoo. You have used its force without dignity." Kontaka dies, and his zombie women collapse.

All is not yet well, however, for Elsie picks up the knife herself and walks to the tied Elvira. "I am going to kill you," she tells her. "You will then become my zombie." Apparently, Elsie intends to create an army of zombies herself, not for petty personal vengeance like Kontaka, but to conquer the world! Fortunately, Lawrence arrives just then with the police, who shoot Elsie and free Elvira. The End.

With his barrel-chested wrestler's physique (he reportedly worked as a professional wrestler before entering films), stocky stature, and rather blank face, Paul Naschy makes for an unlikely horror icon. But icon he is, not because of his acting prowess or physical presence, but because of his obvious energy and respect for his (often absurd) subjects. Naschy's deadly earnestness is almost contagious, so that the viewer often becomes caught up in his characters' tragic plights. Sadly, *Vengeance of the Zombies* is not one of Naschy's better vehicles, even though it gives him three roles to toy with. The script sorely lacks the pathos of his Daninsky/werewolf character or even of his sometimes pitiable Count Dracula (in the same year's *Dracula's Great Love*). In *Vengeance of the Zombies*, he either wears a black cape and mask for most of the time (as Kontaka), sports horns and body paint as a rather dull devil in a brief dream sequence, or is laughably miscast as a sensitive Hindu mystic. Naschy comes off best when playing tormented characters in roles that demand a lot of physical action. In *Vengeance*, he has little to do but wear turbans, pretend he's meditating, and blandly mouth sorry platitudes like "Don't forget that only through our sorrow can we achieve happiness, which all of us desire." One begins to long for a few of his trademark grunts and howls.

Jacinto Molina Alvarez (Paul Naschy's real name) was born in Madrid in 1934. After living through the Spanish Civil War ("once, when I was playing in the garden with my cousin, a bomb fell very close by, not killing us by a fraction"), he became an architectural student and weight-lifter (in 1958 he won the Spanish National Championship). Upon working as an extra in Nicholas Ray's *King of Kings* (simply "to earn some money"), Naschy "began to feel the addiction" of cinema. Of course, he had been interested in movies since childhood, particularly horror and fantasy, after he snuck into a local theater as a boy to see *Frankenstein Meets the Wolf Man*. "I was very impressed by this film," Naschy recalled, "and from that moment on, I knew that I wanted to go into acting, especially the fantastic and horror cinema, and above all as the character of the Wolf Man by which I was completely fascinated." After more bit parts and a stint as an assistant director, Naschy managed to sell a werewolf script he'd written called *La Marca del Hombre Lobo* to a German production company who then brought in a Spanish co-producer. Still, the screenwriter had no delusions of stardom at the time. "The only thing left was to find someone to play the part of the werewolf," remembered Naschy. "There were a number of auditions... none of them successful. Even Lon Chaney, Jr., was contacted, but by then he was too old and ill, and had to refuse the offer. When it looked as though everything was about to fall through, the German producers offered the role to me. I was very surprised at first, but it was in fact the only solution. I was tested; they liked the results; and so there I was, playing Waldemar Daninsky in *La Marca del Hombre Lobo*" (1968; misleadingly re-titled *Frankenstein's Bloody Terror* for release in the U.S.). Fearful that the ethnic name of Jacinto Molina would not appeal to an international audience, the producers induced the fledgling actor to concoct a new onscreen moniker. ("I changed my artistic name for the film to Naschy," related the actor, "inspired by the famous Hungarian weightlifter.") The film became a financial hit in Europe and Naschy went on to appear in over 60 films over the next two decades (over half of

A future zombie (Aurora De Alba) in a scene from the Franquist (censored) version of *Vengeance of the Zombies*. *Vengeance of the Zombies* remains one of Naschy's duller efforts.

which he also wrote or co-wrote under his real name), many of them in the horror genre—including *nine* more Waldemar Daninsky werewolf movies! With 1976's *Inquisition*, Naschy/Molina began directing many of his own films as well. To date he's directed over a dozen features plus a handful of documentaries for Japanese television. After his production company went bankrupt in the late 1980s, coupled with a near-fatal heart attack resulting in triple-bypass surgery in 1992, Paul Naschy has semi-retired from the industry. But perhaps during the next full moon...?

(Amazingly, Naschy *and* Waldemar Daninsky have been recently resurrected after all; *Lycantropus*, a new Daninsky werewolf film, was released in Spain in April of 1997. Naschy both wrote and starred in this two million dollar production [nearly *10 times* the cost of his last werewolf picture!]. As of this writing, Naschy's 11th wolfman outing has yet to find an American distributor.)

Vengeance of the Zombies remains one of Naschy's duller efforts, lacking the energetic quirkiness of his better werewolf pictures. It's plagued with long stretches of stilted dialogue (delivered in that rapid, toneless manner that only cheap dubbing actors can supply) and lengthy filler scenes (endless "establishing" shots of London streets or scenes of Krishna riding around the city in a taxi running errands). In one interminable scene, Lawrence conducts a convoluted discourse on black magic and voodoo ceremonies for the Inspector. For several minutes his awkward lecture drags on (and on and on) before he concludes with the rhetorical (and ironic) question, "What more is there?" Nothing, for he's said it *all*—in boring detail. Yet, comically, he immediately resumes his speech, going on for another several minutes about the proper *places* to conduct the ceremonies! At this point the scene crosses the line of exposition to become farce.

"It's a demented film," admitted Naschy himself. "At the time, I was very interested in the gurus and Hindu mystics, as well as the theme of voodoo. So as I had done before in *Los Monstruos del Terror* [1970; released as *Assignment Terror* in the U.S.], I decided to combine the two ideas." Though he did indeed combine the two concepts, he failed to integrate them, so that the Indian mystic angle becomes completely superfluous. No clashes of faith materialize, no exploration of Hindu or Voudoun myths, not even a single battle between Indian and African magic. The only thing this bizarre juxtaposition adds to the film is the dubious sight of the chunky (and obviously European) Naschy wearing Hindu robes and turbans.

As far as voodoo goes, apart from Lawrence's confused and lengthy lecture on the topic (in which he spouts bizarre, apocryphal "facts" like "a [voodoo] initiate [is] called 'The Minister' who, in order to obtain his wishes, had to conjure evil spirits, which were called 'Montes'"), the film seems to be taking voodoo down a stony path—an *Oliver* Stoney path, that is. If these voodooists can be believed, there's a conspiracy afoot, with no less than *world domination* at its core! Kontaka's supposed goal was "to spread sacred voodoo all over this earth" while Elsie (sent to watch over Kontaka and keep him on the straight and narrow) professes, "my mission is to create an empire, an empire of the dead who will conquer the living." Besides coming out of left field, these last-minute grandiose pronouncements illustrate yet another difference between reel voodoo and real Voudou. Unlike Christianity, Voudoun is *not* a proselytizing religion, for there is no such thing as a Voudou missionary (evil, scarred madman or otherwise) intending to spread his religion "all over this earth."

In Naschy's screenplay, the characters indulge in all manner of nonsensical behavior. For instance, after finding a decapitated housekeeper and being menaced by a scythe-wielding servant, Elvira first goes into hysterics (naturally enough), then abruptly turns tender toward Krishna, stroking his hair and kissing him. It's a moment both inexplicable and ridiculous. And the actors do little better, for during the frequent (and long) dialogue scenes the thespians rarely react with any verisimilitude (perhaps they're as bored as the audience with the never-ending talk), adding to the film's feeling of fabrication.

Sadly, even the zombies let us down. "The one thing that seduced me above all was the idea that the most beautiful women could be tremendously sinister," stated Naschy about his story. "I made these women as powerful as a vampire might be, although on this occasion they were zombies." They're plenty powerful all right (impressively ramming a graveyard cross through a policeman or—almost comically—using a morgue attendant's soda can as a lethal weapon), and they do *smile* creepily on occasion. But these walking dead are sorely let down by both their director and makeup man. Director Leon Klimovsky insists upon filming them in slow motion—even their attacks (which makes their victims' slo-mo struggles look ridiculous and unreal when accompanied by real-time screams and stammers). The constantly sloweddown action and lethargic movements in the zombie scenes quickly become tedious.

Even worse, the zombies' clownish makeup, with a stark white base and black shoe polish around the eyes, looks amateurish. And it's applied in such a slapdash manner that one can sometimes see the streak-marks made by the makeup artist's (using the term loosely here) fingers. What's worse, the makeup simply stops at the neck, so that the pasty complexion of the face contrasts jarringly with the healthy pink flesh tones of the actresses' shoulders, arms, and hands—completely ruining the undead illusion. This uneven pancake makeup simply calls attention to its falsity and robs the zombie women of whatever (slomo) punch they could have delivered. Rather than *Vengeance of the Zombies*, a more accurate title would have been *Vengeance of the Ugly Mimes*.

Leon Klimovsky's direction is adequate (stubborn insistence on slow-motion zombies excepted) but uninspired. He shoots with a minimum of setups and angles, getting just enough footage of basic master and close-ups to get the scene in a presentable fashion—and then moves on to the next. It's what one would have expected of Roger Corman on one of his cheap 1950s films had he been given color film stock and a license for gore.

Klimovsky was Naschy's favorite director to work with, "not because he was the best necessarily," qualified the actor, but "as a person, it was very pleasant working with him. He's a good craftsman and stylist. The only problem with him is that he worked under the belief that he could do the job without spending a lot of money. [Corman all over.] What I mean is that he would always go for the lowest estimate available, despite the producers' offers to give him as much as he needed, and this was eventually bad for the films because in some respects they came out seriously compromised." Klimovsky directed eight Paul Naschy films: *The Werewolf vs. the Vampire Woman* (1970; the best known—and arguably the best—of the Waldemar Daninsky series), *Dr. Jekyll and the Wolfman* (1971); *Vengeance of the Zombies* (1972), *Una Libelula para Cada Muerto* (A Dragonfly for Each Corpse; 1973); *El Mariscal del Infierno* (The Marshall of Hell; 1974), *Muerte de un Quinqui* (Death of a Hoodlum; 1975), *The People Who Own the Dark* (1975); and *Secuestro* (Kidnapping; 1976). Among Klimovsky's many non-Naschy titles are *The Saga of the Draculas* (1972), *The Vampire's Night Orgy* (1973), and *The Night of the Walking Dead* (1975).

Vengeance of the Zombies suffers from an excruciatingly bad '70s jazz/pop music score which has absolutely nothing to do with what's happening onscreen. Composer Juan Carlos Calderon can't possibly have *watched* the picture, for the music bears no relation to a scene's mood (light ersatz jazz playing during what should be a moment of intensity and tension, for instance). And as a final, insulting exclamation point, when the zombies collapse upon Kontaka's death (in slow motion, of course), the music drones to a stop on the soundtrack as well—as if somebody simply pulled the plug on a record player! Incredible. Naschy realized the movie's music was pathetic, but could do nothing about it. "I think the film would have been greatly improved with another musical score, but that's pretty much the general rule in Klimovsky's films since he didn't take care of the music. Some of these films would benefit greatly if the soundtracks could be changed, but… we have to accept them as they are."

With all its faults, *Vengeance of the Zombies* does produce an occasional spark of interest, be it from an unusual zombie attack (in which one of the undead kills a man by taking the unfortunate's soda can and slowly ramming it into his neck) or from a powerfully shocking scene (Kontaka using a voodoo doll to force a man to stick a knife into his own neck and draw it slowly across his throat in a spray of blood). Too bad the poor script, disappointing makeup, dull acting, and pedestrian direction never allow the spark to become a full-fledged flame.

In talking of his career, Paul Naschy stated, "I was capable of mistakes—to do it well or to do it poorly—but what I assure you is that I did it with feeling and with affection. I love the fantastic cinema… I would give years of my life to continue making fantastic films." *Vengeance of the Zombies* definitely falls into the "mistake" category. Even so, while it remains a pretty poor specimen of voodoo cinema,

at least it's better than those other Spanish entries— *The* (execrable*) Night of the Sorcerers* (1973) and the ludicrous *Voodoo Black Exorcist* (1975).

In the late 1970s, Independent Artists re-released *Vengeance of the Zombies* as *Walk of the Dead* in an attempt to cash in on George Romero's successful zombie opus, *Dawn of the Dead*. IA also tried to disguise the film's foreign origins by anglicizing the names of various cast and crew. Actress Mirta Miller became *Martha* Miller, director Leon Klimovsky was listed as Miles Nelson, and (oddly) Paul Naschy was changed to *Richard* Naschy. In addition, IA inserted William Castle-like "Fright Warning" cards throughout the film. It didn't help.

[1] All quotes attributed to Paul Naschy are from interviews conducted by Jose Luis Gonzalez and Michael Secula printed in *Videooze* no. 6/7 and Jose Ignacio Cuenca printed in *Fangoria* no. 134.

CREDITS: Original Language Title: *La Rebelion de Las Muertas* (Rebellion of the Female Dead); Alternate Titles: *The Rebellion of the Dead Women; Revolt of the Dead Ones*; *Walk of the Dead*; Director: Leon Klimovsky; Executive Producers: Ricardo Munoz Suay, J.A. Perez Giner; Story and Screenplay: Jacinto Molina; Photography: Francisco Sanchez; Editor: Antonio Ramirez De Loaysa; Music: Juan Carlos Calderon; Sets: Gumersindo Andres; Head of Production: Modesto Perez Redondo; Makeup: Miguel Sese; Effects: Manuel Gomez; A 1972 Spanish/Italian Profilms production released by ZIV International; 89 minutes

CAST: Paul Naschy [Jacinto Molina] (Krishna Fanatim/Kontaka Fanatim), Romy [Carmen Romero] (Elvira Irvin), Mirta Miller (Kala), Vic Winner (Professor Lawrence Redgrave), Maria Kosti [Kosty] (Elsie), Aurora De Alba (Olivia), Luis Ciges (MacMurdo), Pierre Besari (Ti-Zachary), Antonio Pica (Comisario), Elsa Zabala (Zombie Woman), Montserrat Julio, Ramon Lillo (Inspector), Norma Kastell (Zombie Woman), Ingrid Rabel, Asuncion Molero (Zombie Woman), Fernando Sanchez Polack (Grave-robber), Alfonso De La Vega

Voodoo vampire vixens from the 1973 Spanish sexploitation film, *The Night of the Sorcerers*. (Spanish pressbook and photos courtesy Eric Hoffman and Lynn Naron)

THE NIGHT OF THE SORCERERS (1973)
Voodoo, Spanish Sexploitation-Style

Liz (soon-to-be victim): "Does this have to do with the voodoo?"

Carol (recently converted demon leopard-woman): "Yes, the voodoo; and you are the queen tonight!"

In the 1970s, Spain became a hotbed of horror—at least on the silver screen. Countless low-budget genre films (usually loaded with spurting blood and naked females) poured across its border, some even crossing the Atlantic for brief showings at all-night drive-in fright-fests. Among the most prolific Spanish filmmakers churning out horror after horror were Jess (Jesus) Franco, Leon Klimovsky, Paul Naschy (Jacinto Molina), and Amando De Ossorio.

Though for many years a prominent industry figure in his home country, Spanish director Amando De Ossorio (who speaks no English) is best known to American viewers (if known at all) as the creator of the *Blind Dead* films (*Tombs of the Blind Dead*, 1971; *Return of the Blind Dead*, 1973; *Horror of the Zombies*, 1974; and *The Night of the Seagulls*, 1975). In this quartet of terror, the mummified cadavers of the Knights Templar rise up as unseeing zombies to wreak havoc in Spanish villages, on rural trains, and even on a Flying Dutchman-like galley.

The *Blind Dead* pictures possess some eerie photography and creepy title creatures (appearing as desiccated corpses shrouded in moldering hooded robes, reaching out with claw-like bony hands) whose slow but steady advance, guided by the sounds of their victims' terrified breathing and rapid heartbeat, generate some genuine chills. Unfortunately, most of De Ossorio's other movies (lacking the terrifying presence of the zombified Templars) prove dull and uninteresting. *The Night of the Sorcerers* is no exception.

In speaking of horror films in general and his *Blind Dead* series in particular, De Ossorio told *Deep Red*'s Dale Pierce that "one of the key elements that makes suspense build in the films is because [the zombies] move so slowly and the tension mounts a step at a time. Viewers know the Templars are coming, but they have to wait and wait and wait. This makes the films all the more frightful because suspense and mounting tension is the secret to making a horror film frightening." In *The Night of the Sorcerers* (a truly "frightful" film—though, sadly, not in the literal sense), De Ossorio takes this slowness and "tension building" to the extreme, so that the viewer indeed has to "wait and wait and wait," wading through scene after lengthy scene of bad acting between shallow characters, ill-lit and tedious "love" scenes, and poorly dubbed exposition. By the time something finally does happen, De Ossorio's all-important "tension" has completely dissipated because the viewer has lost all interest.

The story begins in "Bumbasa, 1910" where a group of voodooists decapitate a woman during a ritual ceremony and bathe in her blood. A band of (presumably British) soldiers surround the clearing and open fire. With all the natives dead, the victim's decapitated head suddenly comes alive and, now sporting vampire-like fangs, starts to scream.

Forward to "Bumbasa, the present," and two Land Rovers approach a river to set up camp. Consisting of Professor Jonathan Grant (Jack Taylor), photographer Carol Harris (Loretta Tower; aka Lorena Tovar), guide Rod Carter (Simon Andreu), his girlfriend Tanica (Kali Hansa), and Liz Meredith (Maria Kosti), whose father financed the expedition, the group is there to "make a photographic survey about animals on the verge of extinction." Friendly local fur trader T'Munga (Joseph Thelman) shoos off some inquisitive natives for them and offers to show the newcomers around. Taking them to "the clearing of the witches" (where the sacrifice and massacre took place 60-odd years before), he tells them of the voodoo ceremony consecrated to "the devil of the jungle" which converts the victims into leopard women. "During the day they're leopards that wander about the jungle," he says. "By night they change into devils with human bodies." According to legend, at the time of the full moon the voodoo witches rise up from their graves to seek new victims for their ceremony.

That night Carol sneaks back to the clearing, thinking she might get photos of a voodoo ritual. It being a full moon (naturally), she falls victim to the resurrected witches, who perform the decapitation/blood-drinking ceremony and turn her into a leopard woman.

The following day, the others search for Carol but find only her dropped camera. That night, the leopard women sneak into the interlopers' camp and kill Professor Grant (drowning him in a developer's tray (!) as he's working on the film from Carol's camera). Carol, now a leopard woman, lures her friend Liz back to the sacrificial clearing, then bites her on the neck. After decapitation, Liz joins their ranks.

That night, Rod intends to follow the sounds of the drums, vowing, "I promise you you'll hear *another* rhythm!" After he moves off into the forest, T'Munga shows up at camp and tries to rape Tanica, who manages to stab him to death for his efforts. Then

A voodoo sorceress prepares another victim for indoctrination into the cult of the leopard women in *The Night of the Sorcerers*.

the professor's corpse comes alive and advances toward Tanica. She escapes its grasp and sets the tent aflame, trapping the zombie inside, and flees into the jungle after Rod.

Both Tanica and Rod are captured by the undead witches and leopard women. While the witches hold Rod, the vampiric leopard women bite Tanica on the neck and ready her for the decapitation ceremony. At the last moment, Rod breaks free, grabs Tanica, and tosses his gunbelt into the fire. As the ammunition explodes, sending bullets thudding into the undead voodooists in a reprise of the original massacre, Rod flees with Tanica back to their Land Rover.

Eluding their demonic pursuers (even running down several of them), the pair escape and drive off. When Rod asks the bitten Tanica if she's all right, the woman answers, "I'm feeling much better *now*—" and smiles, showing the tell-tale fangs and breathy panting of the demon leopard women.

Frankly put, *The Night of the Sorcerers* is a mean-spirited, poorly made exploitation picture that relies on nudity, brutality, and gore rather than story, acting, and characterization. And what's worse, it's not even competent on this level, for it breaks the first rule of exploitation filmmaking: Shock, sicken, and titillate, but never, never *bore* your audience.

The opening sequence is a thoroughly cruel and tasteless scene in which a horn-hatted, leopard-skinned, straw-skirted cartoon of the stereotypical "jungle savage" literally whips the clothes from a (white) woman's body and then ritualistically rapes her as she's tied standing up. The scene goes on and on with the camera lingering on her lashed body as her clothes are torn away and she shrieks with pain in an overtly distasteful bout of brutal voyeurism.

Then the natives lay her nude body out on the sacrificial slab and a woman cuts her head off with a machete. With the thick vicious orange blood running out of the neck stump, the frenzied voodooists gather around and anoint themselves with the victim's plasma. This opening is both tasteless and ineffectual, shot for nudity and gore's sake alone, since the viewer has absolutely no background or context at this point. We don't know *who* these people are or *what* this ritual/sacrifice means. It's simply an excuse to show breasts and blood—in an extremely sadistic and unpleasant manner.

As a capper to the sequence, the woman's decapitated head suddenly jumps up onto the altar by itself, turns, opens its eyes and mouth (to show a row of vampire-like fangs), and hisses/screams into the camera. While this last bit is definitely novel and admittedly unexpected, it's also completely inexplicable.

Though this opening set-piece may be exploitative and tasteless, at least it's *active*. De Ossorio next treats the viewer to several minutes of pointless filler in which the protagonists unload their gear, set up camp, and put up the tents. It's like watching a Ranger Rick camping booklet come to badly dubbed life. De Ossorio then extends the ennui by shooting a *loooong* love scene between Rod and his girlfriend on the riverbank. It's not even effective as sexploitation since the soft-core sequence is so poorly lit that it defeats its intended purpose.

In between exchanges of awkward and poorly dubbed dialogue, De Ossorio periodically sends his characters and camera on lengthy rambles through the pitch-black forest. The scenes are so dark that the viewer can only tell something is happening by the occasional tempo changes in the heavy-handed "suspense" music blaring on the soundtrack. (Perhaps the poor lighting was an attempt to disguise the fact that the Portuguese countryside in which De Ossorio filmed looks nothing like the Dark Continent it was supposed to be.)

Most of the subsequent "thrills" are pure repetition, as De Ossorio resorts to re-staging (with little variation) the opening sequence twice more. The first encore (with Carol) is an almost blow-by-blow copy of the distasteful scene as she gets *her* clothes ripped from her body (though, for variety, it's a bikini-clad leopard woman wielding the whip this time rather than a grass-skirted man), is decapitated, and performs her own bodyless scream. Then, a little later, it's Liz's turn, though (thankfully) the leopard women bypass the whipping and make do with a perfunctory neck-biting before going straight to the expected head-chopping.

"I personally place a lot of emphasis on special effects," reported De Ossorio, "because that is one of the main points the audience is looking for in these times. The better the special effects, the larger the crowd. Sometimes it is the special effects in itself that will make a movie popular." Despite his professed emphasis, *The Night of the Sorcerers* has very little in the way of effects, special or otherwise. The only striking sequences, apart from a prop whip leaving snail tracks of stage blood across an actress' naked torso, are the three decapitation scenes. Unfortunately, the dummy head and body (the *same* one stands in for all three victims, with the cuts getting shorter and shorter—no pun intended—in an attempt to disguise this fact) look like, well, a dummy head and body.

Carol (Lorena Tovar) is about to lose her head and so join the ranks of the voodooists' vampiric leopard women.

De Ossorio can't even get his stock footage right. At one point, Temunga talks of the legend of the devil leopard ("…and the devil leopard is tracking us in the underbrush") and the scene cuts to a stock shot of an ambling *cheetah*!

The cast can do little with the nonexistent characterization and stilted dialogue handed them. And the awkward, unnatural dubbing adds the final weight that makes their performances sink like a stone. Sample inexplicable exchange:

Tanika: "Your silly bad manners are really too much. You are just a stupid child."
Liz: "The only thing I may say firmly is if anything has happened to Carol, I'll stop only when the guilty have been found."

The only American in *The Night of the Sorcerers* cast was Jack Taylor (born 1936), who carved a niche for himself as a lead actor in Spanish horror films of the 1960s and '70s, working frequently for the likes of Jess Franco (in films such as *Succubus*, 1968; *Count Dracula*, 1970; and *The Bare Breasted Countess*, 1973), Leon Klimovsky (*Dr. Jekyll and the Wolfman*, 1971; *The Vampire's Night Orgy*, 1973), and De Ossorio (*The Night of the Sorcerers*, *Horror of the Zombies*, 1974).

According to Jess Franco, Taylor ultimately became what all directors dread—an *actor's* actor. "The problem with Jack now," Franco told *Fangoria*'s Donald Farmer, "is he's taking himself *very* seriously. He became kind of an Actors Studio actor. Now he needs the script two months before shooting." Why this is the case is anybody's guess, for one could never suppose such pretensions from his lackluster performance here. Taylor's bland good looks match his gen-

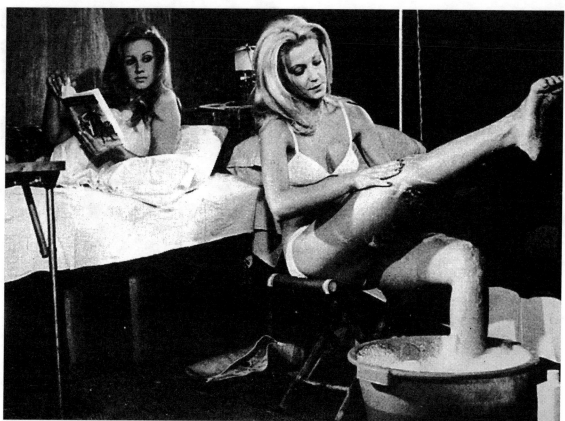

Titillation amongst the terror as Liz and Carol (Maria Kosti and Lorena Tovar) enjoy a quiet, semi-nude moment in *The Night of the Sorcerers*.

erally banal portrayals, making him stand out from his Spanish films only by the fact that his is usually the only name an American viewer can properly pronounce.

The Night of the Sorcerers failed to generate much enthusiasm at the box office. "The film had all the ingredients of a great horror movie," opined De Ossorio grandiosely. "It just didn't go over as well as I thought it would. Perhaps it was because the location was not what one might consider typical for either a horror movie or one of my films. I don't know. Perhaps in trying to be original, I drifted too far from the acceptable horror frame. I thought it had everything that would make a great scary story, but it didn't provoke the reaction I thought it would outside of Spain. Perhaps bad editing and the toning down of important scenes killed it off." Or perhaps, *senor* De Ossorio, it was simply a bad movie.

"You can really tell when you've got a good film," declared De Ossorio, "when you take the impossible and have the people sitting in the theater forgetting about reality and believing, for the moment, what they are seeing. When you have them caught up in that momentary fantasy, where they are one with the action on the screen, you know you've done your job well as a director." Considering the fact that for much

of *The Night of the Sorcerers*, the "people sitting in the theater" can't even *see* what's on the underlit screen—and what they *can* see is far from realistic, it's safe to say that by his own standards, De Ossorio must know that he did *not* do his job well as a director.

CREDITS: Original Language Title: *La Noche de los Brujos*; Alternate Title: *Night of the Witches*; Director/Screenwriter: Amando De Ossorio; Executive Producers: Ricardo Munoz Suaym and Luis Laso; Director of Photography: Francisco Sanchez; Sets and Environment: Cruz Baleztena; Makeup: Miguel Sese; Editor: Antonio Ramirez; Production Manager: Modesto Perez Redondo; Music: Fernando G. Morcillo; Special Effects: Jesus Iglesias; English Version Directed by: A.M. Santigosa; A Spanish production released by Profilms/Hesperia; 95 minutes

CAST: Simon Andreu (Rod Carter), Jack Taylor (Professor Jonathan Grant), Kali Hansa (Tanica), Maria Kosti (Liz Meredith), Loretta Tower [Lorena Tovar] (Carol Harris), Joseph [Jose] Thelman (T'Munga), Barbara King (Agnes)

In *The Vault of Horror*'s best segment, Tom Baker plays a painter who, via voodoo, acquires the power to dispatch his enemies with a particularly diabolical artistic flair.

THE VAULT OF HORROR
(1973)
Voodoo Meets Dorian Gray

Voodoo sorcerer: "What do you wish?"
Artist: "To buy voodoo."

Amicus' ineffectual follow-up to their hugely successful *Tales from the Crypt* (the company's most financially successful film) proved a disappointment both for Amicus (it failed to even come close to the gross receipts earned by *Tales*) *and* for viewers.

The film begins as five men step onto a high-rise elevator which inexplicably takes them to the sub-basement. There they find an octagonal room with five chairs. Only when the elevator door closes after they exit do they realize that it has no buttons. Obviously stuck there, the impromptu quintet simply decide to sit down and "make the best of it." After pouring drinks, they each in turn relate their own personal "dream, vision, phobia, obsession, fear—whatever you want to call it."

The first "dream" (called "Midnight Mess") follows Rogers (Daniel Massey) as he tracks his sister (Massey's real-life sibling Anna Massey) to a small town where he murders her for her inheritance. Strolling across the street to a restaurant to have a leisurely dinner after dispatching his sibling, he soon finds that he's the sole mortal in a restaurant catering strictly to vampires (his now-revived sister among them)—and that he's become the main course.

In the second story, "The Neat Job," Terry-Thomas plays a man so obsessed with order and neatness that he drives his new wife (Glynis Johns) around the bend—with the expected (and amusing) results: His dismembered and eviscerated body ends up in a series of neatly labeled jars, each gruesome bit in its proper place on the tidy shelf.

In the third tale, "This Trick'll Kill You," a magician (Curt Jurgens) journeys to India to find something with which to spice up his act. He comes across a young girl's magic rope trick, but when she refuses

In the "This Trick'll Kill You" vignette, magician Curt Jurgens will go to any length to obtain the secret of an Indian rope trick—even murder.

to sell him the "trick," he murders her—only to run afoul of the revenging rope itself.

In the fourth lackluster vignette, called "Bargain in Death," a horror fiction writer (Michael Craig) is buried alive after faking his own death in an insurance scam—which, of course, goes horribly wrong.

The final (and best) episode is the voodoo story: "Drawn and Quartered." When an artist named Moore (Tom Baker), living and working in a primitive hut in the jungles of Haiti, learns that his agent (in cahoots with a wily gallery owner and unscrupulous art critic) has been selling his paintings for huge sums without passing the cash on to the author, he vows revenge. To this end he goes to see the local voodoo sorcerer. "Put the hand you paint with into the pot," instructs the bokor. When the artist reluctantly thrusts his fist into the boiling cauldron, he draws it back unscathed.

Back at his hut, Moore takes time out from working on his self-portrait to do a quick sketch of a pot sitting on his table. Unsatisfied with his doodling, he rips the paper into four pieces and the vase suddenly falls, breaking into four pieces! As an experiment, the incredulous artist draws a piece of bread lying on the table, then erases one corner. Immediately a rat scurries in to nibble that very corner. Next Moore draws a small scar on the face of his self-portrait. Nothing happens immediately, but that night he

dreams of the sinister bokor and falls out of bed—scratching his face in that exact same spot.

Moore journeys to England (taking his now-finished self-portrait, of course, which he locks securely in a safe) to confront his three enemies. "You cheated me," he tells the smug gentlemen, "all three of you, and I'm going to have revenge."

With that, he goes to work painting portraits of each of them. One portrait he blinds with a knife. That night, the man's wife discovers his infidelities and throws acid into her cheating husband's eyes.

Moore then rips out the hands in the portrait of the second man, resulting in the unfortunate gallery owner having a gruesome run-in with an industrial paper cutter.

Saving his agent for last, Moore takes the portrait to the man's office and confronts his enemy face to face. The wary agent pulls a gun from his drawer, but Moore simply draws a red hole in the painted forehead and then watches as the man incredulously turns the gun on himself.

Suddenly, Moore is gasping for breath—he has placed his own self-portrait in an air-tight safe! Rushing back to his studio, he gets the door open just in time and sets the painting safely on an easel. In his haste, however, the artist has left his watch on the agent's desk and realizes he must retrieve the incriminating object. Dashing out into the traffic to catch a taxi, he's hit by a truck at the same time a sign painter working outside his studio accidentally knocks an open can of thinner off his scaffold. It falls through the studio skylight and onto the self-portrait. As the truck wheels roll over Moore's head, the self-portrait becomes a grotesque mix of running colors when the thinner washes over it.

Back in the sub-basement, the elevator doors suddenly open to reveal a graveyard beyond. As each man moves off into the cemetery, they vanish one by one. "That's how it is," observes the last, sadly, "and how it always will be. Night after night we have to retell the evil things we did when we were alive. Night after night, for all eternity." He turns and walks back into the mausoleum as the vault doors close.

The Vault of Horror is arguably Amicus' worst anthology, thanks mainly to Milton Subotsky's weak scripting and Roy Ward Baker's desultory direction. ("Milton wasn't very good at script writing," opined frequent Amicus director Freddie Francis to this author, explaining that though Subotsky "was not a writer, he had to write the scripts" because Amicus couldn't afford to *buy* them.)

The film's connecting device, which is *so* important to anthology films in both setting the tone for the tales to come and for grounding the stories in (some sort of) reality, comes off as contrived and slap-dash. Unlike Subotsky's first anthology, *Dr. Terror's House of Horrors* (1965), whose wraparound was an intriguing story in and of itself, *The Vault of Horror*'s connecting link is rushed and implausible, making it even more difficult than usual to take the terror tales seriously.

As well as often scripting his pictures himself, producer Milton Subotsky was in love with the editing process (having come from a semi-professional background in both screenwriting and editing). *The Vault of Horror*, in particular, fell under Subotsky's knife. "I feel the exciting aspect of our films is that we try not to bore an audience," the outspoken producer told *Cinefantastique* (Summer 1973). "We cut them so tightly and so fast that the first version of *Vault of Horror* was two hours and now we've got it down to 87 minutes. We cut it as tightly as we possibly can, and nothing stops for a second." This "tight cutting" most probably did irreparable harm, since presumably those excised portions were exposition and character development. One of the major faults with anthology films is the frequent lack of characterization—simply because there's no time for it. *The Vault of Horror* possesses this particular foible in abundance.

In addition, all but one of the five (poorly developed) protagonists are completely unlikable. In fact, most are greedy murderers. This leaves the viewer floundering about without any character to hang their hopes on, distancing them from the stories being told.

Baker's straightforward direction adds little to the underdeveloped tales. Rather than utilizing intriguing angles or unusual perspectives to augment the macabre aspects of the individual plots, Baker simply relies on the incidents themselves to generate impact. And, for the most part, the stories are simply too weak.

While a well-acted film (an Amicus trademark), *The Vault of Horror* simply looks cheap and dated. Apart from the one relatively long story (the voodoo tale), no segment utilizes more than one or two sets. And these are usually decorated (as are the hapless actors themselves) in the mod/garish (non)fashion that simply *screams* out early 1970s.

Director Roy Ward Baker himself made no bones about *The Vault of Horror*. "It wasn't any good," the director bluntly told John Brosnan in *The Horror People*, "it was a bore. We had a good cast but the script was really rubbish. That good cast was absolutely wasted and the producer, Milton Subotsky, says so himself."

Subotsky did indeed say so himself. The producer's initial enthusiasm for the project ("It's very inventive and it's funny," he told *Cinefantastique*'s Chris Knight shortly after the film's completion) quickly gave way to a more objective disappointment. "I don't know what went wrong with that one," the producer admitted only three years later in *The Horror People*. "Maybe I chose the wrong stories. You can never tell until a picture is finished whether it's good or not… Maybe we were too funny in *Vault of Horror* because we were really kidding it. It was probably too tame."

That "kidding" went so far as to have one character in "Bargain in Death" read the movie tie-in paperback of *Tales from the Crypt* while awaiting his catalepsy-inducing drug to kick in. "It's full of laughs and self-parody," stated Subotsky during production, "kind of tongue-in-cheek." Unfortunately, the laughs fail to come off and the viewer ends up *biting* that tongue in his cheek out of frustration.

"Milton wasn't his own best screenwriter," opined Roy Ward Baker in *Fangoria* magazine. "I told him, 'I don't think the picture is much of a success. I'm sorry about that, but I couldn't capture the strip cartoon idea.' Milton said, 'Don't be silly. It's not your fault. The script was no damned good, and that was me.'"

The film only really comes alive during its fifth and final episode—the voodoo vignette. Unlike most of the other segments, "Drawn and Quartered" is played absolutely straight. No in-jokes, sight gags, or over-the-top vampire fangs disrupt the story's carefully contrived concept. As such, it remains the most effective of the five segments.

The murderous magician gets more than he bargained for from his ill-gotten rope trick.

Like Amicus' earlier voodoo-inclusive anthology, *Dr. Terror's House of Horrors*, the voodoo segment is awarded the most time of the five tales; at 24 minutes it receives nearly a *third* of the film's running time! In addition to a better build-up and more intricate plotting, more care was taken with the settings in this segment than in the other, briefer, episodes. Unlike the other vignettes, "Drawn and Quartered" features a variety of sets plus a frantically paced sequence shot outside in the streets of London (with one exception, the other stories are all depressingly set-bound). This opens up the voodoo segment which, along with its intriguing premise, makes it the most polished and satisfying of the five tales.

*Un*like with *Dr. Terror's*, however, voodoo is taken very seriously in *The Vault of Horror*. When the painter, after removing his hand from the voodoo cauldron, impatiently asks half-contemptuously, "Now what? Do I get a little doll to stick pins into?," the unperturbed bokor responds matter-of-factly, "You are an artist. You don't need doll." Indeed, rather than the usual trite "voodoo doll" device, this story creates an appropriate and clever voodoo variation on *The Picture of Dorian Gray*. The quiet seriousness of the scene leaves no doubt that something sinister has just transpired.

As the bitter artist, Tom Baker (Britain's favorite "Dr. Who") exudes a glowering, imposing presence, and makeup man Roy Ashton provides him with striking red hair and an imposing Gauguin-like beard to complete the picture of a driven artist. Of the five main characters, Baker's is the only one that inspires any sort of viewer sympathy.

Denholm Elliott (always a joy to watch) is utterly convincing as the smarmy, cheating agent. His talent shines during the scene in which he struggles mightily against his own hands as they begin to turn the gun toward his own face. Elliott looks both incredulous and horrified as he vainly strains against his own possessed limbs.

Perhaps because he was allowed more than 10 minutes to tell his tale, director Roy Ward Baker seems to have taken more care with the voodoo story than with the others. Some fast-paced editing and effective foreshadowing from Baker at the climax, as the scene cuts from the frantic artist running across the traffic-congested streets futilely trying to hail a cab to shots of the oblivious workman edging ever closer to that fateful can of thinner poised above the studio skylight and the Dorian Gray-like painting, create the film's only real moment of effective suspense.

The only other segment besides the voodoo story that proves at all memorable is "Midnight Mess," thanks solely to its clever climax. Unfortunately, for some reason it's marred by the insertion of a still at a crucial moment—when the camera shows Daniel Massey's gruesome fate. Reports from the time of filming indicate that this scene was shot in the normal fashion (Massey even boasted to *Cinefantastique* magazine that he cleverly added some subtle convulsions to the sequence, "the same as when you see a bull dying in the bull ring—there is always a terrible sort of twitching as the blood pours out of him"). Either the footage was lost or ruined or (most likely) removed at the behest of the anti-twitching MPAA when the film made it to American shores. In any case, when it's time to show Massey hanging upside down with a tap sticking out of his neck as the vampire waiter smilingly fills a glass from this ghastly "vintage," it's patently obvious that the scene is a still photograph which the camera awkwardly holds on for several seconds. Consequently, a moment of shock and macabre humor becomes a technically jarring and ineffectual one—yet another example of the film's inferiority.

Variety's "Verr" (3/21/73) felt that *The Vault of Horror* "is less notable for its chill factor than for its showcasing of a number of name performers who react to the ham macabre like celebs who used to relish the pie-in-the-face from Soupy Sales. Quality for the material is uneven, ranging from camp comedy to the belabored grotesque." "Verr" singled out the weak wraparound, noting, "the five stories are bracketed with a creaky device about five men in an elevator that is more functional than imaginative."

Critic and future filmmaker Joe Dante, writing in *Castle of Frankenstein*'s Summer 1973 issue, was even harsher, claiming that "it beats *The Deadly Bees* as Amicus' worst film." (While this particular slam may be something of an overstatement, it certainly reflects the genre fans' attitude at the time of release.)

More interesting than the film itself were some of the promotional ploys leveled at potential ticket buyers. At the film's American premier at New York's Broadway Penthouse Theatre, for instance, each ticket holder was asked to scream before entering the theater in a PR contest to find "the best screamer." EC comics writer/publisher Bill Gaines was in attendance (but whether he screamed or not is unknown).

The Vault of Horror hasn't received the favorable attention garnered by its more-famous and better-liked predecessor, *Tales from the Crypt* (and rightly so). Those few modern critics who've bothered to write about it at all are usually dismissive. Dennis Fischer, in *Horror Film Directors*, briefly notes that "despite a good cast, the script just didn't work, and Baker does not get too visually inventive with his material." *Leonard Maltin's 1995 Movie and Video Guide* also noted "fine cast with so-so material." In *The Encyclopedia of Horror Movies*, Phil Hardy labeled it "the least interesting of the [Amicus anthology] series" and complained "Baker's flat direction can't overcome the lengthy and plodding expository scenes."

Ironically, none of the five tales in the movie actually appeared in the comic *Vault of Horror*. "Midnight Mess" is from *Tales from the Crypt* no. 35 (April-May 1953); "The Neat Job" was printed in *Shock SuspenStories* no. 1 (February-March 1952); "This Trick'll Kill You" was published in *Tales from the Crypt* no. 33 (December 1952); "Bargain in Death" is from *Tales from the Crypt* no. 28 (February-March 1952); and "Drawn and Quartered" was printed in *Tales from the Crypt* no. 26 (October-November 1951).

For the voodoo fan, *The Vault of Horror* actually surpasses its anthology companion, *Dr. Terror's House of Horrors*, for novelty and entertainment. In every other respect, however, *Vault* comes in a distant second. Except to get a peek at the one rather clever and innovative voodoo story, there's no real reason to open the door to this *Vault*.

CREDITS: Director: Roy Ward Baker; Producers: Max J. Rosenberg and Milton Subotsky; Executive Producer: Charles Fries; Production Executive: Paul Thompson; Screenplay: Milton Subotsky; Based on the stories written by Al Feldstein and Bill Gaines as originally published by William M. Gaines in the comic magazines entitled "The Vault of Horror" and "Tales from the Crypt"; Director of Photography: Danys Coop; Music Composed and Conducted by: Douglas Gamley; Art Director: Tony Curtis; Editor: Oswald Hafenrichter; Production Manager: Teresa Bolland; Production Supervisor: Art Stolnitz; Assistant Director: Anthony Waye; Camera Operator: John Harris; Continuity: Betty Harley; Set Dresser: Fred Carter; Construction Manager: Bill Waldron; Casting Director: Ronnie Gartis; Chief Makeup: Roy Ashton; Chief Hairdresser: Mibs Parker; Wardrobe Master: John Briggs; Sound Editor: Clive Smith; Sound Mixer: Danny Danfel; Dubbing Mixer: Garry Humphries; Alternate Title: *Tales from the Crypt II*; A British production released March 1973 by Amicus/Cinerama; 87 minutes; Rated PG

CAST: "MIDNIGHT MESS": Daniel Massey (Rogers), Anna Massey (Donna), Michael Pratt (Giles), Erik Chitty (Old Walter), Jerald Wells (Walter); "THE NEAT JOB": Terry-Thomas (Critchit), Glynis Johns (Eleanor), Marianne Stone (Jane), John Forbes-Robertson (Wilson); "THIS TRICK'LL KILL YOU": Curt Jurgens (Nebastlaz), Dawn Addams (Inez), Jasmine Hilton (Indian Girl), Ishaq Bax (Fakir); "BARGAIN IN DEATH": Michael Craig (Maitland), Edward Judd (Alex), Robin Nedwell (Tom), Geoffrey Davis (Jerry), Arthor Mallard (Gravedigger); "DRAWN AND QUARTERED": Tom Baker (Moore), Denholm Elliott (Dlitast), Terence Alexander (Breedley), John Witty (Gaskill)

Scream Blacula Scream's effective storyline resembles the 1970 film *House of Dark Shadows*, with voodoo magic standing in for medical science as a potential cure for vampirism. (Pressbook cover courtesy Lynn Naron)

SCREAM BLACULA SCREAM (1973)
Voodoo Dolls and Vampire Capes

"To us voodoo is simply a religion based on faith—
a powerful, powerful faith."
— Pam Grier as Lisa

In 1972 the screen's first black vampire took the drive-ins by storm, thanks in no small part to the imposing and cultured presence of Shakespearean actor William Marshall playing the title role. Though cursed with a ridiculous name (which, nonetheless, proved extremely exploitable), Marshall brought a stately charisma to *Blacula*[1] and added some much-needed respectability via his suggestions regarding the character. "The image that I suggested," Marshall told this author, "would be more meaningful to people—an African prince who had been nudged by his elders to go to Europe to do something about the *theft*, the continued thievery where African people were concerned."

Naturally, fiscal success led to a sequel, and American International talked their new star into reprising his role in their proposed *Blacula Is Beautiful* (a working title thankfully soon abandoned). "They believed it could do as well as the first one," recalled Marshall. This time, however, AIP proved less appreciative of the actor's input. "They were wary of me by then and didn't want to hear anything I had to say." As a consequence, the actor holds little love for *Scream Blacula Scream*.

When asked his opinion of the sequel, William Marshall complained that, "It didn't add anything to the first one." His viewpoint, however, peeks strictly from behind Mamuwalde's cape, and in that sense he's right—*Scream Blacula Scream* added nothing to the character of "Blacula." What it did add, however, was a new twist (voodoo) on a tired old theme (vampirism).

When the mamaloi of a modern-day voodoo congregation dies, her brash young son Willis (Richard Lawson) tries to foist himself upon them as their new priest. "The leadership goes to me, it's mine!" he shouts. "*I'm* the new papaloi!" The voodooists have other ideas, however, and choose Lisa (Pam Grier) as their spiritual guide. Incensed, Willis stalks off to plan his revenge. To this end, he visits a dethroned voodoo priest (Bernie Hamilton) who presents him with a bag of human bones along with the admonishment

that they contain great power (though he *fails* to mention that the remains are those of a certain vampire...).

That night Willis performs a voodoo ritual over the unholy relics. As a storm rages outside, fire shoots up from the bones, but the supernatural conflagration quickly sputters and dies. Thinking he's failed, a dejected Willis doesn't notice the shadow moving on the wall behind him—until the now-resurrected vampire known as "Blacula" (William Marshall) sinks his fangs into his neck.

Ordering Willis (now his vampiric slave) to remain at the house, Mamuwalde (Blacula's real name) attends a party at the home of Lisa's ex-detective boyfriend, Justin (Don Mitchell). Charmed by Lisa (and vice versa), Mamuwalde eventually vampirizes her friend Gloria (Janee Michelle) as well as several other men and women over the next few evenings.

When Lisa performs her priestly duty by sitting up with Gloria's body, Gloria revives as a vampire and attacks her former friend. Mamuwalde breaks in and Gloria suddenly cowers in fear before skulking out. Mamuwalde then pleads with a terrified Lisa to use her voodoo powers to "exorcise this demonic creature that inhabits my body." Though fearful, Lisa agrees.

Meanwhile, Justin has been reading up on the supernatural and has concluded that the recent rash of killings is the work of vampires. When blood-drained corpses start disappearing from the morgue, and the victims' bodies fail to show up in crime-scene photos (vampires, of course, cast no reflection and so cannot be photographed—the same apparently applies to soon-to-be-vampires), Justin's former boss, Sheriff Dunlop (Michael Conrad), is half-convinced as well.

Mamuwalde takes Lisa back to a quiet room in Willis' mansion to conduct the voodoo ceremony that will cure him of his vampiric curse. There, Lisa takes clippings from his hair and prepares a voodoo doll in his likeness.

When Justin learns Lisa is missing from her home, he rounds up the Sheriff and a dozen uniformed policemen. Justin arms the skeptical posse with wooden stakes extracted from a nearby picket fence and they enter the mansion.

As the police confront Mamuwalde's coven of undead (putting those fence rails to good use), Lisa's voodoo exorcism (chanting and swaying over the doll) begins to take effect. "It's working!" shouts Mamuwalde triumphantly, "I can feel it!" Just then, Justin bursts into the room and an enraged Mamuwalde hurls the intruder to the floor while Lisa pleads for his life.

Mamuwalde grabs Lisa (still clutching the voodoo doll), intending to make their escape and resume the curative procedure. But more police attack, and Lisa, horrified by her patient's animal ferocity, rejects

Blacula (William Marshall) menaces one of his own vampiric acolytes (Janee Michelle) in this lobby card pose.

the vampire's pleas to go with him. Justin recovers and charges Mamuwalde, but the vampire gains the upper hand. Just as he's about to put the bite on Justin, Lisa stabs a wooden arrow into the voodoo doll. At this, Mamuwalde cries out and staggers backwards. Lisa stabs again and again into the doll until the dying black prince finally raises his arms upwards and gives one last agonizing cry. The scene freezes and it is THE END.

Scream Blacula Scream is one of the few films to depict the *healing* power of voodoo. In fact, it picks up the flag hastily dropped by *The Vampire's Ghost* which proclaims that voodoo can be a powerful tool for good in the fight against evil. As Mamuwalde himself tells Lisa, "Voodoo in the proper hands can unlock many mysteries. Yours is a power unlike mine. It can be used for good as well as evil." While not particularly profound, at least it's a more balanced portrayal of the concept.

Unfortunately, little else is made of the voodoo angle in *Scream Blacula Scream*. After the very first scene, there's no exploration of (nor even a further appearance by) the voodoo group itself, so its dynamics and motivations remain mute. And after Lisa briefly refers to voodoo as a religion based on faith (see opening quote), this concept also disappears with-

out a trace. In fact, the only time voodoo truly comes into play is at the picture's beginning (Willis' resurrection ritual) and end (Lisa's abortive curative ceremony and subsequent use of the doll to strike down the vampire). While the film carries a germ of voodoo extrapolation, the seed fails to sprout.

As entertaining blaxploitation/horror, however, the picture fulfills its promise to a much higher degree. Thanks in large part to leads William Marshall and Pam Grier (and, to a lesser extent, some effective touches of humor), *Scream Blacula Scream* remains a fairly involving horror hybrid.

With his imposing 6'5" frame, his deep baritone voice, and his charming and commanding presence, William Marshall takes total control whenever onscreen. Trained on the stage (with a number of Shakespearean successes to his credit—not to mention at one time serving as understudy to Boris Karloff's Captain Hook in *Peter Pan!*), Marshall's command of the English language and nuance of voice serves him well in the occasionally awkward role of Mamuwalde/Blacula. His powerful delivery makes even such potentially pretentious (and preposterous) lines like, "I'm moved by powers no human is capable of comprehending," both sincere and affecting. Making something of nothing even in *this* instance,

180

Marshall's pinpoint inflection and emphasis on the word "human" adds a subtle and poignant note of sadness.

At one point, Mamuwalde accepts an invitation to return the next day by answering, "Evening would be better for me; I'm rather a night person." Marshall's slight accent on "night" adds to the secret humor of the statement. The actor's disarming charm then comes fully to the fore as, smiling, he continues, "I have the awful habit of sleeping away the daylight hours." Rather than going over the top with his eyes all a-twinkle and his tongue protruding visibly from his cheek, Marshall keeps his smile and twinkle subtle, thus displaying the *character*'s wry humor rather than the *actor*'s broad wink.

When asked what he thought of the voodoo vs. vampirism concept in *Scream Blacula Scream* Marshall replied "not much" and laughed. Fortunately, he still took his job seriously and, while letting a bemused humor come to the fore when appropriate, he

"It didn't add anything to the first one," remarked star William Marshall. While he's right in that it didn't expand upon the character of "Blacula," *Scream Blacula Scream* did add a new twist (voodoo) to a tired old theme (vampirism).

thankfully played his character straight, becoming a truly ferocious figure when aroused while at the same time projecting a powerful pathos.

As Lisa, Pam Grier does an admirable job in what could have been a walk-through role (or a stock "tough babe" part similar to those she so often played in her numerous action pictures). In addition to looking good in pantsuits and throwing a mean karate chop, Grier shows in *Scream Blacula Scream* that she indeed *can* act. When confronted by her friend rising from the dead and Blacula's subsequent frightening appearance, she effectively portrays a near-hysterical fear while still remaining lucid enough to demand an explanation through her terrified tears. Grier reveals a solid strength in Lisa while at the same time displaying a near-overwhelming (and natural) terror that makes her more human and more real.

Much of the fun of watching *Scream Blacula Scream* comes from its liberal doses of humor—some of it sly (such as Mamuwalde's occasionally droll dialogue) and some blatant. When the newly vampirized Willis starts to preen before a mirror only to realize

that he can no longer see his own reflection, for instance, he lets out with "Hey look man, I don't mind bein' a vampire and all that shit but this really ain't hip. I mean a man has *got* to see his face." Crestfallen, he then keeps pestering a half-bemused, half-annoyed Mamuwalde with questions like, "Hey man, how do I look?" adding with all sincerity, "It's important." There's something about vampire vanity that tickles the funnybone.

Also amusing are the shots of Mamuwalde in bat form (in effectively animated silhouette) flapping down a modern traffic-filled avenue, past high-rise buildings, and through busy intersections—an anomalous sight that not only produces a chuckle but perhaps underscores the tragic gulf between the hapless vampire and the bustling world of humanity all around him. Fortunately, however, when the fangs come out and the action begins, all pretense of levity stops and vampires become a deadly serious subject.

Speaking of vampires, this film portrays them in a rather unusual light. Looking normal and thoroughly human when relaxed and sated, Blacula's undead fol-

Appearing human and normal when relaxed and sated, these vampires sport ferocious fangs and a hideous pallor when their bloodlust rises.

lowers take on a deathly pallor only when their bloodlust is aroused. Oddly, however, they also move in a slow, almost somnambulistic manner and so appear more like shuffling zombies than vicious vampires. It makes for an intriguing contrast and, because of their zombie-like gait and appearance, one that ties vampirism even more closely to voodoo. Alternatively, when Blacula swings into full vampiric action, coarse hair lines his cheeks and eyebrows to give him a ferocious animalistic image—and there's nothing slow or ponderous about *his* lethal movements.

The picture also possesses an effective and involving storyline—thanks to a liberal borrowing from a certain Gothic soap opera, for *Scream Blacula Scream* bears more than a passing resemblance to the popular feature film *House of Dark Shadows* (based on the cult hit daytime drama *Dark Shadows*) released in 1970. Both pictures center on an unhappy vampire seeking a cure from a sympathetic female (with *Scream* changing *Dark Shadows*' medical doctor into a voodoo priestess) while at the same time reluctantly wreaking undead havoc all around them. *Scream* even "borrowed" *House*'s striking imagery of a troupe of uniformed policemen facing off against the lead

vampire's minions. In substituting a voodoo for a scientific treatment and a black vampire for a white one, *Scream Blacula Scream* added even further interest to an already potent and pathos-laden (not to mention audience-tested) premise.

Technically, *Scream Blacula Scream* is competent—but no more. The same can be said for Bob Kelljan's earnest but uninspired direction. "I didn't feel the dramatic touch of a great director," deadpanned William Marshall. To Kelljan's credit, however, he at least *tries* different things, tossing in varied camera angles and techniques (extreme close-ups, high-angle shots, *un*steady cam, etc.). Unfortunately, they seem more arbitrary than impact-oriented and the rather obvious, unsubtle approaches often prove more distracting than enhancing.

A few things work quite well, however, such as the shock effect generated by first focusing on a character cautiously creeping about the vampire-infested mansion, then cutting to a close-up of Blacula, arms outstretched, as he zooms out of nowhere toward the camera (along with a jarring note on the soundtrack to complete the startle effect). Of course, this is simply a rehash of the same shock stunt Kelljan pulled in his two previous *Count Yorga* movies. Consequently, for those who've seen those earlier films, familiarity brings with it a liberal dose of contempt. (Kelljan also reuses from his *Yorga* pictures the [admittedly effective] ploy of having his human protagonist verbally spar with the vampire in a polite-but-guarded "discussion" of vampirism.)

Another device Kelljan uses is to visually link two scenes with a similar image. As the bones burst into flame during Willis' resurrection ceremony, the film cuts to a shot of Lisa suddenly starting awake and glancing at the fire in her fireplace—as if some kind of mental contact had been made. Kelljan then zooms into the fire, and when the camera zooms out again, it's now focused back on Willis' supernatural flames—an obvious but nonetheless effective transition.

These are the exceptions, however, and most of the director's staging is of a more perfunctory manner. Blacula's resurrection, for instance, is a pivotal scene rife with excitement and possibilities which, under Kelljan's drab direction, ends up as an opportunity missed. When the supernatural fire dies down, Willis, angry and dejected, goes into the next room to get a drink. We then see the shadow of a man on the wall behind him, and the camera cuts to a close-up of black-clad legs and feet (and cloak) approaching the seated Willis. Willis then turns, and Blacula reaches down to bite him on the neck. The mundane staging generates little suspense, less excitement, and no terror.

Though cinematographer Isadore Mankofsky's lighting occasionally throws a token shadow, the film as a whole appears over-lit, fully displaying the pale, washed-out color so typical of the 1970s (particularly on TV—a place where director Kelljan soon sought career refuge).

Bob Kelljan (born Robert Kelljchian) began his career as an actor in New York. Coming to Hollywood in 1960, he appeared on television (including *The Twilight Zone* episode "The Jeopardy Room") and in features (such as *The Glass Cage*, *Psych-Out*, and *Hell's Angels on Wheels*). As a result of his association with actor Michael Macready, Kelljan turned director in 1969 with *Little Sister* (aka *Flesh of My Flesh*) which he also wrote. Kelljan next wrote and directed the highly successful *Count Yorga, Vampire* and its follow-up, *The Return of Count Yorga*. After a few more films (including *Scream Blacula Scream*, *Act of Vengeance* [aka *Rape Squad*], and *Black Oak Conspiracy*) he turned to television where he helmed the telefilms *Cry for Justice*, *The Plague*, *Angels on Ice*, and *Angels in Vegas*. He also directed in episodic television, working on series like *Fame*, *Beach Patrol*, and *Police Story*. Kelljan never completely abandoned his initial in-front-of-the-camera roots, however, for he continued to teach acting classes in Hollywood. He died in November 1981 at age 52 (from cancer), only six weeks after completing a *Hill Street Blues* episode.

Several *Scream Blacula Scream* actors encountered voodoo again over the course of their careers. Only a year after the *Blacula* sequel, Richard Lawson (Willis) played a cop investigating the voodoo vagaries of *Sugar Hill* while Janee Michelle (Gloria) graduated from supporting vampiress to lead voodoo victim in *The House on Skull Mountain*.

Scream Blacula Scream remains an unusual, if flawed, entry in both the voodoo and vampire cinema subsets. Though it fails to carry its intriguing voodoo premise to its full conclusion, it still remains an entertaining film with a few shocks, a few doses of humor, and a few good performances to recommend it.

[1] Marshall felt the title was ludicrous. "It was *not* going to sell with that title," he recalled, laughing. "I was quite wrong about that."

CREDITS: Director: Bob Kelljan; Producer: Joseph T. Naar; Executive Producer: Samuel Z. Arkoff; Screenplay: Joan Torres, Raymond Koenig, Maurice Jules; Story: Joan Torres, Raymond Koenig; Director of Photography: Isadore Mankofsky; Editor: Fabian Tordjman; Post-production Supervisor: Salvatore Billutteri; Music Composed and Conducted by: Bill Marx; Title song "Torment" lyrics by Marilyn Lovell, music by Bill Marx; Art Director: Al Brocchicchio; Production Manager: Frank Beetson; Makeup: Alan Snider; Special Effects: Jack De Bron; Sound Mixer: Don Johnson; Released July 1973 by American International Pictures; 96 minutes; rated PG

CAST: William Marshall (Mamuwalde), Don Mitchell (Justin), Pam Grier (Lisa), Michael Conrad (Sheriff Dunlop), Richard Lawson (Willis), Janee Michelle (Gloria), Lynn Moody (Denny), Barbara Rhoades (Elaine), Bernie Hamilton (Ragman), Beverly Gill (Maggie), Don Blackman (Doll Man), Van Kirksey (Professor Walston), Arnold Williams (Louis)

Voodoo god incarnate Baron Samedi (Don Pedro Colley) claims "the price I asked for our bargain" at the close of *Suger Hill*. (Courtesy Eric Hoffman)

SUGAR HILL (1974)
"Meet Sugar Hill and Her Zombie Hitmen…"

"She found all the forces of evil,
Put them in a voodoo trance,
She used all her tools to put the fools away,
And evil never had a chance."
    —from the theme song
    Supernatural Voodoo Woman

The 1970s were something of a cultural wasteland in America, full of bad fashion (polyester leisure suits and voluminous bellbottoms), bad hair (who can forget the gigantic afro phase?), and bad music (one word: Disco). Consequently, a "modern" American movie from the '70s (particularly one that strove for a "hip" contemporary look) is *instantly* recognizable for the cultural curiosity it is.

Though this author "came of age" during the 1970s, he holds little nostalgic love for it, a personal prejudice perhaps, but one that seems justified when the decade's shortcomings are so bluntly exposed by films like *Sugar Hill*. It's not a bad movie; in fact it possesses a solid story, some moments of effective atmosphere, and decent production values. It's just hopelessly trapped in the thick amber of its time period. The dated dialogue and charmless "jive" talk ("That's a very foxy lady"), the ridiculous she-bop Motown theme song ("Supernatural voodoo woman does her thing at night/ Supernatural voodoo woman, do her wrong and you won't see the light"), and the wide lapels on powder blue pantsuits only serve to distract from the tale being told. Consequently, it's sometimes difficult to take seriously. Even so, for those with more tolerance for the sights and sounds of "K-Tel" and the like, *Sugar Hill* offers up a well-produced and often atmospheric tale of voodoo vengeance.

Marki Bey plays Diana "Sugar" Hill, whose lover, a nightclub owner named Langston (Larry D. Johnson), is beaten to death in his club's parking lot by a gang of thugs headed by crime boss Mr. Morgan (Robert Quarry). Thirsting for vengeance, Sugar returns to the old bayou plantation house where she grew up to seek the aid of Mama Maitresse (Zara Culley), a voodoo witch.

The old sorceress leads Sugar to a secret mist-shrouded graveyard in the swampland where she calls upon "Baron Samedi, keeper of the dead, king of the graveyards." When the Baron (Don Pedro Colley) appears, Sugar offers him her soul in exchange for his aid, but the voodoo god ("a great lover," cackles Mama Maitresse) lasciviously counters, "It's not your *soul* I want." [1] Baron Samedi then raises up a band of zombies, the corpses of buried slaves, and instructs Sugar to "put them to *evil* use, it's all they know or want."

In a dockside warehouse, Sugar confronts the first of Morgan's men, Tank (Rick Hagood). "You and your punk friends killed my man," she pronounces, "and the sentence is *death*!" The zombies descend on him and hack him to death with machetes. Police detective Valentine (Richard Lawson), an old flame of Sugar's, finds a slave shackle near Tank's body and dead skin on the victim's neck, and begins to wonder...

Sugar learns that Langston has left the club to her, and now Morgan tries to induce her to sell. Sugar humors the crime lord while continuing her plan of vengeance. In quick succession, she and her zombies dispatch two more of Morgan's men—by tossing one into a pen full of ravenous pigs and using a voodoo doll to force the other to stab himself to death. Sugar then anonymously sends the man's heart to Morgan in an urn. [2] Needless to say, Morgan has become both angry and frightened at these attacks from his unseen enemy and sends the rest of his gang out to find whomever is responsible.

While Detective Valentine, suspecting the involvement of the supernatural in these bizarre deaths, seeks answers from an expert on voodoo, Sugar continues her vengeful rampage. She kills the three remaining henchmen (via a straight-razor judiciously applied to a voodoo doll, a coffin full of snakes, and an attack by the zombies).

Baron Samedi warns Sugar that Valentine is getting too close, and subsequently puts him out of the way with a carefully placed pin in a voodoo doll, causing the nosy detective to fall down the stairs and break his leg.

Sugar then culminates her vengeance by luring Morgan and his girlfriend, Celeste (Betty Anne Rees), to Sugar's family mansion. There, Morgan is confronted by the zombies—as well as the now-reanimated corpses of his own men. The terrified mobster flees by jumping through a window. He races off into the swamp, but Sugar and her zombies trap him once more. In trying to escape, Morgan falls into a pool of quicksand and drowns. [3]

"Well woman," concludes Baron Samedi, "You've destroyed them all—nicely, neatly, superbly." The Baron then hands Sugar his silver-tipped cane as a memento and takes the screaming Celeste into his arms (as "the price I asked for our bargain"). With a hearty laugh, the king of the dead disappears.

The genesis of *Sugar Hill* began in Haiti itself, for that's where screenwriter Tim Kelly acquired his interest and inspiration. Kelly, a prolific playwright (with over 300 plays currently in print) who for a time made some extra cash penning blaxploitation pictures (and one other horror, *Cry of the Banshee*, which he remembers as "a painful experience"), had visited Haiti several times and "was absolutely fascinated by the island and wanted very much to do something in that genre" (as he related to this author). Feeling that "there was nothing [in films at that point] that was really hooked into the basic aspects of the voodoo religion," he wrote a script in 1972 called *Black Voodoo* "that was absolutely loaded with historical stuff that was completely accurate." Paul Maslansky, a producer who was looking to direct his first feature, took Kelly's script to AIP and received the green light—after a significant rewrite, of course, to make the concept fit the exploitable AIP mold. "At that time," recalled Kelly, "AIP was really intent on making *revenge* movies." So Kelly took *Black Voodoo* and (for the modest sum of $12,500) turned his historically accurate voodoo script into " the perfect wedding of the black exploitation film with something that was meant to be a little more serious."

Originally intended to be filmed in New Orleans (which makes more sense given its subject matter), the location was changed to Houston when AIP encountered "some sort of trouble with the teamsters," remembered Kelly. For the four week shoot, director Paul Maslansky filmed in actual locations (real houses, hospital, office, mansion, etc.) rather than on a soundstage. As a result, the surroundings are realistic and more convincing than most, from the dusty deserted mansion to the eerie swampland.

Also convincing—and genuinely creepy—are the film's zombies. "They did good makeups on the voodoo people, the zombies," opined star Robert Quarry. With their bulging, filmy eyes a milky white, their hair matted with leaves and spider webs, and their pasty gray skin highlighted so that one can almost *see* the bones beneath the dead flesh, they present a terrifying image of death revived. In one shuddery shot, two of them sit up simultaneously from their shallow graves, turn their heads slowly toward one another, and *smile*—a horrible, ghastly rictus grin. These are creatures of *evil*.

Director Paul Maslansky (making his directorial debut *and* swan song—he never directed another picture though he continued as a highly successful producer) and cinematographer Robert Jessup take care with their supernatural charges, filming them to chilling advantage. In the resurrection scene, for instance, close-ups of gray hands poking up through the dead leaves of the mossy forest floor progress into atmospheric low-angled shots of the horrible corpses rising stiffly from the earth while the swirling mist turns the midday light into a hazy twilight punctuated by flashes of preternatural lightning.

As a voodoo film, *Sugar Hill* possesses more integrity than most—thanks to scripter Tim Kelly's genuine fascination with the Haitian religion. The story begins, for instance, with a voodoo ceremony in which authentically dressed devotees dance and whirl, some clutching sacrificial chickens or sacred snakes. Suddenly, one of the participants starts screaming ecstatically, apparently possessed by a loa, and the others rush to gather around her writhing body.

While visually intriguing and well-staged, this authenticity-minded beginning also illustrates the film's '70s quaintness: Instead of the expected rapid drumbeats, we hear the Motown rhythm of "Supernatural Voodoo Woman" playing on the soundtrack. Though this musical anomaly remains more than a little disconcerting, the sequence ends rather cleverly when the dancers suddenly collapse and we hear applause as the camera zooms in on a sign reading "Club Haiti." It was all just an outdoor nightclub act.

In amongst the "hip" talk, screenwriter Kelly sprinkles some thought-provoking and credible dialogue. When Mama Maitresse admonishes Sugar, "Child, you have always been a *dis*believer; why do you now believe?," Sugar answers, "Because I want *revenge*!," making an interesting comment on the power of faith.

Later, in a ceremonial exchange, Mama Maitresse asks, "Where does the sun rise?," and Sugar answers, "In the east, Mama." The old woman continues, "Where does the sun *set*?," to which Sugar ritualistically responds, "In Guineé, Mama." Guineé was the term used by the Haitian slaves to designate their distant homeland in Africa and remains a symbolic Eden to the Voudounist.

The picture's subject matter apparently spooked some of its participants. "Some of the people were quite uncomfortable with making the film, because they really were a little upset about the voodoo aspect," recalled Kelly. "I'm speaking of the local people they used in Houston" who felt "that maybe you shouldn't fool around with this stuff." Nervous bit players aside, no serious mishaps (voodoo-induced or otherwise) occurred during the four-week shoot.

Sadly, *Sugar Hill* remains a decidedly flawed film. Beyond its appalling wardrobe and dated dialogue, the picture's main weakness lies in its acting. Apart from Robert Quarry, most of the major players are either amateurishly flat (the actors playing Morgan's henchmen) or too strained for credibility (Zara Culley as Mama Maitresse and top-billed Marki Bey).

According to AIP publicity, "Ms. Bey researched her part among various voodoo cults in and around the L.A. environs, thereby acquiring the proper authoritative menace to make her role as a voodoo high priestess believable." If so, it didn't work. Though pretty enough to look at, she brings little depth or distinction to her role. Bey was less-than-thrilled with her starring assignment, and this may have tempered her performance. In fact, co-star Robert Quarry remembered to this author that, "she hated it, hated the whole thing," even though Bey was the highest paid member of the cast (Quarry was second).

Quarry had nothing but nice things to say about Ms. Bey. "Oh, Marki, she was darling. I don't think she ever made another movie. [She made one more, *Hangup*, released later this same year.] Marki had just come from the Pearl Bailey all-black *Hello Dolly*, playing Irene, the second lead. And she was as pretty as could be and she was as nice as could be. We shot for about a week, and when the dailies started coming in, [AIP president] Sam Arkoff didn't think she looked black enough so they had an Afro wig made for her and darkened her makeup. So half of the time she had sort of light red hair with a very pale skin which

The fashion police? No, it's *Sugar Hill*'s "zombie hit men."

they covered over. Well, I'm not sure, but Sam Arkoff with his usual class probably said, 'She don't look like a nigger to me.' Mr. Class. So they insisted they put her in an Afro wig. She was beautiful."

Quarry, however, was not so enamored of his other co-star, Don Pedro Colley (playing Baron Samedi), calling him "one of the most pretentious bastards. He had a better dressing room than I did. That was in his contract, that he had to have a van and the whole thing. He was so full of affected shit. He behaved like he was the star of the movie. I mean, in *his* mind he was the star of the movie. So it was always 'Makeup! Costume! Wardrobe!' Don thought he was a *big movie star*."

Colley's performance certainly reflects this "star" attitude. Colley plays Baron Samedi in a broad, exuberant fashion—wide-eyed, big-voiced, and full of theatrical poses and dramatic gestures. Though a voodoo god incarnate is an admittedly unusual role which calls for an unusual portrayal, Colley makes him something of a caricature and so fails to convince. (This concept of a voodoo god appearing on Earth strays far from the Voudoun canon, since the loas manifest themselves through *human beings*—via temporary possession—rather than owning corporeal forms themselves.) Colley's cause isn't helped by the echo

chamber reverberation that his voice receives on the soundtrack—an obvious and distracting technical artifice.

As Morgan, Robert Quarry provides the only naturalistic and convincing performance in the film. His surface urbanity hides a brutal ruthlessness that periodically peeks out from under the mobster's thin facade via his subtle expressions and unsmiling eyes.

Initially, producer Elliot Schick and director Paul Maslansky felt that Quarry was *not* the right actor for the part of crime-syndicate head Mr. Morgan. In fact, they felt he was not even the right *color*. "I was forced to do the movie," recalled Quarry. "I had a pay or play contract. They were going to make an all-black movie, but that meant that they were going to have to pay me and not play me, and Sam [Arkoff] wasn't going to do that. Elliot Schick and Paul Maslansky, who were doing this all-black exploitation horror film, were not thrilled to suddenly end up with me playing the head of the Black Mafia. It made about as much sense as me playing Bernadette of Lourdes. So I was just suddenly flown off to Houston to do this movie. I hadn't even read the script. When I got there I read it and I thought what the hell am I doing playing *this* part? I mean this was a black man's role. And they had a black actor set for it, but Sam said no, we'll use

187

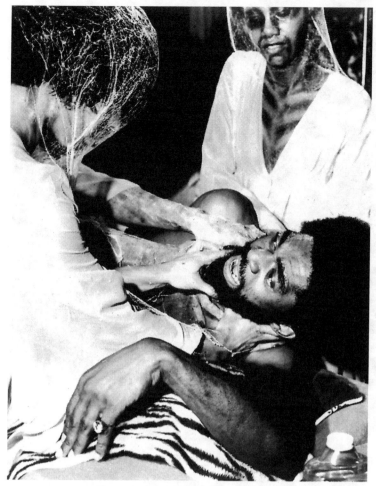

Massage parlor patron Fabulous (Charles B. Robinson) gets more than a rubdown from the *Zombies of Sugar Hill* (the film's television title).

[laughs]. She got a big hand, you know, everybody thought that was terrific she'd done that. She was a little ham." Virginia's "ham" paid off nicely for the canine thespian, for the director rewarded her sterling performance with a big steak at lunch that day.

Though he had small roles in a number of films, and scored some stage success in New York prestige productions like *Richard II*, *The Taming of the Shrew*, and *Who's Afraid of Virginia Woolf*, Quarry didn't become a commodity until the low-budget drive-in horror *Count Yorga, Vampire* (1970) did unexpected blockbuster business. After the huge success of *Yorga*, AIP (who picked up the independent film for distribution) put Quarry under a five-year contract. The actor subsequently starred in two more vampire films, the inevitable *Return of Count Yorga* (1971) and *The Deathmaster* (1972), as well as *Dr. Phibes Rises Again* (1972), *Sugar Hill* (1974), and *Madhouse* (1974). Quarry believes that AIP president Sam Arkoff saw him as a rival/successor to Vincent Price. This apparently caused some initial friction (which was soon smoothed over) between the two actors when they first worked together on *Dr. Phibes Rises Again*. In the late 1970s, Quarry's acting career went on hiatus, due primarily to a serious car accident that kept him from seeking work for three years (as well as ending the life of his beloved poodle). The actor made a comeback of sorts when he began appearing in low-budget independents in the late 1980s such as *Cyclone* (1987), *Beverly Hills Vamp* (1989), and *Haunting Fear* (1990), usually directed by the prolific Fred Olen Ray (who affectionately refers to Quarry simply as "Uncle Bob").

Being one of the few whites in the predominantly black cast of *Sugar Hill* caused a few problems for Robert Quarry (both on and off the set), even in the civil rights-conscious year of 1971. Just how far attitudes had *not* come was brought home to him one evening when he took his co-star to dinner.

"Marki [Bey] would never go out," remembered Quarry. "And I finally got her to go out to dinner with me one night. And she said, 'Well, I don't want problems.' We walked into a restaurant, a very fashionable restaurant. And we walked in at six

Quarry. And I ended up doing the movie. And then as it turned out, it was a very happy working relationship with Paul and Elliot, because I was doing good work—even though it was just all wrong for the movie."

Despite everyone's protestations (including Quarry's), Arkoff's money-conscious insistence paid dividends, for Quarry's fine performance is one of the film's prime assets. "I was kind of amazed [when I saw it recently]," concluded the actor, "I wasn't that embarrassed by it."

Quarry brought more than just *his* talent to the part, he brought his *dog's* too. For the scene in which Morgan and his girlfriend receive the heart in a jar, the poodle Morgan plays with on the couch is actually Quarry's own beloved dog, Virginia. ("I had just done the play *Who's Afraid of Virginia Woolf*, so when I got her I called her 'Virginia Woof.'") Virginia was an instant success. "During rehearsal," remembered Quarry, "they opened the jar and she just kind of sat there. When they went for the take, I opened the lid and she went 'aaah' and jumped off the couch and ran o'clock, because Marki wanted to eat early and go to bed. So we went in there and there wasn't a person in the room and they said, 'Do you have a reservation?' And she was now in her light skin and red hair. Only in the South would anybody have known that she was 'a black,' an Afro-American. I said 'We'd just like to have dinner.' And I could see her shrinking back—because she knew what it was. He wasn't going to seat us because, you know, black and white do not *go together* in Houston, Texas, even in 1972 or whenever the hell it was. I mean civil liberties were in and they no longer had segregated toilets and segregated theater seats or segregated anything, but they had their own *way* of segregating themselves. So I said, 'Excuse me a minute Marki, I want to talk to this man.' And I went and I said, 'Listen, what is this *shit* that you're giving me? Is it because the young lady with me is black?' And he said, 'Oh no, no, no.' And I said, 'I'll tell you what's up. I know a *lot* of people. You start screwing around with me with this shit and I promise you I'm calling every newspaper man and newspaper woman I know in this town and telling them what you've done.' 'Oh, we've got a table for you.' Well now by that time the evening was ruined for poor Marki. She never went out again, she stayed in the Holiday Inn and ate breakfast, lunch and dinner there. It was just awful."

Though Quarry had spent several years in Houston with a respected theater troupe, he suddenly found himself *persona non grata*. "I was there making an all-black movie. And I had a lot of friends, very rich, very influential friends that I had made when I was there in 1960 [with the Alley Theater], 10 years before. And they read 'Alley Theater actor returns to star in movie'—and it was called an 'All-Black Cast.' Well I think they were so afraid I was going to bring a *nigger* to lunch. I mean that was their attitude. Nobody called me, nobody asked me, nobody said, 'how are you.' They just *ignored* my being there since I was there under those circumstances. And it was just shabby."

Quarry ran into some racially oriented difficulties *on* the set as well. "Many of those people [who played the zombies and such] were local people they picked up there in Houston; they didn't use actors. So, of course, the black actors there hated me because I was calling them 'nigger.' I mean that was what the script did. Well, it's all right for a black to call a black nigger, but they were seeing a *white* guy doing this. And they didn't know from acting. They thought that was what I was like, that it was *my* doing. So we had

Meet *Sugar Hill*

...it's not a place —it's a brand new face, she's the hippest chick in town!

Ya dig?!

a very nice actor named Charlie Robinson [who played 'Fabulous,' Morgan's right-hand man], who was then at the Alley Theater and who later was in the TV series *Night Court* and *Love and War*. Charlie was the one who had to straighten 'em all out. So he went to all these extras—I mean, I thought they were going to *kill* me, they started *at* me—after I'd been screaming, 'back you black bastards, you fuckin' coons,' or whatever the wonderful dialogue was, which as I said was perfectly all right to say if you were black but not for Mr. White Chops over here to be doing it. And he explained to them that it was just acting and that that was the part and what it was all about. So we settled down and it was all right."

"*Sugar Hill* was not a title I wanted" complained screenwriter Tim Kelly. "Sugar Hill was at one time the most wealthy area of Harlem, sort of the Beverly Hills of Harlem, and I thought that that title was kind of vague. I wanted something up there that said what it was all about—like *Black Voodoo*." Why AIP, a company famous for coming up with an exploitable title first and the movie second, would choose such a nondescript and unilluminating name as *Sugar Hill* for their new horror feature remains a mystery. (Had AIP co-founder Jim Nicholson still been onboard, this

"They did good makeups on the voodoo people, the zombies," opined *Sugar Hill* star Robert Quarry. Indeed they did.

film would have undoubtedly sported a much more effective—and exploitable—moniker, since Nicholson was renowned in the industry for his ability to create catchy film titles.) One possible explanation is that AIP was trying to follow in the lucrative footsteps of their previous vengeful-female blaxploitation feature, *Coffy* (1973). (If "Coffy" was good then "Sugar" must be better?)

Even so, the company seemed to recognize their marketing error, for their publicity refers to the film "proving to all and sundry that Sugar Hill is a curvaceous female creature—and not the geographical location the term so connotes..." At least when AIP sold the film to television, they changed the title to *The Zombies of Sugar Hill* (still no great shakes, but at least it gives the viewer a clue as to content).

AIP urged their exhibitors to promote *Sugar Hill* with such diverse tactics as a "Reptile Lobby Display" ("obtain several snakes and place on display in your outer lobby with information pertaining to the picture and/or voodoo ritual"), a "Candy Bally" ("print labels reading, 'I'm Sugar Hill, Try Me!' and affix to small plastic bags of any kind of candy"), and an "Ouanga or Voodoo Charm" giveaway consisting of "small plastic bones in a bag."

Plastic trinkets aside, the film itself didn't disappoint its intended audience (though modern viewers

don't fare so well). Thanks to some well-staged and atmospheric sequences, Robert Quarry's convincingly ruthless portrayal, and the genuinely frightening zombies, *Sugar Hill* still remains a fairly entertaining blast-from-the-past curiosity.

[1] This intimation that the voodoo god has no use for Sugar's soul but instead wants her live body for his pleasure is a rather amusing (and exploitative) twist on the Voudoun practice of offering up one's body to be possessed (or "mounted") by the loa so that the voodoo god can speak and act in the material world.

[2] This scene (along with several of the death sequences) was drastically cut for the TV version (renamed *The Zombies of Sugar Hill*) so that the viewer never sees what's inside the canister. According to Quarry, "there was a heart that was ripped out and it was pulsating, bleeding, and steaming. It was a cow's heart or something that they'd cut out and put in. But it was all wired to sort of pulsate in the bowl."

[3] Of course I got a mouthful of that *crap*," remembered Quarry about filming his death scene. "Jesus, but I couldn't get it out of my ears, I couldn't get it out of my hair. God, I was hours trying to wash that shit out. That stuff was very unpleasant."

CREDITS: Alternate Titles: *Voodoo Girl*; *The Zombies of Sugar Hill*; Director: Paul Maslansky; Producer: Elliot Schick; Executive Producer: Samuel Z. Arkoff; Screenplay: Tim Kelly; Director of Photography: Robert Jessup; Production Manager/First Assistant Director: Frank Beetson; Post-Production Supervisor: Slavatore Billittero; Editor: Carl Kress; Casting: Betty Martin; Casting in Houston: Earl Chasen and Charles P. Robinson; Dance Sequence Choreographed by: William Chaison; Music: Nick Zesses and Dino Fekaris; Song "Supernatural Voodoo Woman" sung by The Originals; Makeup: George "Hank" Edds; Special Effects: Roy L. Downey; Released January 1974 by American International Pictures; 91 minutes

CAST: Marki Bey (Diana "Sugar" Hill), Robert Quarry (Morgan), Don Pedro Colley (Baron Samedi), Betty Anne Rees (Celeste), Richard Lawson (Valentine), Zara Culley (Mama Maitresse), Charles B. Robinson (Fabulous), Larry D. Johnson (Langston), Rick Hagood (Tank Watson), Ed Geldhart (O'Brien), Albert J. Baker (George), Raymond E. Simpson III (King), Thomas C. Carroll (Baker), Big Walter Price (Preacher), Charles Krohn (Captain Merrill), J. Randall Bell (Dr. Parkhurst), Peter Harrell III (Police Photographer), Judy Hanson (Masseuse), Gary V. Chason (Lab Technician), Roy L. Downey (Stevadore), Garritt Scales (Crew Chief), John F. Scarborough (Uniformed Cop)

THE HOUSE ON SKULL MOUNTAIN (1974)
Voodoo: A Family Affair

"A raven flew over and dropped an ouanga,
  and then the casket started to smoke.
  Ouanga means somebody will die."
—Ella Woods as the worried servant girl, Louette

This deservedly obscure PG-rated (though it's so tame that it could just as easily have earned a G), independent black horror film was shot in and around Atlanta, Georgia. A group of local businessmen hired Ron Honthaner, the former associate producer of TV's *Gunsmoke*, to direct. This was Honthaner's first—and apparently last—directing assignment (unsurprising, considering the poor result).

Just before the elderly Pauline Christophe (Mary J. Todd McKenzie) dies in her mansion perched atop Skull Mountain, she sends out letters summoning her four descendants to her home (though none of them have ever met Pauline before nor have they met each other). There's the straight-laced and middle-aged Harriet Johnson (Xernona Clayton), the beautiful Lorena Christophe (Janee Michelle), the "hip" Phillippe Willard (Mike Evans), and, surprise, a white anthropologist named Andrew Cunningham (Victor French)—obviously the *white* sheep of the family. They arrive just in time to witness Pauline's funeral at the house's private cemetery.

The family lawyer (Senator Leroy Johnson) reads a posthumous statement from Pauline in which the old woman talks of her family legacy of power. The imposing family servant, Thomas Petoine (Jean Durand), explains that the Christophe family is descended from Henry Christophe, a former slave who led the rebellion against the French, and who became King Henry the First of Haiti. Thomas also mentions that the Christophes were powerful voodoo practitioners.

That night, Thomas performs a voodoo rite (manipulating a doll over a miniature coffin) to lure the drunken Phillippe (thinking he sees Lorena beckoning to him enticingly) into the house's empty elevator shaft. Cunningham finds an ouanga charm next to Phillippe's lifeless body and begins to wonder…

While Cunningham and Lorena frolic in Atlanta the next day (and apparently fall in love—despite the fact that they're supposedly cousins), Harriet is lured into Pauline's formerly locked bedroom where she's bitten by a snake. As Cunningham rushes her to the hospital, Thomas stabs a pin into a voodoo doll and the woman dies.

Thomas next uses his voodoo powers to take control of Lorena's spirit, forcing her to rise and come to him. When Cunningham finds Lorena gone, the maid, Louette (Ella Woods), jealous of Thomas' attraction to Lorena, shows Cunningham a secret passage in the cellar. He follows it to a hidden cavern in which a voodoo ceremony is in progress, presided over by Thomas.

Cunningham sees Louette tied to a post (how she got there before him—trussed up for sacrifice no less—is never explained), and Thomas kills the girl with a knife. The voodoo priest then summons forth Lorena. At this, Cunningham steps forward and engages Thomas in a machete duel. When Thomas gets the upper hand, Cunningham grabs the voodoo priest's skull-topped standard and parries Thomas' blow with it, causing the machete to crush the sacred skull. At this, everything and everyone (except the dead Louette) supernaturally vanishes.

Cunningham rushes back to the house where he finds Thomas hovering over the entranced Lorena. "For generations," expounds the sorcerer, "the Petiones have lived in caution, obscurity. Our powers have *weakened*, held in check by the Christophes. But now, through Lorena, the powers of the Christophes will be *mine*!"

Entranced by the voodoo sorcerer, Lorena (Janee Michelle) dances at a secret ceremony held in the caves under *The House on Skull Mountain*.

Thomas then summons forth the corpse of Pauline from her grave. When the zombie enters the room, Thomas orders it to kill Cunningham. The quick-thinking anthropologist (who's made a study of Haitian voodoo) makes a plea to the voodoo gods. "I call upon you Erzule, and you Damballah, father of all Christophes, protect us; restore this creature's soul." At this, Pauline's corpse points her finger at the sorcerer, her face becomes a (superimposed) skull, and Thomas gives a terrified cry, crashing backwards through the window to his death on the flagstones below. Pauline's corpse retreats, never to be seen again.

The operative word for *The House on Skull Mountain* is "dull." Most of the film's running time is taken up with the characters sitting around talking. Even worse, there's the pathetic and forced time-eating falling-in-love montage sequence when Cunningham and Lorena go to Atlanta. Scenes of the two kissing cousins holding hands, laughing, eating, visiting a player piano museum (?!) while tepid music plays on the soundtrack, brings the film's already glacial pace to a complete standstill.

Even the "money" scenes carry little in the way of thrills. For instance, the zombie resurrection sequence, which *should* be a frightening highlight, is completely mishandled. It begins when the grave's tombstone suddenly (and inexplicably) bursts into flame and a hand pokes up through the dirt and leaves. The (normal-looking) curled fingers then swivel about almost comically—like some bizarre periscope. That's it. The next we see is Pauline's wispy body (with nary a trace of grave dirt about it) enter the bedroom where our protagonists await.

To add insult to injury, the film's solitary zombie is a big disappointment. This walking corpse (of Pauline Christophe) looks like nothing more than a toothless old lady having a bad hair day. There's no special makeup, no rotting skin, not even any filmed-over eyes. Instead, with her thin frame and elderly face, she looks more like a confused grandma than a living dead creature of destruction. This zombie is anything *but* menacing.

The ceremonial sequence in the cave, which has the potential for some solid voodoo excitement, is so repetitious and uninspired that it too fails to become the highlight that it should. When Thomas approaches the terrified Louette with his sacrificial knife, instead of plunging it into the girl, he engages in a lengthy exchange with another voodooist in which the two men pass the knife back and forth, back and forth, again and again. When they finally get down to business and Thomas stabs the girl, the viewer, instead of cringing at the barbarous act, can only breathe a huge sigh of relief that they finally *did* something.

Even the machete fight lacks verve, and it ends on a ridiculous and awkward note. When Thomas accidentally hits the sacred skull with his machete, the entranced Lorena screams, Thomas gives an angry cry, and the screen fades—*slowly*—to black (as if to signify the end of the scene). When the picture fades in again (slowly) on a flaming torch, the camera shows an incredulous Cunningham holding the torch in the now-empty cave. The poor staging and slow fades rob the moment of its bewildering impact.

Occasionally, all the talk does generate a spark of interest, however, particularly when it involves voodoo. Screenwriter Mildred Pares obviously did her homework, for *The House on Skull Mountain* is one of the few films to get its voodoo background right.

Sprinkled amongst all the dull dialogue are several illuminating passages, like Thomas explaining, "When the loa Damballah possessed the slave Henry Christophe, these beads were a sign to remind him of all that he owed Damballah when he became a king." (This illustrates the relationship between the loas and human beings—one of possession, aid, and veneration.)

A later exchange brings up the Voudoun/Catholicism dichotomy:

Cunningham: "If Pauline was really descended from Henry Christophe, she probably believed in voodoo.
Lorena: "Pauline was Catholic."
Cunningham: "One doesn't exclude the other. In Haiti, for example, the Virgin Mary is just another aspect or manifestation of the goddess Erzule, which is a voodoo goddess."

Visually, *The House on Skull Mountain* looks and feels like a 1970s TV movie, full of the telltale static set-ups, perfunctory close-ups, and sudden zooms that marked television productions of this decade (unsurprising, perhaps, considering the director's television background). The old dark house setting is so overlit that any chance for atmosphere disappears along with the potential shadows. Even when the lights go out due to a storm (a hoary old cliché to be sure), there's no appreciable difference in the light level.

Fortunately, director Ron Honthaner does manage to inject a few creative touches into the mix, so that it's not a *complete* loss. Our first good look at the house (apart from a pathetically unconvincing Lionel train-style model of the titular manse and mountain) shows a skull-shaped door-knocker which promptly dissolves into the face of the aged Pauline on her deathbed inside—the symbolic death's head transposed onto a *living* one.

In another scene, Lorena sits in front of a dressing table with an oval mirror. The camera pulls back and the lighting changes slightly so the reflection of her dark hair against her white nightgown and the position of her body make the mirror appear like a gigantic skull (a subtle superimposition and a discordant note on the soundtrack drives the image home).

The biggest "name" in *The House on Skull Mountain* cast was Victor French (as Cunningham), a strapping bear-like actor who generally appeared in Westerns such as *Charro!* (1969), *Rio Lobo* (1970), and *Chato's Land* (1972). He was also a regular on the *Little House on the Prairie* TV series. A publicity article for the film states that French "had been known to turn down offers of roles ranging from television to motion pictures and stage." Apparently, in 1974 at least, the actor's "philosophy of professional selectivity" deserted him.

Janee Michelle (Lorena) appeared in a handful of films from the late 1960s and early 1970s, including one other voodoo entry, *Scream Blacula Scream*. She also worked frequently on television in such series *as Love American Style*, *The F.B.I.*, and *Ironside*. *The House on Skull Mountain* was her last feature.

Apart from Mike Evans (playing Phillippe), who appeared in a few TV movies and had a recurring role on TV's *All in the Family* and later on *The Jeffersons*, the rest of the cast was comprised of local actors and unknowns. The film's financiers apparently pulled a few political strings, however, for they somehow talked a local Senator (!), Leroy Johnson, into playing Mr. Ledoux, the lawyer (he has one scene).

As one would expect from such a lusterless cast, acting is *not* the film's strong suit. Victor French basically walks through his part, his face rarely changing expression. Mike Evans plays Phillippe as the stereotypical hip dude, complete with cock-o'-the-walk strut, jive talk, and "cool" attitude. It simply grates. Janee Michelle, though attractive, infuses little personality into her pivotal role, making for a colorless heroine (no pun intended). The remainder of the cast are obvious amateurs and it shows—with one exception. Jean Durand as Thomas possesses a quiet and powerful presence. Aided by his frequent and subtle pointed looks, assured dialogue delivery, and occasional half-smiles, he creates the impression of a man in control and one who knows much more than he tells.

According to the film's publicity, Durand (who was actually born in Haiti and spoke French, Creole, and Spanish as well as English) was well-suited for his role of voodoo priest: "Durand... is in reality a serious student of this ancient religion and is a master of several chants and dances." When the article tactfully notes that Durand has been deliberately passed over by most Hollywood casting agents "because of his unmistakable Haitian accent," it quotes the actor as philosophically recalling that "Sidney Poitier also had his problems when he began in films." It goes without saying that, since *The House on Skull Mountain* proved to be the only time Durand came close to a starring role (with only a few brief appearances in minor films such as *Penelope*, *Eighteen & Anxious*, and Russ Myer's laughable *Blacksnake* to "fatten" his resume), he fell well short of Mr. Poitier's level of success. A pity, perhaps.

Despite some notable attempts at voodoo accuracy and an occasional directorial flourish, this *House* is merely a low-rent dwelling inhabited by wasted opportunities. *The House on Skull Mountain* would be better named *The House on* Dull *Mountain*.

CREDITS: Director: Ron Honthaner; Producer: Ray Storey; Co-Producer: Tom Boutross; Executive Producer: Joe R. Hartsfield; Screenplay: Mildred Pares; Director of Photography: Monroe Askins; Art Director: James Newport; Music: Jerrold Immel; Film Editor: Gerard Wilson; Set Decorator: Dorothy Crone; Assistant Director: Stephen P. Duran; Property Master: Charles Hughes; Sound Mixer: Bill Oliver; Makeup: Ken Chase; Hairstylist: Faye Burruss; Costumer: Joan Lewis; Script Supervisor: Eve Light; Key Grip: Gene Griffith; Camera Operator: Robert Dening; a Chocolate Chip and Pinto co-production released 1974 by 20th Century-Fox; 84 minutes

CAST: Victor French (Andrew Cunningham), Janee Michelle (Lorena), Jean Durand (Thomas), Mike Evans (Phillippe), Xernona Clayton (Harriet Johnson), Lloyd Nelson (Sheriff), Ella Woods (Louette), Mary J. Todd McKenzie (Pauline Christophe), Don Devendorf (The Priest), Jo Marie (The Doctor), Senator Leroy Johnson (Mr. Ledoux), Ray Banner (Deputy Sheriff), O.J. Harris (Dancer)

VOODOO BLACK EXORCIST (1975)
Voodoo Meets *The Mummy*

"Heads decapitated, sarcophaguses, mummies,
voodoo rites, lying scientists…
I don't like this."
—Disgruntled police inspector

Appropriately enough, this ridiculous feature was
saddled with a ludicrous name, a moniker that makes
about as much sense as the film's unintelligible
storyline. In an obvious attempt to cash in on the popularity of *The Exorcist* (1973) as well as the then-boom-
ing blaxploitation genre (with successful pictures like
Shaft, 1971; *Blacula*, 1972; *Coffy*, 1973; and the like),
the distributors took this muddled tale of a voodoo-
created mummy longing for his lost love of a thousand years past and called it *Voodoo Black Exorcist*.
Yes, the story does contain "Voodoo," and yes, the
main character is technically "Black" (though a very
light, light brown would be more accurate); but where
the "Exorcist" part fits in is anybody's guess.

The film begins with a pre-credit sequence in
which a man interrupts two lovers romping in the surf.
In the ensuing fight, the interloper is killed, and the
scene switches to a night-time voodoo ceremony in
which the woman-in-question is beheaded and her
lover stabbed with a sacred pin and collapses. The
voodooists then seal the man in a ceremonial coffin
which they leave inside a cave.

A thousand years later (in present day), Dr.
Kessler and his secretary/lover Sylvia are transporting the sarcophagus and mummy to Port-au-Prince
onboard a Caribbean cruise ship. Down in the hold,
the sarcophagus opens and the mummy steps forth.
Out on deck the wrinkled creature transforms back
into his human-looking self and kills a ship steward
by decapitating him. The mummy also gets a glimpse
of Sylvia and realizes she's the reincarnation of the
woman ("Kenya, the most beloved of women") he
died for a millennium ago.

Using his sacred "curare ring," the mummy en-
slaves a crew member who tries to steal the sarcophagus' valuables. Then the creature (who periodically
reverts back to his horrid appearance) kills Dr. Craig
(whom Dr. Kessler was supposed to meet) at the Port-
au-Prince airport. The mummy reveals itself to
Kessler and concocts a plan in which he will pose as
Dr. Craig. Kessler goes along with the charade so he
can learn from the 1,000-year-old creature.

Things soon go awry, however, when the mummy
orders his slave to kidnap Sylvia and bring her to the
original burial cave. "Once you and I were in love,"
the creature tells the timid Sylvia. "They *separated*
us! But I *found* you again. Now we'll be together
forever." Kessler, accompanied by a police inspector
and his men (toting machine guns and flame throwers),
follows them to the cave. Kessler wants the mummy
alive, but the Inspector has other ideas. "Don't make
trouble," the policeman admonishes, "we've got quite
enough of it now."

Kessler slips away from the police party to find
the mummy, but is killed by the creature's servant for
his troubles, whereupon the police promptly shoot the
servant. Then, when the Inspector spots the mummy
carrying Sylvia in his arms, a trigger-happy lackey
opens up with his flame-thrower, burning both monster and heroine to a cinder. The End.

Other than the fact that this apparently Spanish/
American co-production was filmed in Jamaica, Haiti,
and Santo Domingo (not to mention onboard a
Starward "Love Boat"-style cruise ship), little is
known about this obscure voodoo entry. No trade publications covered it, and few of the modern genre lite-
rati (known for their love of minutiae and the obscure)
have ever even *mentioned* it.

Apart from the authentic locales and a solitary
voodoo ceremonial sequence at the film's beginning,
there's nothing in *Voodoo Black Exorcist* to recommend. Though it seems like sacrilege to mention the
two films in the same breath, *Voodoo Black Exorcist*
is really a remake of the Universal Boris Karloff vehicle *The Mummy* (1932), with voodoo standing in
for Ancient Egyptian magic and cheesy gore standing
in for powerful mood. Both films are about ancient
mummies who died for love and who, upon their accidental resurrection, encounter and pursue the modern reincarnation of their lost lovers. Though thematically similar, artistically the two films couldn't
be further apart. *The Mummy* is a poetic, timeless
classic of understated mood. *Voodoo Black Exorcist*
is simply a dull, poorly produced hack job on all
counts.

The script makes little sense. The mummy comes
to life in the ship's hold for seemingly no reason—
except that it was apparently time for it to start stalking about. The creature then uses a ceremonial blade
to decapitate a crewman and dumps the head in
Sylvia's bed, saying "I bring you proof of my vengeance. Your killer is dead, oh Kenya." Does the
mummy think that this unlucky ship steward is the
reincarnation of his ancient lover's executioner? If
so, that's one incredible coincidence (though, I suppose, no more unlikely than having the current incar-
nation of his 1,000-year-old lover turn out to be the

Ad for the (justifiably) obscure *Voodoo Black Exorcist*. (Courtesy Lynn Naron)

secretary of the very scientist in charge of his undead body).

The mummy's actions often prove inexplicable. In Port-au-Prince, for instance, he lies in wait for an exotic dancer and then murders her in her dressing room. Who this two-bit stripper is or why he would want to kill her is anybody's guess (although after seeing her pathetic dance routine, one can almost condone his actions).

Inconsistencies and out-and-out *non sequiturs* abound. After the sacrificial ceremony during the opening sequence, for instance, a narrator babbles something about bad things repeating in a thousand years and we're abruptly treated to several minutes of stock footage of the Apollo moon mission (!) followed by space/astronaut drawings and still photos of a modern city shown under the credits. Why? One can only shake one's head and wonder.

Later, the mummy has his slave flatten Dr. Craig with a steamroller at the airport, but the police inspector states that the man was "run over with a bulldozer." And even something so simple as consistent character names seems to be beyond this film's grasp, for Sylvia is sometimes "Sofia" and Dr. Kessler at times becomes "Dr. Kess*ling*." These silly anomalies indicate the level of care (or lack of it) taken with both the script and dubbing.

The film also suffers from awkward, almost nonsensical dialogue, whose ridiculousness is only exacerbated by the lifeless dubbing. "I had the impression of being turned inside out, into a state of no gravity," states Sylvia flatly after "dreaming" of her past life. "I began to wonder who I was or what I was doing. I couldn't tell anything, I don't know why." Nor can the audience "tell anything" from this muddled monologue.

To pad out the running time director M. Cano resorts to frequent (red-tinted) flashbacks of tepid love scenes and the sacrificial ceremony (admittedly, the film's one exciting sequence) which the viewer has already seen at the beginning in full color. Cano also seems to adore close-ups for close-ups' sake, employing them indiscriminately and often. The faces constantly filling the screen (even the furry face of a caged kitty) become both annoying and disorienting, for often they come without prior background establishing shots so the bewildered viewers can only wonder *why* they're staring at a particular actor's nosehair.

Editor Frederic Vich's sorry scissor-work doesn't help matters (though, to be fair, he obviously had very little to work with in the first place). As the ancient sarcophagus is wheeled into the ship's hold, the film inexplicably cuts to an extreme close-up of a caged cat. Why? Who knows. Later, Vich inserts red-tinted flashback shots from the beheading sequence into a scene of a steward drinking sherry. Why? Again, who knows. And this mess required the further services of an "Editing Supervisor" in the form of someone named Tonny Loaysa. Why? Who knows.

Robert Ochoa's shaky photography perfectly complements the inept editing and graceless direction. For minutes on end the viewer is subjected to long stretches of mummy point-of-view shots as the creature promenades about the ship deck. This mummy-cam proves so unsteady as the creature totters about for no particular purpose that the viewer gets an authentic taste of seasickness.

Even the mummy makeup (courtesy of Sergy Casttle) proves ineffective, for he looks like nothing more than an actor covered in wrinkled Kleenex and chocolate syrup. At best, he appears the victim of an over-enthusiastic tanning salon rather than a petrified 1,000-year-old cadaver.

Amazingly, the picture is not all bad. The initial ceremonial sequence is impressive, with dozens of native participants energetically whirling to the drumbeats, some wearing the traditional Voudoun garb of white shirts and red scarves on their heads while others are nearly naked (including a number of topless women who are, refreshingly, not the expected silicone-enhanced Hollywood-type bimbos). In a flurry of frenzied dancing, drumming, and torch wielding, a man beheads the kneeling woman. Then, shockingly, the voodooists grab the severed head and triumphantly hold it aloft, passing the gruesome trophy from one to the other. One man even kisses it (!) while another holds it above him to bathe in the dripping gore. Too bad the impact of this startling sequence is lessened by the unconvincing, plastic-looking mannequin head. (This production had further difficulties with its severed heads—the crew member's decapitated dome found in Sylvia's bed looks suspiciously like a Styrofoam head covered in wrinkled brown paper and topped with a bad toupee.)

With a worthy model (Universal's *The Mummy*) to pattern itself upon and possessing the timeless theme of eternal love and tortured separation, *Voodoo Black Exorcist* could have become an enjoyable hybrid of voodoo cinema and that time-honored mummy subgenre. Instead, not only is this one of the worst voodoo movies ever produced, it also wins the prize of worst mummy movie as well.

CREDITS: Director: M. Cano; Producers: Rosgard of Miami and Mingyar of Madrid; Screenplay: S. Monikada; Director of Photography: Robert Ochoa; Art Director: Manahem Velasco; Set Dresser: E. Tower; Editor: Frederic Vich; Editing Supervisor: Tonny Loaysa; Music: Fernand Morcillo; Production Manager: Ben Marrt; Special Effects: Antony Molina; Makeup: Sergy Castle; Assistant Camera: Frank Conde; Script Girl: Rosa Biadiu; A Spanish/American co-production; 1975

CAST: Aldo Sambrell, Tanyeka Stadler, Alexander Abrahan, Ferdinand Sancho, Alfred May, Eva Lion, Richard Rod, Henry River, Mary A. River, Kess Bridge, Louis Marin, Antony Houss

An (ahem) eye-popping shot from the close of *Zombie*. (Ronald V. Borst/Hollywood Movie Posters)

ZOMBIE (1979)
Gore! Gore! Gore!

"As a man of science I don't believe in voodooism,
but the phenomenon defies logical explanation!"
—Richard Johnson as Dr. Menard

When George Romero's (non-voodoo) zombie sequel *Dawn of the Dead* (1979) took European theaters by storm, continental producers sat up and took notice. "The two Romero 'living dead' films [*Dawn* and its predecessor *Night of the Living Dead*] were instant horror classics in Italy," recalled Italian director Lucio Fulci, "indeed, throughout Europe." [1] The first to hop aboard the zombie bandwagon (or *hearse*, as the case may be) were Italian producers Ugo Tucci and Fabrizio De Angelis. Teaming up with the prolific Lucio Fulci, they constructed a gory European knock-off which in some places managed to out-gross its American model (in *both* senses of the word).

After *Zombie*'s immediate fiscal success both in Europe and America (where it was released with a publicity-generating self-imposed X rating), flesh-eating ghouls began pouring across the Italian border to invade the cinematic world. "We had no idea [*Zombie*] would become so popular," recalled Fulci. "The enormous success was a revelation to my producers, who were totally unprepared for it. So [Fabrizio] De Angelis offered me this five-films-in-five-years contract, with screenwriter Dardano Sacchetti working on the stories, in which he spilled out his deepest fears, if not his very guts." As a result, Fulci spewed forth three more bloodstained zombie pictures: *The Gates of Hell* (1980), *House by the Cemetery* (1981), and *The Beyond* (1981; aka *Seven Doors of Death*). Fulci was soon followed by a horde of like-minded continental filmmakers who quickly churned out titles like *Burial Ground* (1980), *City of the Walking Dead* (1980), *Dawn of the Mummy* (1981), *Oasis of the Zombies* (1982), and *Night of the Zombies* (1983), solidifying a new cinematic subgenre through sheer weight of numbers alone. (Oddly enough, none of these subsequent films utilized voodoo as the source of their zombies, relying instead upon mad science, Satanism, and even ancient Etruscan sorcery.)

While most of these zombie follow-ups were top-heavy with exploitable nudity and gore, they proved decidedly light on characterization, story, and simple entertainment value. Sadly, the same can be said of this cinematic subset's prototype—*Zombie*.

An apparently abandoned sailboat drifts into New York harbor. When the harbor patrol boards her, a walking corpse kills a patrolman before being knocked overboard. Newspaper reporter Peter West (Ian McCulloch) teams up with Ann Boles (Tisa Farrow), the daughter of the boat's missing owner, to investigate. They journey to St. Thomas where they talk a young American couple, Brian (Al Cliver) and Lisa (Auretta Gay), into taking them in their power cruiser to the remote island of Matule (the last place Ann had heard from her father).

When they stop so Lisa can go scuba diving, she encounters first a shark and then an underwater zombie, who soon becomes locked in a life and (un)death struggle with the shark. In the ensuing fracas, Lisa makes it to safety but the shark rams the foursome's boat, damaging the drive shaft.

The quartet coax their limping vessel to Matule where they're met by Dr. Menard (Richard Johnson). One of the few white men on Matule, Menard tells of "the horrors that are destroying our island, transforming it into a wasteland of terror." Said horrors take the form of corpses rising from their graves to eat the living. "The natives say it's something to do with voodoo," states Menard, "some evil witch docter creates these zombies. But I'm sure there's a natural explanation and I'm *determined* to find it!" In his tiny makeshift hospital, Menard has been trying to do just that—with little result. In fact, Ann's father, Menard's friend, had succumbed to the disease and Menard was forced to destroy his zombified friend with a bullet in the brain.

Menard asks the four Americans to take his Jeep to his cottage and keep his wife company while he attends to his work. When the quartet arrive at the house, however, they find Mrs. Menard has become a meal for the advancing zombies (who, heretofore, had only been seen on the *other* side of the island).

They flee through the jungle back to the hospital. On the way, however, they lose Lisa to a zombie attack when buried Conquistadors rise up from a centuries-old cemetery. Peter, Ann, and Brian finally make it to the hospital and barricade themselves in with Dr. Menard and his two assistants. The zombies soon lay siege, and the living battle the dead with rifles and molotov cocktails.

Menard and his assistants fall prey to the zombies, but Peter, Ann, and Brian escape from the burning building. Brian, however, instantly comes face to face with the now-zombified Lisa, who promptly takes a chunk out of Brian's arm before Peter can shoot her in the head.

The trio make it back to their boat and set off for civilization, nursing the damaged drive-shaft. Brian,

however, soon succumbs to his wound. Then, over the radio Ann and Peter hear a New York broadcast: "In every borough in the city, from Brooklyn to Manhattan, from Harlem to Queens, the zombies are taking over...." The broadcast ends with the announcer shouting, "I've just been informed that zombies have entered the building. They're at the door! They're coming in! Aaaaarg—," and we see a final shot of zombies shambling across a New York bridge.

In Italy, *Zombie* was released as *Zombie 2* in an attempt to cash in on the popularity of George Romero's *Dawn of the Dead* (which was titled *Zombie* in Europe)—even though Fulci's film has nothing to do with Romero's (particularly considering Fulci's zombies are a product of voodoo rather than science; *Night of the Living Dead* and its sequels offer radiation from a recently returned Venus probe as the probable explanation for the dead returning to hungry life).

Dawn of the Dead's producers frowned upon the misleading sequel-implication tactics employed by *Zombie*'s Italian distributors. "Dario Argento was the Italian producer of *Dawn of the Dead*," stated Richard P. Rubinstein, the American half of the *Dawn* producers team, "and neither Dario nor any of his people were involved in *Zombi 2*. If the American distributor claims otherwise, he's likely to find himself in a lawsuit." (Hence the simple title of *Zombie* in the U.S.) [2]

"I don't like *Dawn of the Dead*," opined Lucio Fulci. "It was Argento's re-editing that made it as good as it was. It was erroneously considered a horror film, it's more of a sociopolitical movie. My film, *Zombie*, was more of a pure horror film. I think of *Zombie* as being along the lines of Jacques Tourneur and his movies, as more absurd, more fantastic." Fulci apart, most cineastes think Tourneur movies and *Zombie* have about as much in common as chocolate truffles and pickled pig's feet.

The film's sole *raison d'être* is gut-munching corpses. (For a movie called *Zombie*, I suppose this might be understandable.) Everything, however, including script, characters, and acting, takes a back seat to blood and guts and putrescence. In this respect, *Zombie* remains a seminal flesh-eating-ghoul picture since it exists solely for its gory set-pieces. Admittedly, these can be quite effective—if the desired effect is a stomach flip or a disgusted cringe. Numerous instances of zombies ripping chunks of flesh from necks and arms, the dead hungrily gorging themselves on ripped entrails, or the once-seen-never-forgotten splinter-in-the-eye sequence all bombard the viewer with gruesome (and convincing) close-up detail.

One scene, however, because of its sheer novelty value and some deft handling and (environmentally imposed) restraint, transcends its sordid roots to become *Zombie*'s most thrilling sequence. It's two min-

Sights (ouch) such as this infamous eyeball-impalement scene make *Zombie* the goriest voodoo film to date.

utes of bizarre, jaw-dropping amazement that almost makes sitting through the film's other 89 minutes worthwhile... almost. I'm speaking, of course, of the famous zombie-vs.-shark sequence. In it, a convincingly made-up waterlogged corpse grabs and wrestles with a nine-foot denizen of the deep. In the exhilaratingly filmed fracas, the zombie bites a chunk of flesh from the shark's underbelly while the predator's huge gaping mouth rips an arm from the ghoul. The sequence is so excitingly staged and effectively shot that it becomes wholly convincing.

This underwater battle, the true highlight of the film, almost didn't occur. For the scene, a nine-foot shark and its handler were recruited from a nearby aquarium and shipped to the specially designed marine tank at the Elios R.P.A. Studio in Rome. After numerous dry runs (so to speak) with just the tranquilized shark and its trainer, it was time for the actors to get in the tank. Perhaps unsurprisingly, the actor hired to play the zombie chickened out at the last minute. "I couldn't blame him," admitted Fulci, "but we were left in a terrible situation. We were finally able to get the trainer to put on the zombie's

costume and makeup—I told him we'd make him a star. And, for an amateur, he was quite believable in the part." Indeed, he really seems to be *trying* to bite that huge shark!

"I've always held great admiration for the marvelous horror classics made in America," pronounced Fulci just prior to *Zombie*'s American release. "Fright films such as *I Walked with a Zombie*, *Voodoo Island*, and *The Walking Dead* were all in the back of my mind." (From looking at *Zombie*, one suspects that it was the pathetic *Voodoo Island* rather than the other two bonafide classics he mentioned that crept to the *front* of Fulci's mind.) "My own interpretation, however," continued the director, "has many new twists and surprises never before seen in a film of this type." True to his word, these "new twists" (in the form of the zombie-shark battle and the infamous eyeball-impaling scene) did indeed prove "surprising."

Zombie was shot over a two-month period on location in Santo Domingo and New York, and at Rome's Elios R.P.A. Studios for less than $500,000. To give Fulci his due, he did attempt to create moments of *frisson* with a bit more artistry and style than

For *Zombie*, distributor Jerry Gross obviously had his finger on the pulse of promotional giveaways. (Courtesy Ronald V. Borst/Hollywood Movie Posters; photo Lynn Naron)

that usually found in shots of actors chewing on sheep intestines. In one sequence, for instance, the camera tracks slowly forward to peer through a window at a woman (the ill-fated Mrs. Menard) taking a shower. As the camera moves in for a titillating close-up, blue-gray fingers suddenly rise up from the bottom of the frame in the extreme foreground (complete with shrill notes on the soundtrack), generating a startling shock. The camera then changes focus to show in clear detail the rotting fingers scrabbling at the window glass while the now-fuzzy-imaged woman continues her ablutions in the background, oblivious to the horrific danger just outside. With this, Fulci demonstrates that he can create both shocks and suspense without any spurting blood or exposed internal organs. Sadly, this remains the exception and he generally abandons Tourneur territory in favor of the local sausage factory.

Unlike many of his imitators, Fulci shows a cleverness in his staging and a proficiency with the camera, using alternating point-of-view shots and movement to augment his gory subject matter. In the film's most outrageous gore sequence (in fact, its signature scene), Mrs. Menard is besieged by the zombies at her house. An arm suddenly crashes through the closed door and grabs her hair, leaving a jagged piece of wood pointing straight out from the penetrated portal. As the hungry corpse pulls the victim's screaming face toward the splintered stake, Fulci shifts the camera from the side view to the front, so that it's now *our* arm that draws the woman toward her doom. We next see in extreme close-up from the victim's perspective the ragged splinter looming ever larger as it draws nearer, pointing at *our* eyes now. The changes in point-of-view (first neutral, then from the attacker's vantage, and finally from the victim's) make this sickening scene that much more involving and disturbing. Then comes the "payoff," of course, when we see (in lingering close-up) the splinter enter the victim's (now a dummy) eye, slowly penetrating further and further until Fulci finally cuts away to the (live) actress' shrieking face with the broken-off shard of wood imbedded in its new fleshy home.

In another scene, a dying man raves, "They'll be here soon—to destroy us all!" and Fulci cuts to a close-up profile of a slow-moving man. The camera begins to circle the figure, panning around in front of him as he shambles forward. Continuing around to the other side, we see that half of the man's face is a decaying, putrid mass—he's actually a walking corpse! Then, to hammer the revelation home with repulsive overkill, Fulci zooms in to show live maggots wriggling about in the man's dead flesh.

Fulci defended his brutal and excessive approach thus: "Cruelty is more immediately involving for an audience. More personal, emotional. Now, if you take a cruel act and depict it beyond the point where an audience expects it to go... Cinema is an interactive spectacle. I like to take advantage of this... I place the camera so that the audience is complicit in this cinematic crime. They are now past the point of simply being aware of a brutal act—they are now the perpetrators.

"My films are no more than nightmares, at the end of which one wakes up, relieved and relaxed. I feel the cinema of the fantastic is deeply liberating, for young people in particular, due to this 'audience participation.'"

Lucio Fulci originally had no aspirations to become a filmmaker. In fact, he studied and practiced medicine, but left the profession after a falling out with the hospital at which he worked. "On my way home on the bus," recounted Fulci, "I read an ad on the back of another passenger's newspaper about a new film school that was about to open. I applied and learned from some of Italy's great cinema minds." Fulci initially worked as a screenwriter and assistant producer, then graduated to director in the late 1950s—starting out with musical comedies (!). After a long and gore-strewn cinematic career, Fulci died on March 13, 1996 of diabetic shock.

While (for good or ill) *Zombie*'s gore and "cruelty" may be affecting and well-staged, there's just no getting past the film's major liabilities.

The (living) people in *Zombie* exist solely as zombie-fodder. The script contains no human conflict (one aspect that made *Night of the Living Dead* so compelling) nor even much interaction. They're there simply to attract the hungry dead. ("In fact," related lead actor Ian McCulloch to *Fangoria*'s Martin Coxhead, "[Fulci] wasn't really bothered about the subtleties you could put into the script or the fine points of your performance. He knew exactly what he wanted on the screen, exactly what the visuals were to be, and he concentrated on those.") Because of the poor characterizations, we have no affinity for nor empathy with the characters in peril. Consequently, rather than inspiring terror, the various gruesome set-pieces simply inspire disgust. This points up one of the significant differences between *Zombie* and Romero's *Night of the Living Dead* and *Dawn of the Dead*: Romero's films effectively develop their characters to draw us into the horrific proceedings; *Zombie* does not.

As a consequence, after the umpteenth scene of oozing corpses engaged in throat-ripping and entrail-munching, boredom begins to creep into the sickening scenario. Like a porno movie, *Zombie* initially titillates (or regurgitates—depending on one's constitution) but ultimately becomes both repetitive and uninteresting.

Zombie's cast are wasted in their thankless roles as walking bullseyes, which seems a pity considering that two of the leads are more than competent actors (Richard Johnson of *The Haunting* fame, and Ian McCulloch, who showed he could essay roles more demanding than that of a simple corpse magnet in films like *It!* [1967] and *The Ghoul* [1975]).

While Tisa Farrow (Mia's sister) looks remarkably like her famous sibling, all similarities seems to end there, for she appears stiff and uncomfortable in the few mildly demanding scenes she's given. "I wanted to use Tisa Farrow again [for *The Beyond*]," related Fulci, "but she's rather a bizarre girl; the last I heard, she had become a taxi driver in Manhattan!"

Zombie treats voodoo just as superficially as it does its characters and story. Though Dr. Menard occasionally mutters something about "investigating the phenomenon" of voodoo, he (and the viewer) never encounters *any* voodoo rites or practitioners. Apart from some infrequent background drumming and chanting, no voodoo visuals materialize. Voodoo is merely an (unseen) excuse to get the corpses up and running (or at least stumbling).

Even the few token lines of voodoo expostulation prove less than illuminating. Brian states that, "basically [voodoo] is a mixture of two religions: Catholicism brought here by the Spanish Conquistadors; and African tribal rites that were brought here by the slave trade." In reality, the Voudoun religion did not "mix" African rites and Catholicism, but merely grafted a few Catholic icons onto its African-based template (an expediency which allowed the religion to survive and evolve in the face of centuries of tyranny). The tenets of Voudou remain uniquely their own.

If one is looking for some effective "chunk-blowing" scenes staged with a bit of flair, one need look no further than *Zombie*. If, on the other hand, one desires a well-constructed story, fleshed-out characterizations, or insightful exploration regarding the subject of voodoo, one had best leave this particular *Zombie* rotting in the ground (or on the video shelf).

[1] Quotes by Lucio Fulci are from interviews conducted by Robert Schlockoff (*L'Ecran Fantastique*), Jim Wynorski (*Fangoria*), Loris Curci (*Fangoria*), and Howard Berger (*Fangoria*).

[2] Fulci *did* lens a (belated) sequel to *Zombie*, er, *Zombi 2* in 1988 called… *Zombie 3*. Perhaps not surprisingly, it actually has nothing to do with the previous film, as the (leaden) plot focuses on a small Asian town whose inhabitants become homicidal maniacs (*not* revived corpses) when exposed to a toxic nerve gas leak. Fulci claims he stalked off the troubled production and that it was finished by Bruno Mattei.

CREDITS: Original Language title: *Zombie 2*; British Title: *Zombie Flesh Eaters*; Director: Lucio Fulci; Producers: Ugo Tucci, Fabrizio De Angelis; Screenplay: Elisa Briganti; Director of Photography: Sergio Salvati; Film Editor: Sergio Salvati; Special Effects and Makeup Supervisor: Giannetto De Rossi; Production Designer: Walter Patriarea; Music: Fabio Frizzi and Giorgio Tucci; Production Manager: Antonio Mazza; Unit Managers: Walter Massi and Tullio Lullo; An Italian Variety Film production released Summer 1979 (Europe) and July 1980 (U.S.); 91 minutes

CAST: Tisa Farrow (Ann Boles), Ian McCulloch (Peter West), Richard Johnson (Dr. Menard), Al Cliver (Brian Hall), Auretta Gay (Susan Barrett), Stefania D'Amario (Nurse), Olga Karlatos (Mrs. Menard)

Lisa Bonet writhes in orgiastic abandon during a ceremonial scene that proves more cinematic than authentic.

ANGEL HEART (1987)
Voodoo Noir

"I ain't up on all this voodoo shit;
I'm from Brooklyn."
—Mickey Rourke as Harry Angel

"I read [William Hjortsberg's critically acclaimed novel] *Falling Angel* when it was first published in 1978 and rather liked it," offered writer/director Alan Parker to *Fangoria*'s Anthony Timpone about *Angel Heart*'s genesis. "Robert Redford snapped it up, but couldn't see himself as Harry Angel. Then someone dropped the project on my desk." Parker himself subsequently "snapped it up" and set about adapting the book as a screenplay. He made the main character of Harry Angel more sympathetic and expanded the story's New York-bound setting to include both The Big Apple *and* The Big Easy. According to Parker,

"Hjortsberg [no stranger to the movies, having penned the screenplay for Ridley Scott's *Legend* the previous year] agreed with my transposing half the story to Louisiana, and said he once thought about doing it himself. I sent my script to him for his approval, and he was very generous. Writers usually hate directors and say we're all butchers, which we probably are anyway [laughs]."

Parker (who says he chose to shoot half the film in New Orleans for "selfish directorial reasons") looked long and hard to find just the right locales in The Big Easy. "I tried to find a part of New Orleans that wasn't a postcard cliché," he stated. "New Orleans is a hard city to find, especially the stranger side. Usually, the city is like a vain actress who only presents her best profile. But we found New Orleans' creepier side." Indeed they did.

In 1955 New York, small-time private detective Harry Angel (Mickey Rourke) meets with a mysterious client named Louis Cyphre (Robert De Niro) and his attorney, Mr. Winesap. Cyphre wants Angel to find someone called Johnny Favorite, who was "a crooner before the war." "I gave Johnny some help at the beginning of his career," explains the enigmatic Cyphre. "Mr. Cyphre has a contract," continues Winesap. "Certain collateral was involved to be forfeited in the event of his death." Johnny was drafted in 1943 and subsequently "was badly injured about the head and face. He had amnesia." Upon his return to the States, he entered a private sanitarium but was subsequently whisked away by two people who paid a crooked doctor $25,000 to keep up the pretense that he remained a patient there.

Angel's investigations lead to that very doctor, an elderly drug-addicted medico named Fowler (Michael Higgins). After interrogating the old man in his home, Angel locks him in his own bedroom for a couple of hours "cold turkey" in the hopes he'll be more cooperative. When Angel returns, however, he finds the doctor dead, an apparent suicide.

Angel meets again with Cyphre and tries to back out from the case ("I usually handle small-time stuff, insurance jobs, divorces, things of that nature"), but the money Cyphre offers proves irresistible. Continuing his investigation, Angel learns that Johnny was engaged to one Margaret Krusemark (Charlotte Rampling), whose father "owns half of Louisiana." Though a member of high society, Margaret was into black magic and was even derisively dubbed "the witch of Wellsley."

Journeying to New Orleans, Harry tracks down both Margaret and a former friend of Johnny's, an old guitar player named Toots Sweet (Brownie McGhee). He also finds that Johnny's "secret love" (a voodoo priestess) has died. Angel eventually learns more from the mambo's beautiful 17-year-old daughter, Epiphany (Lisa Bonet), herself a mamaloi, who admits to being Johnny Favorite's child.

After both Toots and Margaret turn up dead, grotesquely mutilated, Angel fears he's being set up. He goes to see Margaret's father, Ethan Krusemark (Stocker Pontelieu), and intimidates him into spilling the whole sordid story. Kruzemark relates how Johnny, an avowed Satan-worshiper, "sold his soul for stardom. Except he thought he could outwit the Prince of Darkness... Johnny came upon an obscure rite in an ancient manuscript. He needed a victim, someone his own age—to steal his soul." So Johnny and Margaret picked up a young soldier and performed a ceremony whereby Johnny cut out the boy's heart and ate it. ("It was still beating when he wolfed it down!" exclaims a near-enraptured Kruzemark.) Through this unholy rite, Johnny took that soldier's identity in an effort to elude his "debtor." When he shipped out to North Africa in the guise of his victim, however, he was injured, came home with amnesia and, via plastic surgery performed on his battered

Robert DeNiro as the enigmatic (and *diabolic* as it turns out) Louis Cyphre.

countenance, received a new face. Margaret, who truly loved Johnny, and her father then whisked the shell-shocked Satanist out of the sanitarium and dropped him off in Times Square, the very place from which Johnny had stolen the young soldier's life and embarked upon his new identity. This attempt to jog Johnny's memory apparently failed and they lost hold of him.

Shocked and sickened by this tale, Angel runs to the bathroom to vomit. When he returns, Kruzemark is dead, his face shoved into a pot of boiling gumbo. After a romantic—and violent—encounter with Epiphany, Angel finally learns the whole, horrifying truth, both about his client ("Louis Cyphre—Lucifer," he realizes) *and* himself, in the film's powerful denouement, an ending that once seen is not soon forgotten.

At 18 million dollars, *Angel Heart* is the most expensive voodoo film made to date. Amazingly (for money rarely guarantees quality and more often than not results in an *inverse* ratio—the more cash, the less innovation), it's also one of the best, thanks to a unique and involving storyline, evocative photography, superb acting, and inspired direction.

More than almost any other film involving this era, *Angel Heart* succeeds in its marvelous evocation of time and place, transporting the viewer back to the

Death by boiling gumbo in *Angel Heart*.

seamy realism of 1955 New York, New Orleans, and rural Louisiana. Through its realistic production and set design and Michael Seresin's rich, moody lighting, one can almost *feel* the New York grit under Harry Angel's fingernails and the Louisiana dust clogging his throat.

Writer/director Alan Parker consciously strove for realism, both in its detail and in the film's broader scope. "From the very beginning," stated Parker, "I didn't set out to make a supernatural story. I didn't fall into the clichés you usually see in that kind of movie. I was making a totally *real* detective story that's entertaining because of that *and* the supernatural elements. At no point did I allow myself, or anyone else on the movie, to think of *Angel Heart* as anything but real and believable. People selling their souls to the devil occurs every day of the week. And in the movie industry, more than every day!"

Written and shot in a noirish style, *Angel Heart* is an exquisitely photographed film which often emphasizes both beauty and horror almost simultaneously. The opening credit sequence in which the camera roams a nighttime New York street, for instance, is so effectively lit that the scene seems bathed in an eerie blue and silver light, evoking the glittering, dark night of winter (the story takes place in January) and transforming the slush-soaked, dirty street into a landscape of near-abstract beauty. This makes it doubly shocking when the camera comes to rest on

a blood-soaked corpse sprawled amongst the refuse and soiled snow. (This introductory sequence foreshadows one of *Angel Heart*'s primary themes: Nothing and no one in this film are quite what they first seem.)

When the story shifts to Louisiana, Michael Seresin's camera and lighting captures the beauty of a misty bayou twilight, replete with its quiet humidity and dusky stillness. Under Parker's direction, Seresin fills the film with darker images as well, such as silhouettes seen through backlit windows, long, forbiddingly black hallways, and the shadows of barred grates and slowly rotating fans that evoke a sense of mystery and menace.

Parker employs the fan as a symbolic object, for Cyphre's appearances are invariably accompanied by an eerie, metallic creak and a shot of slowly rotating blades. When Angel first meets Mr. Cyphre, the detective glances up at the two fans in the room and gives a brief, involuntary shudder (it's the dead of winter, after all, so why would his client want a cool breeze?). It's as if the Winds of Evil—or of Destiny—blow at Cyphre's presence. Parker uses this emblem to represent Cyphre's all-invasive influence even when he himself is absent. For example, when Angel locks Dr. Fowler in his bedroom, the room's window fan begins to slowly spin, auguring the evil to come (when Angel returns, he finds the doctor shot through the eye). The scene ends on a wonderfully composed shot of the fan's rotating shadow thrown over a spot of threadbare carpet on which rests one of the doctor's old shoes—lying on its side as if it had been kicked off in some violent struggle. It makes for a disturbing and portentous image.

Though aiming for (and getting) a brooding, noirish mood, Parker peppers his script with moments of effective dark humor. After finding that seemingly everyone he comes in contact with ends up murdered, Angel tells Epiphany that, "There's too many dead bodies floating around," adding, "even for Louisiana." Even at the end, when Angel's world comes crashing down around him, Cyphre makes a joke out of death. "Winesap?" echoes Cyphre after Angel's inquiry; "He's dead—*nasty* accident. Don't worry, no one will mourn one less lawyer in the world."

London-born filmmaker Alan Parker began his career in the early 1970s in British television and commercials. He soon turned to feature films, and his subsequent eclectic career has seen him helm such disparate big screen projects as *Bugsy Malone* (1976), the exceedingly powerful *Midnight Express* (1978), the exceedingly popular *Fame* (1980), the exceedingly bizarre *Pink Floyd—The Wall* (1982), the largely unseen *Birdy* (1984), and the topical *Mississippi Burning* (1988).

Robert Redford showed good judgment when he decided he did not fit this particular anti-hero mold, for, after watching Mickey Rourke's intense, quirky, and appealing portrayal, it's impossible to see anyone else as Harry Angel. In Parker's words, Rourke exhibits "something wicked, anarchic and charming." Disheveled, unkempt, and rumpled, Rourke ingratiates himself with his seedy charm and unassuming likability. Small touches, such as when he casually retrieves a lady's hat blown off by the wind or briefly touches the cheek of a small child sitting on the stairs as he wearily passes by, help forge a bond with the viewer so that we become caught up in Harry Angel's plight. Consequently, his frantic, fruitless denial at film's end ("I know who I am!" he shouts over and over with less and less conviction until, finally, he truly *does* know who he is—to his ultimate despair) becomes both horrifying and poignant.

"Louis Cyphre had to be someone of incredible presence and stature," explained Parker about his choice of actors to play the Devil himself. (Parker at one point considered Marlon Brando for the role.) "Even though Angel's the principal player and Cyphre's a subsidiary and intermittent one, Cyphre's presence had to permeate the whole film. You had to *feel* him. Plus, I wanted an actor whose work is based on truth and reality."

In assaying Satan, De Niro comes as close to "truth and reality" as one could want in such a role. With his penetrating gaze, commanding-yet-ingrati-

Lucifer's lawyer loses his head in a messy scene cut before *Angel Heart*'s release. Pictured (with head attached) is writer/director Alan Parker.

ating demeanor, a bemused, knowing attitude full of secret humor *and* secret menace, and a personality as oily as his hair, De Niro indeed makes the Devil a very real, albeit subtly disturbing, person. When Angel and Cyphre meet in a church, Angel tells him of Toots Sweet's demise and how "he got choked to death with a part of the body meant for pissing with." At this, De Niro raises his fingers to his lips in an almost effeminate gesture and gently admonishes, "This is a church, Mr. Angel," in a tone undercut with just a hint of mock sincerity.

More disturbingly, when Angel meets with Cyphre for the second time (in a deserted restaurant), De Niro picks up a hard boiled egg and begins to daintily peel it. "You know, some religions think that the egg is the symbol of the soul." After a pregnant pause, he adds, "Would you like an egg?" Then, in extreme close-up, De Niro, his eyes black and dead-looking, face totally expressionless, slowly and deliberately bites the egg in half, chewing up the meat just like the Devil chews up men's souls. It makes for a chilling image. If Satan does exist, he might very well look and act like Robert De Niro in *Angel Heart*.

While brutal, grotesque killings feature prominently in the story (a man shot through the eye, death by boiling gumbo, a heart cut from a woman's chest,

Playing a 17-year-old mamaloi, Lisa Bonet (of TV's *Cosby* fame) proves to be the thespian featherweight amongst big-screen champs Mickey Rourke and Robert DeNiro.

even a victim choked to death by his own severed penis), Parker never shows the actual act but only its gruesome aftermath when Harry stumbles upon the grotesque scenes. (The director even tastefully keeps the last-mentioned victim offscreen altogether, choosing to have Angel learn about it *verbally* rather than visually.) While still retaining the horrific impact such scenes inspire (via quick shots of the mutilated corpses and longer shots of Harry Angel's shocked and sickened reactions), this helps keeps the film grounded firmly on the side of art rather than exploitation.

Like the best film noirs, *Angel Heart* is unafraid to take a subversive stance, showing a sly irreverence for society's sacred cows of authority. In this case, said animal proves to be organized religion (specifically, Christianity). When Angel first goes to meet Cyphre, he finds an old-style gospel revival meeting going on in the building's downstairs meeting hall. As Angel watches, the energetic preacher shouts, "I want you to open up your *hearts*—and open up your *wallets*!" to an enthusiastic chorus of "yeahs" and "amens" from his enraptured (and gullible) parishioners. What makes this stereotypical (and, sadly, all-too-real) scene so ironically amusing is that directly above this religious panhandling sits Satan himself. The close physical proximity of the Devil speaks satirical volumes on the "religious" transaction occurring below.

In another scene Cyphre tells Angel, "I have old-fashioned ideas about honor. You know, an eye for an eye, things like that." Even Lucifer can find some-

thing in scripture to fit his purpose. (Obviously, the Bible has something for everyone.)

"They say there's just enough religion in the world to make men hate one another but not enough to make them love." Beyond the fact that it's Satan himself spouting such wisdom, he's doing it while in a *church*! Then, amusingly, when Angel gets fed up with his client's vague answers and asks, "Who the fuck *are* you, Cyphre?," the disguised Devil only lifts his fingers to gesture about him and, with an almost impish smile, gently whispers, "Watch your language."

Though *Angel Heart* may be one of the best films ever to feature voodoo, it's not necessarily one of the best Voodoo Films. "For most of its length, *Angel Heart* is a Chandleresque film noir that turns into something quite different in its explanation," observed Alan Parker. As such, voodoo appears in the picture simply as background, a colorful (and brief) backdrop in front of which this noirish tale of evil and destiny plays out. Beyond that, the "something quite different in its explanation" turns out to be Satanism rather than voodoo. Though labeled a voodoo film, *Angel Heart* concerns itself more with Devil-worship than hoodoo (particularly considering one of the film's pivotal characters is Beelzebub himself). Revealingly, the fateful sacrifice and soul-transference was undertaken by avowed Satanists (the Krusemarks), *not* by followers of the voodoo faith.

The picture plays it safe by casting Voudoun in a slightly savage, even sinister light (via the bloody ceremony observed by the ignorant Harry Angel in

206

which Epiphany, in an erotic trance, slits the throat of a chicken and bathes in its blood), and so retains its topic's exotic, dangerous charm. On the less exploitative side, the film throws a few verbal bones to the politically correct viewpoint of Voudoun as a legitimate (and benign) form of worship. When Angel sarcastically observes, "That's a mighty cute religion you people got," Epiphany shoots back with, "Yeah, well, nailing a man to a cross ain't so cute either." And later she defensively assures the skeptical P.I. that, "We don't go around murdering people, all right Mr. Angel?" So, at least by implication, Voudoun is removed from the devilish doings in which Harry Angel finds himself embroiled. Yet, the film's final shot (in which Epiphany's child points a damning finger at the condemned Harry and the tot's eyes suddenly take on the same devilish glow sported earlier by Lucifer) seems to link Voudoun with Satanism after all—for Epiphany stated earlier that her child was conceived when she was "mounted by the gods" during spirit possession. The logical conclusion then, is that she was "mounted" by Satan. So perhaps *Angel Heart*'s attitude toward Voudoun may not be so "PC" after all.

Apart from this superficial, backhanded (and ultimately negated) defense of Voudoun, the film offers no further exploration of the religion. The only voodoo-related activity we see is Toots Sweet worried by a dried chicken foot found on a urinal (the man also answers Angel's taunts with, "We ain't all Baptists down here, sonny") and the brief (one-and-a-half minute) backwoods ceremony in which Epiphany (without any background or explanation) lasciviously rolls in the dirt covered in chicken blood. Not much in the way of enlightenment.

To his credit, however, Parker did utilize actual Haitian ceremonial music for this sequence, and choreographer Louis (*Fame*) Falco studied genuine Voudoun ceremonies before creating the film's dance arrangements. (Due to an amusing coincidence, this ceremonial sequence took on a devilish connotation during filming. "Ironically," chuckled Parker, "the slate number of Lisa Bonet's voodoo dance scene was 666! The focus puller, who's from England and doesn't know about such things, yelled 'Scene 666, take one!' I couldn't believe it!")

While both Rourke and De Niro provide effective, even scintillating performances, the film's third lead, Lisa Bonet, presents a disappointing contrast. Though possessing an undeniable beauty and appealing vulnerability, this former Cosby-kid's featherweight, shallow acting pales in comparison to her heavyweight co-stars. (Even as the older daughter on the long-running TV sitcom *Cosby*, she appeared toneless and uninteresting.) Though at one point Angel tells her that her beautiful eyes can't hide her fear, the viewer sees absolutely *nothing* in those gorgeous orbs, nor does *any* deep emotion ever register on her face either. Bonet projects such a blunted effect that she appears more mannequin than mambo.

In addition to this serious casting error, Parker and company stumbled again at the end when Cyphre finally confronts Angel with his real identity and forces the sublimated memories of Harry's brutal acts to the surface. After calmly and coolly (even bemusedly) delineating Angel's crimes and explaining that his soul is not truly his own, Cyphre's eyes suddenly glow with a supernatural light when he points a demonic finger at Angel and growls, "Only the soul is immortal—and yours belongs to *me!*" This blatant crossover into supernatural effects (repeated with similar glowing eyes and gesture by Epiphany's child for the film's final scene) strikes a dissonant chord with the rest of the reality-based feel of the picture. Rather than chilling, such banal demon-devices simply jar with the film's tone, appearing both out of place and absurd. Better had Parker let Cyphre's words and Angel's reactions generate the revelation's inherent *frisson*.

A few minor missteps aside, *Angel Heart* remains an innovative, engrossing, and artful voodoo entry. With voodoo utilized only for backdrop, it adds little to Voudoun's cinematic canon, but it treats its topic as well as most and shows that voodoo has its place among the very best (directors, actors, production designers, cinematographers) that the silver screen has to offer.

CREDITS: Director: Alan Parker; Producers: Alan Marshall, Ellito Kastner; Executive Producers: Mario Kassar, Andrew Vajna; Screenplay: Alan Parker; Based on the novel *Falling Angel* by William Hjortsberg; Director of Photography: Michael Seresin; Camera Operator: Michael Roberts; Original Music: Trevor Jones; Editor: Gerry Hambling; Production Designer: Brian Morris; Costume Designer: Aude Bronson-Howard; Choreographer: Louis Falco; Art Directors: Kristi Zen, Armin Ganz; A Carolco International production released March 1987 by Tri-Star; 113 minutes; Rated R

CAST: Mickey Rourke (Harry Angel), Robert De Niro (Louis Cyphre), Lisa Bonet (Epiphany Proudfoot), Charlotte Rampling (Margaret Krusemark), Stoker Pontelieu (Ethan Krusemark), Brownie McGhee (Toots Sweet), Michael Higgins (Doctor Fowler), Elizabeth Whitcraft (Connie), Eliott Keener (Sterne)

THE BELIEVERS (1987)
Santería and Sorcery

"Santería is a thousand years older
than Christianity, brought by slaves
to the Caribbean, their African gods
hidden in Catholic saints."
—Martin Sheen as Cal Jamison
reading from a book on Santería

The Believers is based ("very loosely," according to scripter Mark Frost) on Nicholas Conde's 1981 novel *The Religion.* "Conde's book was optioned a couple of times in Hollywood," explained Frost to *Fangoria*'s Roger Berrian. "I was brought into the project when John Schlesinger had it at 20th Century-Fox. We did quite a bit of research on Santería. Then the picture went to Orion, and we finally began shooting last year [1986] in New York and Toronto."

The only full-fledged voodoo film to date that deals with the Hispanic voodoo variation of Santería, *The Believers* presents a fairly sympathetic picture of the religion while still remaining an entertaining (if flawed) horror film. Not an easy task, actually.

When the wife of police psychologist Cal Jamison (Martin Sheen) dies in a freak accident, he returns with his eight-year-old son Chris (Harley Cross) to New York City and a job with the NYPD. In his capacity as staff psychologist, Cal tries to help a detective named Tom Lopez (a pre-*L.A. Law* and *NYPD Blue* Jimmy Smits) who, after finding a ritualistically murdered boy in Spanish Harlem, has seemingly gone out of his mind with terror ("They know who I am!" he raves). Cal learns that Lopez, a follower of the Santería religion, thinks he's been cursed by the boy's murderers.

Lopez escapes from Bellevue Hospital and phones Cal to meet him, warning "you're in danger, you and your son." But before Cal can reach him, Lopez, sick and in intense pain, grabs a knife from behind a diner counter and fatally stabs himself in the stomach. An autopsy reveals a grisly anomaly—living snakes in Lopez's abdomen!

Cal's son Chris had earlier found a ceremonial shell in the park near the site of an animal sacrifice. This shell turns out to be a symbol belonging "to a god of destruction and pestilence," and his finding it has marked Chris for sacrifice ("Chris was chosen when he found the shell," one of the evil cultists later tells Cal, "it was a sign").

Cal seeks out a man named Oscar Serine (Raul Davila) to learn more about this mysterious Santería. "This is not Santería," Serine tells him when he examines Chris' shell, "it is black magic—Brujeria." Serine explains that, "There was a ritual when a tribe was threatened by drought or flood or destruction by its enemies. Three children were offered to the gods, elder sons sacrificed by their fathers, the last child on the summer solstice, to gain power, to destroy their enemies." A second boy has been found ritualistically murdered and, with the solstice only four days away, Cal fears that his own son will be the third and final victim. Serine, a santero (Santería priest), performs a protection ritual for the panicked psychologist which (it turns out) has little effect.

Those close to the case continue to die, including the hard-bitten Lieutenant McTaggert (Robert Loggia), who has uncovered evidence that this cult is overseen by a prominent financier and community leader, Robert Calder (Harris Yulin). Afflicted by a terrifying paralysis, McTaggert entreats Cal to "destroy Calder" and then takes his own life. Even more horrifying, Cal's new girlfriend, Jessica (Helen Shaver), develops a boil on her face from which pours forth a legion of tiny spiders, leaving her in the hospital in critical condition.

Cal must then face the ultimate betrayal when Dennis (Lee Richardson), the grandfatherly friend (and Cal's former professor and mentor) to whom he has temporarily entrusted the safety of his son, turns out to be a member of the Brujeria cult. "We want you to join us," he tells a confused and horrified Cal after giving him a drugged drink. Though Cal tries to snatch his son and flee, the sect's malevolent priest, Palo (Malick Bowens), overpowers him. Taken to an old warehouse and surrounded by the cult followers (all wealthy and "respectable" community members), Cal must fight off the power of both Palo and the drug to rescue his son.

The Believers is one of the few films in voodoo cinema to take a respectful (rather than exploitative) view of its subject. "[Santería] is a religion with much strength and dignity," opined screenwriter/associate producer Mark Frost, "a force for good that is often used for healing." Beginning with Frost's script, this respect for its topic traveled through the director down to the cast.

"We made a very strong point in the movie of separating this mad cult, which is sacrificing children, from the practices of Santería, which is, in New York City, a very important part of the Hispanic community," reflected star Martin Sheen (in *Fangoria* magazine). "I am a practicing Catholic. I believe a lot of things, but I don't *know* anything. I would be a fool to criticize anyone else's beliefs or the way they choose to practice their faith. I remain open in heart and mind to anyone's form of worship, and that includes Santería."

"I must emphasize that there is a distinction between Santería, which we treat, I hope, with a good deal of care and respect, and Brujeria, which is the practice of black magic," added director John Schlesinger. "We haven't gone as deeply into Santería as probably any true santera would like, but we've been as true to it as we possibly could under the circumstances."

To aid in this quest for authenticity, Schlesinger utilized a source from his own cast. Actress Carla Pinza (who plays Cal's Santería–practicing house-keeper, Carmen) is actually a real-life santera. Revealing this fact only *after* she'd landed the role, she was immediately drafted as a technical advisor in addition to her acting duties. "Carla was also our go-between with the elders of the Santería church," recounted Frost. "They read the

The cult's malevolent sorcerer, Palo (Malick Bowens, center), leads his flock in their quest for power through human sacrifice.

script and gave us their explicit approval. They even helped with suggestions. So we had their blessings in making the picture—which the more superstitious of us thought was a good idea."

In one sequence, Schlesinger (working with editor Peter Honess) mixes shots from two different scenes to draw a subtle comparison between Santería and Catholicism. Shots of Carmen lighting candles, dipping Chris' shell into a glass of purifying water, and intoning a litany in Spanish are intercut with scenes of Chris lighting a candle ("for Mom") in a Catholic church where a priest ritualistically manipu-

lates the trappings of *his* faith (chalice, holy cloth, etc.). The juxtaposition of the two different ceremonials emphasizes the similarity—and solemnity—of faith. The sequence ends (somewhat tellingly) with Chris gazing at a rather gory icon of Christ lying supine after the crucifixion, the camera roving over the realistic statue to show the gaping raw wounds in the icon—a gruesome and disturbing sight.

The Believers is the only film to date that includes a scene of spontaneous (and unbidden) spirit possession—a little-known and fascinating Voudoun phenomenon. It occurs when the cult's sorcerer, Palo,

In *The Believers* child sacrifice is at the heart of Brujeria, a black magic perversion of Santería. (Courtesy John "J.J." Johnson)

inadvertently becomes possessed by the loa at a swank fund-raising party hosted by Calder. When the tuxedoed drummers begin beating out a rapid rhythm as Calder's assistants flow through the crowd collecting donations from the well-heeled guests, Palo's body begins to shudder. Then, as if summoned by the drumbeats, his arms and legs stretch and move of their own accord in graceful rhythm while, most disturbingly, his eyes roll back in his head until only the whites show in his strained face. At this, several of the elegant party guests take on a look of ecstatic reverie. Though coming unbidden and at a highly inappropriate time, it's as if Palo has been summarily "mounted" by a loa. Such an impromptu possession can indeed happen, according to Maya Deren—who experienced such an occurrence first hand. ("Toward the end of my stay in Haiti," wrote Deren in *Divine Horsemen*, "I had ordered a set of drums and arranged to have them baptized and 'put to sleep' overnight with a special ceremony. I was very anxious to make a wire recording of this relatively infrequent ceremony which I had never seen and which I would not have another opportunity to witness before my departure. I began by making the technical arrangements for recording and, since the drum ceremony would take place after the regular songs of salutation to the loa (which I had already recorded frequently and had no interest in duplicating), I was free to participate in the early part of the ceremony. It was during this period that Erzulie [one of the Voudoun gods] mounted my head. When I regained consciousness, about four hours had passed, and I was informed that I was very lucky since Erzulie herself [using Deren's own body] had performed the complete drum ceremony.")

Though of noble intent, Schlesinger and company did not *always* succeed in treating their topic "with a good deal of care and respect." While taking pains to separate Santería from the murderous sorcery labeled Brujeria and while defending its legitimate religious practice ("Santería is a 1,000 years older than Christianity"; "Santería is a force for good"; etc.), the film possesses an underlying current upon which flows a feeling of distaste for the subject. When Cal confronts his kindly housekeeper about her Santería "blessings" in the form of votive candles and statuary, he points out that Santería rituals sometimes involve animal sacrifice. At this, Carmen (a true devotee) hangs her head as if ashamed at such a revelation.

Even more telling, when Sezine performs a protection ritual for Cal, Jessica (whom the viewer has come to like and admire) evinces first an uncomfortable nervousness ("this doesn't feel right") and then an ill-concealed disgust at the ceremonial proceedings (which involve sacrificing a chicken for its blood).

Veteran director John Schlesinger (*Midnight Cowboy*, 1969; *Marathon Man*, 1976; *The Falcon and the Snowman*, 1985, etc.) knows his business. For *The Believers* he utilized varied camera angles, thematic symbols, and subtle foreshadowing to generate a feel of unease in an otherwise "normal" milieu.

The film's opening shot has Cal jogging toward us down an empty, early-morning street before a milk truck suddenly tops the rise behind him, appearing to pursue the running man. Gradually, the camera's focus shifts so that Cal becomes blurred and the truck stands out in detailed relief while Cal jogs across and out of the frame and the milkman pulls over to deliver his wares. The "milk theme" continues with a low-angle shot of a woman (Cal's wife) reaching down for the milk carton left on her doorstep, the positioning and camera angle making the innocuous item loom menacingly large in the foreground. These mildly disturbing images serve as portents of the horror to come, for we soon see Cal's wife electrocuted by a faulty coffee maker—while standing in a puddle of *spilled milk.*

Schlesinger continues with this benign-turned-deadly thematic device when Cal's friend, Marty, spills his coffee cream on his desk. At this, Sheen stares at the white puddle, forcing the viewer (like Cal) to reflect upon the painful emotions lurking just beneath the character's exterior—grief, anger, and misplaced guilt (for it was *he* who'd spilled the milk). Schlesinger cleverly ties these visual threads together to add depth to the characters and situations (as well as giving that old platitude "no use crying over spilled milk" a whole new and ironically dark connotation).

Schlesinger also opens his epilogue sequence with a scene that neatly bookends the film both visually and thematically. Like the opening, it begins with the camera on an empty stretch of road before a man and a vehicle suddenly top the rise and enter the picture. Only this time, Cal is *driving* the vehicle (a Jeep) rather than running in front of it as if being pursued. It's symbolic of his having taken control of his own destiny—he's in the driver's seat now, as it were. No longer pursued by the juggernaut of fate (the tragedy-bearing milk truck), Cal is in control, driving (rather than fleeing) to his new home and new family (his son and pregnant new wife, Jessica).

But all is not well in this symbolic dairyland. Unpacking a bag of groceries in the kitchen, Cal pulls out a *milk carton* from the bag—just as his dog begins barking and growling out at the barn. It's no accident that this once-benign article appears again at the exact point Cal's world once more turns upside-down (by his subsequent discovery of his new wife's sacrificial shrine in the barn—the film's disturbing denouement).

Schlesinger exercised an admirable restraint in the gore department (much as Alan Parker did with *Angel Heart*), making those few shots of grue or instances of violence that much more affecting. The bloody acts are never shown, and the ghastly handiwork only briefly glimpsed, their horrific impact generated by the actors' reactions rather than lingering shots of gory FX. (In fact, the film's two most effective and horrific scenes of mayhem—the mother's electrocution and Jessica's arachnid attack—come without any blood at all.)

"I don't like gratuitous violence," stated Schlesinger. "We wanted to imply as much as we

Actress Carla Pinza plays Carmen, a Santería-practicing housekeeper who tries (unsuccessfully) to cast a spell of protection. Ms. Pinza is a real-life santera (Santería priestess) and served as a technical advisor on *The Believers* as well as an actress.

could without it becoming too explicit and appalling. The actual ideas are really horrifying. The question was how to make it possible for an audience to witness it without it being so uncomfortable as to be impossible to watch. If we literally showed child sacrifice, *I* wouldn't have been able to do it." (In fact, Martin Sheen was attracted to the project primarily because of Schlesinger's presence. "I knew John had a method of doing the material that would very clearly raise it up to an 'A' level that would not be exploitative in any fashion. There was good cinema technique being done here.")

The evil cultists drug Cal (Martin Sheen) in an effort to induce him to sacrifice his own son. "One life from each of us is all he asks," declares his once-trusted friend (Lee Richardson).

"*The Believers* will do for dermatology what *Marathon Man* did for dentistry," laughed screenwriter Mark Frost about the film's horrific centerpiece. He's referring, of course, to the scene in which a huge boil on Jessica's face erupts to disgorge a bevy of living spiders. "I didn't know how much I was acting when the spiders were walking around my face," actress Helen Shaver admitted in *Fangoria* magazine. "That was kind of an improvised form of acting, like, 'Oh, God, can I stay still while they're doing this? It took *six* hours of close-ups.'" Though the scene lasts less than a minute, Shaver's marathon efforts proved worthwhile. In a series of quick cuts, shots of spiders crawling over her face (her eyes wide open in terror while inarticulate, high-pitched sounds of horror issue from her constricted throat) alternate with her panicked flailing at her face and hair to make this sequence one of the most (literally) skin-crawling in cinema history. Schlesinger ends it with a bang too: In close-up, a spider crawls up her cheek toward her wide, staring eyes—which she violently closes just as the arachnid reaches her vulnerable orb. At this the screen suddenly goes dark, ending the scene—as if shutting one's eyes will indeed shut out the horror.

Though thoughtfully directed and excellently acted all round, *The Believers* doesn't quite succeed in becoming the ultimate voodoo movie. The biggest problem with *The Believers* is a general unevenness that tends to dissipate its overall effect. While Schlesinger creates several truly terrifying scenes that grab the viewer and shake him or her, and sets up a realistic milieu surrounding the practice of Santería (centering around the day-to-day rituals and prayers of Carmen, Cal's housekeeper), he is unable to maintain this sense of suspense or atmosphere throughout the script's numerous scenes of cloying warmth and friendliness (between Cal and his friend Marty, Cal and his son Chris, Cal and Jessica, Jessica and Chris, Chris and Dennis, Dennis and Cal...). The disparities never quite gel into a cohesive whole. Though screenwriter Mark Frost attempted to do justice to the subject of Santería and generally succeeded, he couldn't quite pull off the same success with his script's characters and tone.

Comparisons to the same year's *Angel Heart* seem inevitable. Both voodoo pictures were shot roughly at the same time and released only three months apart. While it's difficult to argue that *The Believers* is as good a *film* as the atmospheric, noirish *Angel Heart*, it definitely stands as a better *voodoo* movie, since *The Believers* places voodoo firmly in the fore rather than relegating it to simple background color like its sister production. As scripter Mark Frost explains, "*Angel Heart* is wrapped up with a Christian conception of the Devil. It deals tangentially with voodoo, but the villains in that piece are actually practicing a Western form of black magic. Our picture deals more with the African roots of the religion." And deal with it it does, making *The Believers* one of the most intriguing and well-intentioned (albeit uneven) voodoo variations in cinema.

CREDITS: Director: John Schlesinger; Producers: John Schlesinger, Michael Childers, Beverly Camhe; Executive Producer: Edward Treets; Associate Producer: Mark Frost; Screenplay: Mark Frost; Based on the Book *The Religion* by Nicholas Conde; Director of Photography: Robb Maller; Music: J. Peter Robinson; Costume Design: Sahy Cunliffe; Editor: Peter Honess; Production Design: Simon Holland; Released June 1987 by Orion; 100 minutes; Rated R

CAST: Martin Sheen (Cal Jamison), Helen Shaver (Jessica Halliday), Harley Cross (Chris Jamison), Robert Loggia (Lieutenant Sean McTaggert), Richard Masur (Marty Wertheimer), Elizabeth Wilson (Kate Maslow), Lee Richardson (Dennis Maslow), Harris Yulin (Donald Calder), Raul Davila (Serine), Malick Bowens (Palo), Carla Pinza (Mrs. Ruiz), Jimmy Smits (Tom Lopez)

SCARED STIFF (1987)

Of Hexes and Curses

"The slaves I hid have put a curse on George;
he's changing. I am afraid."
—Nicole Fortier as Elizabeth Masterson

1987 proved a busy year for screen voodoo, with no fewer than four features in release (plus another borderline hoodoo in the form of *The Offspring*). Two of the quartet (the impressive *Angel Heart* and the lesser-but-still-worthy *The Believers*) were big-studio productions while the other two (*Scared Stiff* and the direct-to-video *Zombie Nightmare*) were inexpensive independents. A busy year, yes, but not necessarily a *great* year, as evidenced by this sorry entry. Though it may not be the worst of the four (*Zombie Nightmare* has the edge there), *Scared Stiff* runs a close second.

Screenwriter Mark Frost (who also penned *The Believers* and later co-created *Twin Peaks* with David Lynch) took his new voodoo screenplay to Daniel F. Bacaner (executive producer of *Blood Simple*). Bacaner liked what he saw and agreed to produce it as a low-budget (1.3 million dollar) independent feature. However, before cameras rolled on the Florida shoot, Bacaner, along with director Richard Friedman, heavily rewrote Frost's script. Something was definitely lost in translation.

The confusing story centers on a somewhat less than typical family of the eighties—a yuppie psychiatrist (Andrew Stevens), a female rock star on the comeback trail (Mary Page Keller), and her seven-year-old son, Jason (Josh Segal)—who move into an old house once owned by a notorious slave-trader named George Masterson (David Ramsey).

Back in 1857, a voodoo curse was placed on the slaver by his mistreated slaves which gradually turned him into a hideous monster. We learn this via diary entries and visions experienced by Kate (the rock star/mom) who, incidentally, was recently a mental patient, so of course no one lends credence to her mounting fears. The curse apparently worsened Masterson's disposition as well as his looks, for he ended up killing his wife and young son, age (you guessed it) seven. So, naturally, David (the yuppie psychiatrist) gets a funny gleam in his eye and starts chasing his loved ones around the mansion.

When the possessed David abruptly transforms into the Masterson monster after Jason clubs him on the head with a lamp, the house seemingly becomes some kind of dimensional portal (or perhaps an hallucination machine). Suddenly, Jason and his mother are in a long, dark hallway lined with doors, behind which lie various nightmarish visions and different time/space scenarios (1857 settings, African jungle, etc.).

When Masterson finally catches Kate, Jason fights back by rejoining the two broken halves of a protective voodoo talisman. At this, the monster drops the woman and staggers backwards as two spears come whizzing out of the air (thrown across time and space by the voodoo-practicing natives in Africa we'd seen in earlier flashbacks) to imbed themselves in the creature's chest. Masterson's body then (strangely) breaks up into pieces which fly apart and disappear, leaving Jason and his mom back in the (present day) house.

Unfortunately, David is also there, and he's still acting possessed. A knife and fall dispatches the menacing psychiatrist, and the film ends with Jason visiting his now-catatonic mom in the mental hospital presided over by the new Chief of Psychiatry—Dr. George Masterson!

With *Scared Stiff*, confusion reigned *off*screen as well as on (see bewildering scenario above) when director Richard Friedman left the project several days before completion of principal photography. (Reportedly, that old "creative differences" dragon reared its ugly head.) Producer Daniel F. Bacaner stepped in to finish the shoot.

The title of this tired film is a misnomer, since it inspires more yawns than scares. Over half the picture's 84-minute running time elapses before anything even mildly interesting happens (Masterson's initial appearance in monster-guise, for instance). Most of the first half focuses on the shallow relationship between the three cardboard characters (David, Kate, and little Jason) and their slooooow discovery of the story behind the Masterson house.

The picture's second half becomes a confusing dance with (un)reality as Kate (and later Jason) periodically and arbitrarily enter and exit the past (or alternate dimension?) inhabited by George Masterson. The absurdity culminates with Kate's journey through a misty, candlelit hallway which features a different time/dimension behind every door (including such silliness as an attack from Jason's Indian-head lamp grown to giant proportions and a rampaging grand piano). These anything-can-happen fantasy devices undermine the story's tenuous hold on reality so that the (already-bored) viewer can never establish any kind of framework on which to hang the proceedings. (The innovative *Nightmare on Elm Street* series had used similar fantastical alternate-reality ploys but wisely kept them within the parameters of the victims' dreamworld and so adhered to its own rules of

In *Scared Stiff* a voodoo curse transforms slave owner George Masterson (David Ramsey) into a monster (whose unique appearance proves to be one of the film's few assets).

reality; *Scared Stiff* seemingly offers *no* rules.) Consequently, any flame of interest still flickering after the first 40 minutes of ennui soon sputters and dies.

The film's dialogue is alternately banal and clichéd, especially the pseudo-psychiatric lingo spouted by Andrew Stevens as the (very unconvincing) psychiatrist. Stevens' performance is just too plastic to inspire any empathy or liking, so when the possession finally comes there's no pathos or even interest in his character (he's just the handiest body present for the malignant spirit). The remainder of the cast is flat, when they're acting at all.

While the film is competently shot, Richard Friedman's straightforward and uninspired direction adds little to the floundering story. Soon after *Scared Stiff*, Friedman helmed the awful *Doom Asylum* (1987; an ultra-cheap mad killer pic made for a paltry $90,000) followed by yet *another* awful mad-killer movie, *Phantom of the Mall* (1988) (though with a more respectable two million dollar budget this time).

Not only can money not buy happiness, in Friedman's case it apparently can't buy quality either.

Some of *Scared Stiff*'s effects (such as video game-style opticals in which a computer graphic shoots out of Jason's monitor to create a gigantic image of the talisman in mid air—complete with goofy green glow) are more appropriate for a Saturday morning sci-fi show than an atmospheric horror picture. (In truth, these effects appear so cheap and shoddy that they're not really appropriate to *any* picture.)

Another ridiculous effects moment that proves less than special occurs when Jason's toy cars and trucks suddenly come to life and start driving around his sandbox on their own. This has to be one of the silliest (and most pointless, since the scene offers no payoff) supernatural manifestations in cinema history—possessed *Tonka trucks*!

Despite dressing itself up with voodoo curses and talismans, *Scared Stiff*'s basic plot appears both worn and thin. The possessed-husband/lover-menacing-his-family device has been done before to much better effect (*The Amityville Horror*, *The Shining*, etc.), and the only innovative aspects present the use of the voodoo curse and the occasional physical transformations are handled poorly.

The solitary voodoo ceremonial scene (set on the Ivory Coast in 1857) is a brief and confusing sequence involving savage-looking natives marching around a prostrate man (or corpse?) spitting fire like circus performers or waving spears while chanting something that sounds like "Mabuta Wapee Damballah." The Africans throw blood on the body and this somehow effects the curse being pronounced by slaves half-a-world-away who sit around a small brazier saying, "Curse you Masterson, curse your house and all that is Masterson." The film cuts back and forth from the two scenes without any explanation or visual linking device, so one can only *guess* that they actually have something to do with each other. To add to the confusion, the climactic confrontation shows the natives hurling their spears from the African jungle to somehow cross both time and space and thud into the chest of the Masterson monster in Georgia… or something.

The film utterly fails to explore any of the issues its slave-setting raises (such as the role of voodoo in the life of the slaves; voodoo as a source of spiritual refuge and escape from the impossibly harsh realities of bondage; the white masters' fear of voodoo as a source of strength and unity among their human chattel; voodoo as a symbolic link—the only one these oppressed people have—to their distant homeland). Instead, the script simply uses voodoo as an excuse to conjure up yet another supernatural monster.

To give credit where credit is due, however, this particular voodoo monster proves more novel than the usual walking zombie. While for most of Masterson's initial monstrous appearances he resembles nothing so much as an over-fanged vampire with bad skin, the final makeup (courtesy of New Jersey-based makeup artist Tyler K. Smith) in which Masterson's head becomes a living African death-mask remains startlingly unique.

Also, a couple of bright spots occasionally shine forth from the tedium. During the climactic hallucination/alternate dimension sequence, for instance (in which the heroine gets a surprise behind every door she opens), she's greeted by a mental patient with a perverse sense of humor who shows her he's "cured" by literally unzipping the top of his skull and exposing his pulsing brain for her inspection.

Sadly, a novel makeup job and an occasional momentary flash can't wipe out nearly 84 muddled, sleep-inducing minutes. A more accurate title for *Scared Stiff* would have been *Bored Stiff*.

CREDITS: Director: Richard Friedman; Producer: Daniel F. Bacaner; Associate Producer: Charles S. Carroll; Screenplay: Mark Frost, Daniel F. Bacaner, Richard Friedman; Director of Photography: Yuri Denysenko; Production Design: Wynn P. Thomas; Costume Design: Beverly Safier; Musical Score Produced and Composed by: The Barber Brothers; Mechanical and Prosthetic Effects: Tyler K. Smith; Editor: Nick Gerard Stagliano; A Fremont Group production released November 1987 by International Film Marketing; 84 minutes

CAST: Andrew Stevens (David Young), Mary Page Keller (Kate Christopher), David Ramsey (George Masterson), Josh Segal (Jason), William M. Hindman (Dr. Ben Brightman), Jakie Davis (Detective Whitcomb), Nicole Fortier (Elizabeth Masterson), Brian Smith (Detective), Tony Shepherd (Wally), Tom Kouchalakos (Michael Murphy), Jennifer Hingel (Jennifer), Richard Jason (Elizabeth's son), Pete Conrad (short man), Carol Gun (Sherry), Ellen Simmons (Claire), Chris Gilbert

Conrad Roberts plays Christophe, a recovered "zombie" patterned after the real-life case of Clairvus Narcisse as detailed in Wade Davis' fascinating book, *The Serpent and the Rainbow*.

THE SERPENT AND THE RAINBOW (1988)
Hollywood Comes to Haiti

"In the legends of voodoo the Serpent
is a symbol of Earth.
The Rainbow is a symbol of Heaven.
Between the two, all creatures
must live and die.
But because he has a soul Man
can be trapped in a terrible place
where death is only the beginning."
—opening written narration

When, at the urging of producers David Ladd and Doug Claybourne, director Wes Craven read Wade Davis' nonfiction *The Serpent and the Rainbow* (about the Harvard ethnobotonist's search for a "zombie poison" in Haiti), he immediately signed on for the project. "It was fascinating and I knew that anything made from it would be wonderful," Craven told *Fangoria*'s Marc Shapiro. Though containing isolated moments of exciting activity, Davis' anthropological account was not exactly the stuff of celluloid dreams

(or nightmares) and so substantial changes were needed to bring the tale to the big screen. "We have fictionalized the story to a certain extent," admitted Craven. "In the book, Davis was pretty much left alone to do his work, even though the country itself was going through one of its revolutionary periods... We created an antagonist for the Davis character, Dr. Dennis Alan, to go up against. The villain [named Petraud, head of the dreaded Ton Ton Macute *and* an evil voodoo sorcerer] is the symbol for all the terrorism going on in the country, and Alan takes it upon himself to get rid of him." Scripters Richard Maxwell and A.R. Simoun also added a love interest and Craven himself penned a series of his trademark dream sequences to spice up the scenario. "But essentially it is still Davis' story of looking for the zombie drug," assured Craven. "All the elements of voodoo, zombies, and Haiti's exotic mystery were so good that it would have been a mistake to mess with them."

Employing the book's author as a guide and technical advisor, Craven shot for a month in Haiti in February 1987. Through Davis, Craven sought the blessing of a Voudoun priest (an American-educated houngan named Max Beauvoir), who performed rituals offering the protection of the loas for the production's cast and crew. "[Producer] David [Ladd] and I attended real voodoo ceremonies," declared

Craven, "and talked with real voodoo priests. We told them we wanted to do a movie about voodoo and that we wanted to treat the subject fairly. And to prove how serious we were, we asked that we be given protection, through a voodoo ceremony, before filming actually started."

Despite such spiritual precautions, shooting in the poorest country in the Western Hemisphere proved a daunting task. With disease running rampant and sanitation nearly nonexistent (food and water were often contaminated and raw sewage ran in open ditches along the streets), Craven reported that, "nearly three-fourths of the cast and crew had come down with something… just about everybody was suffering from nausea, vomiting, or dizziness."

While physically draining, the strain took its toll mentally as well, afflicting several cast and crew members with hallucinations and outright psychosis. "One person came out of a voodoo ceremony," recalled Craven, "turned around and immediately hallucinated about seeing an animal with eyes like television screens staring back at him. An actor was exploring the remains of an old fortress when he saw the ghost of a Haitian general on horseback. The worst incident involved one staff member who went completely insane after being in the country for only four days. He was shipped home and remained in a total paranoid state for four more days after he returned to the States. On the fifth day, he awoke perfectly normal."

According to Craven, entire villages were depopulated as the poverty-stricken locals swarmed to the shooting site and eagerly signed on for the prospect of making a few dollars as extras in the film. As well as providing authentic local color, these extras generated some serious problems as well. "We were faced with riots because the estimated 2,000 extras we were using kept asking for more money," remembered Craven. "We were confronted by stone-throwing crowds on at least three occasions." These hostile mobs resulted in Craven and crew hightailing it out of Haiti a day early. "We were right in the middle of shooting when all 2,000 extras went on strike. They surrounded the entire company and began throwing stones. They were ready to do us in. The producers and I had an immediate conference with them and negotiated a higher fee for them. At that point, we realized how dangerous it had become for us. We left the country the next day." Location shooting was completed over the next eight weeks in the more stable environment of the neighboring Dominican Republic.

The film begins in Haiti in 1978 with an intimidating nighttime voodoo demonstration through the streets of Port-au-Prince. A man, painted as a skeleton and wielding a pistol, sets a coffin on fire in front of a government building. Upstairs a doctor pronounces his patient dead. The next day, as they lower the deceased's coffin into the ground, the unfortunate's sister wails "Christophe!" and we see a tear slide down the cheek of the entombed "corpse."

Switching to the "Amazon Basin 1985," anthropologist Dr. Dennis Alan (Bill Pullman) meets with "the most powerful shaman in the Amazon Basin." The shaman gives him a potion to drink ("He has something he wants to show you," explains Alan's guide). The elixir causes the anthropologist to hallucinate—first that a jaguar seemingly befriends him, and then that arms reach up from the jungle floor to drag him screaming beneath the earth. Coming out of his "trance," he finds his pilot dead and the shaman's hut deserted. "Something more evil and powerful than the shaman and his men has killed my pilot," Alan's narration tells us. "I know this as clearly as I feel the darkness and cold closing in on me." In his desperate flight through the jungle, Alan sees a jaguar ("his animal spirit, his totem") and follows the beast, who safely leads him to a roadway and thus back to civilization.

Back at Harvard, Alan is contacted by Biocorp, a large pharmaceutical company who wants to send him to Haiti to investigate the case of Christophe Durand (Conrad Roberts), who'd been buried seven years earlier and has just shown up in a Port-au-Prince clinic—alive. "Somebody brought him back from the grave," says the Biocorp executive (Paul Guilfoyle), "and I want to know how they did it." Theorizing that some sort of "zombie drug" was involved, they might create from it "a totally new anesthesia that could revolutionize medicine."

Arriving in Haiti, Alan meets Dr. Marielle Duchamp (Cathy Tyson), who'd treated Christophe at the clinic. A practicing voodooist ("my father was a houngan") as well as a psychiatrist, Marielle leads Alan to the confused and tormented Christophe, who tells them that a powder was used to "kill" him and make him a zombie. A friendly voodoo priest, Lucien Celine (Paul Winfield), steers Alan to a bokor (sorcerer) named Mozart (Brent Jennings) who can make such a powder.

In the meantime, Captain Petraud (Zakes Mokae), the head of the Ton Ton Macute (Haiti's secret police), pays Dr. Alan a little visit and warns him to stay out of affairs that do not concern him. With a shock, Alan recognizes the man as a figure from his nightmare hallucination in the Amazon jungle, and Marielle delivers the disturbing news that Petraud is also a voodoo sorcerer. Soon Alan's nights take a terrifying turn as Petraud begins to manipulate his unconscious and invade his dreams.

After thwarting Mozart's initial attempt at trickery, Alan gains the affable bokor's trust, and Mozart (for a thousand dollars) works with Alan to prepare a sample of the zombie poison. Before the process is completed, however, Petraud snatches Alan and proceeds to first terrify, then physically torture the meddlesome anthropologist.

Finding the bleeding Alan in the street, Marielle (who has become Alan's lover) nurses him back to health. But before Alan can link up with Mozart again and acquire the precious poison, Petraud's men break into Marielle's hiding place and bundle Alan aboard the next outbound plane with a warning that death awaits his return. Despite all of Petraud's efforts, the crafty Mozart manages to deliver the zombie powder to Alan anyway, just before takeoff.

Back in Boston again, Alan and Biocorp begin analyzing the zombie powder. At a small dinner party given by the drug executive in honor of the anthropologist's success, the hostess (Dey Young) seemingly becomes possessed and lunges at Alan with a knife. "You've been warned," she hisses in Petraud's voice. "You're going to die!"

Despite the obvious danger, Alan decides to return to Haiti. "He's going to get to me wherever I am," he realizes. "I've stolen his darkest and most powerful secret. He'll want to get even and, if he can't get me, he'll go for Marielle." Upon arriving in Haiti, Alan is taken under Lucien's protection. But the powerful houngan proves no match for the evil Petraud, and Lucien abruptly succumbs to the bokor's malevolent magic, dying in Alan's arms. (Petraud has also killed Mozart for helping Alan, decapitating him in a ritual sacrifice.) Just then, a man walks up to Alan and blows a yellow powder into his face... the zombie poison! The quick-acting poison causes Alan to stumble a few feet while he pleads "Don't let them bury me—I'm not dead," before he drops, apparently lifeless. Of course, he is *not* dead, and Petraud buries him alive with great relish, taunting the helpless unfortunate with the fact that he plans to sacrifice Marielle that very night.

The poison wears off after a few hours and Alan begins to scream in his dark prison. Christophe, lurking about the cemetery (the former "zombie" is "obsessed with death"), hears his cries and frees the shaken anthropologist from his tomb.

As Alan stumbles back to the city to find Marielle, the country erupts in turmoil. Baby Doc Duvalier and his family have fled and the ecstatic populace dance in the streets. The noise of rioters interrupts Petraud's intended sacrifice of Marielle, and the bokor's followers flee. Alan enters the building, but Petraud, possessing the jar that holds Alan's "soul," sends terrifying hallucinations to bedevil the doctor. "Your soul is mine!" Petraud's voice booms inside Alan's head, "I control your thoughts now."

Alan finally reaches Petraud's basement lair and the two engage in a brutal struggle, with the sorcerer

tossing Alan about with seemingly supernatural strength. Marielle awakens and smashes the jar containing Lucien's soul. At this, a wavering image of Lucien rises up and Petraud grabs his head in pain. Then the glimmering form of a huge jaguar emanates from Alan's body—his totem spirit. With his newfound strength, Alan tosses the bokor into the rows of "soul jars," from whose shards rise hundreds of points of light that whirl about and descend upon the screaming Petraud until the sorcerer's body literally bursts into flames before ultimately vanishing altogether.

It's not quite over yet, however. Upstairs, a now-charred Petraud literally comes flying out of nowhere to attack Alan. "You're coming with me to hell!" he shouts. But Alan beats Petraud at his own game and magically manipulates the man's own torture chair which straps Petraud into itself and carries the screaming man through the floor into the earth.

With Petraud now gone, Marielle observes, "The nightmare is over." The two lovers then walk out into the dawn and the celebrating crowd.

"The project was attractive to me," Wes Craven explained to *Cinefantastique*'s Fred Szebin, "because it enabled me to fuse everything I learned from making horror films into a love story and a political drama, while exploring the hitherto unexamined voodoo religion to tell an adventure tale about one man's trip into the heart of darkness. This film offered a much richer palette than I had been afforded before."

A richer palette indeed, as the authentic source material and locales provided opportunities for Craven to capture—more than any other fictional film before or since—the feel of Haiti and of Voudoun. Scenes of abject poverty appear with an alarming casualness, offering glimpses of the wooden shacks and rusted roofs, rutted dirt streets, and the local populace barefoot and clad in ragged clothing. Such dismal sights alternate with scenes of sublime beauty as a candlelit Voudou procession moves through the forested mountains or Voudoun acolytes bathe in the restorative waters of a sacred waterfall (a Voudoun "cathedral," as one character calls it). "There is great beauty and compassion in [Voudoun]," states Marielle, and Craven's camera bears this out. *The Serpent and the Rainbow* is perhaps the only film to effectively capture the almost desperate appeal of the Voudoun worldview felt by Haiti's impoverished millions.

Thanks to its nonfiction source material, *The Serpent and the Rainbow* turned out to be the silver screen's most *accurate* depiction of Voudoun as well—up to a point, of course. Naturally, the director took Davis' factual but slightly sensational book and (for a mere seven to 10 million dollars—sources vary) turned it into a fictional and *highly* sensational movie. And "sensational" is the word, for *The Serpent and the Rainbow* is a superior specimen of voodoo cinema.

For most of its running time, the film deals in a naturalistic and mature manner with such central Voudoun topics as possession by the loa ("In Haiti," explains Marielle, "our god is not just in his heaven, he's in our bodies, in our flesh"), the incorporation of Catholic iconography into Voudoun worship ("Haiti is 85 percent Catholic and 110 percent voodoo; for us, Erzuile and the Virgin Mary are the same"), and, of course, zombies.

Regarding zombies, *The Serpent and the Rainbow* comes the closest of all its cinematic brethren to an accurate depiction of the phenomenon (discounting, of course, the film's climactic mystical pyrotechnics as the expected visual poetic license). Not surprisingly, however, the film both romanticizes and simplifies the motivation behind zombification. The "recovered" zombie Alan contacts in the film, Christophe Durand, is the big screen counterpart of the real-life Clairvus Narcisse, whose extraordinary case had drawn Wade Davis to Haiti in the first place. In reality, however, Clairvus was not "a grade school teacher [who] wasn't afraid to speak out for the people, for freedom"

In real Voudoun, being possessed by a loa can be a physically draining experience that not all practitioners seek out. In this scene, the loa Erzule comes unbidden to mount the reluctant heroine (Cathy Tyson).

(as his character is described in the film), but a greedy, ambitious pariah at odds with his family (even coming to blows with siblings) and his community. "Clairvus had been involved in innumerable disputes with his various brothers," reported Davis in his book. "Land [the most important economic factor in rural Haiti] was often an issue but there were others." In addition, Clairvus "had compromised innumerable women," and "had profited at the expense of the community." Because of this, Clairvus was judged and condemned by a tribunal of the secret Bizango society, the unofficial authority among the rural Haitian peasantry. According to those Davis interviewed, the complaint was undoubtedly lodged (and the process paid for) by members of Clairvus' own embittered family. So while the reel story casts this former zombie as a martyr to an evil sorcerer's political ambitions, the *real* story shows him to be a hated outcast tried and condemned by his own community—his own *relations*—for his irresponsible and antisocial behavior.

Such dramatic simplification comes not unexpectedly, however, and indeed adds to the theatrical value of the story (as well as creating a fascinating antago-

nist in the form of the ruthless bokor, Petraud). Towards the film's end, however, such poetic license gets completely out of hand, transforming this serious character/culture study into the typical Hollywood horror, filled with unkillable supernatural sorcerers and occult pyrotechnics.

The picture's major failing comes from the director's seemingly inescapable proclivities. Though Craven sought authenticity by filming his opus in Haiti and the Dominican Republic, some of the filmmaker's trademark technique ultimately works *against* the picture's efficacy. With the frequent insertion of bizarre dream-images and occasionally over-slick lighting and dialogue that just screams "Hollywood," *The Serpent and the Rainbow* loses much of its authentic edge. What it sacrifices in verisimilitude, however, it admittedly gains in its "horror" effect, although even in this Craven goes overboard at the end by turning his Ton Ton Macute sorcerer into a Freddy Kruegerish dreamkiller-clone (complete with a clichéd one-last-rise-from-the-dead denouement). Craven owes much to the fiscal success of his 1984 groundbreaker, *A Nightmare on Elm Street*. In fact, admitted the director in Stanley Wiater's *Dark Visions*, "it was instru-

"Don't bury me...I'm not dead!" cries the miniature coffin in this promotional giveaway which comes complete with "a vial containing our version of 'Zombie Powder.'" (Ronald V. Borst/Hollywood Movie Posters; photo Lynn Naron)

mental in me getting *The Serpent and the Rainbow* simply because of the magnitude of that phenomenon. I was considered by people such as producer David Ladd, who normally wouldn't have considered me except he was aware of the money that film generated." Unfortunately, Craven went a bit too far in paying his respects to *Nightmare*, taking the maturity level of *The Serpent and the Rainbow* down a peg by introducing the seemingly unstoppable supernatural killer able to invade dreams and alter reality.

The only other significant fault found in *The Serpent and the Rainbow* is in the choice of lead actor. Though the remaining players paint memorable portraits of their characters, Bill Pullman's maverick anthropologist fails to convince as the single-minded field researcher determined to succeed in his mission at all costs. Pullman's boyish good looks and breezy demeanor don't carry the weight and conviction needed for such a portrayal. One wonders why this rather superficial interloper doesn't just leave the country when told to do so.

Fortunately, the film's other actors do an admirable job of bringing their intriguing characters to fleshed-out life, particularly Brent Jennings' turn as the easy-going, roguish Mozart and South African Zakes Mokae's intensely malevolent portrayal of the soul-stealing Petraud. Aided by Maxwell and Simoun's thoughtful script, Mokae's assured playing (his character nearly always shows a prominent mouthful of teeth, their white expanse more significant of *aggression* than of friendliness) make this politically powerful bokor a believably three-dimensional character rather than the standard evil bogeyman he could have become (and, in effect, sadly *did*

become at the overblown climax).

In his first confrontation with Alan, Petraud reveals something of the driving force behind his brutal actions. "This country lives on the edge, Dr. Alan. One weakness in the wrong place and over it goes right back into slavery again. Just like with the French. The United States would like anarchy here, I'm sure." Now Mokae lowers and hones the timbre of his voice into a hard, menacing edge as he peers closely into the face of his uncomfortable listener and his false smile evaporates in the heat of his hostility. "Well, this isn't Grenada, Dr. Alan. I'm here now." Mokae draws out the word "noooow" to a low rumble, venom dripping from the once-innocuous word. Besides the actor imbuing his character with a startling depth of menace, this speech also gives Petraud a powerful motivation and depth of character. He's not simply a "mad dog" after all (as Lucien labels him), but a man who, in his own twisted way, feels he's doing what is right—or at least what is justified.

While Craven indeed brought his "dreamkiller" disposition to the story, he also brought his considerable genre-oriented acumen to bear on the project, resulting in one of the better horror films of the decade. On the surface, Craven generates moments of pure terror and near-madness, such as when Petraud tortures Alan with an iron spike poised above his naked loins. (Thankfully, Craven plays the moment for dread and suspense rather than exploitation and gore, leaving the viewer's imagination to fill in the shuddery blanks.)

In perhaps the film's most terrifying sequence (at least for those claustrophobics and arachnaphobics among us), Petraud buries Alan alive. The bokor taunts the protagonist as he lies immobilized in the open coffin, thrusting Marielle, his newfound love, into Alan's (and our) line of vision and hissing, "her head will be taken as an offering tonight!" Then, when the feelings of horror and helplessness could not possible get any greater, Petraud opens a jar and shakes out a large hairy spider onto Alan's supine body before closing the coffin lid and growling, "to keep you company." The shuddery scene ends with the sound of dirt raining down on the coffin lid while we see in close-up the spider slowly crawling over Alan's paralyzed face, the legs moving near his staring *eyes*.

As per his métier, Craven likes to juggle with reality, keeping the viewer off guard as to what is real and what is a dream or hallucination, often blurring the two states so that they overlay one another and it becomes difficult to tell where one ends and the other begins. While he tends to overdo it at film's end, for much of the picture, this technique proves disturbingly effective.

After drinking the Amazonian shaman's potion at the movie's opening, for instance, Alan collapses. He awakens in a jungle clearing and spies a leopard in the tree above him. The animal leaps down and Alan flees for his life. The big cat quickly catches him, but instead of rending the man limb from limb, it rolls onto its back and playfully wrestles with Alan. As the relieved anthropologist gently tussles with the animal, laughing with delight, the camera cuts to a close-up of the smiling shaman looking on benignly, then back to Alan as he wrestles and plays with… nothing. The powerful leopard is merely a vision in his drug-enhanced mind. With this, Craven gives an initial jolt to the unsuspecting viewer (though merely a gentle one—later instances will be moments of loathing and terror rather than of delight and relief) and shows how dreams and reality can blur in the face of that imperfect tool we call "perception."

Even at this early stage, Craven doesn't let his protagonist (or his viewer) off so lightly, for the director ends this idyllic hallucinatory episode on a terrifying note. When a strong wind arises, Alan seemingly comes to his senses and realizes there is, in fact, no leopard. The shaman pulls his ceremonial cloak up around his head to shelter from the tempest. Alan approaches the covered man and gingerly draws back his shielding arms—revealing the evil, snarling countenance of a black man (whom we later learn is Petraud). Startled and frightened by the vicious face, Alan next screams aloud when hands suddenly thrust up through the forest floor and drag him down into the earth.

Aided by cinematographer John Lindley and camera operator Ken Ferris's fluid camerawork, Craven employs both a steady and *unsteady* hand to set a tone or enhance a mood. For instance, as Alan flees alone through the Amazon jungle, the camera follows close behind—as if a presence in pursuit. Then, as the light begins to fail, it stays in close-up on Alan while he fights through the tangled leaves and vines, the camera jostling and tipping as if it too were impeded by the stifling greenery. Such clever and intimate camerawork adds a claustrophobic sense of immediacy to the sequence.

Later, when Alan first arrives in Haiti, the camera moves with him through the crowded streets, casting about with its lens as if it were the character's eyes. We hear Alan's voice narrating "…what I hadn't expected was that the dark presence from the Amazon would instantly come over me here, as real as a cold hand falling on my shoulder." Gliding smoothly through the surroundings, the camera subtly rocks and tips like the rolling of a ship at sea, making the common marketplace sights seem off-balance and out-of-synch and visually augmenting the character's feeling of unease.

Craven knows his craft as well as he knows his genre. With *The Serpent and the Rainbow* he brings all his considerable talent to bear on the topic of voodoo, creating, if not a completely perfect portrayal, then at least one of the more thoughtful, frightening, and entertaining entries in voodoo cinema.

Interestingly, despite his film's kowtowing to the obviously supernatural, Craven's personal views on the topic of the occult take on a more objective (and realistic) tone. "I don't know about the occult per se," he explained in *Dark Visions*. "I do know that the human mind can be persuaded to perceive almost anything that it already completely believes in. And, at a certain point, the line between belief and reality gets very, very cloudy.

"For example, in Haiti I saw people do things that we would consider physically impossible—not walking on air or anything like that—but eating broken glass, leaning against very sharp machetes without them piercing the skin, things like that. You could call it supernatural. I prefer to think of it as 'today's magic is tomorrow's technology.'"

Something to think about anyway.

CREDITS: Director: Wes Craven; Producers: David Ladd, Doug Claybourne; Executive Producers: Rob Cohen, Keith Barish; Screenplay: Richard Maxwell, A.R. Simoun; "Inspired by the book *The Serpent and the Rainbow* by Wade Davis"; Director of Photography: John Lindley; Camera Operator: Ken Ferris; Costume Designer: Peter Mitchell; Music: Brad Fiedel; Film Editor: Glenn Farr; Production Designer: David Nichols; Special Makeup Effects: Lance Anderson, David Anderson; Special Mechanical Effects: Image Engineering; Supervisor of Special Visual Effects: Gary Gutierrez; Art Director: David Brisbin; Set Decorator: Rosemary Brandenburg; Released in January 1988 by Universal; 105 minutes; Rated R

CAST: Bill Pullman (Dennis Alan), Cathy Tyson (Marielle Duchamp), Zakes Mokae (Dargent Petraud), Paul Winfield (Lucien Celine), Brent Jennings (Mozart), Conrad Roberts (Christophe), Michael Gough (Schoonbacher), Theresa Merritt (Simone), Paul Guilfoyle (Andrew Cassedy), Dey Young (Mrs. Cassedy), Badja Djola (Gaston), Aleta Mitchell (Celestine)

Producer/writer Darin Scott (holding shovel) clowns with director/writer/actor Rusty Cundieff on the set of *Tales from the Hood*.

TALES FROM THE HOOD (1995)
Voodoo's Celluloid Conscience

"I found this doll in a house in the South.
It is an *amazing* thing."
—Clarence Williams III as Mr. Simms

As voodoo cinema's third anthology film (*seventh* if you include the pseudo-voodoo entries *Asylum*, *Trilogy of Terror*, *Creepshow*, and *The Offspring*), *Tales from the Hood* proved far and away the best.

Backing for this black-oriented horror film (and first ever black anthology movie) came from an unlikely source—acclaimed African American filmmaker Spike Lee. "It just kind of happened," recounted director/co-writer Rusty Cundieff to Anthony C. Ferrante in *Fangoria* magazine. "Spike had seen

Fear of a Black Hat [Cundieff's rap mockumentary], called me up and said, 'I want to do something with you.' [Producer/co-writer] Darin [Scott] and I were in the middle of working on the *Hood* script and I said, 'This is what we want to do,' and he liked it. He read the script, gave a couple of notes and that was pretty much the extent of it." Along with his "couple of notes," Lee also secured the six million dollars needed to bring these *Tales* to life.

"The strength of anthologies," postulated Cundieff, "is that you can take something that doesn't need two hours and really make it powerful for 15 or 20 minutes." With *Tales from the Hood*, Cundieff did just that, fashioning several hard-hitting "message" tales that inspire both thought and shivers.

Filmed in Los Angeles in the summer of 1994, the picture begins when three gang members (Joe Torry, De'Aundre Bonds, and Samual Monroe, Jr.) arrive at the mortuary of Mr. Simms (Clarence Williams III), who has stumbled upon a cache of drugs which he plans to sell to the boys. The rather eccentric mortician gives the impatient gang-bangers a tour of his funeral parlor (and its temporary residents) and relates the four stories involving his current "patrons."

The first tale has a murdered black activist return from the grave to take revenge on the three crooked (and racist) cops that killed him. The second segment is a sensitive, well-constructed story of child abuse—but with a grotesque (and satisfying) EC-style twist in its tail.

Voodoo comes into play in the third vignette. When the three homeboys spy a strange little doll sitting on a shelf, Mr. Simms explains that, "The doll is a way station for lost souls. Sometimes when a person's body has been through a lot, the soul is displaced. This doll is a place for the soul to survive until it can move on..."

While running for governor, Southern politician (and former Ku Klux Klan member) Duke

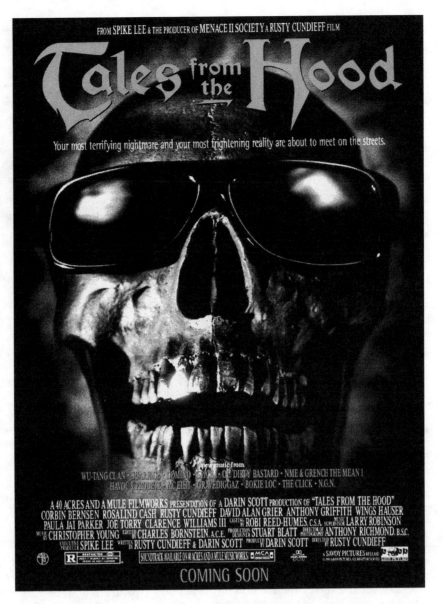

Metger (Corbin Bernsen) is under siege from the media, particularly because he has chosen an old plantation house—the sight of a slave massacre over a century before—as his home and headquarters. Legend has it that an old voodoo woman placed the unhappy souls of those murdered slaves into small dolls, which remain hidden in the house to this day. In fact, one whole wall of the mansion's living room consists of a colorful mural depicting the old woman surrounded by her tiny creations. Metger scoffs at the idea and continues to work with his image consultant (Art Evans) on improving his electoral chances.

Metger's media troubles soon pale in comparison with the siege under which he then finds himself. When a small black doll mysteriously appears, his consultant falls down the stairs to his death and Metger is plunged into a deadly cat-and-mouse game with the living doll. After Metger seemingly gets the best of his animated antagonist (via a well-aimed shotgun blast), several more dolls appear until, finally, every last doll from the painting materializes and swarms over the screaming racist en masse.

In the fourth and final story, a prisoner named Crazy K (Lamont Bentley) volunteers for a radical experiment in which an emphatic doctor (Rosalind Cash) employs *Clockwork Orange*-style techniques and hallucinatory imagery to try to divest him of his hateful tendencies. The experiment seemingly fails and we see the three gang-bangers gun down Crazy K (a rival gang member) in the street. In the film's final twist, however, we learn that Crazy K was not the only casualty in the crossfire, for Simms next shows his three "guests" a series of coffins that contain... themselves. Suddenly, Simms transforms into the devil himself and the three screaming youths realize they've just entered Hell.

Racist Southern politician Duke Metger (Corbin Bernsen) goes one-on-one with a living voodoo doll in the "KKK Comeuppance" segment of *Tales from the Hood.*

Though a superior specimen of the omnibus species, *Tales* couldn't altogether escape the inevitable curse of the anthology, and its episodes vary in quality and effectiveness. The first two stories, "Rogue Cop Revelation" and "Boys Do Get Bruised," are superbly crafted vignettes, delivering their messages on socially volatile topics (police brutality and child abuse) through engrossing build-up and top-notch acting that culminates in a cathartic climax both shocking and satisfying.

The fourth segment, "Hard Core Convert" (described by writer/director Cundieff as a cross between *A Clockwork Orange* and *Menace II Society*), works less well due to its heavy-handed tone, force-feeding its message (the evils of black-on-black violence [1]) to the viewer via blatant dialogue and obvious attitude. The episode still exudes an effectively disturbing air, however, via its near-medieval, inquisitional-style ambiance.

Sadly for the voodoo fan, the film's third episode ("KKK Comeuppance") remains its weakest. As racist politician Duke Metger, Corbin Bernsen (from TV's *L.A. Law* and the *Major League* films) fails to convince in his thinly disguised David Duke role, so that his titular "comeuppance" carries less weight with the viewer. Though he goes through the motions, the bland Bernsen never exudes the hypocrisy and hate-

fulness that would make his character a worthy target of retribution. It just seems like he's at the wrong place at the wrong time, and so much of the tale's power is lost.

The (stop-motion animated) dolls themselves inspire a few effectively chilling moments, however, particularly when they mass at the climax, milling about menacingly. (Said doll effects were produced by the Chiodo Brothers [Charles, Stephen, and Edward Chiodo], makers of the amusing and underrated *Killer Klowns from Outer Space*], who supervised a "Doll Effects Crew" of *18* people!) And the idea of the wall mural changing as the dolls manifest themselves (blank spaces appearing in the painting where the individual figures once stood—as if they simply stepped from the 2-D image into 3-D reality) generates a real *frisson.* Even with some effective doll doings, however, the story's foregone conclusion and Bernsen's ineffectual characterization (in an essentially one-character vignette) doom it to failure.

Voodoo-wise, "KKK Comeuppance" again disappoints. Apart from a few hastily delivered lines about a slave massacre, the story gives us nothing in the way of historical or religious background. The "voodoo bitch" mamaloi (as Metger yells at her portrait) remains merely a painted image in the wall mural until the very end, when she finally appears (to no great purpose) as her dolls attack en masse. Sitting calmly in a rocking chair, she says little and does less, leaving the viewer quite unilluminated.

To its credit, this socially conscious segment at least touches on (if somewhat obtusely) the issue of Voudou as a last refuge for those in bondage during the reign of slavery. Though naturally sensationalized here (in the form of possessed dolls reaching across time to seek retribution), the implication of the role that Voudou could (and often did) play in the pitiless life of the slave provides food for thought. Though those indentured Voudoun practitioners of the past could not *really* store the souls of the afflicted in dolls as this terror tale suggests, they could, in effect, store the hopes and community spirit of their oppressed peoples within their belief system (which, perhaps, may be a form of soul-storing after all). If these tiny terrors are the living embodiment of the voudooists' spirits, then Metger's consuming fear of these little dolls echoes the white plantation owners' dread of their slaves' unifying religion from two centuries before. Voudoun was indeed something to be feared in the eighteenth-century (at least by the white colonial "masters" of the time), not because of the efficacy of spells or incantations, but because it became both an exclusive symbol and a unifying force among the slave population (an emblem that served its followers well in the successful Haitian slave revolt at the turn of the century).

Social and religious implications aside, one of the things that sets *Tales from the Hood* above its competitors is its exceptional and realistic level of acting (Corbin Bernsen aside)—with one exception. As Mr. Simms, Clarence Williams III goes so far over-the-top that he becomes a cartoon character. When one of the homeys, incredulous at his host's stories (*and his bizarre demeanor*), shoots back "say what?!," the viewer can only echo the query. Williams rolls his eyes, flares his nostrils, and grins to such an extent that one simply cannot take his character seriously. Though initially *fun* to watch, Williams' outrageous approach ultimately becomes both wearisome and distracting, removing the viewer from the tales' carefully built-up sense of serious realism.

Co-star Joe Torry related (to *Fangoria*'s Dan Scapperotti) how he was blown away by Williams' portrayal, labeling him "a great talent." "He smashed every character you had," explained Torry. "I mean, I came prepared, and then here's Clarence and *bam, bam*. And I thought, 'Damn, he's way up there! We have to match him.' Just at a table meeting, I knew that I had to put my seat belt on and learn from him." Fortunately, Torry and his fellow thespians stayed securely buckled up rather than flying about trying to "match him."

Intelligent, scary, and chock full of social conscience (little wonder with Spike Lee lurking behind the scenes), *Tales from the Hood* stands as a shining example of what a horror anthology *should* be. Too bad the voodoo episode proved to be the weak link in this otherwise weighty celluloid chain.

[1] This emphasis on the calamity of "black-on-black" violence strikes me as a dangerously selective attitude in itself. Is "black-on-black" violence any more heinous than, for instance, black-on-white, or black-on-yellow, or white-on-white violence for that matter? Violence is abhorrent no matter what the participants' skin color; a focus on "black-on-black" almost implies that one should *especially* avoid doing harm to those of one's own "race"—a bias with insidious implications.

CREDITS: Director: Rusty Cundieff; Producer: Darin Scott; Executive Producer: Spike Lee; Line Producer: Elaine Dysinger; Screenplay: Rusty Cundieff, Darin Scott; Director of Photography: Anthony Richmond; Music: Christopher Young, Music Supervisor: Larry Robinson; Editor: Charles Bornstein; Production Design: Stuart Blatt; Set Decorator: Amy Ancona; Special Effects and Makeup Supervisor: Kenneth Hall; Makeup Effects: KNB EFX Group, Inc.; A 40 Acres and a Mule Filmworks production released June 1987 by Savoy Pictures; 97 minutes

CAST: "WELCOME TO MY MORTUARY": Clarence Williams III (Mr. Simms), Joe Torry (Stork), De'Aundre Bonds (Ball), Samual Monroe, Jr. (Bulldog); "ROGUE COP REVELATION": Wings Hauser (Strom), Tom Wright (Martin Moorehouse), Anthony Griffith (Clarence), Michael Massee (Newton), Duane Whitaker (Billy); "BOYS DO GET BRUISED": David Alan Grier (Carl), Brandon Hammond (Walter), Rusty Cundieff (Richard), Paula Jai Parker (Sissy); "KKK COMEUPPANCE": Corbin Bernsen (Duke Metger), Roger Smith (Rhodie), Art Evans (Eli); "HARD CORE CONVERT": Rosalind Cash (Dr. Cushing), Lamont Bentley (Crazy K)

Appendix A:
PSEUDOO-VOODOO
(Borderline Hoodoo, Near-Misses, and Lost Films)

Asylum (1972; Amicus; Great Britain) Alternate Title: *House of Crazies*; Director: Roy Ward Baker; Producers: Max J. Rosenberg, Milton Subotsky; Screenplay: Robert Bloch; Photography: Denys Coop. CAST: Peter Cushing, Britt Ekland, Herbert Lom, Patrick Magee, Barry Morse, Barbara Parkins, Robert Powell, Charlotte Rampling, Sylvia Syms, Richard Todd, James Villiers.

The first episode of this Amicus horror anthology, entitled "Frozen Fear," details the rather (ahem) chilling account of a wife's frozen, dismembered corpse coming to life and attacking her unfaithful, murdering husband. The wife apparently lived in Africa for a number of years and has been "taking voodoo lessons from a black charlatan" (as the husband sneeringly puts it). "It's not voodoo," corrects his spouse. "There are natural forces which are stronger than life *or* death." Though denying she's involved in voodoo, the wife does wear a bracelet which she labels an "ouanga." This is the only voodoo reference made, and no further explanation for her subsequent piecemeal resurrection is forthcoming.

This exceedingly creepy tale (with the various arms, legs, and head wrapped neatly in brown paper and twine writhing and rolling about on their own) is the strongest episode in what proved an otherwise weak entry in the anthology sweepstakes. "It really is quite frightening," remarked director Roy Ward Baker to *Cinefantastique* magazine, "and you don't see any arms or legs or any blood, it's all wrapped up in the brown paper. Now that, to me, is the right way to do it. Everyone has remarked that this is a particularly good sequence." The film's distributor seemed to think so too, for they played up this episode in its advertising with lines like "Look at the leg that creeps—but there's no body" and "It's not easy breathing in a paper bag... Especially if you're only a head."

Barbara Parkins was initially reluctant to play the role of Bonnie, the third point of the murderous romantic triangle, whose battle with body parts provided the film with its most memorable sequence. "I had reservations about appearing in a horror picture," admitted the actress in *Famous Monsters* magazine, "but the people who made *Asylum* have such a track record with past terror pictures that I couldn't resist. I went to the theater one evening to see Sir Ralph Richardson in a new play and I went backstage afterward to congratulate him on his performance and we talked awhile. I told him I was considering the part... and he urged me to do it. He had just finished starring in *Tales From the Crypt* [another Amicus anthology] and said he hadn't had so much fun in years."

Bride of the Gorilla (1951; Realart) Director/Screenwriter: Curt Siodmak; Producer: Jack Broder; Photography:

Unlike *Weird Woman*, *Burn, Witch, Burn* replaced voodoo with a more Satanic witchcraft. (Courtesy L. Naron)

Charles Van Enger. CAST: Lon Chaney, Jr., Barbara Payton, Raymond Burr, Tom Conway, Paul Cavanagh.

On a plantation in the Amazon jungle, an old servant woman, whom one native policeman refers to as a "witch," uses a poisonous plant to curse the man who murdered her master. The afflicted man (Raymond Burr) seemingly transforms into a gorilla at inopportune times and roams the jungle.

Due to its jungle setting and "curse" scenario, *Bride of the Gorilla* has sometimes been referred to as a voodoo film when in actuality it has nothing at all to do with voodoo. It's possible that the old witch practices Candomblé (a South American voodoo variation), but nothing in the movie confirms this.

Burn, Witch, Burn (1962; Anglo Amalgamated/AIP; Great Britain) Alternate Title: *Night of the Eagle* (British); Director: Sidney Hayers; Producer: Albert Fennell; Screenplay: Richard Matheson, Charles Beaumont (based on the novel *Conjure Wife* by Fritz Leiber); Photography: Reginald Wyer. CAST: Janet Blair, Peter Wyngarde, Margaret Johnston, Anthony Nicholls, Colin Gordon, Kathleen Byron, Reginald Beckwith, Jessica Dunning, Norman Bird, Judith Stott, Bill Mitchell.

Unlike *Weird Woman* (1944), this second version of Fritz Leiber's novel *Conjure Wife* dispensed with voodoo altogether, opting instead for the more home-grown (at least for England) Satanic-style witchcraft. The story centers around a college professor who discovers that his young wife has been practicing protective black magic in order to ward off the evil witchcraft she thinks is being practiced against her husband. Apparently, two years ago the couple had taken a research trip to Jamaica, and the wife had become involved with "that old warlock Carrubius and his phony black magic" (as the husband dismisses it). While this suggests a background in Obeah (the Jamaican form of voodoo), the wife only uses terms like "witch" and "witchcraft." Even the books she consults (bearing titles like *Rites and Practice of Black Magic* and *The Devil*) preclude any suggestions of voodoo. None of the rituals or occurrences imply the workings of West Indian sorcery, including the very un-voodoo-like use of tarot cards and the conjuring up of a hellish giant eagle (demon-conjuring is *not* a trait of voodoo and its variations), and the Jamaican visit is never shown nor elaborated upon.

While disappointingly light on voodoo, *Burn, Witch, Burn* is heavy on atmospheric chills, as it's one of the best supernatural thrillers ever produced. An intelligent script by horror specialists Richard Matheson and Charles Beaumont (who received a paltry $5,000 apiece for their efforts), mood-building direction and evocative camerawork by Sidney Hayers and Reginald Wyer, and effective acting (particularly in Margaret Johnston's subtly off-center portrayal of the bitter antagonist) make this a worthy companion to such British horror classics as *Dead of Night* (1945) and *Curse of the Demon* (1956).

In England, the film was released as *Night of the Eagle*. American distributors AIP changed the title to *Burn, Witch, Burn*, added a narrative prologue (in which Paul Frees intones for the audience's protection "an ancient incantation of the rite which dispels all evil spirits which may emanate from the screen during *Burn, Witch, Burn*"), and gave American actress Janet Blair top billing over English actor Peter Wyngarde (who was billed first on British prints). By any title, it remains one of the most gripping and effective horror films of the decade.

Child's Play (1988; MGM/UA) Director: Tom Holland; Producer: David Kirschner; Screenplay: Don Mancini, John Lafia, Tom Holland; Photography: Bill Butler. CAST: Catherine Hicks, Chris Sarandon, Alex Vincent, Brad Dourif, Dinah Manoff, Tommy Swerdlow, Jack Colvin.

"There's more to the story than the voodoo," commented director/co-scripter Tom Holland to *Fangoria*'s Kim Howard Johnson. One should hope so, since there's very *little* voodoo in the story. The film begins with serial killer Charles "Chucky" Lee Ray (played by the soon-to-be-typecast-as-psycho Brad Dourif) shot by a detective and taking refuge in a toy store. Dying, he transfers his soul into the nearest body, that of a two-and-a-half-foot tall doll called "The Good Guy." The possessed doll then falls into the hands of six-year-old Andy Barclay. Chucky kills a few people (including his low-life former partner and the man who taught him the soul-transference technique) and sets his diminutive sights on finding a new home for his evil soul (preferably one not made of plastic)—in the body of little Andy. Andy's mother, aided by the detective, must battle the devilish doll for the life of her son.

Voodoo is the mechanism which allows Chucky to inhabit the doll. Unfortunately, this rather intriguing premise remains completely unexplored, with the voodoo element relegated to the soul-transference scene and a brief confrontation with a man that appears to be a voodoo priest. (With the scanty background given, the supernatural element could just as easily have been the result of Satanism, Druidism, or some other arbitrary occult power.) Admittedly, the dying killer shouts "Give me the power, I beg of you" and intones (in what sounds like French) a litany that includes the words "Damballah," "Santería," and "Macumba" while an unnatural lightning storm forms overhead. And when Chucky pays a visit to his voodoo mentor, "John" (who's none too pleased with his acolyte's misuse of power: "You perverted everything I've taught you and used it for evil, and you have to be stopped!"), Chucky uses the man's own "mojo" (in the form of John's personal voodoo doll) to dispatch him. Yet it's never revealed why or how or when or to what purpose Charles Lee Ray studied under this apparent voodoo-master, nor who this sorcerer is exactly. (In fact, the "V" word never comes up at any time during the film.)

While perhaps a disappointment to the voodoo cineaste, *Child's Play* is a resounding success for those viewers enamored of killer dolls. An odd cinematic subset to be sure, the killer doll concept, when handled effectively, can be a genuinely frightening idea (dredging up those ancient childhood fears wrought by nighttime imaginings of toys taking on monstrous forms in a darkened bedroom). *Child's Play* fully exploits this fearful context by making the victim-to-be a six-year-old boy. Spot-on acting (including a wonderful performance from the young Alex Vincent, whose piteous and terrified crying scene grabs the viewer's heart and squeezes), believable characters (who remain so by their natural *dis*belief), suspenseful staging, and exciting action sequences (particularly a pins-and-needles car chase—involving only *one* car!—as Chucky tries to kill the driver) make *Child's Play* one of the more effective and entertaining horror entries of the 1980s. Moviegoers thought so as well, for the film took in eight million dollars in its first five days of release (ultimately earning over 40 million domestically) and spawned two (decidedly inferior) sequels.

Child's Play proved rewarding not only financially but personally as well—for at least two participants. During production, a romance blossomed between star Catherine Hicks and special effects artist (and Chucky designer) Kevin Yagher. The two were eventually married after *Child's Play 2* wrapped.

Child's Play 2 (1990; Universal) Director: John Lafia; Producer: David Kirschner; Co-Producer: Laura Moskowitz; Screenplay: Don Mancini; Photography: Stefan Czapsky. CAST: Alex Vincent, Jenny Agutter, Gerrit Graham, Christine Elise, Brad Dourif, Grace Zabriskie.

"Chucky is a classic villain," opined director John Lafia in a Universal publicity release, "in the tradition of *Frankenstein*, the shark in *Jaws*, or *The Terminator*. He's unstoppable." Though the "classic villain" status may be wishful thinking, the two-and-a-half-foot plastic doll with the soul of a serial killer did indeed prove unstoppable—thanks to impressive box-office returns on the first *Child's Play*.

Via voodoo, serial killer Charles Lee Ray transfers his soul into a two-and-a-half-foot-tall "Good Guy" doll. Sadly, no further voodoo variants arise in this fright film franchise and "Chucky" simply struts through the three *Child's Play* installments as the world's most diminutive murderer. Pictured: *Child's Play 3* (1991).

When MGM/UA declined to follow up their successful hit with a sequel, citing "moral grounds" as the reason (though more likely it was the studio's then-troubled financial situation that dictated a cutback in production), Universal optioned the rights and hired original scripter Don Mancini (whose credit for the original *Child's Play* screenplay had to be protected by a Writer's Guild arbitration when director Tom Holland claimed the script was all *his* doing) to resurrect the popular killer doll.

Set two years later, the now eight-year-old Andy is in the care of foster parents while his mother (apparently unhinged—or at least *believed* crazy) is under psychiatric care. The Play Pals Toy Company acquires the demolished Chucky doll and reconstructs it (thinking that some technicians had altered its voicebox or something as a joke) in their (vague) plan to offset the bad publicity Andy's claims have generated. Of course, the repaired doll still houses the evil soul of serial killer Charles Lee "Chucky" Ray, and the now-restored Chucky tracks down Andy in an attempt to possess his body before it's too late and the killer is trapped in his unwanted doll-form forever. (Since Andy was the first person to whom Chucky revealed himself, his is the only body that will do... or something.) Aided by a teenage girl (another foster child), Andy ultimately faces Chucky in the Play Pals factory, culminating in all manner of diminutive mayhem and a final messy meltdown.

Child's Play 2 is simply a continuation of the original, with the resurrected Chucky trying to get enough "quiet time" with Andy to perform his soul-transference ceremony. In the meantime, he commits various murders (some, apparently, just for fun). The sequel features no expansion of the original concept or characters, and, consequently, it feels like a tired rehash from the start, becoming little more than a slasher film (albeit with a rather unusual killer). Fortunately, its superior production values and outstanding Chucky effects make it a mildly entertaining (if conceptually bankrupt) hour and 20 minutes. Particularly involving

are those clever instances in which the evil doll "frames" Andy (writing an obscene note to Andy's teacher or breaking Andy's foster mom's treasured figurine), effectively dredging up from childhood that special indignation felt when one told the truth and was not believed.

"I think we play upon the very frightening notion of something seemingly passive and sweet really being a maniacal killer," mused Lafia about the series' attraction. Scripter Don Mancini narrowed it even further: "In a way, the drama of the story lies in the fact that Chucky, a homicidal maniac, can be in plain sight and nobody knows that a killer is in the room."

Unlike in the first film, voodoo *is* specifically mentioned in the sequel, with one character recalling that Charles Lee Ray "murdered a dozen people in a series of ritual voodoo killings." No further elaboration is forthcoming, however, and the voodoo fan must make do with just another repetitious and perfunctory (and interrupted) soul-transference ceremony.

Child's Play 3 (1991; Universal) Director: Jack Bender; Producer: Robert Latham Brown; Screenplay: Don Mancini; Photography: John R. Leonetti. CAST: Justin Whalin, Perrey Reeves, Jeremy Sylvers, Peter Haskell, Dakin Matthews, Andrew Robinson, Brad Dourif.

Set eight years after Chucky's meltdown at the close of *Child's Play 2*, the story has the Play Pals Toy Company starting up production (yet again) of the once-popular Good Guy doll. When the factory recommences operation, blood from the gooey mess that was once the demonic Chucky drips into the first batch of melted wax and, presto, Charles Lee Ray is reborn into the first Good Guy doll off the assembly line. Chucky goes after Andy again, who's now a troubled 16-year-old cadet at a military school. Chucky mails himself to Andy (just how he wraps, labels, and posts the package from *inside* the box is never explained), but it's intercepted by an eight-year-old cadet named Tyler. Chucky then sets his sights on *Tyler's* body, while Andy takes on the role of Tyler's protector.

The only voodoo in *Child's Play 3* is by implication, with Chucky doing his usual shtick of chanting in French and calling upon Damballah to "Give me the power!" in an attempt to transfer his soul from the plastic body into the fleshy one.

By this time, the novelty of this killer novelty had definitely worn off, and Chucky is reduced to uttering such "witticisms" as "Don't fuck with the Chuck." Since Andy is now a teenager at a military academy, the film quickly becomes little more than a clichéd (though admittedly slick) teens-in-peril film. Fortunately, the movie finally comes alive in its final third when Chucky spitefully replaces the blanks in the cadets' rifles with live rounds and wreaks havoc during a nighttime war games exercise, culminating in an exciting chase through a wonderfully ghoulish carnival House of Horrors (which was built upon the famed *Phantom of the Opera* stage at Universal).

Child's Play 3 was filmed in 10 weeks on location in Boonville, Missouri (at the Kemper Military School and College) and rural areas near Valencia, California (the outdoor carnival setting) as well as on sound stages at Universal Studios.

"Chucky is in awe of nothing," explained scripter Don Mancini about the character's appeal. "Much of his humor and popularity are a result of that. He is an anarchist and therefore needs a foil. Authority figures are the perfect foils, and when they are eliminated onscreen, young fans really respond. They love his attitude."

"People enjoy the experience of venting some of the dark feelings we all have in the safety of a movie theater," added producer Robert Latham Brown (who was involved in one capacity or another with all three *Child's Play* films). "There's a little Chucky in all of us. We don't let him out, of course, except vicariously when watching these films."

In Britain there appeared to be a bit *too much* Chucky in at least two boys who, after allegedly watching *Child's Play 3*, murdered a younger playmate, touching off yet another round of "The-Movies-Made-Them-Do-It" alarmist media attacks.

Comin' Round the Mountain (1951; Universal-International) Director: Charles Lamont; Producer: Howard Christie; Screenplay: Robert Lees, Frederic I. Rinaldo; Additional Dialogue: John Grant; Photography: George Robinson. CAST: Bud Abbott, Lou Costello, Dorothy Shay, Kirby Grant, Shaye Cogan, Joe Sawyer, Glenn Strange, Ida Moore, Margaret Hamilton, Robert Easton.

In this low-end Abbott and Costello vehicle, the boys journey to the hillbilly country of Old Kentucky when Wilburt (Costello) learns he's a long lost cousin of the McCoy clan, and that there's treasure buried somewhere thereabouts just waiting for him to claim. Of course, his bumbling soon reignites the old McCoy-Winfield feud (apparently the "Hatfields" were out of town that decade).

Somewhere amongst the lowbrow shenanigans (which include *waaaay* too many silly songs from warbler Dorothy Shay), the duo visits an old backwoods witch called Aunt Hattie (Margaret Hamilton doing her Wicked Witch of the West shtick from *The Wizard of Oz*) to buy a love

potion. Hamilton chants comical nonsense that sounds something like "Ardule la gummee gitchee gazoo" and molds an effigy of Costello when Abbott refuses to pay up front, sticking pins into the doll's derriere until the little fat man can take it no longer. Then, when the witch is not looking, Costello makes an effigy of *her* and the two engage in a comical voodoo doll duel. The scene concludes when Costello notices the old witch's broom (complete with windscreen and windshield wipers!), touches a spot on the handle, and accidentally flies out the door to crash into the trees outside. (So much for voodoo—thrown over for the more traditional witchcraft for one final sight gag.)

The film's level of humor (as well as its attitude toward voodoo) is reflected in this dialogue exchange:

> Abbott: "She's making voodoo."
> Costello: "She's making voo do what?"
> Abbott: "Voodoo!"
> Costello: "I do what?"

Craze (1974; Warner Bros.; Great Britain) Alternate Title: *The Infernal Idol*. Director: Freddie Francis; Producer: Herman Cohen; Screenplay: Aben Kandel (Kenneth Langtree), Herman Cohen; Photography: John Wilcox. CAST: Jack Palance, Diana Dors, Jule Ege, Edith Evans, Hugh Griffith, Trevor Howard, Michael Jayston, Suzy Kendall, Martin Potter.

Jack Palance plays a London antiques dealer who makes human sacrifices to an idol he keeps in his basement. Though the idol (of the god "Chuku") looks African in origin, Palance and his fellow "coven" members speak of witchcraft and black magic but never of voodoo. Nor do they exhibit any voodoo trappings (such as drums, dress, or dance) but instead behave like the usual garden-variety Satanists.

A rather dull affair, *Craze* can boast of very few advocates among critics and fans. Even the film's *director* doesn't like it. "I thought it was an awful picture," Freddie Francis admitted to this author. "But it was nice to work with Jack [Palance] and we became quite good friends."

Creepshow (1982; Warner Bros.) Director: George A. Romero; Producer: Richard P. Rubinstein; Screenplay: Stephen King; Photography: Michael Gornick. CAST: Hal Holbrook, Adrienne Barbeau, Fritz Weaver, Leslie Nielsen, Carrie Nye, E.G. Marshall, Vivica Lindfors, Ed Harris, Ted Danson, Stephen King.

In the wraparound segment of this five-part horror anthology, a young boy (Joe King) is infuriated when his insensitive father (played by an oddly unbilled Tom Atkins) slaps him and throws away his EC-style comic book (titled *Creepshow*, of course). The five subsequent segments ("Father's Day," "The Lonesome Death of Jordy Verrill," "Something to Tide You Over," "The Crate," and "They're Creeping up on You") are the comic book stories come to life. At the end, two garbage men (one played by FX artist Tom Savini) find the horror comic and thumb through it. They see an ad for an "Authentic Voodoo Doll"—and note that somebody has cut out the attached order form. Inside the house, Billy smiles evilly and says "I'll teach you to throw away my comic book," as he gleefully jabs a pin into

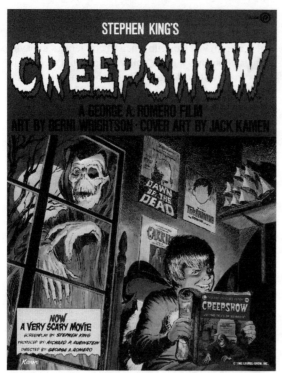

Stephen King's anthology film *Creepshow*. In the movie's wraparound segments, a boy uses a "voodoo doll" to deal with his comic book-hating dad.

cording to the tour guide) contains "photographs that show some of the mysterious practices of this strange cult." Though taking place in New Orleans, the story makes little use of this voodooist setting and instead deals with a Transylvanian curse of werewolfery (complete with gypsies, Central European accents, and talk of "the Old Country").

While the film sports some wonderfully evocative lighting, it goes for naught in this dull effort that seems to take pains *not* to become a horror movie. Even the titular lycanthrope is disappointing, looking like nothing more than a medium-sized dog.

John Abbott, who plays the museum tour guide, starred in a more legitimate voodoo variation the following year, *The Vampire's Ghost* (1945). Of *Cry of the Werewolf*, the actor remembered (to *Movie Club*'s Don Leifert), "I played a museum employee who went around giving a lecture on the exhibits. It was my job to keep the tempo going from one scene to another without pausing." The talented character actor did just that, for these opening sequences proved to be the most interesting in the whole tepid tale.

Dead & Buried (1981; Avco Embassy) Director: Gary A. Sherman; Producers: Ronald Shusett, Robert Fentress; Screenplay: Ronald Shusett, Dan O'Bannon (based on a story by Jeff Miller and Alex Stern); Photography: Steve Poster. CAST: James Farentino, Melody Anderson, Jack Albertson, Dennis Redfield, Nancy Locke Hauser.

After the horror-in-space megahit *Alien*, writers Dan O'Bannon and Ronald Shusett turned their talents toward horror-on-earth with this creepy tale of small-town corruption and (*literal*) decay (since the sleepy seaside village of Potter's Bluff turns out to be populated by the walking dead!). The story follows Dan, the local Sheriff (James Farentino), whose investigations into a series of gruesome murders leads him to continually cross paths with the peculiar Mr. Dobbs (Jack Albertson in his final screen role), the town's "official coroner/mortician." Eventually, Dan discovers that the townsfolk are brutally murdering strangers whom Dobbs then restores to a semblance of life, populating his little burg with walking corpses that need periodic repairs to their decaying flesh (which the artistic-minded mortician happily provides). Dan, much to his horror, finally learns the ultimate truth in a macabre and shocking twist ending guaranteed to raise goosebumps on even the most jaded horror fan.

"What appealed to me [about the story]," explained co-producer/co-scripter Ronald Shusett, "was its outlandish premise and its remarkable twist ending, one of the best I've ever come across. When it happens, it changes everything you've seen in the film up to that point." Indeed it does.

Director Gary A. Sherman (helming only his second feature) infuses the film with an appropriately eerie atmosphere. Under the aegis of cinematographer Steve Poster, Potter's Bluff becomes a landscape illumined by misty, late afternoon light and foggy darkness populated by menacing silhouettes.

A parade of excellent character actors (among them Robert Englund of Freddie Krueger fame, *Northern Exposure*'s Barry Corbin, and Tim Burton's future girlfriend, Lisa Marie, as an ill-fated hitchhiker) create a bevy of ec-

the mail-order doll's neck. Downstairs, his hateful Dad clutches his throat in agony...

Appropriately cartoonish in its characters and situations, *Creepshow* succeeds in bringing the style and feel of the old EC horror comics to vibrant life. Unlike most anthologies, there are no "dud" stories (though some are more successful than others), and each tale holds its fair share of scares (and humor). An (awful) sequel followed in 1987.

The pin-wielding young boy inflicting voodoo vengeance on his father was played by Stephen King's real-life son. (As well as scripting, King himself also acted in the film, playing the title role in "The Lonesome Death of Jordy Verrill"—which, perhaps unsurprisingly, turned out to be the weakest link in the five-story chain.) Said King of his son's film debut: "Jody did have a good time making *Creepshow*, but he did get freaked out for a while. He was eight or nine at the time, and to be in your pajamas with a whole bunch of people around your bed in a strange house can be very unsettling. He just came to a point where it was either freak out or go to work. He went to work" (from an interview by Edwin Pouncy published in *Sounds* magazine).

Cry of the Werewolf (1944; Columbia) Director: Henry Levin; Producer: Wallace MacDonald; Screenplay: Griffin Jay, Charles O'Neal (Story: Griffin Jay); Photography: L.W. O'Connell. CAST: Nina Foch, Stephen Crane, Osa Massen, Blanche Yorka, Barton MacLane, John Abbott.

Though really a werewolf story (hence the title), the film touches on voodoo at the very beginning when we're treated to a tour of the "LaTour Museum." The museum houses a vampire exhibit, a section devoted to a famous gypsy werewolf (Marie LaTour), and a "voodoo room" which (accentric and engaging townsfolk whose outwardly convincing friendliness makes the vicious acts they perpetrate that much more shocking.

Voodoo enters the picture as a *possible* explanation for the gruesome phenomenon. First, Dan finds a book in his wife's possession entitled *Witchcraft and Voodoo*. Next, Dan overhears her lecturing to her class (she's an elementary schoolteacher) about the walking dead. At one point she explains, "…so voodoo is basically a religion. Belief and conversion are absolutely necessary." She goes on to tell the "unsubstantiated story" of "a tribe in central Peru whose residents included a great number of these walking dead who were completely at the will of their master." This seems rather incongruous however, since Peru is a bit off voodoo's beaten path. Toward the end, when Dan demands to know how Dobbs created a townful of corpses, the stubborn old mortician only answers, "call it black magic, call it a medical breakthrough—I'll take my secret to the grave." These are the only voodoo references found in the film, and none of the religion's symbols or trappings appear. Though this may disappoint the voodoo fan, the mysterious vagueness and secrecy fits in well with the film's uneasy milieu.

Though largely (and unfairly) ignored by fans and film historians, *Dead & Buried* remains a macabre, engrossing,

Mexican lobby card for the 1961 lost film *The Dead One*. (Courtesy Lynn Naron)

and ultimately shocking take on the sometimes stifling and deceptive realm of small-town Americana, becoming the ultimate Norman Rockwell nightmare.

The Dead One (1961; Favorite Films) Director/Producer/Screenwriter: Barry Mahon. CAST: Monica Davis, John McKay, Linda Ormond, Clyde Kelly, Darlene Myrick.

"THE GREATEST VOODOO FILM EVER MADE!" shouted the ads for *The Dead One*. This grandiose (and highly unlikely) claim is at present difficult to dispute, since as of this writing *The Dead One* appears to be a lost film. Made by exploitation/nudie veteran Barry Mahon, the story centers around a woman who uses voodoo to raise up the

corpse of her dead brother in an effort to keep a property inheritance from going to her cousin. This ultra low-budget drive-in feature was shot in and around New Orleans (including the Kenilworth Plantation on the city's outskirts). "SEE beautiful dancing girls in Bourbon St. nite clubs in New Orleans. SEE the voodoo princess call on the dead ones to Kill! Kill! Kill!" (Maybe someday we *will* SEE this voodoo vision from the maker of such grindhouse oddities as *Nude Scrapbook* and *Sex Club International*. One shudders to think of it.)

The Devil's Own (1966; Hammer; Great Britain) Alternate Title: *The Witches*. Director: Cyril Frankel; Producer: Anthony Nelson Keys; Screenplay: Nigel Kneale; (Based on the Novel *The Devil's Own* by Peter Curtis); Photography: Arthur Grant. CAST: Joan Fontaine, Kay Walsh, Alec McCowen, Duncan Lamont, Gwen Ffrangcon-Davies, John Collin, Ingrid Brett, Leonard Rossiter, Michele Dotrice, Carmel McSharry, Martin Stephens, Ann Bell.

The only voodoo found in this tale of modern-day (or at least 1966) witches in a small English village comes during the brief two-and-a-half minute pre-credit prologue. In it, a schoolteacher (Joan Fontaine) at an African missionary compound hurriedly packs up her books while deafening drums beat ominously all around her. Suddenly, a weird knife with its hilt fashioned into a voodoo doll flies through the door to thud into the room's table. The schoolmarm frantically blocks up the door as her two terrified native helpers bolt. Abruptly, the door smashes inward and a figure wearing a huge, horrific primitive mask enters. The woman screams and the screen fades into the credit sequence.

The rest of the film deals with this same woman coming to a small English village (after recovering from the nervous breakdown she suffered because of her African experience) to teach school. Once there she finds that much of the town is involved in witchcraft (of the standard Satanic variety), which culminates in her attempt to stop a human sacrifice.

As could be expected (since it's a Hammer film), *The Devil's Own* is well-acted but slow, with little happening until the story winds down to its rather uninteresting conclusion. (To be fair, Hammer did eventually make one good witchcraft movie, 1968's *The Devil's Bride*.) *The Devil's Own* witchery and supposedly "wanton" coven activity seem dreadfully tame, and the evil high priestess is vanquished with a whimper rather than a bang. Scripter Nigel Kneale (*Enemy From Space, The Abominable Snowman, First Men in the Moon*, et al.) would have done better to expand the voodoo-themed prologue rather than abandoning it in favor of the dull small-town witchcraft scenario, since the opening two minutes prove to be the film's highlight.

Apart from Hammer's casting coup of corralling Academy Award winner Joan Fontaine for the lead role, *The Devil's Own* is noteworthy only because it turned out to be child actor Martin Stephens' (star of both *Village of the Damned* [1960] and *The Innocents* [1961]) final screen appearance.

The Four Skulls of Jonathan Drake (1959; United Artists) Director: Edward L. Cahn; Producer: Robert E. Kent; Screenplay: Orville H. Hampton; Photography: Maury Gertsman. CAST: Eduard Franz, Valerie French, Henry Daniell, Grant Richards, Paul Cavanagh, Paul Wexler.

In a far cry from his fascinating turn as Dr. McFarland in *The Body Snatcher* (1945), a rather dissolute-looking (and obviously slumming) Henry Daniell plays Dr. Emil Zurich, a centuries-old being with "the head of a white man on the body of a jungle Indian." With the aid of his servant Zutai ("a living dead thing"), Zurich carries out the Drake family curse by dispatching the (literal) heads of the Drake household. The result of an Amazonian witch doctor's handiwork, Zurich must collect and shrink the heads of the Drake family in order to achieve "eternal peace." Rather than voodoo, Ecuadorian black magic (and head-hunting) is behind the tepid thrills of this dull programmer.

The Four Skulls of Jonathan Drake was released on a double-bill with the almost-as-dreadful *Invisible Invaders*.

The Ghost Breakers (1940; Paramount) Director: George Marshall; Producer: Arthur Hornblow; Screenplay: Walter De Leon; Photography: Charles Lang, Theodore Sparkuhl. CAST: Bob Hope, Paulette Goddard, Richard Carlson, Paul Lukas, Willie Best, Anthony Quinn, Noble Johnson.

In what has proven itself to be one of the funniest horror-comedies of all time, Bob Hope plays a radio personality who aids a plucky young girl (Paulette Goddard) in her investigation of the haunted castle she's just inherited off the coast of Cuba. Though mainly concerned with ghosts (and the various human villains—and accompanying red herrings—skulking about), the story also tosses out a few voodoo bones in the form of a "death ouanga" left in Paulette's stateroom, and one old woman residing on the island with her "zombie son."

King Kong's Noble Johnson (with a bald head and grotesque makeup distorting his features) plays the supposed zombie (the scariest of the decade apart from Darby Jones in *I Walked with a Zombie*). Unfortunately, after a few moments of menace, the scriptwriters place him inside a suit of armor (!) and then have our heroes lock the metallic monster inside a closet. Apart from these two brief hoodoo happenings, no other voodoo variants present themselves.
Sample Dialogue:

Richard Carlson: "A zombie has no will of its own. You see them sometimes, walking around blindly with dead eyes, following orders, not knowing what they do, not caring."
Bob Hope: "You mean like Democrats?"

The House That Dripped Blood (1971; Amicus; Great Britain) Director: Peter Duffell; Producers: Max J. Rosenberg, Milton Subotsky; Screenplay: Robert Bloch; Photography:

Noble Johnson's frighteningly grotesque zombie briefly menaces Bob Hope and company in one of the screen's best horror-comedies, *The Ghost Breakers*.

Ray Parslow. CAST: Christopher Lee, Peter Cushing, Nyree Dawn Porter, Denholm Elliott, Jon Pertwee, Joanna Dunham, Joss Ackland, John Bennett, Chloe Franks, Tom Adams, Ingrid Pitt.

Robert Bloch (author of the novel *Psycho*) adapted four of his own short stories for this third Amicus horror anthology. The four tales center on the various occupants of a sinister country house which "reflects the personality of whoever lives in it." The first story, "Method for Murder," stars Denholm Elliott as a writer seemingly haunted by his own fictional character. The second episode, "Waxworks," features Peter Cushing literally losing his head over a wax figure. The third tale, "Sweets to the Sweet," involves a matter of family witchcraft that is needling Christopher Lee. The fourth segment, "The Cloak," is a comical vignette about vampirism caused by wearing a special cape.

In the "Sweets to the Sweet" episode, a man's daughter fashions a wax doll and then sticks pins into the effigy in order to torment and ultimately destroy her hated father. Though this smacks of the stereotypical "voodoo doll" method, the prepubescent witch gets her powers from Satan rather than Damballah. She only exercises her latent supernatural abilities (inherited from her evil deceased mother) after she discovers the "Witchcraft" entry in her encyclopedia.

Of the seven horror anthologies Amicus produced between 1965 and 1973, this may very well be the best. Despite its lurid title (director Peter Duffell wanted to call it *Death and the Maiden* but producer Max J. Rosenberg insisted on the more commercial moniker), *The House That Dripped Blood* possesses an intelligent, solid script that takes both its horror and comedy seriously, producing a more balanced and resonant result than most uneven anthologies can muster. Add some deft direction by veteran British TV director Duffell (who helmed a number of acclaimed *Avengers* episodes) making his feature film debut, evocative camerawork by Ray Parslow, and sensitive playing from a seasoned cast, and *The House That Dripped Blood* remains *The House That Dripped* Talent.

I Married a Savage (c1950; cast and credits unknown)

In this "adults only" feature which appears to be from the late 1940s or early 1950s, a man marries a snake dancer who turns out to be a voodoo priestess. Though the film's trailer has survived the ravages of time, the movie itself hasn't fared so well and appears to be a "lost" film. The picture seems to have been unofficially based on the Cornell Woolrich story "Kiss of the Cobra."

Interview with the Vampire (1993; Geffen) Director: Neil Jordan; Producers: David Geffen, Stephen Woolley; Co-Producer: Redmond Morris; Screenplay: Anne Rice; Photography: Philippe Rousselot. CAST: Tom Cruise, Brad Pitt, Antonio Banderas, Stephen Rea, Christian Slater, Kirstin Dunst.

Popular horror novelist Anne Rice adapted her own innovative novel to the screen in this sumptuous, visually enthralling, yet ultimately cold mega-budgeted production. The film was a financial hit, aided, no doubt, by the media furor and attendant publicity that arose when Rice complained long and loud over the studio's choice of Tom Cruise to play the vampire Lestat. When the picture finally came out, Rice apologized and applauded Cruise's performance (which undoubtedly added a few *more* coins to the coffers).

Ironically, the film's major failing was not the work of Cruise, who brought an engaging energy to his role, but the performance of Brad Pitt as the vampire protagonist and main character, Louis. Pitt's demeanor is so desultory and listless that he becomes a whining bore (to paraphrase Lestat's complaint at film's end). Pitt's deadpan narration and blank countenance rob the story of its intended focus, leaving the film an attractive but hollow shell.

Voodoo enters the story briefly when Louis' plantation slaves rise up against their master and his vampire companion. In one brief scene, the slaves dance around a bonfire while one manipulates what looks like a voodoo doll.

The Invisible Menace (1938; Warner Bros.) Director: John Farrow; Screenplay: Crane Wilbur (From the Play by Ralph Spencer Zink); Photography: L. William O'Connell. CAST: Boris Karloff, Marie Wilson, Eddie Craven, Regis Toomey, Henry Kolker, Cy Kendall, Charles Trowbridge, Eddie Acuff, Frank Faylen, Phyllis Barry, Harland Tucker.

The only voodoo found in this murder mystery set on an Army base (located on a fog-shrouded island) is a brief flashback episode which takes place on the then-American occupied island of Haiti. The flashback centers around an innocent engineer (Boris Karloff) framed by his boss and his cheating wife for stealing the government payroll. Included (for no discernible reason except, perhaps, to establish that the natives are restless) is a brief and admittedly atmospheric scene of a black man in headdress dancing to a drum beat around a blazing bonfire while wielding a machete. Though no one ever mentions voodoo, the implication is clear.

The Leech Woman (1960; Universal-International) Director: Edward Dein; Producer: Joseph Gershenson; Screenplay: David Duncan (story by Ben Pivar and Francis Rosenwald); Photography: Ellis W. Carter. CAST: Colleen Gray, Grant Williams, Phillip Terry, Gloria Talbot, John Van Dreelen, Estelle Hemslee, Kim Hamilton, Arthur Batanides.

In this well-acted, mildly entertaining entry in Universal's late-1950s genre sweepstakes, an unscrupulous doctor and his aging alcoholic wife travel to Africa where they find a tribe that has discovered the secret of eternal youth—in the form of a rare plant combined with fluid from the male pineal gland. The wife kills her caddish husband, steals the plant pollen, and goes on a pineal-hunting spree back in the States.

Despite a prolonged visit to the jungles of darkest Africa (or at least the jungles of a darkened soundstage), there's no voodoo to be found in *The Leech Woman*. What one *does* find is plenty of stock jungle and animal footage (much of it lifted from Universal's 1954 film, *Tanganyika*). The cost-conscious inserts occasionally become laughable, such as when the characters look in one direction to see a lush jungle forest and then a moment later look in another direction to see lions roaming the African savannah (!). Even so, at least this *Leech Woman* doesn't suck the life out of its audience via bad acting (which so many of its contemporaries do) and is refreshingly clear of the giant bugs and atomic mutations then running rampant through the cinematic countryside.

Shot in 10 days in January of 1959, *The Leech Woman* sat on the shelf for a year and a half before Universal released it as the bottom half of a double bill, supporting Hammer's *The Brides of Dracula*.

The Legend of Hillbilly John (1973; Jack H. Harris Enterprises) Alternate Titles: *Who Fears the Devil*; *My Name is John*; Director: John Newland; Producer: Barney Rosenzweig; Screenplay: Melvin Levy (Based on the Book *Who Fears the Devil?* by Manly Wade Wellman); Photography: Flemming Olsen. CAST: Hedge Capers, Severn Darden, Sharon Henesy, Sidney Clute, Denver Pyle, William Traylor, Harris Yulin, Susan Strasberg, Alfred Ryder, R.G. Armstrong, Chester Jones, Val Avery, Percy Rodrigues.

In this little-known (and little-seen) folk-tale oddity, singer Hedge Capers (in his first—and possibly only—movie) plays John, an Appalachian youth who takes up the family task of "defyin' the Devil" when his Grandpappy John (Denver Pyle) succumbs in the line of duty. To this end, John crafts a set of pure silver guitar strings (the Devil and his minions can't stand silver) and begins his search to "find the Devil and face him down." On his journeys he encounters a greedy undertaker and his run-in with a "witch-girl,"

from ghostly
hark mountain
this eerie story
of witches...
voodoo...devils...
monsters
ANTHONY J. HOPE presents a Film by BARNEY ROSENZWEIG
THE LEGEND OF HILLBILLY JOHN
mountain folk swear it's true
HEDGE CAPERS • SEVERN DARDEN • SHARON HENESY • DENVER PYLE
PERCY RODRIGUES • ALFRED RYDER • SUSAN STRASBERG • HARRIS YULIN
Executive Producer ANTHONY J. HOPE • Screenplay by MELVIN LEVY • Based on the book by MANLEY WADE WELLMAN
released by Jack H. Harris Enterprises, Inc.
Directed by JOHN NEWLAND • Produced by BARNEY ROSENZWEIG
Music by ROGER KELLAWAY • Songs by HOYT AXTON & HEDGE CAPERS
Color G
Despite the ad's mention of voodoo, the topic is merely a brief afterthought in this 1973 cornpone curiosity. (Courtesy Eric Hoffman)

an evil strip-mining baron whose soul is bound up with a giant "Ugly Bird" which he uses to frighten the locals into submission, and ultimately to a cotton plantation where the black pickers live in fear of one "Voodoo Captain Lojoie H. Desplain IV" (Percy Rodrigues). When an old man stands up to the Captain (who's systematically cheating the workers) by holding up a "homemade gris gris" (a hoodoo charm), the Captain only laughs—until John steps up and plays a tune on his silver strings, vanquishing the evil exploiter. The film ends with John walking through a misty morning toward the Capitol building in Washington D.C. (apparently a hotbed of Satanic activity).

Filmed on location in North Carolina, Arkansas, and Washington D.C., *The Legend of Hillbilly John* is a cornpone curiosity of its time—one part simplistic allegory, one part ecological message (the film opens with lines about man "paving over mother earth" while construction equipment clears a forest), and one part hippie hoe-down (endless folk songs and free love sensibilities—offscreen, of course, since the film is rated G). It fails to work because of its overly rustic quaintness (with the hero little more than a noble simpleton) and exceedingly dull pace (the film frequently slows to a crawl during the innumerable folk ballads crooned by Capers).

Though Capers possesses a pleasant voice and an appealing innocence, he sorely lacks the screen presence his larger-than-life folk-hero role required. (According to the film's publicity, Capers won the part over the likes of Beau Bridges, Glen Campbell, Jimmy Dean, Bob Dylan, Peter Fonda, Art Garfunkel, Arlo Guthrie, Ricky Nelson, Bobby Sherman, and James Taylor!)

On the plus side, the picture sports some beautiful scenery and an effectively demonic giant bird-creature (courtesy of Gene Warren [*The Time Machine*]). Also, Director John Newland (best known as the host of the television series *One Step Beyond*) managed to secure a number of quality character actors for cameos, including Severn Darden (the best thing about *Werewolves on Wheels*, 1971; *Conquest* and *Battle for the Planet of the Apes*, 1972 and '73; *Mother, Jugs, and Speed*, 1976; *Hopscotch*, 1980), Denver Pyle (*The Alamo*, 1960; *The Man Who Shot Liberty Valence*, 1962; *Bonnie and Clyde*, 1967; the hit TV series *The Life and Times of Grizzly Adams* and *The Dukes of Hazzard*), Harris Yulin (*Night Moves*, 1975; *James A. Michener's Dynasty*, 1976; *Scarface*, 1983), and R.G. Armstrong (*El Dorado*, 1967; *Race with the Devil*, 1975; *Heaven Can Wait*, 1978; *Evilspeak*, 1981). Newland also talked Susan Strasberg (Broadway's Anne Frank and daughter of Actors Studio founder Lee Strasberg) into appearing as the "witch-girl." Among her film credits are *Picnic* (1955), *Taste of Fear* (1961), *Frankenstein* (1973 TV movie), and *The Manitou* (1977). Sadly, apart from Harris Yulin (who has the film's only truly juicy role as the skeptical, greedy undertaker), this fine cadre of actors generally goes to waste.

The voodoo in *The Legend of Hillbilly John* remains slight, and the plantation episode lasts less than five minutes. Apart from the gris-gris incident and the Captain referring to himself as "Voodoo Captain...," no hoodoo horrors appear (unless one counts John's tepid song of triumph: "After the storm, African winds blow cool and light..."). And since John's silver strings defeat the Captain, one can only suppose that he's actually an agent of the Devil rather than of Damballah.

Live and Let Die (1973; United Artists) Director: Guy Hamilton; Producers: Albert R. Broccoli, Harry Saltzman; Screenplay: Tom Mankiewicz (based on the novels by Ian Fleming); Photography: Ted Moore. CAST: Roger Moore, Yaphet Kotto, Jane Seymour, Clifton James, Julius W. Harris, Geoffrey Holder, David Hedison, Gloria Hendry, Bernard Lee, Lois Maxwell.

In Roger Moore's first turn as James Bond, the premier agent from His Majesty's Secret Service faces a ruthless diplomat from a small Caribbean island who plans to corner the heroin market. The villain's island poppy fields are "protected by the voodoo threat of Baron Samedi" (a huge, bald-headed man representing the voodoo god of the underworld). Apart from gun barrels hidden behind voodoo masks and a fake Busby Berkeleyish ceremony, voodoo is only a faded backdrop for Bond's adventure. *Live and Let Die* remains one of the more dated and dull Roger Moore/Bond outings.

Major League (1989; Paramount) Director/Screenplay: David S. Ward; Producers: Chris Chesser, Irby Smith; Photography: Reynaldo Villalobos. CAST: Tom Berenger, Charlie Sheen, Corbin Bernsen, Margaret Whitton, James Gammon, Rene Russo, Wesley Snipes, Charles Cypher, Bob Uecker.

This amusing and affecting baseball comedy, in which the Cleveland Indians' new owner tries to assemble a team so bad that they'll finish dead last and allow her to move the club to Florida, features a character named Pedro Cerrano (Dennis Haysbert) who defected from Cuba because he wanted religious freedom. "What's his religion?" asks one character. "Voodoo," replies another. Cerrano sets up a small shrine in his locker to the voodoo god "Jobu" (a plastic doll that looks a little like Albert Einstein) to which he offers cigars and rum before each game. "Straight ball, I hit it very much," explains the big Cuban in his broken English. "Curve ball, bats are afraid. I ask Jobu to come, take fear from bats."

As expected, voodoo becomes the butt of several jokes, including the instance in which Cerrano wants to sacrifice a live chicken before a big game, and the team's catcher gets him a bucket of Kentucky Fried Chicken (extra crispy) instead. In the end, the frustrated Cerrano (who still has trouble hitting curve balls) calls upon his own strength rather than that of his deity: "You no help me now, I say 'Fuck you, Jobu;' I do it myself." Of course, he then promptly hits a home run (faith in oneself obviously being stronger than faith in one's deity).

Major League 2 (1994; Paramount) Director: David S. Ward; Screenplay: R.J. Stewart. CAST: Charlie Sheen, Tom Berenger, Corbin Bernsen, James Gammon, Dennis Haysbert, Omar Epps, David Keith, Bob Uecker, Alison Doody, Michelle Burke, Margaret Whitton, Eirc Bruskotter, Takaaki Ishibashi.

In this aptly (if unimaginatively) named sequel, Pedro Cerrano (Dennis Haysbert again) has found "inner peace" through the teachings of Buddha. When his game suffers from this new, serene outlook on life, however, he eventually dusts off his old doll of the voodoo god Jobu and places it alongside his new Buddha statuette in his locker shrine.

Obeah! (1935; Acturus Pictures) Director: F. Herrick Herrick; Story: F. Herrick Herrick; Photography: Harry W. Smith. CAST: Phillip H. Lord, Jeanne Kelly, Alice Wesslar.

According to a synopsis in *Film Daily*, this long-lost obscurity centers on an adventurer (Phillip H. Lord) who finds a missing American explorer on a South Sea island. The natives have the explorer under a powerful voodoo spell known as "obeah." When the adventurer tries to break the spell by attacking the natives during their "death ritual," he's forced to flee with the explorer's daughter and a native girl. The trio then search for a hidden treasure indicated on the (now-dead) explorer's map, but the voodoo curse of the high priest pursues them.

Star Phillip H. Lord was best known as a writer/producer/actor on radio during the 1930s and '40s. Among his most popular radio shows were the "Seth Parker" series, *Gangbusters* (which remained on the air for over 12 years), and *Mr. District Attorney*.

According to an item in the 1935 *Film Daily Yearbook*, filming of *Obeah!* took place during the first leg of an around-the-world cruise. It was shot over an 11 month period and covered "20 countries, 18,000 miles, and 6,000 people." As reported, various natives and the ship's crewmembers made up the bulk of the cast.

The Offspring (1987; The Movie Store Entertainment) Alternate Title*: From a Whisper to a Scream* (Foreign release title); Director: Jeff Burr; Producers: Darin Scott, William Burr; Screenplay: C. Courtney Joyner, Darin Scott, Jeff Burr; Photography: Craig Greene. CAST: Vincent Price, Clu Gulager, Terry Kiser, Harry Caesar, Rosalind Cash, Cameron Mitchell, Susan Tyrrell, Martine Beswicke.

This exceedingly dark and humorless horror omnibus "stars" Vincent Price (he worked on the film for only two days) as a small town librarian trying to convince a skeptical reporter that "the history of [Oldfield] is written in blood on pages of human skin" (i.e., it's a baaad place). To this end, he offers journals and town records from which spring four macabre tales of Oldfield's past (set, respectively, in the 1970s, the 1950s, the 1930s, and finally during the Civil War).

The first (and marginally most effective—thanks to the stellar playing of the episode's cast) stars the always excellent Clu Gulager as a quiet, nerdish man whose obsessive unrequited love leads to murder and necrophilia. The ending has his sins revisited upon him nine months later in a rather silly and tasteless denouement.

The second story is yet another take on the "be careful what you wish for" theme as a lowlife criminal runs afoul of a swamp-dweller possessing the secret of eternal life. This segment, though slow-moving, offers up the film's one good kicker, an E.C.-style conclusion both horrific and poignant.

The third tale slides around the edges of voodoo territory. In it, the owner (Rosalind Cash) of a carnival freakshow called "Lovecraft's Traveling Amusements" uses some type of black magic (the "V" word never comes up) to transform various fugitives from the law (including diminutive horror veteran Angelo Rossitto) into freaks in exchange for her "protection." When Steven (Ron Brooks), her resident glass-eater, falls for a local girl named Amarrillis (Didi Lanier), the vindictive "backwater witch" abruptly removes Steven's protective power—with the expected gruesome results. The story's sole voodoo-like moment comes when the witch squeezes some kind of doll in order to induce terrible pain in the misbehaving Steven, telling her writhing victim that she acquired this power over him with just "a bit of your hair, a piece of cloth stained with your blood."

The final story concerns a quartet of brutal Civil War soldiers (led by genre stalwart Cameron Mitchell) who stumble upon the town only to find it populated solely by children whose bitter experiences with the war have caused them to turn against all adults—as well as acquire peculiar and grisly dietary habits.

"Most horror anthologies are dull as hell," opined co-scripter C. Courtney Joyner to *Fangoria*'s Marc Shapiro, "and ones like *Torture Garden* are really bad. There is usually one, maybe two stories you remember and the others are just filler. When we decided on the concept for *Whisper* [the film's shooting title was *From a Whisper to a Scream*] we knew all the stories, including the connecting bit, had to be of equally high quality."

With *The Offspring*, Joyner and company got it only half-right; they succeeded in making their five segments of equal quality—just not of *high* quality. The film's major problem (apart from some labored pacing and occasionally inept dialogue) is that it replaces the shocking irony that punctuates the best horror anthologies (such as *Dead of Night*, *Tales from the Crypt*, and even *Creepshow*) with mere mean-spiritedness, its tales winding down to their nasty forgone conclusion without wit or intelligence.

This low-budget (1.1 million dollar) film, shot in 24 days in Dalton, Georgia during the dog days of summer 1985 (with the wraparound later filmed on a Santa Monica soundstage), ran out of money after the four stories were completed. 24-year-old director Jeff Burr then spent eight months digging up enough financing to finish the film and shoot the connecting story with Vincent Price. In interviews, Price made it clear that this would be his *last* horror picture. (It was not, for he appeared in the even-worse *Dead Heat* two years later.)

The Offspring carried more titles than England's Prince of Wales. Originally announced as *From a Whisper to a Scream*, it became *The Craving*, then *The Outing*, and finally *The Offspring* (at the behest of the film's American distributor who insisted on a one-word title) before it hit a single movie screen.

The Possession of Joel Delaney

The Possession of Joel Delaney (1971; Paramount) Director: Waris Hussein; Producer: George Justin; Screenplay: Matt Robinson and Grimes Grace (Based on a Novel by Ramona Stewart); Photography: Arthur J. Ornitz. CAST: Shirley MacLaine, Perry King, Michael Hordern, David Elliott, Lisa Kohane, Lovelady Powell, Barbara Trentham, Miriam Colon, Rivera Alvarez, Teodorina Bello, Robert Burr, Ernesto Gonzalez.

Shirley MacLaine plays a wealthy Manhattan divorcee whose black-sheep brother, Joel, begins acting violently. It seems that Joel has been possessed by the spirit of a former friend, a Puerto Rican named Tonio, who cut off the heads of several women before he himself was killed by his own father. "Tonio's restless spirit needed a home," Tonio's grieving mother tells the bewildered MacLaine. "Your brother and Tonio were close. The spirit of Tonio entered your brother's body." MacLaine seeks the aid of a spiritualist in Spanish Harlem, and he and his followers perform a rite designed to exorcise the spirit from Joel. It fails, and the tragedy climaxes with the now-fully possessed Joel terrorizing his sister and her children with a switchblade while ranting in a Spanish accent.

The voodoo element enters the story during the exorcism ceremony. The various trappings (Catholic icons, rum bottles) and the behavior of the participants (one man is seemingly possessed, while the priest walks barefoot on flaming alcohol as a demonstration of the protective spirit) indicate that they are practicing a form of Santería. (This brief, realistically portrayed sequence carries an illustrative message on the power of faith when the priest exhorts MacLaine to "Please believe. *Believe*. That's the only way out, you have to believe. That's the only way we can help you. But if you don't believe, we can do nothing.") No further voodoo elaboration is forthcoming, and the film as a whole, though shot in a hard-hitting style and containing some disturbing moments (such as when the possessed Joel forces his young niece to get down on all fours and eat dog food), ultimately fails since the main characters, including Joel, his sister, and even the two children, are all so self-absorbed and unlikable that they generate little sympathy or interest.

Revenge of the Zombies

Revenge of the Zombies (1943; Monogram) Director: Steve Sekely; Producer: Linsley Parsons; Screenplay: Edmund Kelso, Van Norcross; Photography: Mack Stengler. CAST: John Carradine, Robert Lowery, Veda Ann Borg, Gale Storm, Mantan Moreland, Bob Steele.

Despite its Louisiana swampland setting and inclusion of zombies, no mention of voodoo or its trappings are present in this bargain-basement horror. John Carradine plays a foreign (obviously Nazi) scientist who has developed the *scientific* means to create zombies which he plans to use as weapons of war for The Fatherland.

Revolt of the Zombies

Revolt of the Zombies (1936; Academy) Director: Victor Halperin; Producer: Edward Halperin; Screenplay: Howard Higgin, Rollo Lloyd, Victor Halperin; Photography: Arthur Martinelli. CAST: Dorothy Stone, Dean Jagger, Roy D'Arc, Robert Noland, George Cleveland.

In the Halperin brothers' follow-up to their ultra-successful *White Zombie* (1932), a very young (and utterly toneless) Dean Jagger plays a member of an expedition sent to the lost city of Angkōr in search of an ancient formula that can create zombies. He finds it, but decides to use it to further his own selfish ends in a romantic triangle. Rather than voodoo, these zombies (who actually turn out to be living people placed under the hypnotic will of the "zombie-maker" instead of reanimated corpses) are the result of ancient *Cambodian* sorcery.

The Halperins (who created one of the best voodoo films of all time in *White Zombie*) fell a *loooong* way with this film. Plodding pacing, poor production values, awful acting, derisive dialogue, and silly subplots all serve to make *Revolt of the Zombies* the very *worst* horror film of the 1930s.

Scared Stiff

Scared Stiff (1953; Paramount) Director: George Marshall; Producer: Hal B. Wallis; Screenplay: Herbert Baker and Walter DeLeon (Additional Dialogue: Ed Simmons, Norman Lear (Based on a Play by Paul Dickey and Charles W. Goddard); Photography: Ernest Laszlo. CAST: Dean Martin, Jerry Lewis, Lizabeth Scott, Carmen Miranda, George Dolenz, Dorothy Malone, William Ching.

Though this slavish remake of *The Ghost Breakers* (1940) sports the same director and follows that previous film's script almost to the letter (with a half-dozen low-rent musical numbers thrown in for bad measure), it can't hold a candle to its comedy classic companion. Retooled slightly for the talents of Dean Martin and Jerry Lewis (in the roles originally assayed by Bob Hope and Willie Best), the film sends the "boys" to Cuba where they aid a lovely young girl (Lizabeth Scott) who's just inherited a haunted castle.

The voodoo element comes in the form of a death ouanga warning and a zombie who lives with its mother near the castle. Unlike Noble Johnson's truly frightening figure from the first film, *Scared Stiff*'s stiff is simply a big, middle-aged white guy (Scottish stage and screen actor Jack Lambert, complete with thinning hair and five o'clock shadow) sans any special makeup.

The script splits the wisecracks between the two stars (whose mean-spirited relationship quickly becomes tiresome, with Martin constantly telling Lewis to shut up or

CAST: Raquel Torres, Charles Bickford, Nils Asther, George F. Marion, John Miljan, Gibson Gowland.

"Portuga Island," begins the film's opening title card. "Through the night... the weird chant of Voodoo worship. Through the day... the weird industry of Sponge Diving." Though there's plenty of the latter in this melodramatic adventure/romance, there's precious little of the former. Admittedly, *The Sea Bat* is the *first* sound film to mention the subject of voodoo. However, apart from one scene (a rather frenzied moment of "heathen dancing"), voodoo serves only as a distant backdrop, an ignorant evil from which the heroine can be redeemed at film's end.

The story revolves around the beautiful Nina, who spurns the Christian faith of her family when her sponge-diver brother is killed by a huge manta ray (the "sea bat" of the title). "A lot of good *your* God does," Nina bitterly tells a parson and soon begins cavorting with the local natives in their voodoo ceremonies. "Nina is out there now," laments her father, "praying with those voodoo devils. You know what that means? Lowly, slimy natives and a white girl out there praying with them in the jungle mud." (So much for religious or racial tolerance!) The story then focuses on an escaped convict disguised as a preacher who arrives on the island and, through the powerful words of the Good Book, inadvertently redeems both himself and the fallen Nina.

Beyond its Neolithic view of voodoo (when the phony parson sees Nina dancing at the voodoo ceremony, he snorts, "I'm trying to figure out whether this is a jazz cabaret or just a madhouse"), *The Sea Bat* remains (along with 1934's *Chloe: Love is Calling You*) one of the most overtly racist voodoo pictures ever made. Lines like, "What sort of a white girl are you to get mixed up with stuff like that?" and "That's white of you, Nina" (after she does someone a good turn) proliferate.

The film is both low on tolerance and entertainment value. Though the production *looks* fairly substantial (steamy jungle sets, convincing waterfront dives, even some impressive-for-the-time underwater footage of the huge Sea Bat), the film sinks under the weight of its insipid storyline and painfully melodramatic acting.

Even the presence of Boris Karloff (pre-*Frankenstein*) offers little to the viewer, for he plays a character simply called "The Corsican" and only appears briefly in two unmemorable scenes.

Valley of the Zombies (1946; Republic) Director: Philip Ford; Producers: Dorrell and Stuart McGowan; Screenplay: Dorrell and Stuart McGowan (Story: Royal K. Cole and Sherman L. Lowe); Photography: Reggie Lanning. CAST: Robert Livingston, Adrian Booth, Ian Keith, Thomas Jackson, Charles Trowbridge, Earle Hodgins, LeRoy Mason, William Haade, Wilton Graff, Charles Cane, Russ Clark, Charles Hamilton.

Perhaps a better title would be "Valley of the *Vampires*" for this fairly entertaining last-minute Poverty Row addition to 1940s horror movies. Ian Keith plays an undertaker who needs fresh blood transfusions periodically in order to retain his eternal life. When he can't steal it from the local doctor's office, he becomes less picky about how he gets his hemoglobin and begins killing for blood. Soon, freshly

threatening to hit him.) Sadly, Dean Martin is no Bob Hope, and the zingers fall flat coming from this sleepy-eyed crooner. And as for Jerry Lewis... well, Lewis' brand of heavy mugging and high-pitched howling can safely be called an acquired taste. Having no Gallic blood in my ancestry, I seem to lack those particular buds that would allow me to enjoy his facial calisthenics and harpy-like vocalizations. Lewis' only funny moments are those that arise from the clever script or those bits of comedy cribbed from Lou Costello (such as the "armchair" routine from *Abbott and Costello Meet Frankenstein*)—which the short fat man does exceedingly better than the tall thin one.

Lewis flatly stated (to James L. Neibaur and Ted Okuda in *The Jerry Lewis Films*), "We didn't feel that *The Ghost Breakers* needed to be remade in the first place." They were right.

Sample dialogue:

William Ching: "A zombie has no will of its own. Every once in a while you see them walking about with dead eyes, blindly following orders, not knowing what they do and not caring."
Jerry Lewis: "Just like husbands."

The Sea Bat (1930; MGM) Director: Wesley Ruggles; Screenplay: Bess Meredyth, John Howard Lawson (Story Dorothy Yost)

Ian Keith plays a man who's found the secret of eternal life "in the land of voodoo rites and devil potions—the Valley of the Zombies." (Courtesy Lynn Naron)

embalmed corpses (for some inexplicable reason he provides this service to his victims—professional ethics?) are stacking up like cordwood. It's up to a young doctor and his nurse/fiancée, the two main suspects in the eyes of the doubting police (of course), to crack the case and bring this plasma-procuring zombie to justice.

The only explanation given for Keith's hemoglobin-hungry condition is this little monologue delivered by the zombie-fiend: "In my former profession, death was an everyday occurrence. I began to wonder. Would it be possible for a man to *appear* to be dead, and still be *alive*? The thought fascinated me; it became an obsession. I gave up everything to find the answer. And at last I found it, in the land of voodoo rites and devil potions... the Valley of the Zombies." Unfortunately, we never get to see this valley (not even in flashback) nor any further mention of voodoo.

Valley of the Zombies was director Philip Ford's second film (the first of *six* released in 1946), and he does well using shadows and varied angles to create some eerie atmosphere. Ford, nephew of cinema legend John Ford, soon became a B-Western specialist, churning out over two-dozen low-end oaters over the next five years before he began concentrating on television work.

Thanks to a wittier script than one expects from poverty row (a harassed detective, after finding an embalmed victim, employs some amusing alliteration when he states that he's going to try and find "this peculiar party with a passion for pickling"); some engaging acting from Robert Livingston as the breezy young doctor and Adrian Booth (who, under the name Lorna Gray, played Karloff's daughter in *The Man They Could Not Hang*, 1939) as his spunky, wisecracking nurse; Ian Keith doing an excellent impression of a cadaverous Lionel Barrymore (complete with slowed speech and emphatic punctuation); and even a few moments of chilly atmosphere, *Valley of the Zombies* remains an overlooked gem among poverty-row dross. Well, gem might be too strong a word—perhaps a well-polished *rhinestone* is more accurate. It's just unfortunate that the filmmakers couldn't include a little voodoo background; but, with only 56 minutes to tell the hoary story, I suppose *something* had to go.

Voodoo (1933; Principal Adventure Pictures) Producer: Faustin Wirkus.

In 1925, U.S. Marine sergeant Faustin Wirkus was posted to the island of La Gonave about thirty miles off the Haitian coast. The only white administrator on the island of 10,000 inhabitants, he quickly won the loyalty of the natives and soon became known as "King Faustin," acting the part of the people's benefactor for three years.

In the summer of 1932, Wirkus (then retired from the military) returned to the island and brought along a movie camera. This 30-minute semi-documentary was the result. Though now apparently lost, the short film seems to have been a combination of authentic documentary and staged showmanship (an early "docudrama").

According to *The New York Times* review, "when *Voodoo* is describing the customs and the mode of life on La Gonave, it is an authentic, if technically unskillful, travelogue. But when, toward the close, it strives for a synthetic thrill by dramatizing the pagan witchcraft, making Mr. Wirkus the bashful rescuer of a girl intended for the jungle deity, it is patently make-believe."

Voodoo Heartbeat (1972; TWI) Director/Screenwriter: Charles Nizet; Producer: Ray Molina. CAST: Ray Molina, Philip Ahn, Ern Dugo, Forrest Duke, Ebby Rhodes, Mike Zapata, Ray Molina, Jr., Stan Mason, Mary Martinez, Mike Meyers.

Filmed in Las Vegas, this low-budget drive-in horror has apparently joined the ranks of the "lost film." Ads show a craggy-faced man sporting 1970s sideburns and over-large vampire fangs and features catch-lines like "Serum of Satan—one drop... and a raging monster is unleashed to kill... and kill again in an unending lust for blood!" The plot involves spies and an eternal youth serum that transforms people into bloodsuckers. It also reportedly features "an inordinate amount of bikini clad girls performing voodoo rituals" (*The Motion Picture Guide*). Producer Ray Molina stars. "WARNING!" shouted the ads, "Be sure you are mature enough to witness the shocking details of this motion picture!"

Weekend At Bernie's 2 (1993; Tristar) Director/Screenwriter: Robert Klane; Producers: Victor Drai, Joseph Perez; Photography: Edward Morey III. CAST: Andrew McCarthy, Jonathan Silverman, Terry Kiser, Tom Wright, Steven James, Troy Beyer, Barry Bostwick.

This unnecessary sequel to the popular 1989 comedy has the titular stiff brought back to a semblance of life (the body dances around when it hears music) by "The Mobu," a greedy voodoo priestess on the island of St. Thomas in the U.S. Virgin Islands. The Mobu (not to mention our two bumbling heroes and the company's villainous head of security) wants the two million dollars Bernie stole from his corporation before he died (in the first film) and stashed somewhere among the islands. With a foolish smirk on his placid face and a Conga-dancing gait, "Bernie" (Terry Kiser) is the world's silliest pseudo-zombie. The only thing worthwhile (or even mildly amusing) in this insipid comedy are the opening cartoon credits. Once the live action begins, *Weekend At Bernie's 2* dies.

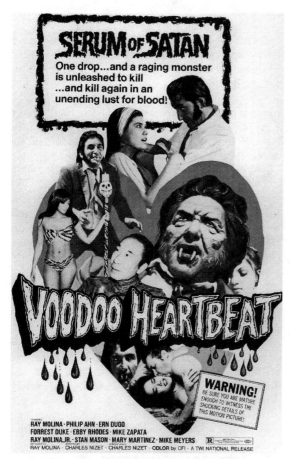

SERUM OF SATAN
One drop...and a raging monster is unleashed to kill ...and kill again in an unending lust for blood!

VOODOO HEARTBEAT

WARNING!
BE SURE YOU ARE MATURE ENOUGH TO WITNESS THE SHOCKING DETAILS OF THIS MOTION PICTURE!

RAY MOLINA · PHILIP AHN · ERN DUGO
FORREST DUKE · EBBY RHODES · MIKE ZAPATA
RAY MOLINA,JR. · STAN MASON · MARY MARTINEZ · MIKE MEYERS
RAY MOLINA · CHARLES NIZET · CHARLES NIZET · COLOR by CFI · A TWI NATIONAL RELEASE

Voodoo Heartbeat: Another "lost" film that's probably better off staying that way. (Courtesy Lynn Naron)

Wide Sargasso Sea (1993; New Line) Director: John Duigan; Producer: Jan Sharp; Screenplay: Jan Sharp, Carole Angier, John Duigan (Based on the Novel by John Rhys); Photography: Geoff Burton. CAST: Karina Lombard, Nathaniel Parker, Claudia Robinson, Ravena King, Martine Beswicke, Michael York, Rachel Ward.

Set in nineteenth-century Jamaica (just after the emancipation of the slaves), this erotic romance/tragedy tells the story of Antoinette, a young plantation heiress whose family arranges for her to marry an English gentleman named Rochester. Initially the two are very happy together, but the girl's unrecognized half-brother begins poisoning the bridegroom's mind with rumors and half-truths. Antoinette seeks the help of her childhood nanny, an Obeah-woman named Christophene, to make her husband love her again. Despite Christophene's warnings ("Obeah too strong for white man; it'll only cause big trouble"), Antoinette uses the potion given her. Realizing he's been drugged, this only drives Rochester into the arms of a brazen servant girl, culminating in a tragic conflagration of obsession and revenge.

Though rather slow-moving and convoluted, *Wide Sargasso Sea* is a beautifully photographed and well-acted tale of clashing cultures, with the subtextural presence of Obeah underscoring the cultural gulf.

The Woman Eater (1959; Columbia; Great Britain) Alternate Title: *Womaneater*. Director: Charles Saunders; Producer: Guido Coen; Screenplay: Brandon Fleming; Photography: Ernest Palmer. CAST: George Coulouris, Vera Day, Peter Wayn, Joyce Gregg, Joy Webster, Jimmy Vaughan.

"As a scientist I'm more interested in things with six legs rather than two; no doubt I'm in a minority," observes astute mad doctor George Coulouris in *The Woman Eater*. This rather entertaining British oddity about a bizarre tree/plant that eats nothing but buxom young girls has often (like *Bride of the Gorilla*) mistakenly been thought of as yet another voodoo variation.

Coulouris discovers the monster plant in the Amazon jungle, worshiped as a god by the primitive tribe caring for it, and brings it back to Merrie Olde England to keep in his basement dungeon so he can experiment with its life-restoring fluid. For those unorthodox laboratory procedures he periodically needs nubile females to feed to the plant. At meal time said legume awkwardly enwraps the girls in tentacles and draws them toward its trunk (there to do God-Knows-What since we're not shown any further digestive developments—we just have to use our "limber" imagination).

The heroine (and potential plant food) is played by Vera Day, who also appeared in *Enemy From Space* (1957) and *The Haunted Strangler* (1958). The production is definitely on the cheap, with the immobile rubbery plant (a mutant rubber tree?) looking grotesque and exotic but not very convincing; but there's an intriguing quality to the bizarre proceedings which often overcomes the shortcomings. And though it gets rather exploitative at times, featuring plenty of sparsely clothed beauties about to become plant food, that old British aplomb rises above it all to lend an air of respectability to the tawdry tale, making it an unusual and moderately entertaining low-end (non-voodoo) thriller. The various magical/ceremonial trappings (witch-doctor dancing to a "tom-tom" rhythm wearing a boa constrictor on each arm) are of an indigenous South American nature rather than of voodoo origin, since the tree-worshiping tribe is referred to as the "last remnants of the Incas."

Zombies of Mora Tau (1957; Columbia) Director: Edward L. Cahn; Producer: Sam Katzman; Screenplay: Raymond T. Marcus [Bernard Gordon]; Photography: Benjamin H. Kline. CAST: Gregg Palmer, Allison Hayes, Autumn Russell, Joel Ashley, Morris Ankrum, Gene Roth.

On the west coast of Africa, a group of treasure hunters search for a lost shipment of diamonds which is guarded by a group of zombies. Other than one character scoffing at "that voodoo stuff," the zombies' origins remain unexplained and unexplored, and there is no direct link nor specific scenes tying these walking corpses (a motley collection of *white* sailors) to voodoo. Missing along with the voodoo is any semblance of entertainment in this dull "thriller." The film plods along at about the same pace as the lethargic zombies, and it often becomes difficult discerning which of the actors are playing the *live* characters.

Appendix B:
BOOB TOOB HOODOO
(Made-for-Television and Direct-to-Video Voodoo)

The Curse of the Doll People (1960; Mexico) Director: Benito Alazrahi; English Language Version Directed By: Paul Nagle; Producer: William Calderon Stell (Pedro A. Claderon and Guillermo Calderon); English Language Version Produced By: K. Gordon Murray; Screenplay: Alfred (Abel) Salazar; Director of Photography: Henry (Enrique) Wallace. CAST: Elvira Quintano, Raymond (Ramon) Gay, Robert (Roberto) G. Rivera, Quintin Bulnes, Alfonso Arnold, Jorge Mondragon, Xavier Loya, Nora Veryan, Luis Aragon.

In the early 1960s, former carnival owner and drive-in theater builder K. Gordon Murray acquired 28 low-budget horror films and eight children's movies from Mexico's Churubusco-Azteca Studios. (*Honey, I Shrunk the Kids* was later filmed at Churubusco-Azteca.) After making a fortune with his various "kiddie matinees," Murray turned his showman's sights toward television, dubbed his 28 Mexican monster movies, and sold the syndication rights to American International Television (the TV distribution arm of AIP). Along with a string of vampire films starring German Robles (such as *The Vampire* and *The Vampire's Coffin*) and a bevy of Aztec Mummy movies, the television package contained this voodoo oddity, *The Curse of the Doll People*.

In it, a voodoo sorcerer, accompanied by his prune-faced zombie, sends out his killer dolls to take vengeance upon those who stole an idol from his Haitian temple. Midgets dressed in half-pint business suits and doll masks creep about with long nasty needles. A woman doctor (an expert on the occult) and her fiancé, along with some very stupid policemen, try to stop them.

Credit the film for using more authentic language than most, rightly labeling the voodoo sorcerer a "bokor" and talking of voodoo as a legitimate religion. But then the convoluted script stumbles off the beaten path by vaguely tying in ancient Egyptian magic in explaining how the bokor actually animates his dolls. (The sorcerer's zombie, named "Sabud," whose face looks like a cross between a monkey and a dried apple, even sleeps in an Egyptian sarcophagus!) And, oddest of all, the evil voodooist is ultimately vanquished when the heroine waves a Christian *crucifix* in his face.

As with most K. Gordon Murray jobs, the dubbed dialogue is often quite funny. "Your fiancé," remarks the sorcerer to the heroine, "is assuredly a drooling idiot!" Zing. As far as the acting goes, however, the cast would be better suited to a film entitled *The Curse of the DULL People*. The picture is padded with scene after scene of people standing around talking, sitting around talking, even *lying* around talking. The dolls themselves manage to contribute one or two shuddery moments as they move ever so slowly toward their intended victim, their faces expressionless, needle in hand, sinister malice in every move… But don't get your hopes up, this is still your typical south-of-the-border celluloid junk—good for a few laughs, one or two shudders, and some atrocious dubbing. But hey, at least nobody *wrestles* in this one.

Curse of the Swamp Creature (1966) Director/Producer: Larry Buchanan; Screenplay: Tony Houston; Photography: Ralph K. Johnson. CAST: John Agar, Francine York, Jeff Alexander, Shirley McLine, Cal Duggan, Charles McLine, Bill McGee, Ted Mitchell, Rodger Ready.

"Never make a swamp picture," warned producer/director Larry Buchanan in a recent interview, "your film comes back and it's all… *strange*." Sadly, in the hands of the creator of *The Eye Creatures* (1965), *Mars Needs Women* (1966), and *Zontar! The Thing from Venus* (1966), "strange" invariably translates into "boring."

In the mid-1960s, AIP contracted with Texas-based filmmaker Larry Buchanan to produce a series of no-budget horror movies (most of them remakes of old AIP sci-fi properties) that could be sold directly to television. Along with the recycled scripts (from such '50s faves as *Invasion of the Saucer Men*, *Day the World Ended*, and *It Conquered the World*), AIP sent Buchanan various fallen "stars" like Tommy Kirk, John Ashley, Yvonne "Batgirl" Craig, and John Agar. It didn't help.

Unlike other Buchanan opuses (like *Zontar* and *In the Year 2889*), *Curse of the Swamp Creature* was filmed from an original script (by failed Buchanan actor Tony Huston). Actually, that's not quite true; Huston stole the basic premise from AIP's *Voodoo Woman*, but made enough changes (none of which are improvements) in the setting and story to fob it off as "original." As a result, *Swamp Creature* lacks even the minimal interest that Buchanan's schlocky remakes possess. Shot in 16mm on a budget of around $25,000, *Curse of the Swamp Creature* may not be Buchanan's worst film (*It's Alive* [1968] wins that [dis]honor), but it comes in a close second. And that's saying something, since Buchanan could easily be labeled the Ed Wood of the 1960s—correction, that should be "the *Dead* Wood of the 1960s" since Buchanan's sorry movies are usually so listless that they prove unwatchable.

Curse's story has a mad doctor turning people into fish-creatures (he refers to his latest creation as "my beautiful indestructible fish-man") deep in the Texas swampland. Voodoo enters the picture when the "swamp dwellers" (poor black folk) come looking for their missing relatives at the doctor's compound. These "natives" communicate via jungle drums (!), worship snakes (rather than voodoo, the characters talk only of "snake magic"), and hang the doctor in effigy. After a threadbare ceremony in which a woman performs what looks like a slow-motion watusi dance around a torch and plastic skull, the leader incites his followers to rise up against the evil doctor: "Our strong magic will destroy him. You must become the instrument of revenge. Go! Do what you will!" They "go" but they don't really "do" anything except mill about on the doc's front lawn. Rather than magic or restless natives destroying the doctor, it's his own ping-pong-eyeballed creation that dumps him into his swimming pool full of (stock footage) alligators.

Bare-bones sets, amateurish acting (star John Agar looks tired and really has nothing to do except sit around and smoke cigarettes), pacing that's more sluggish than the bayou current, deadening dialogue, dim lighting, tinny sound (much of it was shot silent with the sound and dialogue dubbed in later—people frequently say their lines without even moving their lips!), and muddy photography make this picture the very nadir of voodoo cinema. Viewers beware, for *Curse of the Swamp Creature* is actually the Curse of the Couch Potato.

Curse III: Blood Sacrifice (1991; RCA/Columbia Home Video) Alternate Title: *Panga*; Director: Sean Barton; Producer: Christopher Coy; Screenplay: John Hunt, Sean Barton; Photography: Phillip Grosvenor. CAST: Christopher Lee, Jennilee Harrison, Henry Cele, Andre Jacobs, Zoe Randall, Olivia Dyer, Jennifer Steyn, Gavin Hood, Dumi Shongwe.

Filmed in South Africa, *Curse III: Blood Sacrifice* has absolutely nothing to do with the two previous (and also unrelated) *Curse* movies—*The Curse* (1987; a loose adaptation of H.P. Lovecraft's *The Colour Out of Space*) and *Curse II: The Bite* (1988; in which a man's arm transforms into a snake!). In a letter to *Fangoria* magazine, star Christopher Lee explained that, "actually, [*Curse III*] is a 1990 movie, shot in Africa, called *Panga*—the word is regional dialect for machete, a weapon that figures in the storyline. The U.S. distributor that acquired *Panga* evidently retitled the film to create the impression that it is the third entry in an ongoing series of horror movies. It's all news to me." Sadly, *all* these *Curse* films proved to be just that for the video viewer—a curse.

Set in East Africa in 1950, *Curse III*'s story has the young American wife of an English sugar planter (Jennilee Harrison of TV's *Three's Company* "fame") disrupt a native ceremony and rescue their sacrificial goat. Having earned the ire of the evil "nyanga" (witch doctor), her husband and friends soon fall prey to an (unseen) machete-wielding madman. In the end, after a tediously long pursuit, she finally faces her pursuer. Said maniac, however, turns out to be an oversized fish-demon (courtesy of Chris Walas, Inc.) which the wife promptly dispatches with a kerosene lamp. "When a child dies in this region," explains Christopher Lee as the enigmatic Dr. Pearson, "a goat has to be sacrificed as a mark of respect from the families. It's a sacred rite. If it isn't done, the nyanga can summon up the spirit of the sea to take vengeance on the guilty."

Unfortunately for the viewer, said "spirit of the sea" doesn't materialize until literally the last minute (and even then its paunchy appearance proves more Charlie Tuna than horrific gillman). For the previous 89 minutes, the film looks like an African-set slasher movie, full of the expected clichés (false scares, heavy breathing, unsteady POV shots, gratuitous topless scenes, even a couple killed while having sex) found in piles of imitative dreck from the previous decade. It's not even a *good* example of that sorry cinematic subset, for *Curse III*'s predominant characteristic is a general dullness (one "suspense" scene has the heroine wandering through her house for nearly *four solid minutes* before finding the expected bloody body!). Even the usually steadying presence of Christopher Lee fails to relieve the ennui, as he's given little to do but stand around looking as if he knows more than he's telling.

It's a stretch to consider *Curse III* a voodoo movie. No one mentions "voodoo" and none of the natives' activities display any voodoo characteristics (the idea of summoning a demon-spirit in the flesh, for instance, is completely foreign to the religion). Plus, the film is set a continent away from the religion's birthplace (in *East* Africa rather than *West* Africa).

Unless one yearns for the halcyon days of slice 'n' dice cinema and enjoys watching every splatter throwback that comes along, one had best avoid this *Curse* like the plague. (Perhaps inevitably, yet *another* unrelated *Curse* entry hit the video shelves a few years later called *Curse IV: The Ultimate Sacrifice*.)

The Dead Don't Die (1975) Director: Curtis Harrington; Producer: Henry Colman; Screenplay: Robert Bloch; Photography: James Crabe. CAST: George Hamilton, Ray Milland, Linda Cristal, Ralph Meeker, James McEachin, Joan Blondell, Reggie Nalder, Yvette Vickers

In this slow-paced TV movie, George Hamilton plays a man whose brother is wrongly executed for murder (and then turns up as one of the walking dead). With the aid of a beautiful, sympathetic, and sentient female zombie (!), Hamilton unravels the truth about a Chicago-based "Zombie Master" who plans to use his army of undead to infiltrate the government.

"We got Ray Milland to play the Zombie Master," remembered Curtis Harrington in *Psychotronic* (#16). "He plays this arch villain who at the climax of the film is creating an army of zombies to take over the world. He had a speech of an insane megalomaniac at the climax. He did the speech and he did it well. He's a fine actor, but I wanted more. I kept saying, 'Can't you give me... you know... I mean, you're insane... you're trying to rule the world, Ray!' And he suddenly looked at me and he says, 'Curtis, I'm not Vincent Price!'"

Headhunter (1989; Gibraltar) Director: Francis Schaeffer; Producer: Jay Davidson; Screenplay: Len Spinelli; Photography: Hans Kuhle. CAST: Kay Lenz, Wayne Crawford, Steve Kanaly, June Chadwick, John Fatooh, Sam Williams.

Advertised as "Black Magic, Pure Terror," this Florida-shot, direct-to-video yawnfest would be more accurately represented by the tag line, "Low Budget, Pure Boredom." The story has some kind of shape-shifting African demon-monster called "Jakate-Tumo" (or something) decimating Miami's Nigerian immigrant population. "He has come to reclaim the souls that have escaped his reach," a professor of Pan-African studies (and the community's "shaman") tells the two police detectives investigating the rash of grisly decapitation murders. Though the reasoning remains muddled, this vengeful demon has something to do with the Nigerians' lapsed religion, with the monster's object being to cow his escaped flock into submission by taking the heads of those most resistant to him. Voodoo is never mentioned, nor is *any* name given to this particular African-based religion. About all we learn of the topic is that, "in other religions you can be forgiven; in this one, you are punished." And, with *Headhunter*, so is the viewer.

Though both Kay Lenz and Wayne Crawford bring a likabilty to their roles as the two detectives, their efforts sink beneath the weight of the ponderous, unlikely screenplay and the neophyte film-school-style direction inflicted by Francis Schaeffer. While the script focuses on endlessly boring exchanges between the detectives and their cartoonishly racist/sexist boss, Schaeffer tries desperately (and unsuccessfully) to salvage some excitement by overindulging in clichéd steadycam shots, hoary dream-within-a-dream sequences, and even a ludicrous instance in which a knife blade rises up to claim a victim being baptized in a river and glides through the water like some ridiculous shark fin! Even the demon-monster proves disappointing, with its rubbery, generic creature visage looking even more lackluster when juxtaposed with that of *The Hideous Sun Demon* playing on the protagonists' TV.

Good (but wasted) effort from the leads and one or two moments of levity (such as when, at the climax, the detective brandishes a chainsaw and hysterically shouts at the monster, "Alright ooga-booga, let's dance!") can't save this *Headhunter* from the cinema chopping block.

Maniac Cop III (1992; Neo Motion Pictures/First Look Pictures) Directors: William Lustig, Joel Soisson; Producers: Larry Cohen, Joel Soisson, Michael Leahy; Screenplay: Larry Cohen; Cinematographer: Jacques Haitkin. CAST: Robert Davi, Caitlin Dulany, Gretchen Becker, Paul Gleason, Robert Z'Dar, Jackie Earle Haley, Julius Harris, Grand Bush, Doug Savant, Bobby Di Cicco, Frank Pesce.

This third entry in Larry Cohen's *Maniac Cop* video franchise has the vengeful juggernaut in blue, officer Matt Cordell (Robert Z'Dar), raised from the dead by a voodoo sorcerer. *Why* is never fully explained, except for the ever-enjoyable Julius Harris (as the voodooist) muttering something about Cordell's soul never being at peace and consequently allowing himself to be resurrected (though this still begs the question). After taking out a requisite number of scumbags and lawbreakers (as well as the occasional innocent who gets in his way), the zombified Cordell focuses his pistol sights (and razor-edged nightstick) on those who seek to frame gung-ho officer Kate Sullivan (Caitlin Dulany). Sullivan lies in a coma after a nasty shoot-out with a crazed junkie, and Cordell has inexplicably decided he must marry her (!)... or something. Following the mayhem (and confusion) is detective Sean McKinney (the weary-looking Robert Davi returning from *Maniac Cop II*), who looks upon Kate as his "kid sister." The illogical incidents and unlikely circumstances (including the discovery of an underground tunnel leading from the hospital housing Kate to an abandoned church where the sorcerer makes his lair) pile one atop the other until it climaxes in one of the most novel, exciting, and frightening car-chase finales ever put to film. These last few minutes almost make the previous hour and a quarter worthwhile... almost.

Maniac Cop III's confused storyline proved no more chaotic than the production's behind-the-scenes activities. Reportedly, producer Joel Soisson heavily rewrote Larry Cohen's original screenplay and continued to make revisions while shooting progressed so that there never was a completely finished script. As a result, much of the background and involvement with the novel voodoo angle fell by the wayside. "It was actually meant to be shot up in Harlem," recounted director William Lustig to this writer, "with a black detective going into the world of voodoo, all

this mystical stuff, which really *does* exist. Because of the character's background as a child, it affects him and his detective work—which is part of film noir. It was supposed to be film noir." This character history and depth was what initially attracted Lustig to the project in the first place (apart, of course, from a certain lucrative contractual agreement that he helm the series' third installment). "When you're doing these *Maniac Cop* films," continued the director, "you have to find a twist to make the character come into play. What was interesting was that when our hero, the detective, starts to unravel the mystery, the voodoo angle begins to appear and it touches a ghost of his past, of having grown up in a household where this was going on and having rejected it and now having to confront it." Alas, it was not to be.

Obviously, Robert Davi (or *any* white actor, for that matter) was not Lustig's first choice for the role of detective McKinney. The director initially wanted black actor Stan Shaw, but after a series of rejections from his financial backers, he was forced to settle on Davi. With the character's background now lost, Lustig's interest went the same route. "It became a boring picture. There was nothing there—it was a nothing movie. I was uninterested." As a result, midway through filming, Lustig finally abandoned the project, and producer Joel Soisson stepped in to finish the picture. "The movie's a mess," concluded Lustig. "It was one of those committee pictures and those things inevitably become a mess."

Mardi Gras for the Devil (1993; West Side Studios) Director/Screenplay: David A. Prior; Producer: Jill Silverthorne; Photography: Don E. Fauntleroy. CAST: Robert Davi, Michael Ironside, Lesley-Anne Down, Lydie Denier, Mike Starr, Lillian Lehman, Margaret Avery, John Amos.

Though set in New Orleans, this direct-to-video dud deals with a demonic, unstoppable murderer who kills only during Mardi Gras. Rather than voodoo (which one would expect from a supernatural film set in New Orleans—especially one that advertises itself as "in the tradition of *Angel Heart*"), the film's hazy occult background is Satanic in origin, (poorly) represented by an offstage demon voice and distorted shots of the immortal killer (a normal-looking, bearded Michael Ironside) grimacing behind red flames. Playing the detective on the killer's trail, modern B-movie veteran Robert Davi (*Maniac Cop II* and *III*) mumbles and glowers through this lethargic production which features little action, no horror, an inappropriate musical score, and a pathetic non-ending (after shooting and burning the otherworldly slayer to no effect, Davi merely hits him with a board and tells him he can't have his soul after all, at which point the demonic killer simply screams and disappears). "This report, it reads like a bad movie," Davi's disbelieving captain tells him. How apropos.

The Perfume of the Lady in Black (1974; Italy) Original Language Title: *La Profuma Della Donna in Nero*; Director: Francesco Barilli; Producer: Giovanni Bertolucci; Screenplay: Francesco Barilli, Massimo D'Avack; Photography: Mario Masini. CAST: Mimsi Farmer, Maurizio Bonuglia, Mario Scaccia, Donna Jordan, Orazio Orlando, Jho Jhenkins, Nike Arrighi, Daniela Barnes, Alexandra Paizi, Renato Zanengo.

As one might suspect from its awkward title (a direct translation of its original Italian moniker), this European thriller never found American distribution and has only recently made it to American shores on video. One part gore, two parts stylish *giallo*, and three parts *Repulsion* with a dash of "East African black magic" thrown in, *Perfume* is an occasionally disturbing, oftentimes boring, and usually confusing melding of *Repulsion*-type psychological disintegration and *Rosemary's Baby*-paranoia with a cannibal cult wrap-up at the end.

Mimsi Farmer plays a young chemist who meets an African couple who talk of "witchcraft and black magic." After Farmer pricks her finger on the African's tennis racket, she begins having chilling visitations (or hallucinations?) from her troubled past, culminating in a brief murder spree and bloody cannibal feast.

Though the film sports an intriguing premise and an effectively disturbing performance by Mimsi Farmer as the woman tormented by her own inner demons, *Perfume* never jells due to poor characterization (even Farmer's character seems shallow), slow pacing, and first time-director Francesco Barilli's obvious love for imagery over story. There is no mention of "voodoo" per se, simply an implied tie to East African witchcraft, and the (white) group of cannibal cultists which appear at film's end display no voodoo tendencies.

Serpent Island (1954; Medallion TV) Director/Screenwriter: Tom Gries; Photography: Bert I. Gordon. CAST: Sonny Tufts, Tom Monroe, Rosalind Hayes, Don Blackman, Mary Munday.

Though originally intended for theatrical release, *Serpent Island* was sold straight to television in 1955 and subsequently never received a theatrical distribution. After viewing it, one need not ask why. It's basically a three-character story (although two more minor players show up when the trio finally hit the titular island) about a woman seeking a familial treasure on an island off of Haiti and the two men—one good and one bad—who help her.

Ricki (Mary Munday) hires Pete Mason (Sonny Tufts), an out-of-work marine engineer and self-professed "dockside tramp," to sail to the Caribbean (from California!) and help her recover the treasure left there by her ancestor 150 years ago. After much bickering (between Ricki and Pete, Pete and the nasty boat captain, the captain and Ricki, etc.) and sailing (*lots* of stock footage), they land on the island and find the treasure in the form of a golden voodoo statue protected by the locals as a sacred object. After several fist-fights with a big, bald native, a listless encounter with a boa constrictor (to justify the title), and lots of walking through the woods (California's Long Beach and Malibu Cove area), the greedy boat captain is killed by a serpent and the two survivors leave the treasure to its voodoo-practicing caretakers, taking succor in their newfound love ("maybe all treasure in this world isn't gold," philosophizes Pete at film's end).

Though only 61 minutes long, *Serpent Island* seems *much* longer. It's filled with stock footage (Tom Gries wrote his script around available film), talky scenes that go nowhere, and endless shots of actors standing or walking around. The only action in the picture comes from more stock footage—that of the voodoo ceremonies (which are the film's highlights). First-time director Gries managed to procure some genuinely intriguing documentary color footage of authentic Haitian voodoo rituals, showing not only the intricate dancing and drumming but the painting of sacred symbols on the ground, the use of live chickens, and the sharing of sanctified rum. Unfortunately, Gries was unable to integrate these sequences into his tepid tale with anything remotely approaching realism, so that his principal actors seem completely disconnected with the sights they're supposedly watching. Pete's condescending dialogue (such as when he quips to the voodoo priestess, "What do you do here, run the zombie concession?") adds little plausibility.

Since the film was photographed and edited (in his garage!) by Bert I. Gordon (*King Dinosaur*, *The Amazing Colossal Man*, *Village of the Giants*, etc.), it's little wonder that *Serpent Island* lacks even a modicum of visual interest, with the camera seemingly rooted to the spot and unable to move. Of course, there's little of import going on in front of the lens anyway, unless one counts watching Tubby Tufts—er—Sonny Tufts, desperately trying to hold in his flabby stomach.

The film was obviously shot silent with the voices dubbed in later. Along with the rest of the picture's technical aspects, this process proved to be a hack job as well, for the characters often speak without even moving their mouths (and one principal switches back and forth between the actor's real voice and the voice of perennial 1950s narrator Paul Frees—inexplicably employing a Southern accent!).

Mary Munday (married at the time to the director) told Tom Weaver, the film was shot in five days for a cost (minus the stock-footage expense) of about $5,000. To the discerning viewer, it was *not* money well spent.

Shrunken Heads (1994; Full Moon) Director: Richard Elfman; Producer: Charles Band; Line Producer: Keith Payson; Screenplay: Matthew Bright (Original Story Idea by Charles Band); Photography: Stephen McNutt. CAST: Julius Harris, Meg Foster, Aeryk Egan, Becky Herbst, A.J. Damato, Bo Sharon, Darris Love, Bodhi Elfman, Troy Fromin, Leigh-Allyn Baker, Paul Linke.

Shrunken Heads was to be Full Moon's first theatrical release (Full Moon is the name of Charles Band's prolific low-budget production company, best known for its *Puppetmaster*, *Trancers*, and *Subspecies* direct-to-video film franchises). Upon viewing the final product, however, it's little wonder that *Heads* rolled before hitting the bigscreen. Though given a decent budget by Full Moon standards (reportedly between two and three million dollars), the fairly slick surface gloss can't disguise the pabulum underneath.

The (ridiculous) story has three clean-cut 13-year-old boys in a stereotypical *Dead End*-style New York neighborhood run afoul of the slightly older tough-guys and their gangster mentors. When the JDs murder the fledgling teens in cold blood (the film's only disturbing moment), the local newsstand owner, a retired member of Haiti's Ton Ton Macute (the secret police), steps in. Using his sorcerer's powers, he takes the three boys' heads, shrinks them down, and reanimates them. Teaching his new "children" to fly and kill, he sends them out to hunt "evil-doers" and to revenge themselves upon their killers.

Mr. Sumatra (Julius Harris), a retired member of Haiti's Ton Ton Macute, uses voodoo magic to battle street punks in *Shrunken Heads*.

While this sounds like a rather grim and twisted tale, the film's Disneyesque tone negates whatever impact such a bizarre storyline might muster. With its goofy villains (Meg Foster playing a gender-ambiguous, cartoonish gangster obviously inspired by *Saturday Night Live*'s "It's Pat"), pre-pubescent protagonists, and light comedic touches (the heads' victims become zombies who pick up litter and clean off graffiti with toothbrushes), a better title would be *That Darn Shrunken Head*. Add in a cloying budding-romance subplot and shallow, too-good-to-be-true characterizations, and *Shrunken Heads* comes across as a misguided Saturday Afternoon Special.

Shrunken Heads qualifies as a voodoo entry *only* because the film's warlock comes from Haiti. Despite his professed background, Mr. Sumatra's wacky conjuring would leave any self-respecting bokor shaking his (full-sized) head. Shrinking heads in a gigantic bubbling cauldron and then teaching them to fly through the air and zap malefactors with bolts of energy or bite them in the neck is *not* your typical voodoo activity. Most embarrassing of all, however, is that, as Sumatra, poor Julius Harris (doing a warm and fuzzy reprise of the voodoo villain he played two years previous in *Maniac Cop III*) wears a sparkling ceremonial robe (complete with outrageous plumed collar) that looks like it came fresh off the back of a Vegas showgirl.

Trilogy of Terror (1975) Director/Producer: Dan Curtis; Screenplay: William F. Nolan, Richard Matheson; Photography: Paul Lohman. CAST: Karen Black, Robert Burton, John Karlen, George Gaynes, James Storm, Kathryn Reynolds, Orin Cannon, Gregory Harrison, Tracy Curtis.

Though TV viewers from 1975 remember this telefilm solely for its frightening final story (titled "Amelia"), the middle tale of this macabre trio features a taste of voodoo. "Millicent and Therese" centers on two sisters (both played by Karen Black), one a reclusive spinster, the other an "evil" woman who dabbles in the occult. "These books show what [Therese] is like," Millicent tells her sister's disbelieving new beau (John Karlen of *Dark Shadows* fame). "Demonology, pornography, Satanism, voodoo, witchcraft. These books aren't just relics; she uses them to capture the souls of others. By her own admission, Satan guides her." The two siblings hate one another, and it all comes to a head when Millicent decides to "use Therese's own books to destroy her." Removing a volume labeled *Vodoo Rites & Satanism* (note that the prop department misspelled Voodoo as "Vodoo"), she gathers nail parings, hair strands, and buttons from her sister and constructs a voodoo doll—with the expected result. Also expected is the "surprise" twist at the end, which is absolutely *no* surprise to any half-conscious viewer.

Like all anthology films, *Trilogy of Terror* proves wildly uneven. Sadly, both the first story ("Julie"—concerning a sexually repressed teacher [Karen Black] and her blackmailing student) and the second (the voodoo tale) are talky and dull. The final tale (written by horror master Richard Matheson from his own short story "Prey"), however, is an exciting, scary half-hour in which a "genuine Zuni fetish doll" comes to life and terrorizes a young woman (Karen Black again). The segment ends on a final shuddery shot that, once seen, is not soon forgotten.

Producer/Director Dan Curtis was closely tied to television terror in the 1960s and '70s, having created the daytime horror soap opera *Dark Shadows* (1966-1971) and a slew of TV movies such as *The Night Stalker* (1972), *The Night Strangler* (1973), *The Picture of Dorian Gray* (1973), *Frankenstein* (1973, with Bo Svenson as the monster)*, Scream of the Wolf* (1974), *Dracula* (1974, starring Jack Palance), and *Turn of the Screw* (1974). Curtis also helmed the two *Dark Shadows* theatrical features, *House of Dark Shadows* (1970) and *Night of Dark Shadows* (1971), as well as the 1976 Oliver Reed/Bette Davis horror, *Burnt Offerings* (which also featured *Trilogy of Terror* star Karen Black).

Curtis created a belated sequel to *Trilogy of Terror* (unimaginatively titled *Trilogy of Terror II*) for cable TV in 1996 which followed the original's format of three separate stories connected only by the fact that the same actress (Lysette Anthony) stars in each. The anthology contained no voodoo segment this time, but the killer Zuni fetish doll was back to once again wreak its diminutive havoc. Sadly, it proved a fatuous and unnecessary return.

Voodoo (1995; A-PIX Entertainment) Director: Rene Eram; Producers: Donald P. Borchers, Noel A. Zanitsch; Screenplay: Brian DiMuccio, Dino Vindeni; Photography: Dan Gillham. CAST: Corey Feldman, Joel J. Edwards, Diana Nadeau, Ron Melendez, Sarah Douglas, Maury Ginsberg, Amy Raasch, Jack Nance.

"They're not a fraternity, they're some kind of weird voodoo cult!" exclaims Corey Feldman in this direct-to-video venture. Feldman plays a "hip" college student who joins a rather unusual fraternity. Unbeknownst to him, the frat brat leader is actually a voodoo priest and the rest of his new "brothers" are really zombies (a concept that may not be all that far removed from reality, actually). Feldman has been chosen to become the sixth zombie-victim whose sacrifice will allow the priest to attain eternal life.

Apart from the occasional disturbing-yet-enjoyable moment (such as when the voodoo master uses his evil powers to force the Big-Man-On-Campus to turn a shotgun on his equally obnoxious frat brothers), there's little to recommend here. Feldman is smugly unlikable, and the clean-cut whitebread zombie master and his normal-looking undead slaves lack any sense of conviction or interest. "We both love horror," co-scripter Brian DiMuccio told *Fangoria*, "and felt that [voodoo] didn't deliver enough to the horror audience." He was right.

The most interesting (and amusing) aspect of this voodoo misfire occurred *behind* the scenes rather than onscreen. "We had to sacrifice a goat in the movie," related producer Donald P. Borchers to *Fangoria*'s Thomas Crow. "The way you do that gag on our plan is to go to all the prop houses and find an existing taxidermied goat for the sacrificial shot. Then you go to all the animal trainers and do your level best to get a trained live goat that matches the appearance of your stuffed one. That way, the ASPCA won't have a problem with you... We were shooting down at a frat house at USC. On Monday we got the live goat down there, all very nice and behaving ourselves. On Wednesday we brought the stuffed goat down, and all the students thought we had killed the goat and stuffed it! So now we were getting attitude from everybody—the ASPCA, the university— wanting to know where this movie company found the nerve to sacrifice goats on a college campus!"

Voodoo Dawn (1990) Director: Steven Fierberg; Producer: Steven Mackler; Screenplay: John Russo, Jeffrey Delman, Thomas Rendon, Evan Dunsky; Photography: James McCalmont. CAST: Raymond St. Jacques, Theresa Merritt, Gina Gershon, Kirk Baily, Billy "Sly" Williams, J. Grant Albrecht, Tony Todd

Though possessing a few beautiful settings (sun-filled meadow, green leafy forest) and touching (briefly) on the humanistic theme of the plight of the migrant farm worker, *Voodoo Dawn* falls into the same trap that snares many a low-budget, straight-to-video effort: poor characterization and leaden plotting.

John Russo (of *Night of the Living Dead* fame) and his three co-writers concocted a tale of big-city college kids caught up in a struggle between immigrant farm workers from Haiti and an evil voodoo priest named Makoute. For some inexplicable reason, this rogue sorcerer is stalking and killing his former countrymen in order to obtain body parts to assemble a patchwork zombie creation. Why this voodoo version of Dr. Frankenstein does all this is never explained (he already has a handful of *whole* zombie corpses to do his bidding), nor is much else in this poorly scripted and deadly dull movie (has Russo penned *anything* good since 1968?).

Poor Tony Todd (who made such an impression in the 1990 *Night of the Living Dead* remake and the *Candyman* series) has no dialogue as the voodoo villain and little to do except creep about in the dark with a machete. The only intriguing moments in this waste-of-time arise when the friendly mamaloi effectively uses a voodoo doll to make Makoute twist and jerk this way and that—*and* the final shot of one of the zombies (who, lacking significant makeup, simply looks like a slow-walking field worker). Having been run through (sideways) with an iron bar, the perambulating corpse can't get through the door because the ends of the bar jutting out from either side of his body keep catching on the door frame and the mindless automaton simply bumps again and again at the portal. Sadly, one late joke at a zombie's expense and a few pretty images do not an entertaining movie make, and viewers should simply roll over and go back to sleep rather than face this *Voodoo Dawn*.

Voodoo Dolls (1990; Canada) Director: Andre Pelletier; Producer: Roger Racine; Screenplay: Ed Kelleher, Harriette Vidal (based on their novel "The School"); Photography: Christian Racine. CAST: Grace Phillips, Nathalie Gauthier, Howard Balaban, Maria Stanton, Brett Halna Du Fretay, Beth Lachance, Nocole Jacqueline, Graham Chambers.

This direct-to-video cheapie from Quebec begins well enough with an atmospheric black and white prologue filled with clever film-school technique (slo-mo, freeze-frame, quick cuts, etc.). Unfortunately, once the story proper gets underway, the film settles down into just another by-the-numbers bottom-of-the-barrel VCR filler, whose technical competency fails to reach even the level of a low-end Fred Olen Ray or David DeCoteau production.

The convoluted story revolves around The Hanley School for Girls, where a brutal slaying took place 40 years ago (the b&w prologue). Apparently, several of the kitchen help practice "black magic or voodoo or something" (as

Direct-to-video voodoo direct from Canada. (Courtesy Lynn Naron)

one character vaguely explains) and intend to draw the New Girl into their cult of death.

Director Andre Pelletier fills this boring picture with pointless scenes that go absolutely nowhere until the story finally winds down (or *falls* down) to its forgone conclusion. The bargain-basement budget shows through everywhere, from the fact that we only see about five students at this prestigious "school" to some horribly bad non-acting. As the voodoo priest, Graham Chambers is the token black in the cast, but he's also the *toneless* black since he appears less animated than his voodoo dolls.

These dolls provide the one novel notion in this otherwise senseless scenario, for these little bits of straw and cloth possess a life of their own. At one point a whole gang of voodoo dolls attack and kill a lecherous handyman. Sadly, the effects are far from special as the hapless victim rolls around with the obviously inanimate dolls pinned to his shirt while he holds one to his neck and shakes it in a desperate attempt to make it seem alive. Pelletier finally shows some good judgment, since this turns out to be the *only* scene to spotlight these pathetic stuffed menaces (misleading title notwithstanding). For superior (and far less tedious) voodoo doll action, see *Tales from the Hood* or even the south-of-the-border deviation, *The Curse of the Doll People*.

Zombie Cop (1991; Cinema Home Video) Director: J.R. Bookwalter; Producers: Scott P. Plummer, J.R. Bookwalter; Screenplay: Matthew Jason Walsh (story by J.R. Bookwalter); Photography: Brock N. Lenz. CAST: Michael Kemper, Ken Jarosz, James R. Black, Jr., Bill Morrison, James L. Edwards, Christina M. Bookwalter, Bogdan Pecic.

Considering its unprofessional backyard-production qualities *and* the fact that it runs barely over an hour (*including* the long, drawn-out opening and closing credits), calling this amateurish, shot-on-video time-waster a "movie" is an act of astounding generosity. The (silly) story has a serial killer/voodoo sorcerer named Doctor Death (a badly over-acting James R. Black, Jr. sporting an ersatz Jamaican accent) murder a police officer (Michael Kemper) then resurrect him as a zombie. "I curse you," he tells the dying detective, "your bones will walk the earth for eternity." Apart from the fact that the now-zombified policeman looks a bit worse-for-wear (and presumably smells bad as well), little has changed for this "zombie." He retains his full personality and memories and, with the help of his still-living partner, immediately sets out to find the evil voodooist. Meanwhile, Dr. D mutters vaguely about some "master plan" of vengeance against the city, and the remainder of the film has the zombie cop tracking down, chasing, fighting (in pathetically staged half-speed exchanges), and finally triumphing over his afflictor.

Voodoo-wise, *Zombie Cop* stays as dead as its protagonist. Except for the cartoonish figure of Doctor Death mixing blood and a few powders in a bowl, the film features no ceremonials nor explanatory dialogue about the origin of his power or of voodoo in general.

Bad sound, poor lighting, endless (and juvenile) dialogue, and junior high school-level acting make this shoestring schlock a chore to sit through. The only reason *Zombie Cop* has been set loose upon the unsuspecting video-viewing public is that the film's (using the term loosely here) executive producer, David DeCoteau (himself a maker of direct-to-video dreck like *Creepozoids* and *Nightmare Sisters*—though on a far more competent level than this), owns a small-time video distribution outfit.

Zombie Island Massacre (1984; Troma) Director: John N. Carter; Producer: David Broadnax; Screenplay: Logan O'Neill, William Stoddard (Original Story by David Broadnax and Logan O'Neill); Photography: Robert M. Baldwin. CAST: David Broadnax, Rita Jenrette, Tom Cantrell, Diane Clayre Holub, George Peters, Ian McMillan, Dennis Stephenson.

"Toe-tapping Machete Head Dances! Glamourous [sic] Zombie-Style Cosmetic Surgery! Fabulous Air-Conditioned Tiger Pits!" promise the ads for this direct-to-video aberration distributed by the people who brought us *The Toxic Avenger*. A group of tourists in the Caribbean take a side trip to the mysterious island of San Maria in order to witness an "authentic" voodoo ceremony—in which the high priest raises a zombie (afterwards, the local tour guide pays off the "reverend" for putting on the sham show). When their bus is sabotaged, the stranded visitors fall prey one by one to an unseen marauder.

Despite its location and the solitary fake zombie (who does nothing more menacing than sit up), the voodoo angle remains slight as it turns out that the tourists are simply caught in the middle of a multi-million dollar drug deal double-cross; the mysterious killer is actually a hit squad hired by "the Colombians." Rita Jenrette, ex-Abscam congressional spouse and *Playboy* subject, provides the film with its quota of gratuitous nudity. Amateurishly acted, poorly paced, and sloppily scripted, *Zombie Island Massacre* remains a disappointingly vapid voodoo vacation.

Zombie Nightmare (1987; Gold-Gems) Director: Jack Bravman; Producer: Pierre Grise; Screenplay: David Wellington; Photography: Roger Racine. CAST: Adam West, Jon Mikl Thor, Tia Carrere, Manuska, Frank Dietz, Linda Singer.

Of the four voodoo movies released in 1987, *Zombie Nightmare* was the only one to bypass a theatrical release and go straight to video. Since it is the worst of the quartet, this seems only appropriate.

When muscle-bound, baseball-loving Tony (played by former Mr. Canada and weightlifting heavy metal rocker Jon Mikl Thor) becomes a hit-and-run victim, his grieving mother seeks the aid of the local Haitian voodoo priestess, Molly Mokembe (Manuska Rigaud), to avenge his death. The mamaloi raises Tony up as a zombie and sends him out (armed with his trusty baseball bat!) to dispatch the gang of callous teens who ran him down. She also has him kill one of the two men who, 20 years earlier, had tried to rape her. Coincidentally, it was Tony's father who had stopped the decades-old assault and had been killed for his troubles. Even more coincidentally, the current police chief, Captain Churchman (Adam West), was among the assailants and the one who stabbed Tony's dad. At the end, everyone conveniently ends up at the cemetery where the zombified Tony collapses (because "zombies lose their energy after they revenge themselves"), Churchman shoots the voodoo priestess, and the rotting corpse of Tony's dad rises up to drag the screaming Churchman to Hell—or something.

Apart from a confusing ending, this film also boasts cheesy sets (a police station that looks suspiciously like a High School cafeteria), poorly shot filler (teens driving endlessly through town; a listless, never-ending tennis match), poor zombie makeup (at one point Thor wears what looks like an immobile plastic mask), and comically bad acting (Dean Hargopian as the medical examiner doing a bad Bogart impression; Thor's brawny zombie stomping about like a sad parody of the Frankenstein Monster).

Though top-billed, a tired-looking Adam (*Batman*) West has relatively few scenes and walks through his role with a minimum of expression or inflection. By all accounts he was happy to get *any* work at this stage in his career, though in *Zombie Nightmare* he certainly doesn't look it.

One of the film's few bright spots is third-billed Tia Carrere (making her big screen debut) whose effective emoting makes her a standout in the largely thankless role of a terrified teen. Carrere went on from her "sleazy chick" character to bigger and better (?) things, co-starring in the two *Wayne's World* movies and *True Lies* with Arnold Schwarzenegger. (At one point in *Zombie Nightmare*, the versatile Carrere runs for her life from the zombie while managing to adjust her blouse at the same time!)

The film's voodoo ideas prove just as bankrupt as the rest of *Zombie Nightmare*. The "voodoo witch" (as one character describes her) paints her face, lights candles, and mumbles unintelligibly over Tony's coffin. (In the film's funniest moment, Tony's corpse then sits up, shakes its fist, and yells. At this, the mamaloi hands the zombie his beloved baseball bat (!), and the creature eagerly grabs it and sniffs at it like some grotesque gorilla!) That's it for the voodoo involvement. Once again, voodoo becomes merely a simplistic device that sends some monster reeling through another tired old plot. And tired is how the viewer feels after watching *Zombie Nightmare*. Shoddy and dull, *Zombie Nightmare* makes little impact on the discerning cineaste (much less inspiring any nightmares)—though it may indeed cause a few eyelids to droop.

AUTHOR'S NOTE

Years ago, when I studied Comparative Religion in college, Voudoun was (disappointingly) not among those creeds covered. (Nor has it made any significant inroad into present-day curriculum either.) Consequently, I've had to self-educate myself on this topic. Though it has always held an exotic fascination for me, it wasn't until I began delving deeply into the subject in preparation for this book that Voudoun's enthralling beauty and holistic complexity became so readily apparent. Though I am not a Voudounist myself (and, in fact, espouse no particular religion over another), the works of those who are (and of the anthropologists and scholars who have studied the subject first-hand) have taken me on an eye-opening journey into a fascinating worldview as well as providing some little insight into the very nature of faith. It was a trip not to be missed, and I particularly recommend the following books as jumping-off points for those wishing to embark upon an exploratory Voudoun voyage:

> *Divine Horsemen: Voodoo Gods of Haiti* by Maya Deren
> *The Serpent and the Rainbow* by Wade Davis
> *Passage of Darkness: The Ethnobiology of the Haitian Zombie* by Wade Davis
> *Voodoo in Haiti* by Alfred Metraux

ABOUT THE AUTHOR

Bryan Senn is the author of *Golden Horrors: An Illustrated Critical Filmography of Terror Cinema, 1931-1939* (McFarland, 1996) and co-author of *Fantastic Cinema Subject Guide* (McFarland, 1992). He has also contributed to a number of Midnight Marquee Press compilation books, including the continuing *Midnight Marquee Actors Series* (*Bela Lugosi*, *Boris Karloff*, and *Lon Chaney, Jr.*), *Cinematic Hauntings*, and *We Belong Dead: Frankenstein on Film*. He lives in Washington state with his wife and son and several cats.

BIBLIOGRAPHY

Bojarski, Richard. *The Films of Bela Lugosi*, Secaucus, New Jersey: Citadel Press, 1980.

Brosnan, John. *The Horror People*, New York: St. Martin's Press, 1976.

Brunas, Michael, John Brunas and Tom Weaver. *Universal Horrors: The Studio's Classic Films, 1931-1946*, Jefferson, North Carolina: McFarland & Co., 1990.

Cohen, Daniel. *Voodoo, Devils, and the New Invisible World*, New York: Dodd, Mead & Company.

Cremer, Robert. *Lugosi, The Man Behind the Cape*, Chicago: Henry Regnery Company, 1976.

Davis, Wade. *The Serpent and the Rainbow*, New York: Simon and Schuster, 1985.

Davis, Wade. *Passage of Darkness: The Ethnobiology of the Haitian Zombie*, Chapel Hill: The University of North Carolina Press, 1988.

Del Vecchio, Deborah and Tom Johnson. *Peter Cushing: The Gentle Man of Horror and His 91 Films*, Jefferson, North Carolina: McFarland & Co., 1992.

Deren, Maya. *Divine Horsemen: Voodoo Gods of Haiti*, New York: Delta, 1970.

Dixon, Wheeler Winston. *The Films of Freddie Francis*, Metuchen, New Jersey: The Scarecrow Press, 1991.

Dixon, Wheeler Winston. *The Films of Reginald LeBorg: Interviews, Essays, and Filmography*, Metuchen, New Jersey: The Scarecrow Press, 1992.

Everson, William K. *More Classics of the Horror Film: Fifty Years of Great Chillers*, Secaucus, New Jersey: Citadel Press, 1986.

Glut, Donald F. *The Dracula Book*, Metuchen, New Jersey: The Scarecrow Press, 1975.

Haining, Peter (ed.). *The Edgar Allan Poe Scrapbook*, New York: Schocken Books, 1977.

Halliwell, Leslie. *The Dead That Walk: Dracula, Frankenstein, the Mummy, and Other Favorite Movie Monsters*, New York: Continuum Publishing Company, 1986.

Halliwell, Leslie. *Halliwell's Film Guide, Seventh Edition*, New York: Harper & Row, 1989.

Hardy, Phil (ed.). *The Encyclopedia of Horror Movies*, New York: Harper & Row, 1986.

Herskovits, M. J. *Life in a Haitian Valley*, New York, 1937.

Higham, Charles and Joel Greenberg. *The Celluloid Muse: Hollywood Directors Speak*, New York: New American Library, 1969.

Johnson, John "J.J." *Cheap Tricks and Class Acts: Special Effects, Makeup and Stunts from the Films of the Fantastic Fifties*, Jefferson, North Carolina: McFarland & Co., 1996.

Lamparski, Richard. *Whatever Became Of?...11th Series*, New York: Crown Publishers, Inc.

Leab, Daniel J. *From Sambo to Superspade: The Black Experience in Motion Pictures*, Boston, Houghton Mifflin Co., 1975.

Leonard, Sheldon. *And the Show Goes On: Broadway and Hollywood Adventures*, New York: Limelight, 1995.

Maltin, Leonard. *Leonard Maltin's Movie and Video Guide, 1995 Edition*, New York: Plume, 1994.

McClelland, Doug. *The Golden Age of "B" Movies*, New York: Bonanza Books, 1978.

McClelland, Doug. *Forties Film Talk: Oral Histories of Hollywood, with 120 Lobby Posters*, Jefferson, North Carolina: McFarland & Co., 1992.

Metraux, Alfred. *Voodoo in Haiti* (translated by Hugo Charteris), New York: Oxford University Press, 1959.

Miller, Don. *B Movies*, New York: Ballantine Books, 1973.

Miller, Mark A. *Christopher Lee and Peter Cushing and Horror Cinema: A Filmography of Their 22 Collaborations*, Jefferson, North Carolina: McFarland & Co., 1995.

Murphy, Joseph M. *Working the Spirit: Ceremonies of the African Diaspora*, Boston: Beacon Press, 1994.

Nash, Jay Robert and Stanley Ralph Ross. *The Motion Picture Guide*, Chicago: Cinebooks, 1985

Neibaur, James L. and Ted Okuda. *The Jerry Lewis Films: An Analytical Filmography of the Innovative Comic*, Jefferson, North Carolina: McFarland & Co., 1994.

Peary, Danny. *Cult Movies: The Classics, the Sleepers, the Weird, and the Wonderful,* New York: Delta, 1981.

Phantom of the Movies, The. *The Phantom's Ultimate Video Guide*, New York: Dell, 1989.

Pohle, Robert W., Jr. and Douglas C. Hart. *The Films of Christopher Lee*, Metuchen, New Jersey: The Scarecrow Press, Inc., 1983.

Seabrook, W. B. *The Magic Island*, New York: The Literary Guild of America, 1929.

Senn, Bryan and John Johnson. *Fantastic Cinema Subject Guide: A Topical Index to 2500 Horror, Science Fiction, and Fantasy Films*, Jefferson, North Carolina: McFarland & Co., 1992.

Senn, Bryan. *Golden Horrors: An Illustrated Critical Filmography of Terror Cinema, 1931-1939*, Jefferson, North Carolina: McFarland & Co., 1996.

Siegel, Joel E. *Val Lewton: The Reality of Terror*, New York: The Viking Press, 1973.

Stanley, John. *Revenge of the Creature Features Movie Guide* (Third Revised Edition), Pacifica, California: Creatures at Large Press, 1988.

Svehla, Gary J. and Susan Svehla (eds.). *Midnight Marquee Actors Series: Bela Lugosi*, Baltimore, Maryland: Midnight Marquee Press, 1995.

Weaver, Tom. *Science Fiction Stars and Horror Heroes: Interviews with Actors, Directors, Producers and Writers of the 1940s through 1960s*, Jefferson, North Carolina: McFarland & Co., 1991.

Weaver, Tom. *Poverty Row HORRORS! Monogram, PRC and Republic Horror Films of the Forties*, Jefferson, North Carolina: McFarland & Co., 1993.

Weaver, Tom. *They Fought in the Creature Features: Interviews with 23 Classic Horror, Science Fiction and Serial Stars*, Jefferson, North Carolina: McFarland & Co., 1995.

Weaver, Tom. *It Came From Weaver Five: Interviews With Moviemakers in the SF and Horror Traditions*, Jefferson, North Carolina: McFarland & Co., 1996.

Weaver, Tom. *Interviews with B Science Fiction and Horror Movie Makers*, Jefferson, North Carolina, McFarland & Co., 1988.

Weldon, Michael. *The Psychotronic Encyclopedia of Film*, New York: Ballantine Books, 1983.

Wiater, Stanley. *Dark Visions: Conversations with the Masters of the Horror Film*, New York: Avon Books, 1992.

Young, Jordan R. *Reel Characters: Great Movie Character Actors*, Beverly Hills, California: Moonstone Press, 1986.

Periodicals:
American Cinematographer
Box-Office
Castle of Frankenstein
Cinefantastique
Cinemacabre
Cult Movies
L'Ecran Fantastique
Evening Standard
Famous Monsters of Filmland
Fangoria
Film Daily
Filmfax
Harrison's Reports
The Hollywood Reporter
Kinematograph Weekly
Little Shoppe of Horrors
Midnight Marquee
Monthly Film Bulletin
Motion Picture Exhibitor
Motion Picture Herald
Movie Club
New York Daily News
New York Herald Tribune
New York Post
New York Times
Psychotronic Video
Scarlet Street
Sounds
Starlog
Today's Cinema
Variety
Video Watchdog
Videooze